International Patterns of Inflation:
A Study in Contrasts

The Conference Board
American Council of Life Insurance

Collaborating Authors

JAPAN—Nobumitsu Kagami

UNITED KINGDOM—Alan Budd and Geoffrey Dicks

CANADA—Carl E. Beigie

SWITZERLAND—Nicolas Krul

FRANCE—Michel Develle

WEST GERMANY—Frank Wittendal

ITALY—J. Paul Horne

International Patterns of Inflation:
A Study in Contrasts

Ezra Solomon

Editor

Jointly sponsored by the
American Council of Life Insurance
and
The Conference Board

Acknowledgments

In submitting this book for publication I would like to express my gratitude to the American Council of Life Insurance and The Conference Board for their sponsorship of this study; to thank each of my collaborating authors for their contributions and for their patience with the many changes that had to be made in order to adapt their texts to the limitations of length, uniformity and style required by the publishers; to acknowledge the help received from Cynthia Gunn in editing the original country essays, and from Lillian W. Kay who converted and polished the manuscript into publishable form; and finally to offer my appreciation to Ruth Gilombardo and to Arleen Danielson who typed my own contribution as well as large sections of the book.

EZRA SOLOMON
Stanford University
March 20, 1984

Contents

Why This Report

Inflation has been public-enemy number one for almost two decades. The impact of inflation on peoples' lives, fear of inflation, and efforts to cope with inflation and to constrain it—these have been dominant factors in both private and public decision-making throughout the world over the last twenty years. The present project developed out of that environment. A primary concern of our two organizations has been to understand modern inflationary experience and the policy and market responses to it.

We were fortunate that Ezra Solomon, Dean Witter Professor of Finance, Graduate School of Business, Stanford University, accepted the leadership of this undertaking. He assembled a team of authoritative observers to write on developments in countries other than the United States. His own essay covers the United States and places U.S. developments in a global context. This volume will, we believe, be of use to businesspeople, economists and government policymakers alike as a way of tracking eight major economies over two decades of varying degrees of success in coping with inflation.

Our two organizations have found this project to be a rewarding one. We are grateful to the authors for illuminating a difficult and ubiquitous problem.

JAMES T. MILLS, PRESIDENT
The Conference Board

RICHARD S. SCHWEIKER, PRESIDENT
American Council of Life Insurance

Introduction

The eight countries surveyed in this book—the seven largest market economies and Switzerland—account for three-quarters of the free world's economic output and for an even larger fraction of its financial assets. All eight are rich industrial democracies; all have capable central banks and convertible currencies; all encountered a common set of important economic developments during the decade of the 1970's: Two sharp increases in oil prices, each followed by a significant slowing of industrial growth; the collapse of the pre-1971 system of fixed exchange rates; the relentless rise of government spending relative to their national incomes. In spite of such powerful common influences there were uncommon differences in the behavior of inflation rates in the eight countries.

Two examples illustrate the differences alluded to. During the decade of the 1960's, West Germany, France and Italy, the three largest members of the original European Common Market, experienced relatively uniform rates of inflation. As measured by the broadest indicator of national prices, the gross national product price index, inflation in West Germany between 1960 and 1970 averaged 3.7 percent a year, in France 4.4 percent, and in Italy 4.7 percent. In the latter half of that decade, inflation rates in Italy and West Germany were almost identical. Some fifteen years later, between 1976 and 1981, the West Germany rate was still at the 4 percent per annum level. The rate in France had risen to over 10 percent a year, and in Italy to 17½ percent.

Setting France and Italy aside, equally large shifts occurred in the relative price performances of the six other nations surveyed in this study. Between 1960 and 1965 (based again on the gross national product price indexes) the United States, with an annual inflation rate of 1.6 percent, Canada (1.9 percent), and the United Kingdom (3.2 percent) were the three best performers; Japan and Switzerland, each with a rate of 4.9 percent, and West Germany (3.6 percent) were the three worst. Fifteen years later, the relative rankings of these six nations had reversed dramatically. Between 1976 and 1981, Switzerland (3.3 percent), Japan (3.7 percent), and West Germany (4.1 percent) emerged as the three best performers; the United States (8.1 percent), Canada (9.0 percent), and the United Kingdom (14.2 percent) were the three worst.

How and why did essentially common global economic forces lead to such divergent patterns in the behavior of national inflation rates? One answer lies in the different monetary policies that were pursued in each country: namely, the rates at which their individual central banks allowed each nation's money supply to grow. There is clear evidence of powerful correlations between changing trends in monetary growth in each country and changes in that country's rate of inflation. Switzerland, for example, steadily reduced the rate at which its money supply was permitted to grow—from 9.4 percent a year in the early 1960's to 5.2 percent a year in the late 1970's. The United States, by contrast, permitted an acceleration in its monetary growth from 3.1 percent a year in the early 1960's to 7.1 percent a year in the late 1970's. Over the same period, Switzerland's record of price stability shifted from being one of the worst in the group to being the best; by contrast, price performance in the United States shifted in the opposite direction.

One potential approach to our survey of inflation in eight industrialized countries would have been to conduct systematic tests of statistical correlations between money-supply growth and inflationary experience in each country over the past twenty years. This approach was rejected for two reasons. First, such a pursuit would have entailed a study in statistical inference rather than in economic history; it would have produced a set of uniform and largely mathematical results, rather than the historical documentation of very differentiated inflationary experiences and responses to it in individual countries. The second reason for rejecting an empirical approach, based on statistical relations between national rates of change in money supply and national rates of change in prices, was that, no matter how close these relations turned out to be, such a finding would not provide a satisfactory answer to the central issue: Why and how did common global forces produce such uncommon results in national inflation rates? It would merely substitute one question with another. The new question would be: Why and how did eight national central banks, whose staffs were by training and temperament equally in favor of price stability and equally equipped to conduct monetary policies, nonetheless succeed in producing such divergent results?

Arthur Burns, Chairman of the U.S. Federal Reserve System from 1970 to 1977, answered that question in the title of a lecture he delivered to his fellow central bankers at an international meeting in Belgrade on September 30, 1979. His paper was entitled "The Anguish of Central Banking." He was referring to the unhappy combination of two well-known facts: Central banks in all major countries have the power to stop inflation through their ability to control and limit the rate at which credit and money can expand; but, central banks in most major countries have not been able to pursue policies that are single-mindedly directed to their preferred objective of price stability. The explanation for that inability lies in two other facts:

(1) Although inflation can be limited by monetary policy, it is driven by powerful political forces that lie beyond the control of central bankers—forces such as the pressure for faster economic growth, higher levels of employment, higher wages, higher social benefits, higher profits, and increasing shelter for interested groups from economic discomfort brought about by higher interest rates and higher exchange rates.

(2) Monetary policies clearly influence the behavior of the price level, but at the same time they also exert powerful influences over a large range of important variables, some of which have been outlined above. Furthermore, although price stability is the most important objective of central banking, it is not the only objective for which central banks are responsible; as an important arm of government, central banks are also responsible for the solvency of an nation's financial system, for its exchange rates, as well as for such nationally legislated objectives as "maximum employment."

The essays that follow attempt to deal with modern inflation in the context of the issues described above, and to do so on a country-by-country basis. Without ignoring the common forces that led to a worsening of inflation in all countries, the essays attempt to isolate the particular confluence of forces that led to the particular behavior of inflation in each country; to describe policy responses to these inflationary developments; and, finally, to examine the responses to inflation within each country's financial markets.

Part I of this book is a long essay that is designed to introduce the subject as a whole and to cover inflation in the United States—the largest single economy in the group—in the context of global developments. Part II consists of essays by collaborating authors covering developments in each of the seven other countries surveyed. The authors were asked to address inflation at its broadest level, rather than at the more narrowly confined level of statistical inference. Although statistical inference as such was not their major theme, the papers necessarily contain a considerable volume of statistical data. In the interest of readability the authors were requested, wherever possible, to leave statistical documentation to a common set of appendix tables. Part III of the book contains a set of master tables relevant for all of the essays in this book as well as statistical notes that provide essential definitions and sources for these data.

Part I

U.S. INFLATION
IN A
GLOBAL CONTEXT

Ezra Solomon*

*Dean Witter Professor of Finance, Graduate School of Business, Stanford University.

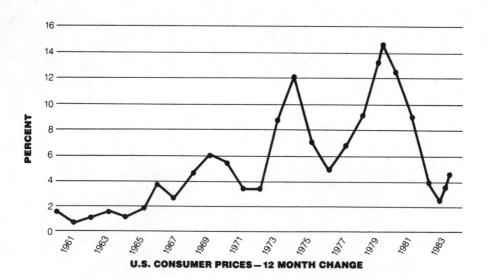

U.S. CONSUMER PRICES—12 MONTH CHANGE

THE ECONOMIC BACKGROUND

THE ECONOMIC HISTORY of the past 15 years has been dominated by two major developments. Both were global in scope and both had global impacts. The first development was a fifteenfold increase in the world price of oil between 1972 and the end of 1980. This increase took place in two quantum jumps: The first, in 1973-1974, raised the average price of oil from around $2.50 a barrel to nearly $12.00 a barrel. After five years of approximate stability, oil prices jumped again in 1979-1980 to around $36.00 a barrel. (For the intricacies of oil pricing, see box on page 4.) The second development was a tenfold acceleration in the rate of inflation in the United States. For five years prior to 1965, U.S. inflation, measured by the consumer price index (CPI), ran at just below 1½ percent a year. After 1965, inflation accelerated in three rising waves, the last of which crested in early 1980 at a rate of just below 15 percent per annum.

If the history of the period 1965-1980 can be explained largely in terms of these two developments, it is equally true that the history of the 1980's is being shaped, and will continue to be shaped, by the responses of the economy and of economic policies to the same two factors.

Oil Prices and Inflation

This essay and the others that follow are concerned explicitly with the second of these two major developments—global inflation. It is impossible to deal adequately with the inflation issue, however, without understanding the profound impact that the jump in oil prices had on the world economy. The two developments are closely related, but the relationships are complex rather than simple:

(1) Although the two jumps that occurred in oil prices were both triggered by severe supply interruptions caused by political events, both jumps were

Oil Pricing

Oil pricing bristles with technicalities that make it difficult to pinpoint exactly by how much prices rose in the two oil shocks of 1973-1974 and 1979-1980: Hence the use of less precise measures such as the "quadrupling or quintupling" for what occurred in 1973-1974 and "tripling" for the 1979-1980 change.

The value of petroleum, and thus its price, varies with its "lightness" (lighter oils are more valuable because they can be refined more easily into gasoline); its "sweetness" (the absence of sulphur and other impurities), and its proximity to final markets. To complicate matters, the price differential for each of these qualities varies over time depending on market factors and fluctuations in oil-tanker rates. Finally, prices can be quoted on two bases: as loaded at port of origin (f.o.b.) or as delivered at final destination (cif).

Before 1975, the price of OPEC oil was generally quoted in terms of a "posted" price in U.S. dollar per U.S. barrel (42 U.S. gallons). These international posted prices were not actual prices; they simply provided the basis for calculating the revenue per barrel that the producing country received from the oil companies which owned, extracted and sold the oil (frequently to themselves). On January 1, 1973, for example, the "posted" price for Saudi Arabian 34° gravity light oil (which has come to be used as the standard or benchmark crude) was $2.59 per barrel. This was the reference price for calculating the royalties and income taxes Aramco (the operating oil consortium) paid to Saudi Arabia. Including an allowance for "lifting" costs and for net profits on Aramco's investment, the effective price at which oil could be delivered in the Persian Gulf was closer to $2.15 per barrel. The delivered price had risen to around $10 per barrel by the end of 1974. Likewise, the posted price for lighter 40° gravity Libyan oil (the lighter the oil the *higher* the gravity number) was $3.77 a barrel in January, 1973, although the effective price was only $2.52. The latter rose to nearly $12 a barrel by the end of 1974.

After 1975, the pricing system changed dramatically because most host countries nationalized their oil-production facilities. The international oil companies were transformed from owners into operators. Once again two pricing quotations emerged. One is the long-term "contract" price at which oil-producing countries sell crude to the operating companies or third parties. These are the official price quotations set by OPEC under Saudi Arabian leadership. The second price is the "spot" price, the effective price at which the same oil is sold on the open market either by the operating companies or by the producing country itself.

Large discrepancies can arise between official, contract prices and spot prices. In the 1979-1980 price explosion, the Saudis tried to hold down contract prices, first to below $20 in 1979 and then to $30 a barrel in 1980. Prices of other oils, including the spot price of Saudi oil itself, rose far more rapidly. The spot price of Saudi light rose to $39 a barrel in some transactions in early 1980 and fluctuated around $36 a barrel for most of the year.

On average, the evidence supports the conclusion in the text that the effective world price of oil rose fifteenfold between 1972 and 1980.

preceded by very sharp declines in the purchasing power of the U.S. dollar, the currency in which oil prices were, and are, denominated. In a sense, general inflation was one cause of the rises we saw in the world price of oil.

(2) In most countries, the jumps in oil prices that occurred in 1973-1974 and again in 1979-1980 were accompanied by worsening inflation in those years.

(3) The most profound effect of oil-price increases was indirect rather than direct: Each of these increases was followed by a sharp decline in growth rates in all major industrial economies. The slowing of growth, in turn, had adverse consequences for the key variables associated with inflation—productivity, wage demands, unemployment and fiscal deficits.

Oil Prices And Growth

Prior to the first oil shock, which occurred at the end of 1973, the industrial economies of the world had enjoyed two decades of expansion at unprecedented rates. As Table 1 shows, between 1955 and 1973 industrial production in the United States rose at an average annual rate of nearly 4½ percent—well above the nation's long-term growth rate. Western Europe, whose growth rate had sunk to very low levels between 1913 and 1938, enjoyed a series of national economic "miracles" in the 1950's and 1960's. Between 1955 and 1973, industrial output in Western Europe rose at a compound annual rate of 5½ percent. Across the Pacific the Japanese economy, which had been reconstructed to its prewar level by 1954, embarked on a lengthy period of extremely rapid industrial expansion that averaged 13½ percent a year for two decades.

The first oil shock brought this remarkable period of industrial growth to an end. Between the end of 1973 and the end of 1978, industrial expansion in Western Europe and Japan fell to just 1 percent a year. For reasons that will be outlined later, the slowdown in the U.S. rate of industrial expansion was not as sharp: With an industrial growth rate of 2.8 percent a year, the United States emerged as the fastest growing of the large industrial economies in 1973-1978. Even so, its growth rate was below that experienced by the slowest-growing economy prior to 1973.

The second oil shock further worsened industrial growth performance. It was followed by a five-year period of near-zero industrial growth in all the major economies with the sole exception of Japan, whose large success in exporting manufactured products allowed its industrial production to grow at 3½ percent a year between the end of 1978 and the end of 1983.

Clearly, the oil price alone cannot be blamed for all of the slowdown the industrial world experienced after the end of 1973. Considerable evidence, however, supports the conclusion that oil was a major factor in that slowdown:

(1) In the 1960's, when growth was vigorous, economists were equally vigorous in developing detailed equations designed to identify and

Table 1
Growth Rates in Industrial Production (IIP) and Real Gross National Product
(GNP) or Real Gross Domestic Product (GDP)
(percent per annum)

Country	1955-1973	IV Q1973-IV Q1978	IV Q1978-IV Q1983[p]
United States			
IIP	4.3	2.8	0.5
GNP	3.7	3.4	1.4
Japan			
IIP	13.5	0.9	3.5
GNP	9.8	3.9	4.0
West Germany			
IIP	5.8	1.3	0.4
GNP	5.5	2.1	1.2
France			
IIP	6.1	1.3	0.3
GDP	5.5	2.1	1.2
United Kingdom			
IIP	3.2	0.3	−0.4
GDP	2.7	1.5	0.5
Italy			
IIP	7.2	1.7	−0.7
GDP	5.3	1.8	1.3
Canada			
IIP	5.8	2.3	0.7
GNP	5.0	3.0	1.3
Switzerland			
IIP	5.3[a]	−1.9	−0.1
GNP	4.4	−0.9[b]	1.3
Average (unweighted)			
IIP	6.4	1.1	1.5
GNP/GDP	5.2	2.1	1.5

[a]From 1959-1973   [b]From 1973-78   [p]Preliminary.

Source: See Statistical Appendix.

measure the sources of growth itself. The explanatory powers of these previously satisfactory equations falls off sharply for the period after 1973; indeed, they account for only a fraction of the post-1973 decline experienced in growth rates. The reason is simple. Prior to 1973, the supply of energy in general, and oil in particular, was so abundant and prices so low and stable that neither the supply nor the price of oil was included in the standard growth equations. The inability of the equations to explain the sudden decline in growth rates after 1973 is a result of this omission. Equally clearly, the shift from plentiful, cheap oil to

Gross National Product (GNP) and Gross Domestic Product (GDP)

The total economic output of a nation can be measured on two different bases—gross national product (GNP) or gross domestic product (GDP). Of the eight countries covered in this book, five prefer the GNP concept—the United States, Japan, West Germany, Canada and Switzerland. The other three—the United Kingdom, France and Italy—use the GDP concept.

The distinction between GNP and GDP is not of major consequence for the large industrial countries. Both measures seek to estimate the total market value of the output of final goods and services that are produced in a given period. The GNP refers to output produced by factors of production *legally* resident in the country covered. By contrast, the GDP refers to output produced by factors of production *physically* located in the country.

To take the United States as an example, U.S. GNP would include the net profits generated by overseas branches and subsidiaries of U.S. corporations, but it would exclude the net profits generated by subsidiaries and branches of foreign corporations located in the United States. U.S. GDP would do the opposite—exclude the former and include the latter.

In 1982, U.S. GNP was estimated at $3,073 billion; U.S. GDP in that year was $3,026 billion. The difference, $47 billion, represents the excess of income generated by U.S.-based factors of production at work in the rest of the world over foreign-based factors of production at work in the United States.

scarce and very expensive oil was a major reason for the sharp industrial slowdown experienced in all major nations.

(2) During the period of rapid growth prior to 1973, industrial output—which is far more energy intensive and, therefore, more sensitive to the availability and price of oil than is nonindustrial output—increased at a more rapid rate than the nonindustrial components of gross product in terms of either GNP or GDP. (For the distinction between gross national product [GNP] and gross domestic product [GDP] see box above.) This is true not just for the major industrial economies as a group, but also for each of them individually. After 1973, and to an even greater extent after the end of 1978, industrial output everywhere has risen at a much slower rate than has nonindustrial output.

(3) The experience of the U.S. economy for the five-year period following the first oil shock provides additional evidence of the powerful effect that the availability and price of oil had on industrial expansion. Between the end of 1973 and 1978, when the growth of industrial output in Western Europe and Japan declined to 1 percent a year, the United States, with

a growth rate of nearly 3 percent a year, emerged as the country experiencing the most rapid rate of industrial expansion in the group.

Part of the explanation for our differentially better performance in the period 1973-1978 lies in the highly expansionary policies followed by the Carter administration, especially in 1977 and 1978. Even more important, the United States was the only major economy that did not experience the nearly fivefold rise in the effective price of oil experienced by other countries. In the United States, effective energy prices merely doubled. This atypical pattern was the result of two factors: In the 1960's, U.S. energy policy was dedicated to suppressing the price of natural gas via mandatory controls (controls that were continued in the 1970's); at the same time, the government—through the use of import quotas—maintained the price of domestic oil at around $1.00 a barrel higher than the world price of oil. Thus when the world price of oil prior to 1973 was around $2.50 a barrel, the U.S. price was around $3.50 a barrel.

After 1973, when the world price of oil almost quintupled to $12.00 a barrel, U.S. policies toward oil were reversed. Through strict price controls, we suppressed the price of most domestic oil at around $5.50 a barrel and continued to suppress the price of our other major fuel, natural gas, at levels that were even lower than $5.50 a barrel on an energy-equivalent basis. Thus, although the price of oil imports to the United States rose to world levels, the average effective price of domestic plus imported fuel rose far less than did corresponding prices in Western Europe and Japan between 1973 and 1978. It is, therefore, not surprising that the first oil shock had a far milder impact on the growth rate of U.S. industrial output than it had on the growth of industrial output in other major nations. Indeed, the United States was the only major country in which oil imports and oil consumption rose between 1973 and 1978.

With the rapid deregulation of oil prices and the rapid easing of controls on natural gas prices after the end of 1978, U.S. energy prices rose toward world levels and the U.S. economy lost the temporary protection from reality it had enjoyed prior to 1978. As a result, the ability of U.S. production to keep on growing evaporated along with that of most other large industrial economies during the five-year period from the end of 1978 to the end of 1983.

Oil Prices and Productivity

The period of rapid industrial expansion prior to 1973 was also a period of rapid increases in productivity, here defined as output per hour of work. Although the United States started the post-World War II expansion with the world's highest level of output per hour of work, the average increase in this critical variable was nonetheless a steady 2.7 percent a year (Table 2). At such a rate, output per hour approximately doubles every 26 years, about the average length of one generation in Western societies.

Table 2

Three Measures of U.S. Productivity Growth, Selected Periods 1955-1983

(percent per annum)

Years	Output per Hour of Work[1]	Output per Worker	Output per Capita
1955-1973	2.7	2.0	2.2
1973-1978	1.2	0.4	1.7
1978-1983	0.6	0.3	0.25

[1]Private business sector only.

Source: U.S.Department of Labor and Economic Report of the President.

Over the long pull, growth in output per hour is a major determinant of the rate at which average per-capita living standards can rise. However, living standards are also affected by other factors, notably changes in the fraction of the population that works in the economic sector and changes in the annual number of hours worked per employee. By any measure, at the rate of improvement experienced prior to 1973, each generation of U.S. citizens could confidently expect to be about twice as well off as that of their parents. In short, the United States enjoyed two desirable economic outcomes prior to 1973; (1) A rapid growth of industrial and nonindustrial activity provided employment opportunities for a growing labor force, and (2) rapid increases of output per hour provided the basis for higher real wages per worker and rising average living standards. The same was true in the other major industrial economies.

A rapid increase in the use of energy, and especially of oil, was a key factor in the growth of productivity and output that the industrial world enjoyed prior to 1973. In Western Europe, North America, and Japan, energy use grew as fast or faster than aggregate output. One simple explanation for the rapid rise in labor productivity experienced in the United States and elsewhere is that the postwar system was rapidly substituting oil for human sweat, not just in the factory but also on the farm and in the home. Obviously, this process of energy substitution requires that energy use be embodied somehow in machinery and equipment of various kinds. Thus, it is also possible to say that a rising stock of capital per worker was *the* key to productivity and growth. Prior to 1973, this was the generally favored explanation. However, of these two alternative views, the former provides a better insight into what has happened since 1973.

The slowdown in industrial growth after 1973 has been accompanied by an equally sharp slowdown in the rate of productivity improvement, especially in the United States. At the growth rate of productivity increases we have experienced since the end of 1978, the next doubling in average output per hour will take a full century, and the next doubling in our average living standards per capita will take 250 years! This is not a forecast, but only an illustration of the profound change that has taken place since 1973.

The most obvious reason for the marked slowdown in productivity growth is the decline in the use of oil per worker that was mandated by the large rise in oil prices. The stock of capital per worker has not changed appreciably since 1973.

Some writers have described what happened to the industrial world after 1973 by likening it to a situation in which OPEC, by raising oil prices so dramatically, had "bombed" 20 percent of the world's industrial capacity. It is a vivid analogy, but it misses the main point. Had OPEC merely bombed 20 percent of our industrial capacity, Pittsburgh and the other steel centers of the world would now be fully employed in rebuilding it. What OPEC did when it raised the price of oil by a factor of 15 was to render *obsolete* some 20 percent of the West's industrial capacity. The vast stock of plant and equipment that was installed prior to 1973 was designed and built on the premise of a plentiful supply of $2.50-a-barrel oil. OPEC destroyed that premise and in the process destroyed the ability of a significant portion of industrial plant that was based on pre-1973 technology and practices to compete for the consumer's dollar.

The sharpest impact of this fundamental change has been on those plants and industries that were the most energy intensive—industries such as steel, large automobiles, airlines, farm and construction machinery, and nonferrous metals. Because these were the industries that spearheaded the rapid growth we enjoyed prior to 1973, their inability to grow rapidly after 1973 has had serious adverse effects on the growth of the post-1973 economy as a whole.

Consequences Of Slow Growth

The slowing of growth in aggregate output and productivity had two important consequences relevant to inflation itself. During the golden age of expansion prior to 1973, governments everywhere—and especially in the United States—decided that conditions were right for accelerating the translation of various ideals of social justice into active legislation.

The ideals themselves had long been around and most countries in Western Europe had already converted them into legislation. For example, "The Economic Bill of Rights" presented by President Franklin Roosevelt in his 1944 State of the Union message provides a cogent list of the items that were eventually converted into legislation in the United States in the 1960's. Among the universal rights for Americans that Roosevelt mentioned were:

The *right* to a useful and remunerative job;

The *right* to adequate food, clothing and recreation;

The *right* of every family to a decent home;

The *right* to adequate medical care;

The *right* to adequate protection from the economic fears of old age, sickness, accident and unemployment;

The *right* to a good education.

He ended his message by saying: "I ask the Congress to explore the means for implementing this economic bill of rights—for it is definitely the responsibility of the Congress so to do."

By 1973, in the context of a rapid rise in total and per capita output, most of these rights had been legislated by the U.S. Congress into entitlements programs. Indeed, the spate of legislative enactments between 1964 and 1973 augmented Roosevelt's visionary program by adding important environmental and safety regulations. The various programs enacted in that decade were designed to create not just a rich society but a society that might be called just, egalitarian or, even, "great." The future costs associated with these programs were not carefully projected. The general assumption was that the projected doubling of per-capita living standards per generation that was then being achieved would easily provide the resources for financing even costly social programs of the types enacted. A similar expansion of social programs took place in Western Europe and, to a lesser extent, in Japan.

The sharp slowdown in per-capita output after 1973 negated the key assumption on which the future funding of the entire set of programs was based. The costs of the programs remain, but the wherewithal for their financing—namely, rapid growth—vanished. As a result, governments everywhere, and notably in the United States, face huge and enduring structural deficits in their budgets: Even if high levels of economic activity can be restored in the mid-1980's, government expenditures mandated by existing legislation will be far in excess of government revenues. Such deficits have serious potential consequences for the conduct of monetary policy, the behavior of interest rates, and for inflation itself.

A second major result of the slowdown in growth was a sharp rise in unemployment in all industrial economies after 1973, and especially after early 1979. In addition to a rising level of unemployment caused by slow employment growth in the face of a rising labor force, unemployment rates have risen in all major countries because work opportunities in the industries most affected by the second oil shock have actually declined.

In the United States, the civilian unemployment rate in December, 1982, just after the trough of the recent recession (November, 1982) was 10.7 percent—a level not seen since the end of the depressed 1930's. (For a distinction between the overall unemployment rate and the civilian unemployment rate see box on page 12.) Although just one year of cyclical recovery reduced that number to 8.2 percent by December, 1983, few observers expected the rate to fall to much below 7 percent in 1984: a rate far higher than the 4½-to-5½ percent levels achieved in previous peacetime periods of prosperity in the past 30 years.

Outcomes on the unemployment front between 1979 and 1983 were even worse in Western Europe than they were in the United States. For example, in West Germany, generally regarded as the strongest economy in Europe, the unemployment rate, which averaged around 1 percent during the prosperous 1960's, rose to the 9-percent level in 1983. The consensus projection is that this

The U.S. Unemployment Rate

Prior to January, 1983, the official U.S. unemployment rate (e.g., the 10.7 percent rate shown in the text for December, 1982) was defined as the ratio of total unemployment to the total civilian labor force. Starting in January, 1983, the official rate was redefined as the ratio of total unemployment to the *total* labor force (i.e., the civilian labor force *plus* military personnel stationed in the United States). The 8.2 percent rate given in the text for December, 1983, is on the civilian basis. On the total labor-force basis, the rate in December, 1983, was 8.1 percent.

rate is unlikely to fall very much even with a continuation of cyclical recovery. In 1983, the Netherlands, next door, experienced a rate almost twice as high as that in West Germany.

Unemployment is the result of economic conditions, but it is also a social phenomenon that can itself drive economic developments via the political process. In the context of the kind of welfare societies and labor agreements that prevail in all advanced economies, unemployment places very large financial burdens on the already-strained budgets of governments and businesses. In addition, unemployment, especially in politically powerful industries of the type most affected in the 1980-1983 industrial slump, invariably creates powerful political pressures for relief in the form of subsidies and protection from foreign competition.

Interaction of "Real" Factors and Inflation

Economists use the word "real" to describe economic variables from which the effects of inflation have been removed—variables such as industrial output, employment and the volume of GNP. The price of oil has been a major determinant of these real variables since 1973. When oil was plentiful and cheap, real growth was strong; basic industry prospered; unemployment was relatively low; real living standards rose; and welfare benefits were expanded significantly. In that context the Western world was able to move toward a freer and more open set of trading arrangements among the major nations—a development that led to an acceleration of living standards for everybody. In the process, each nation's economy steadily became far more open, that is, more dependent both on exports and imports.

The huge increase in the price of oil in the 1970's had opposite effects. Growth slowed; the industrial sectors suffered a serious decline in their prosperity; unemployment rose; average living standards stagnated; and governments everywhere had to face up to the politically difficult task of constraining the rise in previously mandated payments to nonworkers.

It is against such a background that accelerating waves of inflation occurred in the 1970's, bringing with them widespread complications on the purely financial side of the economy. The two most important financial complications were, first, a collapse of a previously stable system of exchange rates and, more recently, the emergence of high and highly volatile interest rates.

The interaction of adverse developments on the real side of the economy and the equally adverse developments on the financial side of the economy that occurred throughout the 1970's is a highly complex one in which causes become effects and effects, in turn, become causes for still other adverse developments. It is against this background that the story of inflation must be told.

AN OVERVIEW OF INFLATION: 1965-1980

The United States experienced three waves of accelerating inflation from 1965 to 1980, each higher than the one preceding. The first wave, which began in late 1965 soon after the escalation of the Vietnam War, carried the rate of inflation, as measured by the consumer price index (CPI), from 1.3 percent a year during the five years prior to 1965 to just above 6 percent a year by the end of 1969.[1] This was followed by three years of disinflation which, assisted by wage and price controls, brought the rate down to 3.4 percent by the end of 1972. A second and larger wave began in early 1973, and crested at the end of 1974 at over 12 percent per annum. Once again policies were shifted in order to bring inflation down and succeeded in doing so. However, by the end of 1976, at the trough of the price cycle, inflation was still running at a high 4.8 percent per annum, far higher than the rate which, just five years earlier, drove the Nixon administration to adopt mandatory wage and price controls. Nonetheless, the disinflationary emphasis was again relaxed when the Carter administration took over in January, 1977. A third, even worse, wave carried the U.S. rate of inflation to nearly 15 percent a year by the Spring of 1980.

The U.S. experience during these 15 years was not unique. Although the particular pattern of price increases varied from one country to the other, all of the industrial economies suffered a progressive worsening in price performance, with global peaks in inflation rates in 1974 and again in 1980. Most major countries, including the United States, have experienced sharp declines in the rate of inflation since 1980.

How and why did inflation, which had been relatively insignificant prior to 1965, worsen so badly thereafter? The economics profession does not agree on a single straightforward answer to this question. As a result, agreement is also lacking on what should be done to restore price stability on an enduring basis, as well as on projections of probable price trends for the rest of the 1980's. There is, however, broad agreement that inflation is a "cancer" that must be eradicated if the economies of the world are to be set again on a path of sustainable growth. The metaphor is appropriate. The world was able to eradicate

---

[1]Unless otherwise stated, the rates of inflation cited in this paper refer to rates experienced over the preceding 12 months.

smallpox because there was a clear understanding of both the disease and its cure. The cause of and cure for inflation, like those for cancer, are either not fully understood or, in the case of inflation, not politically acceptable. Although much progress has been made, the differences in professional opinion regarding the cause of and remedy for inflation are probably wider today than they used to be. At least some understanding of these differences is necessary in order to analyze the history of the past 15 years.

The Causes of Inflation

For many laymen, economics is a subject that makes simple things complicated. In the case of inflation, an opposite perversity is at work—the insistence of many economists on trying to make something that is extremely complex simple. The attempt to find a single, tidy explanation for the complex phenomenon of recent inflation lies at the heart of current controversy and disagreement.

At one extreme lies the monetarist explanation for inflation. As the leading proponent of this school of thought, Milton Friedman, has put it: "Inflation is always and everywhere a monetary phenomenon." In its simplest version, the monetarist view is that inflation is caused by "too much money chasing too few goods." Spelled out a little further, the logic goes as follows:

- Control over the supply of money and its growth lies in the hands of each nation's central bank. In principle, the central bank can set the growth rate of the money stock at any rate it wishes, regardless of what is occurring in the economy. In technical terms, the money supply is an *exogenous* variable; it is determined by forces outside the general economy.
- When the central bank, for whatever reason, permits an excessive growth in the money supply (growth faster than the rate at which the volume of national output is growing), a general rise in the price level must follow.
- Inflation can be corrected or eliminated as simply as it is caused, namely by reducing the rate of money growth to a pace consonant with noninflationary real growth.
- Nothing else matters very much. Excess growth in the stock of money is the single, critical variable that drives inflation.

In opposition to the monetarist view of events is the cost-push school of thought, which argues that the driving force of modern inflation is an increase in the cost of producing goods and services, especially an increase in wages and fringe benefits, the principal component of costs. For proponents of this view, the sequence of events in modern inflation is as follows:

- In modern economies, labor unions have the power (largely through their ability to strike) to bargain for and win compensation increases in excess of productivity gains. Likewise, politically powerful groups are able to mandate rises in payments for items such as social security, unemployment compensation, and welfare that exceed the capacity of the productive sector to finance them.

- Wage increases achieved by one group of workers, either private or public, tend to spread to other large segments of the economy; so do increases in legislated benefits for nonworkers.
- Wages and other employment costs, such as social-security taxes, account for such a large proportion of the total cost of producing goods and services that employers are forced to pass these increased costs to their customers in the form of higher prices.
- The growth of the money supply is at most a passive accompaniment to the basic wage-price spiral. As production costs rise, businesses are forced to finance their rising costs through increased borrowing at the banks (because in the normal process of production and sales, most increased costs have to be met before they can eventually be recouped through higher prices). The rise in bank lending leads to an observed increase in the supply of money. The power of the central bank to stop such a process is extremely limited, especially in the market-oriented democracies.
- In short, the rise in the money supply we observe when inflation is rising is not the cause of inflation but, rather, its result. In technical terms, the money supply is an *endogenous* variable: It is determined by forces operating in the general economy.

If the quarrel between the two views outlined above were merely an academic debate, the world could leave the matter to be settled some day through increasingly complicated statistical tests published in increasingly abstruse articles in learned journals. Unfortunately, the issues have profound implications for the conduct of policies in the real world. If the monetarists are right, modern inflation can be cured—and should be cured—by imposing strict rules on central banks regarding the rate at which a nation's supply of money should be allowed to grow. By contrast, if the cost-push or wage-push view is correct, modern inflation cannot be so cured without wrecking the economy itself unless government controls are also exercised over inflation's true source, namely wages, prices and profits.

It is entirely likely that the truth lies in a middle ground in which portions of both views or theories play an active role: This view is that modern inflation is, in fact, a complex and untidy process; inflationary pressures arise sometimes from the cost side of the equation, sometimes from the purely monetary side, and sometimes from both; the money supply is partly endogenous and partly exogenous. Such an eclectic view is neither as tidy nor as satisfactory as are the extreme views. In such a view of inflation the conduct of monetary policy is an important determinant of inflation, though not the exclusive, all-powerful determinant envisaged by the monetarists. Without having been so planned, most of the papers in this volume have found it necessary to invoke such an eclectic mix of views in order to explain adequately the course of events in the large industrial economies since 1965.

The Situation Prior to 1965

It is useful to begin with a description of the state of affairs that prevailed during the first half of the 1960's, prior to the onset of inflation in the U.S. economy at the end of 1965. Table 3 summarizes key economic indicators for the eight countries included in this study. Compared with the economic situation that has prevailed over the past five years (1978-1983), the world of the early 1960's looks like a paradise. Economic growth by any measure was extremely rapid; employment was rising in all countries; and output everywhere was rising even more rapidly. The rate of inflation varied from country to country, but by any of the measures shown in Table 3 inflation was low everywhere except for a puzzling rise of consumer prices in Japan. The United States, in which consumer prices rose at just 1.3 percent a year between 1960 and 1965, was the best-performing large economy in the group with respect to price stability.

The remarkable stability of prices prior to 1965 was accompanied by an equally remarkable stability in the two major financial variables that are most closely related to inflation, namely, exchange rates and interest rates. Exchange rates among the major currencies were fixed under the rules of the international monetary system known as Bretton Woods. Hardly any severe strains emerged in the foreign-exchange markets. The volume of international trade and investment grew even more rapidly than did the growth of output. Interest rates in the United States were low and stable; for example, the prime rate of interest charged by banks was unchanged at 4½ percent for over five years between the middle of 1960 and the end of 1965.

Although rates of inflation were low in the 1960-1965 period, they were not zero. Furthermore, within each country the major alternative measures of inflation showed different results. These differences provide a useful insight into just what these alternative measures reflect, as well as into the anatomy of modern inflation. Table 3 shows three different measures of inflation for each country: the consumer price index (CPI), which some countries refer to as the retail price index; the wholesale price index (WPI), the name of which has been changed in the United States to the producer price index (PPI); and, finally, the gross national product (or gross domestic product) price deflator.

The first statistic, the CPI, as its name implies, measures the average retail price that a consumer pays for a fixed market basket of goods and services typically purchased by households. The second statistic, the WPI, measures the average price of goods sold in large wholesale lots, principally by manufacturers and wholesalers. The principal difference between the WPI and the CPI is that the former excludes and the latter includes a large component of pure services that consumers buy, such as professional services, the services provided by retail stores, and the services associated with expenditures related to housing.

During the period of very low inflation, 1960 to 1965, inflation measured by wholesale prices was everywhere lower than was inflation measured by the CPI. This difference is extremely wide in the case of Japan, where wholesale

Table 3
The World Before Inflation
(Changes in Various Key Indexes 1960-1965)
percent per annum

Country	CPI Index	WPI Index	GNP Deflator[1]	Industrial Production	Real GNP[1]	Employment[2]
United States	1.3	0.4	1.6	6.3	4.7	2.3
Japan	6.0	0.4	4.9	11.7	10.0	6.1
West Germany ...	2.8	1.3	3.6	5.5	4.9	0.9
France	3.7	2.1	4.1	6.2	5.8	1.1
United Kingdom..	3.3	2.5	3.2	3.3	3.4	1.1
Italy	4.9	2.6	5.6	7.2	5.1	1.1
Canada	1.6	1.6	1.9	7.4	5.6	3.1
Switzerland	3.2	1.8	4.9	5.2	5.0	2.7

[1]GDP or GDP deflator for France, the United Kingdom, and Italy.
[2]The employment concept varies from country to country. See Statistical Appendix for details.

Source: See Statistical Appendix.

prices rose at only 0.4 percent a year as against a rise of 6 percent a year in retail prices. The explanation for the phenomenon in Japan, as well as elsewhere, lies in the difference between productivity growth experienced in the production of goods and lower productivity growth in the production of services. Rising productivity in the goods-producing sector tends to lead to proportionate rises in wages paid by this sector. These wage increases gradually spread to all sectors of the economy, including the retail sector and the government sector. Here, because they are not matched by commensurate productivity increases, the rising wages spill over into rising prices.

Retail prices do not always rise faster than wholesale prices. Indeed, in many years subsequent to 1965, exactly the reverse has been true. The 1972-1974 wave of high global inflation, for example, was partly the result of extremely rapid increases in raw-material prices including, notably, oil. Such increases show up rapidly in the wholesale price index. The relative stability of wages in the service sectors works to hold down the rise in retail prices. Thus during 1974, a year of very rapid increases in raw-material prices, the WPI in the United States rose at 18.3 percent as against 12.2 percent for the CPI. Similar developments took place elsewhere.

The third major measure of prices is the GNP (or GDP) price deflator. This statistic measures the average price of all goods and services produced in an economy. It differs from the CPI in many significant ways. The most notable are that the GNP deflator includes—but the CPI excludes—the price of goods produced for export (the opposite is true of imports); likewise, the GNP deflator includes and the CPI excludes the price of capital goods and industrial buildings; thirdly, the GNP deflator also reflects changes in the composition of goods and services produced in the economy, whereas the CPI and WPI are based on an unchanging set of weights. Over the long run, the effects of these statistical differences tend to get washed out. For example, although import prices have only a small direct effect on the GNP deflator, they eventually creep into the system as a whole and show up indirectly in later years. Similarly, the prices of capital goods and industrial buildings do not have an immediate impact on the CPI but do have an impact later.

By any measure, the period of relative stability of prices and interest rates came to an end at the end of 1965 when the first of three successive waves of accelerating inflation began in the United States. What follows is both a historical and an analytical account of how and why inflation progressively worsened for 15 years, despite attempts to break the inflationary spiral. Attempts to halt inflation in the United States began very soon after inflation started to accelerate in 1966; nonetheless, inflation had become a serious issue in the United States as well as in all of the major economies by 1980. These developments do not mean that governments are incapable—they suggest that the problem is intricate rather than simple. The chronology of each of the three waves of U.S. inflation attempts to capture some of the intricacies that are involved. Each inflationary wave provides a lesson, though not the answer, for how policy should be conducted for the remainder of the 1980's.

THE FIRST WAVE: 1965-1969

The first wave of inflation (1965-1969) was not a global one. It began in this country and remained essentially confined to the United States unitl 1968. By the middle of 1965, the U.S. economy, after four-and-a-half years of very rapid expansion, was operating at close to its full capacity. Unemployment was down to 4.2 percent of the civilian labor force and the overall operating rate of manufacturing capacity was close to 90 percent, a level generally regarded as the maximum efficient rate. This achievement was partly the result of highly expansionary fiscal policies initiated a few years earlier, such as the easing of depreciation rules and the investment tax credits instituted in 1962, and the large tax-rate reductions of about 20 percent granted to individuals and corporations by the Revenue Act of 1964. In addition, the Federal Government had launched its ambitious set of "Great Society" reforms, which increased federal spending for a wide variety of social programs.

Prior to mid-1965, part of the stimulus from increased federal civilian spending was offset by a fairly sharp reduction in defense spending, which fell steadily from 9¼ percent of GNP in 1962 to 7¼ percent by mid-1965. It was in this context that the United States escalated its commitment to the undeclared war in Vietnam. Military outlays rose extremely rapidly (by nearly 20 percent a year) starting in August, 1965, and new orders for defense goods (which are not included in outlays until they are actually paid for) rose even more rapidly.

The large surge in civilian and military demand for both goods and labor created severe pressures on prices and wages in an economy already operating at close to full employment. To accommodate these increases in demand, business had to increase its own demand for plant and equipment, which in the short run worsened the imbalance between overall demand and supply. Furthermore, in order to fulfill the growing flood of orders for defense hardware, some of which required long lead times to produce, defense contractors had to build up their inventories of raw materials and goods in process—yet another factor that exacerbated the imbalance. The stage was set for worsening inflation by October, 1965.

The logical step to restore a noninflationary balance to the economy in mid-1965 would have been to increase taxes immediately. The Administration chose otherwise. The simultaneous quest for guns, butter *and* the Great Society without a commensurate tax increase led to the inflation that followed. The pace of price increases at both the wholesale and retail levels accelerated after mid-1965; by the Summer of 1966, just a year after President Johnson requested and received additional defense funds for the undeclared war in Vietnam, the rate of inflation had doubled to 3.7 percent, a level not seen since the Korean War 15 years earlier.

In the absence of a tax increase, the burden of constraining inflation fell on monetary policy. The Federal Reserve System (the U.S. central bank) acted to restrain the growth of credit and money in the face of extremely strong and rising demands for borrowing by both business and consumers. The competition for funds led to a sharp rise in interest rates, which by the Summer of 1966 reached levels not seen in 40 years. The prime rate of interest charged by banks, which had stabilized at 4½ percent for over five years until the end of 1965, moved up in four rapid steps to 6 percent. The rise in rates was accompanied by a condition of extreme tightness in the credit markets that came to be called the "credit crunch."

Tight money led to a marked slowdown in the rate of economic expansion. The largest impact was on residential construction, a sector that is uniquely dependent on borrowed funds. The rate of new housing starts fell to below one million per annum in the final quarter of 1966, its poorest level since the end of World War II. The growth of industrial production, which had risen by 9 percent from the Summer of 1965 to the Summer of 1966, fell to zero between the Summer of 1966 and the Summer of 1967.

The pace of inflation slowed. The increase in the CPI declined from the 3.7 percent rate reached in October, 1966, to 2.7 percent a year later. Had the Federal Reserve stayed on its course of restraint, the subsequent worsening of inflation that followed all through 1968 and 1969 would have been averted. However, the Fed was either not willing or not able to do so. In any case, after the credit crunch of late 1966, monetary policy was loosened. Housing, and economic activity in general, began a renewed expansion soon thereafter. So did inflation, which accelerated once again until it peaked at 6.1 percent during the 12 months ending December, 1969.

The 1965-1969 period is unique for two reasons: It marks the beginning of modern inflation. It also allows us to analyze inflation itself in a setting that is free of external complications that later became important sources of price pressures. There were no oil shocks and no changes in the dollar's exchange rate from 1965 to 1969; indeed, the price of imports to the United States hardly rose at all during those years and thus served to hold down the U.S. inflation rate. That first wave of U.S. inflation was a purely domestic one.

The evidence shows that fiscal policy was the major driving force of U.S. inflation in the late 1960's. Between fiscal year (FY) 1965 and (FY) 1968, defense spending rose from $50 billion a year to over $80 billion—a 62 percent rise. Federal expenditures on social programs (health, welfare, income maintenance, education and community development) rose even more rapidly, from $30 billion in FY 1965 to $55 billion in FY 1968, a rise of over 80 percent in just three years. Although several small tax increases took effect in early 1966, fiscal policy, on balance, was extremely expansionary. The federal budget deficit rose sharply from $1 billion in 1965 to $25 billion in FY 1968.

Deficits as such do not necessarily cause inflation. A deficit that occurs spontaneously when tax revenues fall during an economic recession, for example, simply tends to offset part of the decline in private demand that caused the recession in the first place. The rising deficits of 1966-1968 were an altogether different matter, however. The economy was not in recession; indeed, it was operating at a level significantly above its full employment potential. The expansive shift in fiscal policy turned out to be highly inflationary in such circumstances.

Although the Administration had been unwilling to ask the Congress for a tax increase in mid-1965, it was forced by the events of 1966 to make such a request a year-and-a-half later in its January, 1967, budget message. Congress was unwilling to give the President the tax increase he asked for without corresponding concessions in the form of spending cuts. As a result, this essential step was delayed for a further year and a half. Approval finally came with the passage of the Revenue and Expenditure Act of 1968, which was signed into law on June 28. The tax increase came three years too late. The damage had been done. In 1969, the United States, which prior to 1965 was the best-performing large economy in the world with respect to price stability, had become the worst performer.

Federal Reserve Policy

Federal deficit spending, even of the 1965-1968 variety, need not result in general price-level increases if monetary policy can be kept commensurately tight. Had it chosen to do so, the central bank could have refused to accommodate the government's inflationary budget policies. It could have done so by not buying any of the new debt the goverment was issuing; that is by not "monetizing" the new debt. The Federal Government would have been forced to go to the private credit markets to finance the growing difference between what it took in in taxes and the even larger amounts it wanted to spend. Given the ability of the Federal Government to command credit because of its insensitivity to interest costs, the private sector would have been deprived of part of the flow of credit on which it regularly depends. Thus, private demand would have had to fall. This is precisely what happened in 1966, when the central bank tried to contain the worsening inflation at its earliest stages. In principle, the Fed could have continued its 1966 policies until such time as the government saw fit to correct its budget policies. In practice, there were tangible impediments to the Fed's ability to act in such a manner, and the experience of 1966 demonstrated what these problems are.

Over the years, thrift institutions such as mutual savings banks, savings and loan associations and, to a lesser extent, life insurance companies have become a very large part of U.S. financial markets. The funds that households place in these institutions represent long-term savings and normally behave as such. However, these funds can also behave like short-term deposits in that they can be withdrawn on demand (in the case of life insurance companies, through policy loans).

A policy of tight money that is single-mindedly devoted to the task of preventing inflation in the face of inflationary federal deficits must lead to an intense competition for funds and, therefore, to rising interest rates, just as occurred in 1966. When market rates of interest rose above the lower rates paid by the thrift institutions (most of which were regulated by interest ceilings), funds were withdrawn from the institutions for direct placement in the market, a process that goes by the inelegant name "disintermediation." Financial institutions become highly vulnerable once such a process begins. Even if regulations on maximum interest rates they were permitted to pay did not exist, the institutions could not compete for new funds by offering higher rates without having to pay similar rates to *all* their depositors. Because most of their assets were held in the form of illiquid, long-term mortgages or fixed-coupon bonds bearing rates of interest below the current market level, the intermediaries would have been driven toward losses and eventually insolvency, thus threatening the entire financial system of the country.

A second consequence of a very rapid rise in interest rates in such circumstances was that the flow of new funds into the housing markets dried up, causing a sharp fall in residential construction activity in 1966. Both of these developments made it difficult, if not impossible, for the central bank to stay on its original course.

It is useful to ask, but not possible to answer, an important question: What would have happened in the United States had the central bank not changed to an accommodative course in 1967? Several developments could have followed. An obvious one is that the Administration, with the support of the Congress, could have simply replaced the central bank's existing management with another less troublesome one. This is exactly what has happened in dozens of other countries. Alternatively, if the Fed's single-minded pursuit of price stability had had widespread support, the result might have been to force Congress and the Administration to change their budget policies much more rapidly. Whatever the answer, the decision that was in fact made in 1967 was for the central bank to ease off in its policy of restraint.

To prevent a continuation of the credit crunch and to avert the risks of recession and financial chaos that a prolonged crunch would have entailed, the Federal Reserve System decided to buy a sizable part of the new debt that was issued to finance the growing federal deficit. From December, 1965, to December, 1969, gross federal debt rose by 15 percent. Federal debt held by the central bank rose by over 40 percent during the same period. Other Federal Government accounts, such as the social-insurance trust funds, also bought substantial portions of the new debt that the government sold. Private investors bought less than $2 billion of the nearly $50 billion of net federal debt issued in those years. When any government buys its own IOU's on such a scale, inflation can never be far behind.

Demand Pull Versus Cost Push

The onset of inflation in the 1960's provides an opportunity to analyze the theory that the push of costs, especially of wage costs, is the cause of modern inflation. Prior to 1965, output per hour of work in the U.S. private economy had risen by 20 percent in five years, a better rate than the historic improvement in that particular measure of productivity. Compensation per hour of work over the same period rose by 22 percent, just about in line with productivity growth. Thus, unit labor costs in the private sector rose by less than 2 percent in five years. In the important manufacturing sector, unit labor costs actually fell, a better performance than was achieved in any other major industrial economy. The superior performance in the U.S. economy showed up in two ways: The U.S. inflation rate of 1.3 percent a year was the lowest among the major nations. Our balance of trade in goods reflected our superior cost and price behavior. That balance, which had fallen to $1 billion a year in 1959, rose to an average of $6 billion a year in 1964-1965.

After 1965, U.S. economic performance deteriorated rapidly both in absolute terms and relative to other economies. From 1965 to 1970 the productivity gain in the private sector was only 10 percent, about one-half the gain experienced in the preceding five-year period. Furthermore, the rate of gain deteriorated rapidly as the decade progressed. Compensation per hour of work rose by nearly 40 percent, far in excess of the productivity gain achieved. As a result, unit labor costs rose by 27 percent between 1965 and 1970, both for the private economy as a whole and for the manufacturing sector. By contrast, unit labor costs in Japan rose only 4 percent and in Switzerland they did not rise at all. As we have already seen, inflation in the United States, measured by the CPI, accelerated from 1.3 percent prior to 1965 to 6.1 percent during the 12 months ending December, 1969. There was hardly any worsening in inflation rates in most of the other major countries. The relative worsening in our competitive position led to a fall in our balance of trade in goods from the $6-billion-a-year level of 1964-1965 to virtually zero by 1969. In 1971, this balance turned negative for the first time since 1893.

It is difficult to blame the dramatic shift that took place between the first and second half of the 1960's on a shift in the behavior of workers, unions, and corporations. Essentially the same workers, the same unions, and the same corporations operated under the same laws and regulations both before and after 1965. It is far more plausible to explain what happened after 1965 in terms of the excess demands placed on the economy by an inappropriately expansive fiscal policy and, after 1966, an inappropriately expansive monetary policy. These were the factors that caused inflation. They also brought about conditions in which productivity could no longer rise rapidly because the entire economy was forced into operating at a level above its normal potential. The inflation that was produced by excess demand and the low productivity increase induced by that excess demand was the *cause* and not the *result* of the subsequent acceleration in wage demands and unit labor costs.

Although wage push does not hold water as the *cause* of the post-1965 inflation, it does provide an important explanation of why inflation tended to get worse once it began. The complex interaction between wages and prices also explains why inflation, once it worsens, is so difficult to reverse.

Disinflation: 1970-1972

The Johnson Administration was by no means insensitive to the danger of inflation; indeed very shortly after inflation's onset, policymakers began to think of ways to stop it. However, the one policy that could be invoked at short notice, namely monetary policy, turned out to have highly disruptive effects on the financial system in the context of fiscal expansion. Fiscal policy itself also turned out to be far less controllable in practice than in theory. In the 1965-1968 period, defense outlays kept growing because the United States could not control the course of events in Vietnam; social outlays kept growing because they were based on legislated entitlements rather than on annual appropriations; finally, budget deficits kept growing because of the uncontrollable political lag involved in increasing tax rates. Nonetheless, all of the forces driving inflation were decisively reversed by the end of 1968.

The tax increase of 1968 converted the huge deficit of FY 1968 into a small surplus by FY 1969—one that still ranks as the only surplus achieved in our national budget since 1960. Monetary policy, which was either erroneously or inadvertently loosened just after the tax-increase bill was passed, was decisively tightened by December, 1968. The effort devoted to the war in Vietnam also reached its peak in December, 1968. At that time, the war was absorbing the equivalent of eight million man-years annually, including persons in and out of uniform. That level of commitment was reduced sharply starting in January, 1969. Finally, there was a change in government. By and large, Republican presidents have displayed a lower tolerance for inflation than have presidents of the opposing party.

In spite of these fairly dramatic reversals both in policy and in attitudes toward policy, the rate of inflation continued to climb throughout 1969, rising from 4.4 percent in December, 1968, to 6.1 percent in December, 1969. The driving force was no longer fiscal-monetary policy. It was a scramble by everybody for larger compensation increases and a larger share in the national income, a scramble that was itself the result of a perceived erosion caused by previous price increases. Although inflation is essentially a zero-sum game (what some sectors lose by inflation must be offset by gains of other sectors), almost all sectors in 1969 perceived that they were net losers and therefore demanded "catch-up" increases to compensate for these losses. So long as the economy continued to expand, these individual attempts at the catch-up game could succeed, at least in nominal terms. The result was worsening inflation.

Fiscal-monetary constraint brought economic expansion to a halt by the end of 1969. The longest uninterrupted expansion in U.S. history (1961-1969) ended. The economy went into the 1969-1970 recession. The rate of inflation declined, but the decline was painfully slow—to 5.5 percent by the end of 1970 and 4.5 percent by the middle of 1971.

The 1969-1970 contraction ended in the final quarter of 1970 and the economy moved into a phase of slow expansion. The danger was that with renewed expansion the rate of inflation would start rising again, as it frequently does during an upswing in the business cycle. There were tangible signs in the Spring quarter of 1971 that these fears might be justified. If the effects of fluctuations in food prices and mortgage-interest rates are removed from the CPI, for example, it becomes evident that average prices in all other sectors of the economy were increasing more rapidly during the Spring quarter of 1971 than they had risen in 1969 or 1970. The same was true of wholesale industrial prices, an index that generally provides a revealing preview of future changes in nonfood retail prices.

The threat of renewed inflation, the inflationary behavior of wage and price demands in key segments in the key economy, the sluggishness of the economic expansion that was under way between the Summer of 1970 and the Summer of 1971 (for example, industrial production barely grew) and, finally, the need to devalue the dollar led the Nixon Administration to announce a dramatic set of policy changes on August 15, 1971. Among the many changes put into effect on that date was a three-month freeze on wages and prices to be followed thereafter by mandatory wage, price and profit controls. By December, 1971, the 12-month rate of increase was down to 3.4 percent, as measured by the now substantially controlled CPI. In spite of a quickening in the rate of economic expansion after mid-1971, controls helped to hold price increases down to the 3.4 percent level until December, 1972, when a second and even larger wave of inflation began.

THE SECOND WAVE: 1972-1974

The second wave of inflation was a global one. In December, 1973, the rate of inflation in the United States rose to 8.8 percent and to 12.2 percent in December, 1974. With the exception of Switzerland and West Germany, far higher rates were experienced elsewhere, as witness the 25 percent per annum rates that struck Japan, the United Kingdom, and Italy. The source of these extraordinary rates of price increase was *not* the large jump in oil prices that occurred in December, 1973. Oil prices did worsen inflation everywhere in 1974, but the inflationary wave itself was fully under way before this complication occurred. The real cause of the 1972-1974 wave of inflation was a global expansion in the money supply. The cause of this expansion, in turn, was the ill-advised way in which the major countries of the world handled the dollar devaluation in 1971-1973, a complex matter to which we now turn.

International Monetary Confusion

In 1971, the major nations of the world were on a system of fixed exchange rates known as "Bretton Woods," after the small New Hampshire town in which plans for the post-World War II international monetary system had been drawn up in 1944. Under this system, each major country agreed to define the value of its currency in objective terms, and to maintain this value through central bank action. One way of defining a parity, which only the United States adopted because only the United States had sufficient gold to do so, was to define the currency unit in terms of gold. Thus the value of the U.S. dollar was set at $35 to one troy ounce of gold. The United States undertook to maintain that value by selling gold in exchange for dollars, or dollars in exchange for gold, to any other central bank in the system at that fixed price. Other countries defined the exchange value of their currencies in terms of U.S. dollars. For example, the Japanese yen was set 360 yen to $1.00, and Japan undertook to defend that parity by exchanging dollars for yen or yen for dollars at that fixed rate.

The system, which was in full effect by the early 1950's, worked remarkably well for 20 years. One major nation or another would find itself unable to maintain its undertaking from time to time. In 1968, for example, France was beset by social and economic problems that put downward pressure on the exchange rate of the French franc because, for one reason or another, parties holding francs wanted to convert them into dollars. In order to maintain the exchange rate in the face of such pressures, the Bank of France had to purchase the excess supply of francs offered in its foreign-exchange markets. To pay for these purchases, the Bank of France had to use the stock of dollars which it held as part of its international reserves, dollars it had accumulated in earlier years. When that stock diminished to dangerously low levels, as it did in 1968, the French government was forced to abandon the previous parity of the franc: It had to devalue the franc in the hope that at a new, lower rate of exchange individuals and businesses would no longer want to get rid of their francs. Such devaluations, and dozens occurred during the Bretton Woods period, sometimes had a traumatic effect on the devaluing countries; but they had no impact whatever on world inflation, just as the almost continuous devaluations of South American currencies have no impact on world inflation. The devaluation of the U.S. dollar starting in 1971 was an altogether different story.

The U.S. dollar was not just the most important currency in the Bretton Woods world, it was the central currency against which all other exchange rates were defined and maintained. There was a second and even more important difference between the U.S. dollar and the other currencies. Through its willingness to allow the dollar to act as the central currency in the system, the United States had effectively given up control over the dollar's exchange rate relative to other major currencies. The dollar-yen rate was set in Tokyo and maintained in Tokyo through the buying and selling actions of the Bank of Japan. The same was true of all other exchange rates. Our only responsibility was to maintain the convertibility of dollars into gold and vice versa. When the time came for the United States to devalue in 1971, the issue caused a great deal of confusion because no mechanism for doing so had been established. One of the implicit assumptions of the Bretton Woods system was that the United States dollar would never have to devalue. It had become abundantly clear by early 1971 that this assumption was invalid.

The reason for the devaluation of the U.S. dollar in 1971 was the same as that for any other currency's devaluation—a decline in its international competitiveness at the old exchange rate. Thus, if Brazil suffers a 100-percent inflation rate while the rest of the world has 5-percent inflation, Brazil discovers that goods and services produced at home will soon become almost twice as expensive as goods and services produced elsewhere. Everybody in Brazil will prefer to purchase foreign-produced goods (offering cruzeiros) and nobody outside of Brazil will be demanding cruzeiros to purchase Brazilian goods, assuming that acceptable substitutes are available elsewhere. Nor would sensible central banks outside of Brazil offer to buy the now-excessive supply of cruzeiros. As a result, the exchange rate of cruzeiros would fall until equilibrium once again was restored.

Between 1965 and 1970, the United States suffered a far sharper worsening of its inflation rate than did its principal trading competitors. We went from being the best-performing large economy in terms of price stability and unit labor costs prior to 1965 to being the worst performer by 1969-1970. In addition, U.S. imports rose rapidly because the U.S. economy was unable to supply all of the goods and services needed to satisfy the unprecedented combination of civilian, military and welfare demand. The supply of dollars from individuals and businesses who wanted to buy non-U.S. products and securities rose far more sharply than the demand for dollars from parties who wanted to buy U.S. products and securities. However, the excess supply of dollars in the foreign-exchange markets of the world did not automatically lead to a decline in the dollar's exchange rate, because central banks outside of the United States simply purchased all excess supplies of dollars to maintain the preexisting exchange rate.

Theoretically, the ability of a non-U.S. central bank to buy dollars with its own currency (yen, deutsche marks, French francs, and so forth) is unlimited. The reason is simple: Each of these central banks holds the patent for manufacturing its own currency and, therefore, can do so in unlimited amounts.

There is a limit to such behavior in practice. Every time a central bank buys anything by using money that it can manufacture with a stroke of the pen, it increases the stock of that money. Eventually, an overcreation of money will lead to inflation. On the other hand, if the central bank of a country stopped buying the excess supply of dollars entering its foreign-exchange markets, the exchange rate of the dollar against its own currency would fall. The prospect of such a fate presented every major country with an enormous problem in 1971. Because the dollar was the centerpiece of the system against which all exchange rates were defined, a fall in the dollar's exchange rate against a currency, the deutsche mark for example, would mean a rise in the deutsche mark exchange rate against every other currency in the world—not only against the dollar.

A rise in the exchange rate of a country's currency is not always desirable. It makes the country's exports less competitive on world markets and, at the same time, it exposes large segments of its own economy to the threat of competition from cheaper imports by lowering the effective price of those imports. For example, if the exchange rate of the Japanese yen were to rise from around 235 yen per dollar that prevailed at year-end 1983 to, say, 120 yen per dollar (to take an extreme case), the dollar price of Toyotas in the United States would double. In that event, few non-Japanese customers would want Japanese automobiles, or Japanese steel, or a wide range of other Japanese products. For an export-oriented country, such a consideration was an important inhibition against allowing its exchange rate to rise against the dollar in 1971.

Thus, the rising flood of excess dollars that flowed into the foreign-exchange markets of the world, starting in 1971, was purchased by the central banks of the countries receiving those dollars. Each such purchase created new money. The dollar outflow arising out of simple trading imbalances was not that large in itself. The swing of the U.S. international account from a surplus in 1965 to a deficit in 1971 amounted to $6 billion a year. Far more serious were the much larger flows of dollars into currencies such as the deutsche mark, Swiss francs, and the Japanese yen that were triggered because most sensible people had come to believe by early 1971 that, sooner or later, the dollar would have to be devalued against these currencies. That devaluation, when it finally came, offered the prospect of enormous capital gains to anybody who had previously shifted out of dollars into these appreciating currencies.

By early 1971, the outflow of dollars had become a flood—especially into West Germany, the country whose currency offered the largest prospect for massive appreciation and which, at the same time, had the freest capital market outside the United States. The pace of the flood accelerated from a $1 billion a year to $1 billion a month and, finally, on May 5 of 1971, to $1 billion an hour. The Bundesbank was forced to abandon its dangerously inflationary policy of mopping up all these dollars. Faced with two unpleasant alternatives—an unwarranted rise in the exchange rate on the one hand and a potentially inflationary rise in the money supply on the other, the German authorities chose to avoid the threat of inflation. They stopped purchasing dollars and thereby allowed the exchange rate of the deutsche mark to rise.

West Germany's closest neighbors, Switzerland, Austria and the Netherlands, whose economies were closely linked to hers and who shared her antipathy to inflation, followed this example within days. The Netherlands allowed the guilder to float upward; Switzerland and Austria responded in more orthodox fashion by raising the exchange parity of their curencies against the dollar by 7 percent and 5 percent, respectively.

By May, 1971, it had become clear that the dollar was overvalued, not just against the deutsche mark and one or two other currencies but against virtually all of the other currencies, and not just by 5 or 7 percent but by a lot more. Some means had to be found to achieve a general and significant devaluation of the U.S. dollar. Unfortunately, the major financial powers of the world were unable to agree on a straightforward way of doing so. Most major countries refused to follow the example set by West Germany and Switzerland: Instead, Japan, France, Italy and the United Kingdom—apparently more willing than Germany and Switzerland to risk serious inflation—continued to peg the dollar's exchange rate against their currencies at its old parity. This peg was achieved partly through the use of artificial controls on the inflow of dollars but mainly through intervention, that is, by purchasing dollars in their exchange markets. These policies eventually led to large increases in their domestic money supplies and, later, to extremely high rates of inflation.

The reluctance to revalue (i.e., up value) national currencies against the U.S. dollar had complex roots. In addition to a basic unwillingness on the part of each nation to risk the loss of export competitiveness, nobody was quite sure about the size of the correction that was required in the dollar-exchange rate. Different econometric models that were addressed to the question produced different results. Furthermore, it was clear that the degree of dollar overvaluation was not the same against all major currencies. Thus, in addition to the problem of devaluing the dollar, the world faced the problem of resetting the entire network of exchange rates among the major currencies.

One solution to the problem of arriving at a new set of exchange rates would have been for everybody to stop intervening in foreign-exchange markets, thereby allowing market forces to determine a new and more appropriate set of rates. Most countries, for multiple reasons, were unwilling to accept such a solution. First, there was a general reluctance to abandon a system of fixed exchange-rate parities that has served the world so well for two decades; second, a world of floating rates would have formalized the role of the U.S. dollar as the official centerpiece of the Bretton Woods system, a role that France, in particular, strongly opposed on grounds of principle; finally, there was a suspicion on the part of some countries, notably West Germany and Japan, that their currencies might be driven up more sharply than others against the dollar and, in the process, driven up against other currencies as well.

Given the unwillingness of the major powers to adopt a floating or market solution, the currency-realignment problem had to be resolved through the process of international negotiation. The negotiation route itself, however, encountered serious obstacles, in addition to those already mentioned. Essentially, there were three obstacles to a negotiated realignment, all of them at least partly political.

The "Contribution" Issue

Changing its currency's exchange parity (either up or down) always presents political problems for a goverent because either move hurts some segment of a nation's economy. Although a simple revaluation of their currencies upward against the dollar would have resolved the problem of devaluing the dollar, it would have entailed political costs to each of the other countries. The problem can be stated as a question: Why should the United States government, the principal culprit, be allowed to get away scot-free while every other government exposed itself to political discomfort? The consensus, led by the French government, was that the United States itself should be required somehow to make a "contribution" to the process.

Balance Sheet Losses

A second issue concerned the financial "loss" that countries that revalued their currencies upward against the dollar would suffer. Each nation's international reserve assets were held principally in gold or dollars, but were shown on their own books in terms of local currencies. Hence, an upward revaluation against the dollar would have caused the stated values of their gold and dollar assets to fall by the extent of their revaluation.

For France, whose citizens are reputed to be the world's largest private hoarders of gold, there was an additional problem. French households had acquired and held gold for centuries on the generally correct assumption that the price of gold would always rise in terms of francs. Because the price of gold was pegged by the United States at $35.00 per ounce, an upward revaluation of the franc against the dollar would mean that the franc price of gold would fall. A Gaullist government that had repeatedly proclaimed the eternal verity of the yellow metal as a standard of value was politically incapable of performing an act that would cause the value of gold to fall against a paper currency.

The Gold Problem

There were obstacles on the U.S. side as well. The only way in which the United States could have contributed to the process would have been to devalue the dollar in terms of gold—that is, to raise the official price of gold above the $35.00-per-ounce level at which it had been fixed ever since the Roosevelt devaluation of 1934. Such a move would have served two purposes: It would have provided a clear signal to the world that the exchange-rate problem it faced in 1971 was essentially a dollar problem, and it would have minimized many of the obstacles that other countries participating in the negotiating process perceived. Unfortunately, there were political, legal, financial and ideological impediments to raising the U.S. price of gold.

One impediment was President Nixon's reluctance to saddle a Republican administration with the stigma of devaluation. This political reluctance was reinforced by a legal interpretation that stated (arguably) that the president did not have the authority to alter the U.S. price of gold without the prior approval of the Congress. Given that both houses of the Congress were controlled by the opposition party, it was clear that such a request would have become the subject of endless debate and delay. The delay, in turn, would have triggered further large speculative dollar outflows: World financial markets, already in great distress, would have become even more chaotic.

The economic obstacle to a devaluation of the dollar against gold arose from the fact that many within the Nixon administration attributed U.S. trading deficits not to an overvalued dollar but to restrictive trading practices on the part of our competitors. For people who held this opinion, the appropriate remedy was for the United States to demand fairer and more open trading practices on the part of other nations.

Ideology was a third obstacle. Under the Bretton Woods system, gold had been pushed into a relatively insignificant role, and the U.S. dollar had effectively become the world's principal international reserve asset. There were many who were not anxious to return gold—that "barbarous relic," as it was sometimes called—to a more central position in international finance. Furthermore, an increase in the official price of gold would have bestowed benefits on the two principal gold-producing nations, South Africa and the Soviet Union, at the expense of most other countries. It would also have benefited countries like France, which had made it a point to hold the bulk of its reserve assets in the form of gold, at the expense of countries like Japan, which held its international assets primarily in the form of dollars.

In the light of all the obstacles that lay in the way of a quick and easy solution to the realignment process, it is not surprising that nothing was accomplished. Dollars continued to flood the world's principal exchange markets after the German crisis of May, 1971. Some countries, such as West Germany, gradually allowed these pressures to push the exchange rate upward. Others, notably Japan, France and Italy, kept on purchasing dollars in order to prevent a rise in their currencies. In policy terms, Germany and Switzerland were willing to give up control of their exchange rates in order to maintain better control over their money supplies. By contrast, countries like Japan, France and Italy surrendered control over their own money supplies in favor of maintaining control over their exchange rates. The different policies showed up a few years later in the form of remarkable differences in the rates of inflation these countries experienced. In December, 1974, West German inflation, as measured by the CPI, was 6½ percent, the lowest among the large nations. Japan and Italy each suffered a 25 percent inflation rate in that year, and the French rate was 15 percent.

Technically, the central banks could have offset the expansive effect that their purchases of dollars had on their money supplies, but in most cases the sheer volume of dollar purchases overwhelmed their capacity to take such offsetting action. Also, they could have presented the dollars they had acquired to the United States Treasury in exchange for gold—a right they had under the Bretton Woods agreement. In fact, as opposed to theory, any such move would have been self-defeating, because the amount of dollars held by these central banks was many times larger than the total stock of gold and other reserve assets ($14.5 billion) held by the United States. Nonetheless, as the certainty of eventual dollar devaluation became increasingly obvious, some central banks did try to exchange the paper assets they were holding into gold. These moves precipitated U.S. action on August 15, 1971.

On that Sunday, President Nixon announced a dramatic combination of economic policies:

(1) The United States closed the gold window; that is, it officially suspended the convertibility of dollars into gold.
(2) The United States imposed a temporary surcharge of 10 percent on most imports into the country, a move that effectively devalued the dollar by 10 percent because it raised the price of imports by that amount.
(3) Most United States prices and wages were frozen for 90 days, to be followed by a comprehensive system of mandatory wage and price controls.
(4) A package of stimulative tax reductions was put forward for swift congressional approval.

The surcharge and the suspension of convertibility by the United States were designed to force the issue of international monetary readjustment. They did bring the parties concerned to the negotiating table, but nothing much else was resolved until the end of the year. The outflow of dollars continued as the negotiations dragged on. Many nations followed the West German practice of allowing their currencies to rise in exchange markets, but nonetheless maintained control over the overall rise in their exchange rates through heavy intervention. France was a notable exception and continued to hold the franc-dollar exchange rate firmly at its original parity. As French policy fully intended, the French franc experienced as large a devaluation against the German mark by the end of 1971 as did the U.S. dollar.

The problem with this outcome was that the dollar had needed to be devalued against the deutsche mark whereas the French franc had not. The even larger problem was that until the French were prepared to let the franc rise against the dollar, the willingness of other nations to do so became increasingly constrained. This was particularly true for West Germany because France is her largest single trading partner and thus, in a sense, her principal competitor. It was also clear that the French government would make no move until the United States agreed to devalue the dollar against gold. This was eventually done in December, 1971: The United States raised the price of gold from $35.00 to $38.00 an ounce, an increase of 8.5 percent or a dollar devaluation of 7.89 percent. The French, in return, agreed to maintain the previous price of gold in terms of francs, which meant that the exchange rate of the franc would rise by 8.5 percent against the U.S. dollar. Other major exchange rates were also set by negotiated agreements, hammered out at an international conference convened at the Smithsonian Institution in Washington, D.C. As part of the agreements, the United States lifted the temporary surcharge on imports that it had imposed on August 15.

In one sense the Smithsonian accord resolved the most pressing issue that faced the international community in 1971: It produced a negotiated multilateral set of new exchange rates that gave the United States the devaluation it had sought for the dollar. Given the obstacles that had to be overcome this, in itself, was no mean achievement. The President of the United States described it as "the greatest monetary agreement in history." As a long-run solution, however, the Smithsonian accord was a failure. In order to reach an accord, the parties had allowed political considerations to dominate matters better resolved through the realities of the marketplace. Thus, one condition for French participation was that the British pound should rise as much against the U.S. dollar as did the French franc, and that the Italian lira should rise by almost as much. The deutsche mark was required to go up by 14 percent and the Japanese yen by 17 percent. The set of rates finally selected was not in harmony with underlying financial realities.

In June, 1972, it became increasingly clear that the pound had been assigned too high a value; a speculative run against the pound began and the British were forced to abandon the parity they had been assigned under the Smithsonian accord. The pound rapidly sank to its pre-Smithsonian level. Even more serious, it became clear that the dollar had not been devalued by as much as economic reality required. There was a run against the dollar in early 1973. The German Bundesbank was forced to buy some $6 billion in less than a day to maintain the Smithsonian parity between the U.S. dollar and the deutsche mark, and the German monetary authorities once again had to allow the exchange rate of the dollar to float—that is, to sink.

The U.S. authorities responded to the situation by devaluing the dollar against gold for a second time, raising the official price of gold to $42.22 per ounce. Shortly thereafter, all major nations abandoned the Smithsonian parities in favor of a generalized system of floating rates. The "greatest monetary agreement in history" had lasted for just over one year. As for gold, the official U.S. price of $42.22 per ounce is now simply a price at which the U.S. Treasury neither buys nor sells the metal!

The Consequences

The mismanagement of currency realignment in 1971-1973 had three serious consequences. The first was a massive increase in the world's supply of money; the second, partly triggered by the first, was the development of a worldwide boom in which industrial production rose at unprecedented rates; the third was the onset of a huge wave of inflation.

The Monetary Explosion

Between the end of 1970, when the weakness of the dollar first became apparent, and the second quarter of 1973, when the dollar was reluctantly allowed to sink to its market-determined level, the world experienced an explosion in monetary growth. The principal reason for this explosion was the attempt by major countries to prevent or retard the rise in their exchange rates against the dollar by purchasing all (or most) of the dollars that flowed into their exchange markets. Table 4 measures the monetary growth that took place during this period in two ways. The first column shows money-supply growth, measured in terms of M-1, for each of the major countries. These rates range from a low of 11.5 percent per annum for Switzerland to a high of 27.2 percent per annum for Japan. Compared with these rates, the rise of 7.2 percent per annum for the U.S. money supply, itself too high from the point of view of price stability, looks like a model of restraint.

The second column of Table 4 shows the aggregate rise in the world's money supply (defined as the total money supply in the eight countries) expressed in terms of dollars. Although the dollar had fallen from grace, it retained its place as the key yardstick in which world commodity prices, notably oil, were expressed. Because each of the other currencies was worth more in terms of dollars in early 1973 than it had been worth at the end of 1970, the dollar-equivalent measure of monetary growth shows an even more explosive rise than the measures shown in Column 1. Aggregate M-1 for the seven non-U.S. coun-

Table 4
Growth in Money Supply (M-1)
IV Q 1970 to II Q 1973

| Country | Percent | |
	In local currency units (average annual[1])	In U.S. dollar equivalent (overall)
Japan	27.2	146.0
West Germany	12.1	100.0
France	12.9	82.1
United Kingdom	13.3	51.6
Italy	20.6	70.6
Canada	13.3	44.6
Switzerland	11.5	94.5
Average (unweighted)	15.8	—
Total (weighted)	—	94.2
United States.................	7.2	19.0
World money supply (weighted)[2]..		55.2

[1]Based on continuous compounding
[2]Defined as total M-1 of all eight countries including the United States

Sources: Federal Reserve Bank of St. Louis, *International Economic Conditions* (various quarterly issues) and *Federal Reserve Bulletin* (monthly issues).

tries in the table amounted to $206.6 billion at the end of 1970. The corresponding figure for the second quarter of 1973 was $401.2 billion—a virtual doubling in less than two-and-a-half years. One did not have to be a monetarist to predict that a virtual doubling of the price level was soon to follow. It did.

The Worldwide Boom and Inflation

The highly expansionary monetary policies that were advertently or inadvertently pursued in 1971 and 1972 generated a worldwide boom, especially in industrial production. The rising demand for goods in 1972 and 1973, itself propelled by excessive monetary creation, led to rapidly rising output everywhere. For the seven largest industrial nations shown in Table 5, the average (unweighted) rise in industrial production between March, 1972, and March, 1973, was over 12 percent. These increases inevitably led to an accelerating rate of inflation. By the end of 1973, just before the even more explosive rise in oil prices began, the unweighted rate of inflation in the eight countries included in this report had climbed to about 10 percent per annum, ranging from a low of 7¼ percent in West Germany to a high of 16 percent in Japan.

The First Oil Shock

The first oil shock occurred in the context of the boom and inflation just

Table 5
Growth in Industrial Production

Country	Percent per annum	
	1965-1971	I Q 1972-I Q 1973
United States	3.4	11.8
Japan	13.6	17.4
West Germany	4.6	7.9
France	5.6	10.5
United Kingdom	2.0	13.4
Italy	6.0	15.7[a]
Canada	4.9	9.6
Average (unweighted) . .	5.7	12.3

[a]Italy from third quarter 1972 to third quarter 1973 because of serious interruptions to output caused by labor disputes in early 1973.

Sources: Federal Reserve Bank of St. Louis, *International Economic Conditions.*

outlined. Because petroleum prices were set in terms of U.S. dollars, oil-producing countries suffered a twofold loss in purchasing power: Each dollar they received was convertible into fewer units of other currencies; and each such currency unit commanded fewer of the goods and services that they needed to import. Thus, pressures mounted for an increase in petroleum prices.

Just how the 1971-1973 wave of dollar devaluation, money creation, and world inflation might have worked itself out in terms of prices in general, and oil prices in particular, is something we will never know. In December, 1973, the course of events was subjected to a large external shock—the curtailment of Arabian oil production and a quantum jump in the price of petroleum. Soon after the outbreak of the fourth Arab-Israeli War on October 6, 1973, Saudi Arabia—acting in concert with other oil-exporting Arab states—cut oil production, embargoed sales to the United States and the Netherlands, and raised the posted price of its benchmark crude to $11.65 a barrel, effective January 1, 1974. This represented a 350-percent increase over the posted price of $2.59 a barrel that had prevailed just one year earlier. For reasons given earlier (see page 4), the increase in the effective price of oil (as opposed to the posted price) was closer to 400 percent. These massive increases were followed by an acceleration in already-high inflation rates. By December, 1974, the average (unweighted) rate of inflation in the eight major countries had climbed to 16.5 percent. Just how much of the price acceleration experienced in 1974 was caused by oil and just how much was the inevitable result of the prior explosion that had taken place in money supplies is still an unsettled debate. At one extreme, there are those who argue that oil was the principal factor underlying the worldwide inflation of 1974. At the other extreme, there is the monetarist view that aggregate inflation is driven primarily by increases in aggregate monetary supplies and that an increase in the price of a single commodity can have no additional inflationary effect because it will be offset by decreases in other individual prices.

The behavior of prices, notably of producer prices, in each of the eight major industrial countries does not support the popular view that oil was a major cause either of the level of inflation experienced in 1974 or even of the acceleration of inflation that took place between 1973 and 1974. The correspondence between inflation and the rate of monetary growth that preceded it is a close one. By contrast, there appears to be no clear-cut relation between the degree of a country's dependence on imported oil and the behavior of inflation in that country. In Switzerland, Japan and France, three countries that are heavily dependent on oil imports, inflation *measured by the producer price index* was no higher during the year following the oil shock than it had been in the year before. In the United States, whose dependence on imported oil was far lower, and in Canada (which was a net oil exporter in 1973), inflation rates climbed sharply in 1974, but these increases can hardly be attributed to the oil-price factor. Although these observations are not conclusive, the evidence supports the view that money and the pull of monetary demand were the critical ingredients in the inflationary wave of 1972-1974. The major impact of the oil shock was to push the industrial world into a severe recession.

THE THIRD WAVE: 1977-1980

The first oil shock pushed the industrial world into a sharp and prolonged recession, the worst experienced since World War II. Recovery from the recession, especially of industrial production, was also relatively slow.

The duration of a recession can be measured in two ways: The official measure refers to the period in which industrial output is actually shrinking. The second measure covers, in addition, the length of time required for an economy fully to return to the level that prevailed at the preceding peak of the cycle. In the United States, industrial output shrank from November, 1973, to March, 1975; thereafter it took until December, 1976, for output to get back to the level achieved in November, 1973.

In the context of severe recession, inflation rates everywhere receded from the peaks reached in 1974-1975. By December, 1976, the U.S. rate had declined to 4.8 percent. In part, this rate reflected extremely good performance in retail food prices; excluding food, the rise in the consumer price index was closer to 6 percent.

The coexistence of very slow growth and high unemployment on the one hand and a high underlying rate of inflation on the other created a serious dilemma for policymakers in all the major nations. Responses to this dilemma differed markedly from country to country. At one extreme, countries such as West Germany, Switzerland and Japan unequivocally gave the highest priority to the inflation problem. All three were successful in nearly eliminating inflation by the end of 1978. By then, the West German inflation rate was down to 2.3 percent, the Swiss rate to a remarkable 0.5 percent, and the Japanese rate to 3.4 percent.

In the United States, after the Carter administration took office in January, 1977, the thrust of policy was shifted from sustained disinflation to the traditional 1960's objectives of fast economic growth, lower unemployment, and a more equitable distribution of income. During its first two years in office, the administration was highly successful in terms of these objectives. Employment expanded by over seven million and, in spite of a very rapid growth in the labor force, the unemployment rate dropped from 7.8 percent at the end of 1976 to 5.8 by December, 1978. U.S. performance on the inflation front was not as good. From 4.8 percent a year in December, 1976, inflation climbed to 6.8 percent in December, 1977, and to 9 percent by December, 1978. The acceleration of inflation in 1977 was largely caused by a rise in food prices and was, therefore, more or less ignored.

In 1978, however, the cause of the rise had shifted squarely to the wage sector and could not be ignored. Those who made policy were forced to reexamine two troublesome questions:

(1) In early 1978, the Carter administration and the Congress had legislated a 15-percent increase in minimum wages. Was this action somehow to blame for the general pattern of wage and price acceleration that followed?
(2) Policy had assumed, just as had been assumed in the 1960's, that an unemployment objective of around 4 percent was achievable without inflation. Indeed, the Humphrey-Hawkins Act passed in 1978, reaffirmed this unemployment objective. Were these traditional assumptions regarding the compatibility of such an unemployment goal with price stability still valid?

Discussion of these issues in the annual economic reports of the Carter administration did not provide clear-cut answers to either question, but did suggest that U.S. policy was being reformulated to give a higher priority to curbing the new wave of inflation. Whatever the correct answers were to these questions, a sequence of external events took over at the end of 1978 that forced policy to give priority to the inflation issue.

The Collapse of the Dollar

The rapid expansion in the U.S. economy relative to its trading partners and the rapid acceleration in U.S. prices and costs in a world in which most national inflation rates were decelerating led to a sizable increase in U.S. trading deficits and to a sharp fall in the exchange rate of the dollar against other major currencies. Between early 1977 and the end of 1978, the deutsche mark rose

30 percent relative to the U.S. dollar and the value of the Japanese yen rose by 45 percent.

As the dollar's exchange rate fell, the price of imports into the U.S. rose sharply. This rise, in itself, did not add greatly to our domestic inflation rate because imports, though growing, represented only 10 percent of the goods and services we used in 1978. However, there were significant secondary effects: Protected by rapidly rising import prices, domestic producers and the unions that bargained with them were able to raise prices and wages more rapidly— and began to do so. As a consequence, in the final quarter of 1978, average prices in the United States rose at over 10 percent a year, a rate more rapid than in any other major industrial nation with the possible exception of Italy.

A second problem was associated with the falling U.S. dollar. The rest of the world, including the newly wealthy OPEC nations, held a large volume of dollar-denominated assets, mainly in highly liquid forms such as bank accounts, Treasury bills, and Eurodollars (dollar accounts held in banks outside of the United States). When the value of the dollar declined, these holders began to dump some of their dollar holdings in exchange for anything else that promised to maintain its value better. A crisis of large proportions might have ensued had widespread dollar dumping been triggered.

A third potential danger involved oil. In the attempt to foster fast growth and keep U.S. consumers happy, the Carter government had continued to suppress the price of domestic oil and gas. As a result of these policies, United States use of petroleum and, hence, petroleum imports into the United States continued to rise rapidly after 1973—the only major country for which this was true. We were importing petroleum at the rate of 8.8 million barrels a day by the end of 1978, some 40 percent above our 1973 level of imports. The annual bill for these imports was running at $45 billion a year, which accounted in large part for the U.S. trading deficit of $42 billion in 1978. It was fortunate for the United States that the price of imported oil was denominated in U.S. dollars rather than in Swiss francs or deutsche marks and, therefore, did not rise when the U.S. dollar itself fell sharply against these other major currencies. The danger to the United States at the end of 1978 was that the oil-exporting nations would carry out their frequently repeated threat to denominate oil prices in terms of some other currency unit, such as the Swiss franc, the West German mark, the Japanese yen, or some bundle of currencies. Had these threats been carried out, the United States would have found itself in the extremely difficult position of having somehow to find sufficient foreign exchange to pay for the oil imports on which the country had become increasingly dependent.

Given the potential dangers associated with the dollar crisis, a dramatic change in policy had to take place. It did. On November 1, 1978, large segments of U.S. economic policy were put into a U-turn:

(1) With the full support of the President and the Secretary of the Treasury, the Federal Reserve System undertook to tighten its previously inflationary monetary policies. Some bank reserve requirements were

increased; in addition, the central bank raised its discount rate by a full percentage point, an almost unprecedented tightening move.

(2) The United States also undertook to put together a $30-billion international borrowing package and to use these funds for the purpose of defending the exchange rate of the dollar. This represented a major shift from our previous policy of benign neglect of exchange rates. In an even greater shift, the large borrowing package included an undertaking by the U.S. government to sell bonds denominated not in dollars, but in deutsche marks and Swiss francs.

At about the same time, in a separate move, the United States undertook to change its energy policies, that is, to allow energy prices to rise to market levels in order to conserve the use of energy, maximize domestic production, and cut back sharply on petroleum imports.

These major policy shifts constituted an announcement to the rest of the world that the United States was at last prepared to give far higher priority to such objectives as price stability, exchange-rate stability, and the reduction of its huge and rising dependence on imported oil—priorities that most of the other major nations had adopted four years earlier. With these moves began the serious adaptation of the entire industrial world to the realities of the post-1973 era, an era of slower growth, higher unemployment, and one requiring energy conservation and constant vigilance against worsening inflation rates.

The Second Oil Crisis: 1979-1980

The shift in policy that occurred in November, 1978, did stabilize the U.S. dollar's exchange rate at the low level to which it had fallen, but any longer-run effects it might have had were swamped by an even larger event—the revolution in Iran and the overthrow of the Shah in January, 1979. As Iran slid into a sea of chaos, its oil production ground almost to a halt. The world was deprived of the approximately 5 million barrels a day that Iran had previously exported, an amount larger than total Saudi Arab oil exports in 1983. The price of oil traded in spot markets leapt as buyers scrambled to obtain supplies, and the basic price of oil virtually tripled over the following 18 months. The sudden increase of $20 per barrel implied a staggering $200-billion increase in the world's already-high annual bill for oil imports. Because other energy prices were also driven upward by the OPEC price increases, the free world's total bill for energy rose by around $500 billion a year.

A useful way to think of what happened in 1979-1980 is to view the oil price increase as the imposition of a tax of some $500 billion a year on consumption—a massive tax increase even in the context of the world economy. The results were predictable. The first impact of such a large consumption tax is to accelerate the rate of inflation; and the second is to trigger a recession. Both occurred in 1980.

The U.S. inflation rate, which had already climbed to 9 percent a year by December, 1978, accelerated to 13 percent by December, 1979, and to just under 15 percent by March, 1980. The annualized rate of inflation in the United States ran at 18 percent a year during the first quarter of 1980. Other countries recorded even higher rates, notably the United Kingdom (25 percent) and Italy (20 percent). Even in the best-behaved economies, such as West Germany, Switzerland and Japan, inflation accelerated sharply.

Responses

The acceleration of inflation in 1979-1980 evoked powerful responses in the United States from both policymakers and private citizens. On the policy front there were two major changes: (1) The attempt to hold domestic energy prices down artificially was abandoned in favor of a policy of phased deregulation for domestic oil and natural gas that would allow these prices to rise to world levels over a period of years. However, the income distribution question, which had been one of the impediments to the earlier adoption of such a sensible move, was reinjected into the deregulation process. A windfall profits tax was imposed on oil producers, and controls were continued over some natural gas prices. (2) The emphasis on the unemployment rate as *the* major objective of U.S. policy was replaced, at least temporarily, by an emphasis on stabilizing the purchasing power of the dollar. To this end the Federal Reserve System, with the full concurrence of the Carter administration, announced (on October 6, 1979) that it would henceforth pursue a policy of seriously constraining monetary growth within a predetermined target range, regardless of consequences that such a policy might have on interest rates and on all of the other factors that are influenced by interest rates.

The shifts in policy emphasis were dramatic, but they were far less dramatic than the contemporaneous shifts on the part of private citizens. Bitten as they had been by three waves of inflation, each higher than the one preceding and each to a large extent unanticipated, large segments of the private sector began to operate in 1979-1980 on the assumption that worsening inflation had become a way of life for the United States: They began to dump dollars and dollar-denominated assets, such as bonds and common stocks, in favor of real assets that offered a far better probability of preserving purchasing power in an inflationary environment.

In early 1980, when many investors moved away from bonds and stocks, both of which had caused them to suffer huge losses, the price of tangible investments rose extremely sharply. The price of gold jumped to $850 an ounce; the price of silver to $50 an ounce; the price of Libyan oil to $45 a barrel. Land prices soared, as did the price of homes; so did the prices of anything that might be labeled tangible or collectible, including coins, Oriental rugs, works of art, and precious stones. Seminars on how to survive the impending collapse of the currency became a major industry. The advice was consistent—dump all assets denominated in dollars, borrow as much as possible denominated in dollars, and place all funds in tangibles. The long game of inflation that the U.S. government had played with its citizens was over. The only policy move available for restoring sanity to the vast capital markets of the United States was a decisive policy of disinflation. That is exactly what followed.

Monetary Policy and Credit Controls

The two policy instruments used by the government to break the rising wave of inflation in 1979-1980 were, first, the application of a far sterner dose of restrictive monetary policies and, later, the imposition of emergency controls over credit expansion.

Monetary Policy

The period 1977-1980 was an extremely turbulent one both for monetary policy and for financial markets. In 1977, in the interest of achieving rapid economic expansion, the Carter administration changed the leadership of the Federal Reserve System. The Federal Reserve Board Chairman, Arthur Burns, a Republican appointment who was becoming increasingly concerned for fear of renewed inflation, was removed from office in 1977 and replaced by G. William Miller, an industrialist who shared the President's views that economic expansion should be given the highest priority and that wage and price pressures could be held down through voluntary constraints. In order to further the administration's objective, Federal Reserve policy was conducted as if its principal purpose was to constrain interest rates from rising too rapidly. The problem with such a policy, especially in the context of rapidly rising inflation rates and mounting credit demands, was that it ran the risk of permitting the supply of money and credit to rise at rates that would worsen inflation itself. In one sense that is exactly what took place during 1978.

The policies that were followed between the end of 1978 and mid-1979 led to several critical developments. *First*, there was the foreign exchange crisis in late Summer of 1978 that forced the Carter administration to take action in November, 1978; *second*, the oil shock of 1979 struck at a time when the U.S. inflation rate had risen above the critical 10-percent level; *third*, inflation climbed to the 14-percent level during the Summer quarter of 1979.

The President responded to these events by asking his entire cabinet to resign: In the new round of appointments that he made soon thereafter, Mr. Miller was removed from the chairmanship of the Federal Reserve System and appointed Secretary of the Treasury; Paul Volcker, who was president of the Federal Reserve Bank of New York at the time, was appointed as the new head of the central bank. Within a few months, the new chairman decided that the way in which Federal Reserve policy was being conducted had allowed money and credit to expand far too rapidly. On October 6, 1979, he announced that, henceforth, in order to concentrate primarily on constraining the growth of money and credit, the conduct of monetary policy would shift the focus of its attention away from its traditional preoccupation with holding interest rates down. In short, the Fed announced that it was prepared to let interest rates go where market forces drove them, but that monetary growth would be restrained until inflation declined to acceptable levels.

Monetary Targeting

The idea of directing monetary policy so as to achieve a predetermined rate of increase in the money supply was not a new one. In 1975, after the severe inflationary experience of the preceding year, the Federal Reserve System, along with many other central banks, instituted the practice of setting monetary-growth targets as one of several policy objectives. At the same time, Congress had requested the Fed to consult with it on a regular basis regarding monetary-growth targets. An amendment to the Federal Reserve Act that was legislated in 1977 mandated consultations regarding monetary-growth targets. The Humphrey-Hawkins Act, passed in the following year, had spelled out at some length the Congress's view on how the Federal Reserve's monetary targets were to be set and monitored.

Nonetheless, prior to the change instituted in October, 1979, the growth rate of the money supply was treated as just one objective within a large constellation of objectives that included credit-market conditions, interest-rate patterns, and the reserve position of commercial banks. The evidence shows that these other intermediate objectives consistently were given more weight than money supply in the formulation of policy actions. All through the first half of 1979, for example, one of the Fed's many operating objectives, the federal funds rate—over which the Federal Reserve System has almost complete control—was targeted to stay within the 10 to 10½ percent range. The rate was kept within the target range, even though inflation climbed rapidly from the 10-percent level to the 14-percent level and the money supply accelerated far above its targeted rates.

If policy formulation had given more than lip service to the latter two variables, the pattern of developments during the first six months of 1979 would have been the reverse of what, in fact, took place; monetary growth and inflation would have risen more slowly and interest rates would have risen much more. The announcement of October 6, 1979, was thus a clear signal of the central bank's intention to shift its basic priorities.

The result of this shift in operating priorities, as was to be expected, was a sharp rise in interest rates after October. By the end of 1979, the federal funds rate had been allowed to rise rapidly from the 10-percent level to which it had been constrained to just below 14 percent. What was less expected was that interest rates would continue to rise well into 1980. During the early months of 1980, the federal funds rate reached the then-unprecedented level of 17½ percent. Other interest rates rose proportionately.

The impact of the change in monetary policy on inflation and inflationary expectations was not as dramatic as the impact it had on interest rates, at least not in the short run. Credit expansion and the large-scale purchases of real assets continued at a very rapid pace. In March of 1980, the administration decided to supplement its policy of tight money with the use of credit controls.

Credit Controls

On March 14, 1980, as inflationary expectations and behavior fueled an increasing volume of speculative activity in the commodities markets, the President announced the imposition of emergency credit controls. He invoked the Credit Control Act of 1969 to authorize the Federal Reserve to restrain a wide range of credit-market activities that previously lay outside the jurisdiction of the central bank.

The actions taken by the Fed included: (1) the imposition of a requirement that all types of lenders, including credit-card companies, maintain a deposit (i.e., a reserve requirement) at the Fed equal to a percentage of all subsequent increases in credit-card lending and in other categories of unsecured consumer credit; (2) an increase in reserve requirements on commercial bank borrowings such as large time deposits, Eurodollar borrowings, and security repurchase ageements—none of which had previously been subjected to significant reserve requirements; (3) an extension of special deposit requirements both to large nonmember banks and to money-market mutual funds; and (4) a special surcharge of 3 percentage points (tantamount to an increase in the discount rate) on certain borrowings by large member banks from the Fed. In a separate move, the Federal Reserve announced a "voluntary" program under which banks and finance companies agreed to limit the growth in their loans to U.S. customers to no more than 9 percent between the end of 1979 and the end of 1980.

The expansion of credit and money slowed abruptly after these harsh measures were announced; indeed, the response of financial institutions, households and banks was far sharper than had been anticipated. Credit-card sales dropped off markedly and total consumer credit outstanding actually fell. Within months, the economy went into a sharp recession. The pace of inflation and interest rates both fell extremely sharply; the federal funds rate, which exceeded 19 percent in early April, fell to below 9 percent in June; the rate on three-month Treasury bills fell from over 17 percent to 6¼ percent; and the rate on certificates of deposit fell from over 18 percent to just over 8 percent. The decrease in interest rates also spread to the long-term sectors of the financial market.

In early July, the President, who was running for reelection in November, ended the emergency credit-control program. Soon thereafter, the economy began to expand once again. The recession of 1980, which lasted less than six months, was the shortest in U.S. history, too short to achieve a durable correction in the pattern of inflationary expectations that had developed over the preceding decade.

As the economy expanded and credit demands rose, the rate of inflation increased once again, and by the end of the year prices were rising almost as rapidly as they had risen before credit controls were imposed. In keeping with the October, 1979, shift in policy, the Federal Reserve System did not accommodate the accompanying rise in credit demands. As a result, interest rates not only reached but surpassed the extraordinary levels experienced during the first quarter of 1980. Around the end of 1980, both the federal funds rate and the rate on certificates of deposit rose above the 20-percent level, and new issues of long-term utility bonds offered yields of 18½ percent. These unprecedented interest rates were a reflection of two separate forces: (1) inflation itself and the expectation of future inflation; and (2) the Fed's new policy of holding down the growth in bank reserves and the money supply. Several lessons had been learned by the end of 1980:

(1) A sustained attempt by the central bank to constrain a rise in interest rates invariably leads to an exessive increase in the money supply. That increase, in turn, generates an acceleration in inflation and eventually leads to an even larger rise in interest rates than would have occurred under a stricter set of monetary policies.
(2) Once inflation begins, an attempt by the government to foster faster economic growth and lower levels of unemployment leads principally to inflationary conditions that eventually reduce growth to levels below those that would have been achieved through more neutral policies.
(3) The eradication of inflation and inflationary expectations requires a sustained, and possibly painful, period of consistent disinflationary policy, especially on the part of the monetary authorities.

Over the succeeding two years the U.S. economy, under a new president, was subjected to just such a serious dose of disinflation.

INFLATION AND FINANCIAL MARKET RESPONSES

The repeated waves of worsening inflation experienced from 1965 to 1980 imposed severe strains on most segments of the U.S. economy. The impact of inflation on the country's financial sector was particularly powerful. It led to striking changes in the form and structure of U.S. financial markets.

The financial system that had developed over the post-World War II decades was singularly ill-equipped to deal either with inflation or with responses to inflation in the marketplace. Piece by piece, the entire set of institutional arrangements, instruments, practices and regulations had to be scrapped and replaced by new and far more flexible substitutes. By the early 1980's, a major restructuring of the entire financial services industry had taken place. At the same time, new market practices and instruments that were developed to deal with business and consumer needs of the 1980's grew rapidly in scope and size.

The high and variable rates of inflation experienced in the 1970's led to high and variable market rates of interest. The level and variability of interest rates was the major force that drove the restructuring process that transformed the shape and nature of U.S. financial markets. They were not, however, the only force at work; rapid technological advances in computers and telecommunications also played a key role.

Inflation and Finance

Textbooks often define inflation as a rapid *general* rise in prices. Such a definition serves to distinguish inflation from the more or less continuous rise and fall in the relative prices of individual commodities and services through which a market system adjusts supply and demand in individual markets. However, the use of the adjective "general" tends to blur a crucial point about inflation itself; namely, that it is never truly general in practice: Some prices move up far more rapidly than others; many prices, such as fixed interest rates on old financial instruments, do not change at all; and some prices, especially of financial assets, actually fall. The fact that the inflation experienced in the United States between 1965 and 1980 was not *general* inflicted severe economic pains on important segments of the economy.

In a wealthy economy like that of the United States, the economic well-being of individuals and households is comprised of several components. The first is the income derived from current economic activity; the second is the flow of interest and dividends from financial assets; the third is the change in the market value of the financial assets themselves. The richer the society, the greater the relative importance of the second and third components. In the United States, for example, income and dividend receipts in 1983 accounted for some $440 billion dollars of personal income, an amount larger than the total flow of wages and salaries in the entire manufacturing sector. Personal wealth, held in the form of financial assets, amounted to nearly $6 trillion dollars—an amount many times larger than the annual flow of personal income from current economic activity.

In 1967, when the recent wave of inflation had just begun, a large fraction of the nation's wealth was held either in the form of fixed-price deposits or in the form of bonds and mortgages that offered fixed interest rates. The remainder of financial assets was held either directly or through mutual funds, in the form of common stock. The sharp rise in the price level after 1967 led to severe losses in the purchasing power of the households that held this vast wealth:

(1) Interest rates, though rising, lagged far behind inflation rates, at least until 1980, because the severity of the subsequent inflation was not fully anticipated. Thus, the purchasing power of income derived from financial assets declined. Furthermore, income taxes (which were levied at

especially high rates on so-called unearned income) worsened the loss of purchasing power. Thus, even when some short-term interest rates (such as the 15-percent rate on Treasury bills) finally caught up with the inflation rate (also 15 percent) in March, 1980, the fact that interest was fully taxable at an individual's marginal tax rate ensured that the after-tax rate of return to the most astute savers, adjusted for inflation, was negative by a wide margin. Millions of savers, who were forced by regulation to accept 5¼ percent on their saving deposits at banks (or 5½ percent at savings institutions), suffered even more grievous losses on the $500 billion of personal assets they held in this form.

(2) An even more important source of loss was the erosion that took place in the purchasing power of wealth that was held in the form of fixed-price financial assets, such as demand deposits, savings deposits, life insurance and annuities, and savings bonds—the four most important forms of individual financial savings. Because the general price level tripled between 1967 and 1983, households that held these financial assets suffered a 66-percent erosion in purchasing power. Ironically, the rise in interest rates that did eventually take place in response to inflation actually increased the loss of purchasing power for yet other investors. This loss occurred because the rise in market rates of interest brought about a fall in the market value of all long-term bonds and mortgages that carried a fixed rate of return. Consider a person who had purchased a $1,000, 30-year U.S. Treasury bond bearing interest at 6 percent a year in 1967, and who still held that bond in 1983. By then the going rate of interest on similar instruments had doubled to 12 percent a year. The market value of the $1,000 bond fell to around $600. In addition, because of inflation between 1967 and 1983, each 1983 dollar was worth only one-third of the purchasing power of each dollar originally invested. Combining both effects, there was a purchasing power loss of 80 percent. Since the Treasury had, in fact, sold billions of dollars of these long-term instruments, savers who held these securities had taken a financial beating of this magnitude.

(3) Inflation was not much kinder to the households that invested in common stock. The nominal market value of common stocks, such as those represented by the Standard and Poor's 500 Stock Index, rose by 74 percent between year-end 1967 and year-end 1983. This rise was more than offset, however, by an even sharper fall in the purchasing power of the dollar. In real or purchasing-power terms, the average common-stock investor lost 42 percent over that 16-year period.

As the economic pain of losses from their holdings of financial assets mounted, the public began to search for ways to protect themselves from further losses. Some moved out of financial assets altogether into tangible assets of various forms, thus disrupting the normal flow of savings into productive investments. Others sought protection by placing their funds in very short-term instruments bearing the maximum rates of interest available. Because of restrictive regulations, the traditional institutions were unable to offer the public the new kinds of assets they sought. Thus, the system itself had to be changed.

The Old Financial System

Before it was gradually destroyed by inflation, the system that prevailed in the 1960's was itself a product of major regulatory changes made during the financial crisis of the 1930's. To describe the system in detail would require an entire volume, but its principal characteristics can be captured more briefly: Financial institutions were highly specialized and compartmented by regulation; interest rates on deposits were controlled at artificially low levels; competition among institutions was constrained; the delivery of financial services to the public was costly; and the entire system was both paper intensive and inconvenient for customers.

Specialization

Financial services required by the consumer were offered by several distinct types of financial institutions, each confined by regulation to a narrow range of products and services, with little or no overlap among institutions. Thus, commercial banks (the oldest type of financial institution) were given a monopoly with respect to demand or checking deposits. They—and only they—could offer checking accounts. These banks were also allowed to offer a limited range of savings accounts.

The savings and loan associations, which did not become a major element in the system until after World War II, were allowed to offer only savings accounts, bearing interest rates set somewhat higher by regulation than the maximum rate that commercial banks could pay. In return for this privilege, they were required to hold the bulk of their assets in the form of long-term residential mortgage loans.

A customer who wanted to buy common stock had to go to a retail brokerage firm that was a member of one of the stock exchanges that had a monopoly of trading in most common stocks. Brokers were not allowed to sell insurance or to offer their customers any interest-bearing liquid-asset accounts.

Finally, life insurance companies had a virtual monopoly over sales of this important form of protection and investment.

Fixed, Controlled Interest Rates

Maximum interest rates that could be offered by the institutions were generally fixed by regulation at extremely low levels. Banks were not allowed to pay interest on demand deposits subject to transfer by checks. The maximum interest they could pay on savings accounts was also stipulated by regulators. Savings and loan associations were likewise subject to interest-rate ceilings, set at a quarter or half point above the rates that banks were allowed to pay. Life insurance companies, which faced little rate competition from other types of savings institutions, also offered low, relatively fixed rates of return on the investment components of life insurance and annuity policies. Customers of brokerage firms paid a fixed minimum commission set by the stock exchanges and received no interest whatever on credit balances held in their accounts. In brief, the principal institutions were not allowed to compete against each other or against other forms of institutions by offering consumers higher rates of return. The system worked because the majority of the public had no alternatives. However, there was a countervailing benefit to society in that the zero or low rates at which the institutions could obtain funds allowed them to lend funds or buy government, corporate and municipal bonds and mortgages at relatively low fixed rates of interest.

Geographic Restraints

In addition to control over competition between different classes of institutions, regulation also controlled competition within functional and geographic areas. The Glass-Steagall Act (1933) forbade commercial banks from engaging in investment-banking activities, that is, the underwriting and sales of securities other than municipal bonds. The McFadden Act (1928) forbade banks from crossing state lines. In addition, a jumble of state regulations prevented banks from competing outside even narrower geographic areas, such as counties, cities and, in the most stringent cases, a single building.

Savings and loan associations were generally subject to less stringent geographical limitations; life insurance and brokerage companies were free to operate on a nationwide basis. The net result of these regulations was that the United States had a larger number of banks and other financial institutions relative to any other major industrial country, a fact that greatly increased the cost of delivering financial services to the consumer.

Expensive Delivery

The combination of laws and regulations led to practices through which each institution was encouraged to develop expensive systems for delivering the limited products they offered. Because they were unable to compete via prices (i.e., via higher interest rates), the deposit-taking institutions were forced to compete in other ways—for example, by offering consumers convenient branches, lots of personal service, free postage, free checking privileges, and indeed, free gifts of toasters and other minor items. Life insurance was sold by expensive door-to-door agents, who had to be well rewarded for their efforts. Retail brokers offered individual customers research services, investment advice, and considerable hand-holding.

All of this was possible because the cost of funds to the institution was kept at artificially low levels, whereas the rates at which the institutions, in turn, could relend was less subject to limitation. However, even on the lending side, most states had strict limits in the form of usury laws that set the maximum rate anybody could be charged on a loan. Forced by regulation to accept artificially low interest rates, those who saved were, in fact, subsidizing the inefficiencies that regulation imposed on the financial system.

Paper Intensiveness

The entire process by which consumers conducted their financial transactions was highly labor and paper intensive, and extremely inconvenient from the point of view of the consumer. For example, if a particular household wanted to convert $10,000 of assets it held in the form of common stock into an automobile of approximately equivalent value, that household had to go through many separate financial transactions: (1) sell the common stock through a retail broker, incurring a high (fixed) selling fee; (2) arrange for the transfer of these funds to a bank account; (3) obtain a cashier's check for the purchase value of the automobile (assuming a cash purchase), which generally required a trip to the bank and more fees; (4) open a savings account for the difference between the sale price of the stock and the purchase price of the automobile. He or she would also have to decide just where the saving should be held. In addition to the consumer's time, the process also required a large flow of paper work and a large amount of clerical time on the part of the institutions.

The Impact of Inflation

The system began to break down in the late 1960's, when rising inflation brought with it a rise in market rates of interest. In 1966, as market rates rose above mandated ceilings, some consumers withdrew funds they had been holding at institutions because these investments were earning intolerably low real rates of interest (the difference between the after-tax nominal rate of interest received and the rate of inflation). The withdrawal of funds, especially from savings and loan associations, dried up the normal flow of new money into the mortgage market and caused a severe recession in the housing industry. This phenomenon, known as disintermediation, was to be repeated in larger and larger volume on each subsequent upswing of the inflation-interest cycle. As we have seen earlier, it reached frightening proportions in early 1980, when consumers not only moved funds out of institutions into more lucrative financial instruments, but also moved out of financial assets into tangible assets on a large scale.

To meet the changing needs and behavior of consumers, the regulators and the institutions they regulated were pressured into developing new instruments through which they could compete for the consumer's dollar. However, because the regulators were unwilling to allow the system to change too rapidly, the new instruments themselves were subjected to new regulatory restraints. In the early 1970's, for example, the interest rate payable by banks on large certificates of deposit (namely, large savings accounts) was completely freed from interest-rate ceilings. However, the minimum deposit required to qualify a deposit as a large CD was set at $100,000, which put it beyond the reach of most individuals. As interest-rate pressures continued to rise, the regulators were forced into freeing the market to a far greater extent than they had originally planned to do.

Two major developments served as important catalysts in the process through which rising inflation and interest rates forced the authorities to deregulate the financial system. One was the emergence of money-market mutual funds; the other was the development of low-cost computer-based data-processing technology.

Money Market Funds

Money-market funds were first created during the second inflationary wave of the early 1970's. The original idea behind the funds was simple. Public access to market rates of interest on liquid investments (as opposed to the artificially lower rates payable on most deposits) was being suppressed by high minimum-deposit requirements imposed by regulators. Why not a fund that pooled smaller amounts from many depositors? Technically these funds were mutual funds and, therefore, subject to the jurisdiction of the Securities and Exchange Commission (SEC), rather than that of the banking authorities. Subscribers to a fund (who were really depositors) acquire shares in the fund. However, because the assets of the funds were placed entirely in very short-term money-market instruments, such as large CD's or Treasury bills, the shares were, in effect, fixed in value—just as deposits in any bank. Because they were both fixed in price and highly liquid, depositors could be given the privilege of transferring their "shares" to third parties through the use of a draft, which for all practical purposes was the equivalent of a check drawn on a bank deposit. The big difference was that depositors in money-market funds earned market rates of interest. Allowing for the relatively small costs of administering the funds, the rates earned by depositors were only about half a percent below the highest rates available in the open market. The important innovation was that shares in the fund were available to anybody who had just $1,000 to invest. In short, this major financial innovation, made possible in part by large improvements in electronic data processing, made a complete end-run around the entire set of restrictive regulations.

Money-market funds grew far more slowly in the early 1970's than either logic or rationality might suggest. By the end of 1974, when inflation was running at 12 percent a year and the maximum rate of interest allowed on savings deposits held at banks and other controlled depository institutions was below 6 percent, money-market funds, which offered far higher rates of return, had grown only to $2.5 billion relative to some $1 trillion held in other deposits—evidence that the bulk of the U.S. population still had faith that inflation was a transient phenomenon. By the end of 1978, as the third wave of inflation was gathering momentum, the aggregate size of money-market funds was still below $11 billion (compared to $1.3 trillion then being held in much lower-yielding deposits at the traditional institutions.) However, when inflation worsened after the end of 1978, the public woke up to the fact that their inertia was becoming increasingly costly. They began to move financial assets into money-market funds in vast quantities. By 1981, five million new accounts had been opened totaling $75 billion, and by 1982 the total assets of money-market funds had tripled to $225 billion. Both the traditional institutions and those who regulated them decided that the time for a serious change had come.

Computer Technology

The money-market funds, which effectively represented very high-yielding demand deposits, competed not only against the low-yielding savings deposits offered by the institutions but also against demand deposits (checking accounts) on which regulation forbade any payment of interest at all. In order to hold on to their demand depositors, the traditional institutions were forced into innovative uses of the new technology that was being made possible by the computer. Their first move in this direction was the development by mutual savings banks of something called NOW accounts, an acronym for a negotiable order to withdraw, an interest-bearing checking account in everything but name. These accounts were first authorized in Massachusetts, but because of competitive pressures they soon spread to all of New England and later to New York. Because of banking regulations, the rates of interest they could offer were limited to those payable on savings accounts that could not be transferred by check. Commercial banks developed their own end-run around the regulations that forbade the paying of interest on checking accounts by developing something called the ATS account—an acronym for automatic transfer to savings. Under this system, a customer would maintain two parallel accounts with a bank: one, a normal checking account, and the other a savings account. Each day, all funds deposited would be transferred to the second account and thus earn interest at whatever maximum rate was allowed. When the customer wrote a check on the demand-deposit account, funds just sufficient to let the check clear would be transferred back into it; the rest would continue to earn interest.

The phenomenon of NOW and ATS accounts provides a simple demonstration that absurd regulations lead to absurd practices. In a series of decisions starting in 1978, interest rates were gradually deregulated; new savings accounts were then allowed to offer rates tied to market rates on six-month Treasury bills. However, the privilege of holding these accounts was restricted to individuals who could deposit at least $10,000. Later, step by step, the regulators allowed the institutions increasing leeway regarding interest rates they could pay on deposits of other maturities. By 1980, the authorities decided that there was no alternative but to deregulate. Nonetheless, even the restrictions that remained by 1982 and early 1983 continued to cause trouble; in three further moves, interest rates on all accounts except for business checking accounts were effectively deregulated. It is a foregone conclusion that this last vestigial attempt at interest-rate control will also disappear in the near future.

The two motives for interest-rate regulations were to keep interest rates low and to prevent competition among institutions. The system worked well only so long as inflation and inflationary expectations remained low. The prolonged rise in inflation and the consequent prolonged rise in market rates of interest that were not subject to control brought the regulatory system that was conceived in the 1930's to an end in the early 1980's.

The Emerging System

The financial system that emerged by 1983 differed from the old system along all of the lines outlined above. Driven by technology, innovation and the need of consumers for protection from inflation and its consequences, the system evolved into something far different from that which existed in the 1960's.

Specialization

By 1983, the system of artificial specialization imposed by regulation had almost—but not completely—broken down. Transaction deposits (that is, deposits transferrable by means of a check), no longer a monopoly of commercial banks, could be and were being offered by credit unions, savings and loan associations, brokerage houses, and money-market funds. More importantly, the wall that had been built by the Glass-Steagall Act for the purpose of preventing commercial banks from entering into other fields of finance had been breached by nonbank entities entering into the field of banking. By 1983, institutions not constrained by the Glass-Steagall legislation had become large providers of traditional banking services. In addition, they engaged openly in investment banking, brokerage, life insurance, and real estate—another end-run around obsolete regulations. Sears, a major merchandising concern with hundreds of offices throughout the United States, acquired a major investment banker, a major savings and loan association, and a major real-estate operation and thus, in effect, become a nationwide onestop financial services institution. Similarly, Merrill Lynch, the largest stockbroker in the nation, through its asset-management account offered its customers interest-bearing demand deposit privileges (indeed, by this yardstick it had become one of the largest banks in the nation), brokerage services, as well as real-estate purchase, sale and transfer facilities. The Prudential Life Assurance company, the largest U.S. life insurance company, acquired a major investment banking company and thus combined several previously segregated financial services under one roof.

The driving force for all of these moves was the realization that what the public needed was not just a bank account, or a savings account, or a money-market fund, but a convenient way to: (1) achieve safe, high returns; (2) transfer assets easily from one form into another; (3) attain easy access to credit; and (4) meet other financial needs. The fact that by 1983 a telephone call or a single plastic card, used at an automatic teller machine that is open 24 hours a day, could achieve all of these purposes eliminated the need for the cumbersome overly specialized and overly protected system of the 1960's.

Fixed Interest Rates

Most rates of interest were fixed and many were subject to regulatory control under the older system. This system has been replaced by one in which interest rates vary with market conditions and in which controls have disappeared except for the disallowance of interest on business demand deposits. These changes have had, and will continue to have, major implications for savers, borrowers and all of the markets in which they operate (such as mortgages, the loan markets, and the foreign-exchange markets).

Geographic Restraints

The McFadden Act, which restrains banks from crossing state boundaries, remains in effect. However, as is true of the Glass-Steagall Act, which is also still in effect, the McFadden Act has been circumvented by innovative developments and by changes in the ways in which regulations are enforced. Thus, Citicorp, the largest bankholding company in the nation, has been allowed to establish financial offices throughout the United States in the form of savings and loan associations, finance companies, credit-card companies, loan offices, and international banking centers. The only thing it cannot do outside of New York State is to accept a demand deposit from an individual—something it obviously does not need to do in order to conduct its principal business of receiving and relending funds on a global basis.

Expensive Delivery System

So long as they recieved a hidden subsidy from regulations that effectively controlled the rate they had to pay depositors, financial institutions were able to survive in spite of their extremely expensive delivery systems. The effective disappearance of such regulatory subsidies has forced financial institutions to change their mode of operation. In short, price competition has replaced nonprice competition: Expensive branches, labor-intensive practices, and free toasters have all but disappeared from the scene. The public has benefited from the change. A few examples suffice to document how pervasive the change has been.

(1) Prior to 1975, retail brokers charged a fixed commission set by the New York Stock Exchange on all transactions in common stocks. These fixed rates

were eliminated in 1975, and the public is now free to bargain on brokerage fees. Discount brokers conduct a substantial volume of securities trades. In addition, customers demand and get market rates of interest on credit balances that they hold at brokerage houses. To make up for the loss in income previously derived from high, fixed commissions and for the cost of interest payable on customers' credit balances, brokerage firms had to move into new lines of business, thereby increasing competition throughout the system.

(2) In order to meet the competition of higher rates available on alternative forms of investment, life insurance companies, too, have had to offer higher rates of return than they formerly did, and also have had to develop new policy forms that give their customers more flexible choices. To compensate for the higher cost of conducting their business, life insurance companies have had to streamline their expensive delivery systems. New marketing arrangements such as sales of group life insurance and annuities, sales via the mail, and sales through a network of retail stores have increasingly replaced sales through costly calls by individual insurance agents.

Paper Intensiveness

Plastic cards, processed through a central computer, have replaced the intensive paperwork required by the older system. Instead of a personal visit to an institution, involving persons on the other side of the counter, most financial transactions by 1983 could be conducted via either a telephone or an automatic teller machine. Many observers believe the process in still in its infancy and that within ten years virtually all financial transactions—including borrowing, lending, investing and the shifting of assets—will be conducted via a computer terminal installed in individual homes. Furthermore, all of these transactions will involve market rates of interest rather than fixed or regulated rates.

In summary, a major transformation has taken place in the financial services industry that serves the U.S. consumer, a transformation that involves all of the dimensions discussed earlier. Interest rates have been freed; strict functional compartmentalization has broken down; rapid data processing and improved communication have reduced the need for personal time and paperwork; both institutions and individuals have been allowed to play a far more active role in selling and purchasing financial services; finally, a national marketplace for financial services has emerged from a marketplace that previously was essentially parochial. On the whole, the emergent system was far better equipped to serve the consumer—and, hence, to deal with the wave of disinflation that began in 1980.

DISINFLATION: 1980-1983

When President Ronald Reagan took office in January, 1981, he was already openly committed to reversing the major directions in which most U.S. policies had moved over the preceding decade. The administration chose not to pin a specific label on its overall program. Nonetheless, the program attracted several descriptive labels from outside observers: Among them, supply-side economics, neoconservatism, monetarism, and free-market economics. All of these labels fit partly, but none of them fits precisely. Eventually, the particular mix of priorities, objectives and philosophies that were instituted in 1981 came to be called Reaganomics.

Taken together, the Reagan program represented a major turning point in the thrust of U.S. policies. Even more surprising than the boldness with which it sought to reverse previous directions was the speed with which many aspects of the program were put in place: Within seven months of the President's inauguration, most elements of his policies had received legislative approval.

The Reagan Program

The program had four major objectives:
(1) To eradicate inflation and inflationary expectations;
(2) To set the stage for a resumption of growth in output per worker, principally through a restructuring of fiscal policies;
(3) To strengthen U.S. defense capabilities; and
(4) To restore the U.S. budget to balance by fiscal 1984.

Taken at face value, these four objectives, in themselves, do not support the thesis of a major change in policy direction. President Carter's final messages to the American people in January, 1981, had outlined more or less the same objectives. The important difference was that the Reagan administration, unlike its predecessor, made it clear that a policy of disinflation would be pursued without compromise.

Monetart Policy and Inflation

Because the Federal Reserve System had determined to adopt an uncompromising policy of disinflation in October, 1979 (more than a year before President Reagan was elected), such a policy was already fully in place when the new administration took office. Nonetheless, its accession to power did make a large difference. Although President Carter initially gave full support to the intended change in the conduct of monetary policy, he effectively withdrew that support on several occasions in 1980 when he chastized the Federal Reserve for the undue tightness of its policies—and especially for the very high rates of interest to which these policies had led. By contrast, the new president was more fully prepared to support the eradication of inflation through monetary constraint, regardless of the undesirable side effect that such a policy might have.

The contrast between the Reagan view and the Carter view reflected more than just the higher priority that President Reagan placed on the need to eradicate inflation; it also reflected a fundamental difference in theory regarding the link between monetary policy on the one hand and inflation on the other. For President Carter, money was at most one factor in the process through which inflation worsens or improves. His final economic report to the people included a lengthy discussion of the causes of and cure for inflation. The discussion gave far less attention to monetary factors than to such other factors as wage behavior and external inflationary shocks from oil and agriculture. The solution Carter sought for inflation lay essentially in measures to control wages and prices through voluntary arrangements supervised by the government, mandatory controls, or through a proposed mix of the two—known as tax-based income policies (TIPS)—under which tax penalties or rewards would be employed as a means of inducing a moderation of wage and price increases. President Carter's clear preference for such a direct approach to the control of inflation reflected his own beliefs as well as those of his principal advisers, namely, that the cost of reducing inflation through monetary restraint alone would be too high in terms of the unemployment it would cause.

The Reagan position on the issue was clearly different. He and his principal advisers firmly believed that inflation could and should be brought down rapidly within the context of a free market through the use of steady monetary disinflation. Although subsequent disagreements between the administration and the Federal Reserve System did arise, those disagreements concerned the conduct of day-to-day monetary policy and not the basic premise that monetary policy should be kept tight enough for a sufficiently long period to bring the U.S. inflation rate down to an acceptable level.

Government and the Economy

The second major premise of the Reagan economic program was that the solution for stagnant productivity did not lie in more government; indeed, the program reflected the belief that the rising scope and share of government in the economy was itself a major cause of the problem. Therefore, the program sought to reduce the role of the government in the economy through fiscal and regulatory reforms.

The largest component of the reforms enacted in 1981 comprised sharp cuts in federal taxes on individual incomes, business incomes, gifts and estates. Taken together, these reductions amounted to the largest single tax cut in the nation's history. The five principal tax cuts were:

(1) a 23-percent reduction in individual income-tax rates that took place in three steps over a 33-month period;
(2) an immediate cut (effective January, 1982) from 70 percent to 50 percent in the maximum tax rate applicable to income from interest and dividends;

(3) a reduction in the maximum tax rate on long-term capital gains from 28 percent to 20 percent;

(4) a provision for indexing tax brackets and exemptions against future inflation, starting in 1985;

(5) a significant liberalization in the rates and conditions through which the acquisition or exchange of capital assets could be depreciated for business tax-accounting purposes.

The tax cuts had a twofold purpose: One purpose was to increase individual incentives to work and to assume entrepreneurial risks; the second and longer-run purpose was to force down the level of federal spending by denying the government the comfortable growth of revenues it had enjoyed under the prior system of unlegislated tax increases through inflation.

The second component of the fiscal reforms instituted in 1981 was a cutback in the growth of many forms of government nondefense expenditures. The spending cuts achieved in 1981 were confined essentially to those sectors of the budget that were subject to annual appropriations, that is, they barely touched the largest entitlement programs such as social security and medicare. As a result, the reduction achieved in government spending was considerably smaller than the expected falloff in revenue entailed by the tax cuts.

The third component was a set of measures designed to institute a far-reaching program of regulatory relief. The purpose was to reverse the previously rising scope of federal regulation over private, state and municipal activities.

Defense Expenditures

The third major objective of the new administration was a major increase in the rate of spending for defense. In the early 1960's, before the Vietnam War, the United States had allocated over 9 percent of its GNP for national defense. In 1962, for example, defense spending accounted for $9\frac{1}{4}$ percent of the GNP and 58 percent of total federal spending. Except for a minor increase during the height of the Vietnam conflict, the share of defense spending in the federal budget and the economy was reduced steadily and rapidly between 1962 and 1980. By 1980, national defense expenditures accounted for only 23 percent of total federal outlays, and just 5 percent of U.S. GNP.

The Reagan administration was of the firm opinion that the cutbacks that had been made in defense spending, especially during the late 1970's, had endangered the national security and that the trend should be reversed. The administration's proposal was to increase defense spending to at least 7 percent of the GNP by 1985, a massive 40-percent increase even if the GNP did not grow, and an even larger increase under the more realistic assumption that the GNP itself would undoubtedly increase between 1980 and 1985. Further, within the broad category of defense spending itself, the Reagan proposals called for a far sharper increase in weapons-procurement programs than in defense-related wage and salary expenditures.

57

Budgetary Balance

The final item in the Reagan program was a commitment to balance the federal budget by fiscal year 1984. In spite of rapidly rising tax collections and the cutbacks in defense, federal spending had exceeded federal revenues by large amounts in every single year during the preceding decade. As a consequence, the national debt had grown from $370 billion at the end of fiscal year 1970 to just over $1 trillion by the end of fiscal year 1981. The first long-range fiscal program presented by the new administration in early 1981 made the following projections:

(1) Federal expenditures as a share of GNP would decline from 22.9 percent of GNP in FY 1981 to 19 percent by FY 1986;

(2) The budget deficit would decline from $58 billion in FY 1981 to approximately zero in FY 1984, and move into a substantial surplus thereafter.

(3) The federal debt, expressed as a percentage of the GNP, would decline from 37.8 percent at the end of FY 1981 to 23.3 percent by the end of FY 1986.

The Recession of 1981-1982

Given the far-reaching changes it sought, the Reagan program was put into place with remarkable speed. With the passage of the large tax bill in early August, 1981, the overall package of reforms was firmly in place. At that time most observers believed that the overall thrust of fiscal policy, especially the combination of large tax cuts and the rapid increase of congressional authorizations for defense purchases, would have a highly expansive effect on the economy. Thus, they also believed that the economy itself would grow rapidly, but that inflation would at best stay very high. The actual outcome was just the opposite. Monetary policy, which had been loosened somewhat between December, 1980, and March, 1981, was tightened over the following six-month period. In spite of the expansiveness of fiscal policy, the U.S. economy went into a sharp recession starting in August, 1981, a recession that turned out to be deeper and longer than any experienced since the 1930's. The key to what happened was the behavior of U.S. interest rates.

Monetary Policy and Interest Rates

In December, 1980, just before the Reagan administration took office, the combination of high inflation and a vacillating mix of economic policies and pronouncements had driven interest rates to unprecedented levels. In that month, the rate on new issues of three-month Treasury bills averaged 15.6 percent, and the prime rate charged by banks climbed to 21½ percent. Both rates were high, not just in absolute terms, but also relative to the 12.4-percent rate of inflation recorded in December, 1980.

During the first nine months of 1981, the central bank persisted in its policy of bringing the inflation rate down through very stringent control over the growth in the nation's money supply. The inflation rate declined slightly but remained stubbornly high all through this period: It edged down from 12.4 percent in the year ending December, 1980, to just under 11 percent in the 12 months ending September, 1981. The combination of tight money and high inflation was the major reason for the persistence of high interest rates. In August, 1981, the three-month Treasury bill rate was back at 15.6 percent; and the prime rate charged by banks, at 20½ percent, was barely down from the 21½-percent peak reached in December, 1980. The market values of bonds and mortgages remained at low levels. By the end of the Summer, stock prices, which joined the bearish parade by June, had fallen by over 15 percent in less than three months. It was not an auspicious beginning for the major program of economic reform that had been enacted, but was not even scheduled to go into effect until the start of the new fiscal year on October 1, 1981.

The continuing losses suffered by the holders of financial assets through most of 1981 were significant, but the more severe problem during the Summer of 1981 was the rising gap between the interest rate and the rate of inflation. This gap, already too high at the end of 1980, rose to even higher levels in the Summer of 1981. The gap measures the *real* rate of interest, the rate that actually matters. By the very nature of their businesses, farmers, builders, manufacturers, or wholesalers own commodities and owe money. They can operate profitably in a world of 20-percent interest rates on the money they owe if the prices of the commodities they hold also are rising at a commensurate rate; even ignoring the tax-effect of borrowing, the price increase provides the wherewithal to pay their financial costs. By contrast, a world of 20½-percent interest rates, such as prevailed in the Summer of 1981 when wholesale prices were rising at less than half that rate, threatened the very survival of many businesses.

The general consumer price index recorded an increase of nearly 11 percent between September, 1980, and September, 1981, but a large part of this increase was a result of delayed price increases in the service sector of the economy. The relevant price index for most businesses is the producer price index. Between March, 1981, and September, 1981, prices measured by that index were rising at less than 6 percent per annum. On this basis, the gap between the prime rate of interest (20½ percent) and commodity price increases (6 percent) represented a real interest burden of over 14 percent a year—a burden that the average business was unable to bear. As one Congressman on returning to Washington after the August, 1981, recess colorfully described it: "My constituents have just three concerns—interest rates, interest rates, and interest rates." The inevitable outcome was the sharp recession into which the economy moved.

The combined influence of the recession, tight money, and high interest rates finally broke the back of inflation. The recession that begin in mid-1981 continued until December, 1982. By then the rate of inflation, as measured by the CPI, had fallen to 3.9 percent and, as measured by the PPI, to 3.7 percent.

Monetary policy—once it was allowed to do what it set out to do without undue interference from Congress and the administration—was successful in reducing inflation to a level far below targets envisioned just two years previously.

Exchange Rates

The policies, including monetary policy, that were pursued after the Reagan administration took office had a large impact on the dollar's exchange rate against other major currencies. At the end of 1980, the exchange rate of the dollar was still at the very low levels to which it had fallen during the foreign-currency crisis of late 1978. On a weighted-averaged basis against ten major currencies, the external value of the dollar was actually somewhat lower in September, 1980, than it had been in September, 1978. On the same basis, the dollar rose by 20 percent between September, 1980, and September, 1981, by a further 9 percent during 1982, and by still another 10 percent in 1983—a cumulative rise of approximately 50 percent against the currencies of the ten most important financial economies.

The strengthening of the dollar had two major consequences for U.S. inflation. One consequence was that it supressed the price of imported goods. Although imports represented only 11 percent of total U.S. consumption, the competition they provided as potential substitutes for U.S. products and services implied considerable downward pressure on the rise of U.S. wages and prices. The strength of the dollar and declining import prices contributed to the sharp drop in our rate of inflation.

The indirect effect of a rising exchange rate worked in the same direction: As the value of the dollar rose, U.S. exporting industries found it increasingly difficult to compete in world markets as well as in domestic markets. That loss of market share made the U.S. recession far sharper than it otherwise might have been. During the first quarter of 1981, before the recession began, total U.S. output (real GNP measured in 1972 dollars) amounted to $1,516.4 billion, of which some $18 billion was produced to satisfy a net foreign demand for U.S. goods. Two years later, in the second quarter of 1983, by the same measure total U.S. output was still only $1,525 billion. During the latter period, the United States was a net importer of goods to the extent of $11 billion. The swing of $29 billion (from plus $18 billion to minus $11 billion) represented nearly 2 percent of total U.S. production. Because of that swing, the demand for U.S.-produced goods and services—and hence for U.S. employees—was some 2 percent (or 2 million workers) smaller in mid-1983 than it otherwise might have been. Although not all of the swing can be blamed on the strength of the dollar, a large part of it was the direct result of the dollar's higher exchange rate.

The fall in demand for U.S. produced goods hit most heavily those sectors of the economy, such as steel, automobiles and construction machinery, in which foreign competition both here and abroad was particularly severe. One salutary result of the developments outlined earlier was that the sharp fall in the U.S. inflation rate was accompanied by an equally sharp fall in wage inflation in the United States, especially in the heavily unionized sectors of the U.S. labor force.

Wages and Unit Labor Costs

Economists who analyze inflation find it useful to divide the overall rate of price increase into two component parts. The first is that part of the overall price increase represented by the rise in labor costs incurred in producing one unit of output. These unit labor costs rise when the avarage rate of compensation to labor rises by more than the rise in average labor productivity. In 1979 and 1980, for example, hourly compensation in the private sector rose at 10 to 11 percent per annum. Productivity (defined as average output per hour of work) actually fell by about 1 percent a year between the end of 1978 and the end of 1980. Thus, labor costs per unit of output were rising by 11 or 12 percent a year. Because labor compensation accounts for some 75 percent of the national income, or nearly ten times the share accounted for by after-tax profits, employers are in no position to meet an 11 to 12 percent increase in labor cost per unit of output without raising prices. In order to hold their profit margins constant, the average rise in product and service prices would also have to be around 11 to 12 percent a year, thus leading to inflation at that rate. This type of inflation, caused by the phenomenon of wage increases in excess of productivity increases, is frequently referred to as built-in inflation or base-line inflation or core inflation.

The second component of total inflation is the result of price shocks that come from outside the wage-price interaction outlined above. Bad harvests, for example, can bring about a rise in food prices. A sharp increase in the price of imports, notably of oil, has sometimes resulted in price increases that are unrelated to the internal wage-price behavior of an economy. The overall rate observed in the CPI represents the joint result of internal base-line inflation caused by the wage-price spiral and the effects of external shocks. Thus, the actual inflation rate of 13 to 15 percent observed during 1980 was the joint result of the 11 to 12 percent push on prices (caused by the behavior of wages and productivity) plus an additional 2 to 3 percent attributable to the jump in oil prices in that year.

One major reason for the reluctance of the Carter administration to adopt a genuine policy of tight money for the purpose of curbing inflation was its belief that the underlying pressure from rising unit labor costs could not be brought down without direct government intervention in the process by which compensation increases are set in the United States. The experience with inflation rates in 1981-1982 contradicted that belief. In the context of recession and of severe competition both in export and import markets, the rise in unit labor costs fell dramatically. By mid-1983, the annual rise in hourly compensation had fallen by half from 10.6 percent in December, 1980, to just 5.3 percent by June, 1983. Furthermore, output per hour of work, which had been declining in 1979 and 1980, rose by 3.2 percent between mid-1982 and mid-1983. As a result, unit labor costs fell from the 11 to 12 percent range of 1979-1980 to just 2 percent a year by mid-1983.

The sectors of the economy that are dominated by the large, and normally the most aggressive, unions experienced an even better performance than is reflected in the average figures outlined above. The large unions (whose wage bargains cover a thousand or more workers at a time) generally led the parade of wage increases prior to 1980. In 1982 and 1983, wage settlements in these highly unionized sectors fell below settlements in the rest of the economy.

The Recovery of 1983

By August, 1982, with the process of disinflation both of prices and wages well under way, the Federal Reserve System eased up significantly on its extremely tight policies. The rate at which the money supply was permitted to grow accelerated steadily from 3.3 percent a year for the quarter ending June, 1982, and 9 percent a year for the quarter ending September, 1982, and to 14.5 percent a year for the quarter ending December, 1982. With monetary ease, interest rates fell sharply after midyear. The contraction in economic activity ended by November, 1982, and the U.S. economy began to expand again.

The pace of recovery in 1983 was swifter than either official or private projections had forecast at the beginning of the year. From year-end 1982 to year-end 1983, real gross national product increased by 6.2 percent, the index of industrial production by 15.7 percent, and civilian employment rose by 4 million. By the Summer of 1983, aggregate economic activity had regained the level that prevailed two years earlier—just before the recession of 1981-1982 began. Industrial production, the sector most damaged by the large jump in oil prices that took place after December, 1978, rose to 153.8 in September, 1983 (1967 = 100). This was just equal to its level in July, 1981, the official peak month of the preceding expansion, but only trivially above the 151.8 level attained nearly five years earlier (in December, 1978) before the second oil shock caused a global slowdown in industrial expansion.

After mid-1983, monetary policy was tightened once again in order to forestall a rekindling of inflation. As a result of this tightening, interest rates rose: The 3-month Treasury bill rate, for example, rose from 8.2 percent in May, 1983, to over 9 percent by February, 1984. The economy continued to expand vigorously in spite of the mild tightening of monetary policy by the central bank. By February, 1984, the index of industrial production had climbed to 160, a level decisively above the 152-154 range that had been frequently attained but never surpassed during the preceding five years. In terms of business-cycle chronology, the recovery phase of the expansion ended in the final quarter of 1983; starting in 1984, the economy moved into a new phase of bona fide growth for the first time in five years.

The rate of inflation, which had come down sharply in 1982, continued to decline in 1983. The twelve-month rate of CPI inflation fell to a low of 2.5 percent during the Summer of 1983. The United States had not enjoyed so low a rate of rise in the CPI since the mini-recession of early 1967. Price performance, as measured by the PPI, was even better; the PPI rate of inflation declined throughout 1983. By December, 1983, the index was only 0.6 percent above its December, 1982, level—a rate of increase lower than the country had experienced since 1964, before the long wave of modern inflation began. Excluding the food segment of the index, the level of production prices in December, 1983, was no higher than it had been a year earlier.

The decisive reduction in inflation rates that took place between early 1980 and the end of 1983 was not confined to the United States; several major economies did as well or better. By year-end 1983, the rate of inflation in Japan, the best performing large economy, fell to just 1.6 percent as measured by the CPI, and to *minus* 2.2 percent for the PPI. For Switzerland, the corresponding figures were 2.1 and 0.9 percent; for West Germany, 2.5 and 1.6 percent; for Canada, 4.5 and 3.6 percent; and for the United Kingdom, 5.3 and 5.6 percent. By contrast, inflation rates continued to run at double-digit levels in France (9.3 and 14.5 percent) and Italy (12.4 and 9.2 percent). Ironically, among the eight countries surveyed, France and Italy were the two economies that also suffered the slowest rates of economic recovery in 1983, as well as the most extensive regimens of governmental controls over economic activity.

The remarkable disinflation achieved in the United States between 1980 and 1983 was largely the result of the high priority assigned to that objective by the administration, a priority that allowed the Federal Reserve to exercise its willingness and ability to bring inflation down in spite of large short-run costs to the economy in terms of employment, output and profits. The very low level to which United States inflation fell in the second half of 1983 was also partly the result of favorable but transitory forces that were not expected to continue into 1984 and beyond. These favorable forces and the potential reasons for their disappearance or reversal in 1984 are summarized below.

(1) At the beginning of 1983, the levels of unutilized labor and industrial plant were very high; both conditions were conducive to disinflation. These conditions had changed significantly by early 1984. The rate of utilization of plant capacity had risen from below 70 percent in December, 1982, to over 80 percent by February, 1984, and was rapidly approaching the 82-percent utilization rate, above which price pressures had begun in previous business cycles. Civilian unemployment had fallen from a rate of 10.7 percent at the end of 1982 to 7.8 percent by February, 1984. In early 1984, although the economy as a whole was still operating at a level below its potential capacity, bottlenecks and delayed supply schedules had already appeared in some industrial sectors, as well as in several categories of skilled labor: two conditions that had led to rapid, though selective, price and wage increase in the past.

(2) In 1982 and 1983, many of the most militant unions had received wage increases that were well below the national average. In industries most affected by the recession (such as steel, automobiles and airlines), some unions had accepted wage reductions. Similar disinflationary cuts were unlikely to be repeated in a more prosperous year like 1984.

(3) In early 1983, faced by world demand for oil that was far below its producing capacity, OPEC reduced the contract price of oil from $34 a barrel to $29. At the same time, the OPEC nations, behaving like a true cartel for the first time, worked out a set of production-sharing agreements designed to reduce the oversupply of oil. These arrangements, together with the rise in oil demand that accompanied economic recovery, implied that further reductions in oil prices would not take place in 1984.

(4) Agricultural prices were weak in 1983 and, as a result, the price of food in that year rose only moderately. Because of adverse weather in the second half of the year and the government's own program for restricting agricultural output, the expectation in early 1984 was that food prices would rise more sharply in 1984.

(5) The exchange rate of the U.S. dollar rose in 1983, thus exerting a downward pressure on the price of imports as well as on the price of U.S.-produced goods that competed with imports. The prospect in early 1984 was that the dollar would not rise further—indeed, that its exchange rate was more likely to fall—thus removing yet another factor that contributed to disinflation in 1983.

The expectation that the U.S. rate of inflation would rise during 1984 from the very low levels achieved in the second half of 1983 was not an alarming one; the rate of inflation has almost always risen after recovery from a recession gives way to renewed expansion. Statistically, a doubling of the U.S. inflation rate from the 2½-3½ percent range achieved in 1983 to the 5 to 7 percent range by the end of 1984 would not in itself signal a serious renewal of inflation. Similarly, the normal cyclical pattern would indicate a rise in interest rates between 1983 and 1984: Indeed, by February, 1984, the U.S. price level and the level of interest rates were already rising along such a path. There was, however, a deeper and far more serious problem in early 1984—the problem associated with a federal budget deficit that was projected to remain extraordinarily high for an economy that had entered the expansion phase.

The Deficit Dilemma

The Reagan program that was legislated in 1981 had succeeded in achieving three of its four announced objectives by the end of 1983. Inflation had been substantially reduced; defense spending had increased rapidly; social programs and regulations over which the administration exercised budgetary control had been reduced as planned. The fourth objective that was announced in 1981 was for the reduction in the federal deficit from $58 billion a year in fiscal 1981 to zero by fiscal 1984. The program for a balanced budget by 1984 missed its mark by a wide margin. The federal deficit did not fall. It rose sharply, from $58 billion in fiscal 1981 to $111 billion in fiscal 1982, to $195 billion in fiscal 1983. In spite of economic expansion, the deficit for fiscal 1984 was estimated at $175 billion. Furthermore, unless major legislative changes were made with respect to expenditures and taxes, the prospect in early 1984 was that the deficits would rise continually into the future.

The sharp rise in the federal deficit between FY 1981 and FY 1983 and the sharp stimulus that these deficits exerted on the economy did not represent a serious problem. The economy was in recession and a considerable part of the rising deficit was a simple result of that recession. Furthermore, about $100 billion of the large stimulus that was provided by the federal deficit served to offset restraining pressures that were generated by a rising surplus in state and local government budgets (estimated at $55 billion a year in 1983) and by the rising deficit in our international transactions (estimated at $40 billion a year in 1983).

The prospect that federal deficits would continue at around the $180-billion level through 1984 and beyond represented a different and entirely inappropriate stimulus. Federal borrowing to finance its deficit during a recessed period of economic activity does little harm because private demands for funds by business, consumers and home buyers generally fall even faster than government demands rise. Furthermore, during a recession the central bank has far more leeway to permit an expansion in money and credit without risking inflation. By contrast, continuation of large federal deficits in 1984 and beyond and the expansionary stimulus and federal borrowing that such deficits implied presented serious dangers to the economy. Credit demands from the private sector inevitably rise in the expansion phase of the cycle. Continued demand for credit by the Federal Government at such a time implied a total demand for credit that the market would be unable to supply except at far higher levels of interest rates. The combination of large fiscal stimulus and private prosperity creates a dilemma for central banking policy—the dilemma Arthur Burns referred to as the "anguish" of central banking.

(1) Monetary policy can devote itself to keeping interest rates from rising too rapidly by supplying its own credit on an increasing scale, a process that must lead to a rapid increase in the rate of monetary growth and to a subsequent rapid increase in the rate of inflation.

(2) Alternatively, monetary policy can exercise restraint over the growth of money and credit in order to prevent a rekindling of inflation. If if does so, interest rates will rise sharply in order to equate the rising total demand for credit to the flow of saving available in the marketplace. The rapid rise in interest rates leads, in turn, to a sharp decline in the price of bonds and stocks, and to a fall in the interest-sensitive demand for

new housing, automobiles and business plant and equipment-developments that generally trigger a recession.

* * * * *

By early 1984, the central question for the future no longer was: Can inflation be reduced in the context of a free market? That question had been answered in the affirmative. However, the answer had been rendered in the context of a recession. The relevant question was: Can the United States achieve sustained economic growth in 1984 and beyond without rekindling serious inflation? Although the answer to the second and more ambitious question will not be known for some years, the conditions on which it depends were perfectly clear in early 1984: Without significant reductions in the size of prospective federal deficits, the U.S. economy would be able to achieve either reasonable price stability *or* an extended period of expansion—but not both. The shape of the economy and the course of inflation in the second half of the 1980's will be determined by how swiftly the administration and the Congress can act in 1984 to resolve the nation's deficit problem.

Between 1965 and 1980, the United States missed three opportunities to stop the accelerating wave of inflation that began in 1965. In 1966, 1969, and 1974, the Federal Reserve System acted boldly in applying monetary restraint to reverse a worsening rate of inflation. Each time it succeeded in doing so, but only at the cost of politically unpopular short-run losses in output. Those successes with respect to inflation were temporary. On each succeeding upswing of the economy, in 1967-1968, 1971-1972, and 1977-1978, the battle against inflation was lost once more and each time for the same basic reason. Although the three episodes differ with respect to details, the general pattern of events in those periods was similar. The pattern went as follows:

(1) The thrust of fiscal policy, driven by short-run political considerations rather than by the long-run economic needs, became highly (and inappropriately) expansionary.

(2) Large federal deficits in the face of rising private demands for credit placed strains on the financial markets and led to severe upward pressures on interest rates.

(3) The central bank found itself faced by a dilemma: It could retard the upward pressure on interest rates by accommodating the market's need for credit. Such a course of action would nourish the boom in economic activity but it would sooner or later also nourish a substantial rise in the rate of inflation. Alternatively, the central bank could starve the credit markets through a policy of severe monetary restraint, single-mindedly devoted to forestalling future inflation. This alternative course of action would lead to a sharp rise in interest rates that would, in turn, starve the boom in economic activity and thus risk yet another recession.

(4) Faced by the dilemma outlined above, the central bank, which like the Supreme Court watches election results, tried to steer an intermediate course: It would follow a policy that undernourished the boom and that only partially offset upward pressures on interest rates.

(5) The central bank's policy of compromise failed on each occasion because inflation rates eventually rose to levels at which the Federal Reserve became convinced that more stringent restraint was necessary. The economy would then go into a recession and inflationary pressures would ease.

The three cycles of inflation and partial disinflation that took place between 1965 and 1980—a pattern whimsically but accurately described by some observers as root-canal yo-yo—took place along a rising inflationary trend: Price increases rose from 1½ percent before 1965 to 3 percent in 1966, to 6 percent in 1969, to 12 percent in 1974, and 15 percent by early 1980. Even more seriously, the eventual correction of each successive inflationary cycle entailed a far sharper cost in terms of lost output and rates of unemployment. In order to stop and reverse the last inflationary cycle (which peaked in March, 1980), the United States had to suffer its longest post-World War II recession and a rise in the unemployment rate to a peak monthly rate of 10.7 percent (as compared to 4.3 percent in 1967, 6.1 percent in 1970 , and 8.9 percent in 1975).

In 1984, the U.S. economy entered into yet another phase of true expansion after five years of stagnation. Once again, the central bank faced the dilemma it had faced three times before: an overly expansive fiscal policy that forces monetary policy to choose between renewed inflation on the one hand and yet another recession on the other. Sustained expansion without a renewal of inflation cannot be achieved until the cause of the dilemma is eliminated—a federal budget that for a bewildering combination of political reasons spends far more than the same policymakers are willing to finance through taxation. An enduring correction for inflation in the context of expansion will require corrections on both sides of the federal budget in 1984. That, in turn, will require a triumph of long-run policy goals over short-run political considerations.

Part II

INDIVIDUAL COUNTRY STUDIES

JAPAN

Nobumitsu Kagami*

FROM 1965 to 1983, Japan experienced three separate periods of rapid price increases, each resulting from different causes. What follows is a chronological account against which we can examine relationships between Japan's inflationary experience and the various factors responsible for it.

Three Postwar Inflationary Periods

Apart from the major inflationary aftermath of the Second World War, inflation became a matter of public concern for the first time in the early 1960's. Inflation in the 1960's was characterized by a marked discrepancy between the movements of consumer and wholesale prices. While Japan's 5.7 percent annual rate of increase in the consumer price index (CPI) recorded in the 1960's was the worst among the major advanced countries, the wholesale price index (WPI) remained virtually flat throughout the period, rising by only 1.3 percent per annum. This was a time when the Japanese economy grew very rapidly. From 1963 to 1973, gross national product (GNP) grew at an annual rate of 10.3 percent. Industrial production grew even faster (12.1 percent), accompanied by major structural changes toward the heavy chemical and engineering industries.

The second major outbreak of inflation took place in 1973-1974, which is still remembered as the period of "mad inflation," or *kyoran-bukka,* in Japanese. The attempt to counter the strong upward pressure on the exchange rate of the yen, both before and after the Smithsonian Agreement in late 1971, led to massive purchases by the Bank of Japan of large inflows of foreign funds, which resulted in excessive monetary expansion in Japan. At the same time, fears over the potential deflationary impact of the yen's first postwar appreciation led the Prime Minister, Mr. Kakuei Tanaka (who took office in May, 1972) to undertake a major fiscal reflation based on the theme of "Restructuring the Japanese Archipelago." Thus by the time the oil producers of the Middle

*Chief Economist and Adviser to the President, Nomura Investment Management Co. Ltd., Tokyo, Japan.

East decided to deploy the oil weapon in the wake of the fourth Middle-East War, inflationary pressures had been allowed to build to crisis proportions with the WPI in October, 1973 already 20.3 percent above the level of a year earlier. The subsequent quadrupling of oil prices, starting in December, 1973, only served to magnify the eventual price explosion.

The third bout of inflationary price movement occurred in 1979 and 1980, largely triggered by a sharp rise in import prices. Whereas the immediate effect of the upswing in import prices was no less significant than in the previous inflationary uproar of 1973-1974, in 1979-1980 it was successfully contained at the beachhead without a serious spiraling effect on domestic costs and prices. Although both the WPI and CPI registered 24 percent and 8.9 percent increases at their respective peaks in 1980, GNP deflator, which measures the price of domestically produced output, stayed relatively stable. It rose by only 2 percent and 3.1 percent, respectively, in fiscal years 1979 and 1980.[1] Little lasting damage was done to the underlying price trend: A downward movement in the WPI began to set in as early as the Spring of 1981, and CPI inflation moderated to the 3-percent level by the middle of 1982.

Rapid Growth and Inflation: 1960-1970

The marked discrepancy between the movements of the Japanese CPI and the WPI during the 1960's is usually explained by differentials in productivity growth between the manufacturing sector, on the one hand, and the service and distribution sectors, on the other. After the middle of the 1950's, Japan entered a period of economic takeoff in which a rapid growth of exports and of private capital investment reinforced each other, resulting in a strong, fast expansion in the heavy chemical and engineering industries. Led by these industries, labor productivity in the manufacturing sector as a whole rose at an annual rate of 10.5 percent between 1960 and 1970, and manufacturing unit labor costs increased only marginally. Consequently, the price of industrial goods remained almost flat, contributing to the stability of the WPI, of which industrial goods represent an 81.6 percent share.

The uninterrupted rapid economic growth in the 1960's was inevitably accompanied by a gradual tightening of the labor market. The effective job offers/ applicants ratio rose from 0.73 in 1963 to 1.35 in fiscal year 1970. The general wage level increased sharply, by 12 percent per annum, during the 10 years from 1960 to 1970. This increase was accompanied by a significant narrowing of wage differentials between the fast-growing manufacturing sector, dominated by big companies, and the service and distribution sector in which small businesses were predominant. Faced with aggressive recruitment by big companies in the manufacturing sector, where productivity growth was fast, companies in the service and distribution sector were forced to offer competitive

[1]Japan's fiscal years run from April 1 to March 31 of the following year.

wages and salaries higher than their own slower productivity growth could justify. The resulting cost pressure was reflected in the relatively rapid increase in the CPI, in which the prices of services and products provided by small companies are far more important than in the WPI.

It is still a matter of debate whether the price increases witnessed in the 1960-1970 period should be classified as inflation. In one view, these increases largely represented changes in the prices of services in relation to those of manufactured goods. The opposing view is that the rise in the price of services should have been offset by a decline in the price of manufactured goods, had this not been prevented by increasingly oligopolistic conditions in the manufacturing sector. On the whole, however, public concern over the persistent rise in the CPI was muted, and the view was widely accepted that higher consumer prices reflected only higher wages paid to labor. The authorities also remained largely unconcerned with price developments. Their main preoccupation was fixed firmly on the objective of sustaining rapid economic growth. Easy monetary policy was pursued, and the money supply was allowed to increase at an annual rate of 15 to 20 percent for most of the decade.

By the mid-1960's, however, an increasing body of evidence began to emerge of a downward rigidity in wholesale prices. The failure of the WPI to fall when growth slowed in 1960 and its quick upward movement in the early stages of a recovery from the recession of 1965 were regarded as sufficient evidence for the existence of a chronic upward pressure in Japan's cost structure. The Committee to Study Prices, Wages and Productivity was formed in 1967 to investigate whether it was appropriate for Japan to introduce an incomes policy, but its report, "Price Stability and Incomes Policy," rendered a negative judgment on the issue.

Wholesale prices began to surge after the Summer of 1968, registering a rise of 3 percent in the year ending August, 1969, in spite of a continuing abundance of supply capacity. Rising import prices were blamed, but many observers also pointed to the persistent upward drift of prices administered by big companies. The Bank of Japan was more concerned with the eventual inflationary implications of the rapid growth in the money supply in 1966 and 1967 and decided to tighten credit by raising the official discount rate in September, 1969, from 5.84 percent to 6.25 percent, the first time the Bank of Japan had changed its monetary stance for reasons other than the balance of payments.

With the help of hindsight, it is clear that the appropriate policy in late 1969 would have been an upward revaluation of the yen. Secret meetings were held within the Ministry of Finance to explore the possibility of a yen revaluation, but the issue was shelved in the midst of the political turmoil that followed the general elections at the end of that year. The authorities turned in the opposite direction after this, and the defense of the yen's parity at all costs became the official policy of the Government until August, 1971. The pressure on the yen intensified. Massive capital inflows followed, mainly of dollars. This resulted in a large expansion in Japan's supply of money and liquidity. Then came the wave of "mad inflation" in 1973 and 1974.

Excess Liquidity and "Mad" Inflation: 1973-1974

The inflation of 1973 and 1974 in Japan was largely caused by the extremely easy monetary conditions that preceded the first quadrupling of oil prices. In some respects, it was a result of overreaction to the fears about the potentially deflationary impact of the exchange-rate increase that was seen at the beginning of the 1970's. Table 1 shows how important official interventions were in the foreign exchange market in 1971-1972 in inflating the supply of high-powered money, that is, money created directly by central bank actions. The efforts to defend both the pre-Smithsonian parity of 360 yen to the U.S. dollar and the Smithsonian parity of 308 yen to the dollar, established in December, 1971, were accompanied by very sharp increases in Japan's foreign-exchange reserves ($10.9 billion and $3.1 billion, respectively, in 1971 and 1972) with a spectacular increase of $5 billion in two weeks alone following the announce-

Table 1
Japan: Foreign Exchange and Monetary Expansion 1968-1974

Year	Growth in High-Powered Money		Contribution of Foreign Exchange Account	Growth In Bank Lending	Growth In Money Supply
	Percent Increase[1]	Amount of Increase (Billions of Yen)	(Billions of Yen)	Percent Increase[1]	(M-2 + CD's) Percent Increase[1]
1968	18.9	705	301	12.6	14.8
1969	19.6	873	349	16.4	18.5
1970	16.6	881	447	16.9	16.9
1971 Mar	15.3	769	676	18.6	18.0
Jun	15.9	803	1680	20.7	24.3
Sep	19.5	970	3917	22.5	23.1
Dec	14.5	901	4400	24.2	24.3
1972 Mar	13.5	785	4356	24.1	24.0
Jun	17.2	1007	3174	23.2	22.8
Sep	18.9	1120	1606	24.5	22.0
Dec	29.0	2058	1740	25.6	24.7
1973 Mar	33.7	2221	1787	25.3	25.1
Jun	37.2	2556	1229	24.1	24.7
Sep	37.6	2656	230	20.9	22.9
Dec	34.3	3139	−1884	16.6	16.8
1974 Mar	27.4	2411	−2468	14.9	15.1
Jun	27.7	2610	−1521	13.7	13.3
Sep	22.0	2137	−1348	11.8	10.9
Dec	16.1	1985	−378	10.8	11.5

[1]Percentage increase relative to year earlier period.

Source: Ryutaro Komiya, "Inflation in 1973 and 1974," *Keizagaku Ronsyu,* Tokyo University, April 1976.

ment by President Nixon on August 15, 1971, that suspended the U.S. dollar's convertibility into gold. The increase in high-powered money by 901 billion yen and 2,058 billion yen in 1971 and 1972 represented 19.5 percent and 29 percent increases in each of those years. Official foreign-exchange market interventions supplied the basis for more than 100 percent of the increases in each year.

The subsequent explosion in the money supply (M-2) was a natural result of large purchases of dollars by the Bank of Japan. In such an easy monetary environment banks competed against each other to expand their lending, which increased by 24.2 percent in 1971 and 25.6 percent in 1972. At the same time, the monetary policy of the Bank of Japan was further eased for the purpose of blunting dollar inflows by a five-step reduction in the official discount rate from 6 percent to 4.25 percent. As the upward pressure on the yen persisted, the authorities began to accept the view that Japan's inflation rate should be adjusted upward to the prevailing world rate. This view provided moral support for the acceleration of the money supply, which grew by 24.3 percent and 24.7 percent in 1971 and 1972, respectively.

Fiscal policy also turned highly expansionary after exchange rates were temporarily realigned by the Smithsonian Agreement in December, 1971. The budget for fiscal year 1972 incorporated a 21.8 percent increase in the central government general account expenditure, with spending on public works increased by 29 percent. Upon taking office in May, 1972, Prime Minister Tanaka added further stimulus in the October supplementary budget, which was then followed by the fiscal year 1973 budget in which total general account spending increased by 24.6 percent and public-works expenditure by 32.6 percent. Combined with the prevailing easy monetary situation, this flamboyant fiscal stance, colored by Mr. Tanaka's euphoric theme of "Restructuring the Japanese Archipelago," was undoubtedly responsible for the rising inflation rate and growing inflationary psychology which became pervasive throughout the country.

Compared with the successive attempts to stimulate domestic demand, the response of the supply side of the equation was far less dynamic. Cartels that developed in the basic material sectors during the recession of 1970 and 1971 were extended into 1972. Production controls on steel and ethylene were maintained until the end of that year. Companies tended to respond to the increasing demand for their output by raising prices rather than by expanding production—behavior not seen in the 1960's. While a growing need to reduce industrial pollution as well as difficulties in securing plant sites had worsened supply constraints, the situation was further exacerbated in 1973 by a shortage of water and by repeated major accidents in chemical plants.

The escalation of inflationary psychology, coupled with the tightening of labor supply, led to sharp rises in nominal wages. On top of the 20.1 percent wage increase agreed upon in the wage negotiations in the Spring of 1973, generous bonuses were paid based on sharply improving profits, resulting in a

Table 2
Contributions to Wholesale Price Increases
(1973-1974)

Year		Actual	Estimate	Supply-Demand Balance	Wage Costs	Import Prices
					Contributions by	
1973		15.9%	16.8 %	9.0 %	1.3 %	6.5 %
			(100.0)	(53.6)	(7.7)	(38.7)
1974		31.3	30.2	−0.7	9.6	21.3
			(100.0)	(−2.3)	(31.8)	(70.5)
1973	III	5.2	6.0	2.1	1.0	2.9
			(100.0)	(35.0)	(16.7)	(48.3)
	IV	8.7	9.1	5.0	1.1	3.0
			(100.0)	(54.9)	(12.1)	(33.0)
1974	I	14.6	11.1	−0.9	1.8	10.2
			(100.0)	(−8.1)	(16.2)	(91.9)
	II	3.4	4.4	−3.5	3.7	4.2
			(100.0)	(−79.5)	(84.1)	(95.4)
	III	2.9	4.6	−2.0	3.5	3.1
			(100.0)	(43.5)	(76.1)	(67.4)
	IV	1.2	1.4	−1.4	1.8	1.0
			(100.0)	(−100.0)	(128.6)	(71.4)

Source: *Review of Financial Developments in 1974,* The Bank of Japan. Estimates and contributions are based on the following regression equation for the period from January-March 1965 to October-December 1974.

WPI = 38.4710 + 0.1055   DI + 0.3241   IPI + 0.2920   ULC + 5.5128DM
     (27.79)   (17.42)   (18.48)   (21.1)   (4.39)
R = 0.9973   SE = 0.9454   DW = 1.25

WPI : the wholesale price index
DI : the diffusion index of businessmen's judgments on supply-demand balance from the Bank of Japan's *Short-term Economic Survey of Enterprises.*
IPI : the index of import prices
ULC : unit wage cost $\left(\dfrac{\text{Index of Manufacturing Employment} \times \text{Wage index}}{\text{Production index}}\right)$
DM : Dummy variable (response to the first oil shock: 1 after October 1973)

21.8 percent increase in the total nominal wages in fiscal year 1973. This was followed by 32.9 percent wage settlements in the 1974 spring offensive, as trade unions' demands for compensation for inflation were largely met. With increased nominal income in their pockets, consumers rushed out on a buying spree in anticipation of accelerating price rises and in the face of growing shortages of many essential consumer products.

Table 2 shows the three main factors in the sharp WPI increases recorded in 1973 and 1974. The analysis is based on an input-output study by the Bank of Japan. As the table shows, the tightening of the supply-demand balance was the primary cause of the price rise in 1973, a manifestation of the inflationary effect of excess liquidity and growing inflationary expectations. In 1974, overseas factors—namely, rising oil prices and falling yen exchange rates—became predominant. Toward the end of 1974, however, the emphasis shifted to the wage-cost pressure brought about by a combination of sky-rocketing wages and declining productivity.

The perverse effect of excess liquidity on inflationary psychology prior to the first oil crisis can also be seen in the exaggerated price response to the oil-price increase itself. The Bank of Japan has calculated that the direct effect of sharp oil-price increases after October, 1973, would have brought about an 11 percent rise in Japan's WPI. In fact, the WPI rose by 22 percent from October, 1973, to March, 1974. Companies clearly raised their prices far in excess of what could be justified on the grounds of the increased energy costs alone. In addition, distributors and retailers widened their profit margins, taking advantage of consumer panic buying.

Imported Inflation: 1979-1980

After a brief period of price stability in the wake of the recession of 1975 and 1976 and the subsequent appreciation of the yen in 1977 and 1978, the WPI began to show ominous signs of an upward move in early 1979. Wholesale prices reached a peak in April, 1980, when the WPI registered a rise of 24 percent compared with a year earlier. The CPI followed the movement of the WPI with a lag of a few months and climbed to its peak in September, 1980, when it was up 8.9 percent over the preceding 12 months.

As can be seen in Table 3, the 1979-1980 bout of price increases was basically the result of imported inflation, triggered by the second oil-price upheaval in 1979-1980, which was further magnified by the concurrent sharp depreciation of the yen. Once import prices began to stabilize in the second quarter of 1980, both consumer and wholesale prices moderated rapidly, and the inflation rate was brought down by 1981 to 4.9 percent in consumer prices and 1.7 percent in wholesale prices. According to the Bank of Japan, four-fifths of the 17.5 percent rise in the WPI from December, 1978, to December, 1979, is ascribable to both direct and indirect effects of higher import prices, which increased by 72.8 percent during the same period. (Imported goods account directly for approximately 10 percent of the wholesale price index.)

Table 3 also demonstrates how the initial impact of rising import prices was absorbed in the process of production. When import prices rise, the immediate effect is to increase the wholesale price of raw materials. This, in turn, is transmitted to prices of semifinished and finished products. Reflecting the sharp upswing of import prices in 1979, the WPI for raw materials rose by 70.4 percent a year at its peak in the first quarter of 1980, an increase of similar magnitude to the one experienced in the previous inflationary period of 1974-1975. Yet the rises in the WPI of semifinished goods and finished goods

Table 3
Import Prices and Wholesale Prices
(Percent changes over year-earlier period)

	Import Price Index	WPI (Total)	By Production Stage			CPI	Nominal Wages (MFG)	Labor Productivity (MFG)	Unit Wage Cost (MFG)
			Raw Materials	Semi-Finished	Finished				
First Oil Shock 1973-1975									
1973 I	12.3	9.4	20.3	12.3	4.9	7.2	19.3	17.5	1.3
II	14.9	12.5	20.4	16.0	7.8	10.5	21.7	16.6	4.5
III	25.7	17.3	32.6	22.0	10.5	13.0	21.5	14.4	6.0
IV	31.0	24.0	35.8	30.0	15.3	16.3	28.1	11.2	15.3
1974 I	60.5	35.4	63.7	39.8	25.0	24.4	20.3	5.0	14.8
II	73.7	35.4	79.2	37.9	23.8	24.0	30.3	− 1.7	32.6
III	71.0	32.5	72.8	32.4	23.1	24.8	31.1	− 5.8	39.2
IV	60.2	23.4	56.6	20.0	19.9	24.6	22.2	−10.9	37.1
1975 I	19.8	7.3	15.6	4.7	8.5	15.5	24.2	−14.7	45.5
II	7.1	3.4	4.7	1.6	6.3	13.4	7.3	− 8.0	16.6
Second Oil Shock 1979-1980									
1979 I	− 6.8	− 0.8	− 5.0	− 0.8	0.3	2.6	5.4	9.2	− 3.5
II	14.4	3.6	10.7	4.0	0.9	3.1	7.0	9.0	− 1.8
III	46.9	10.5	37.2	12.1	2.0	3.4	8.5	9.3	− 0.7
IV	67.7	16.1	54.5	18.3	7.1	5.0	8.1	9.4	− 1.2
1980 I	81.3	21.2	70.4	24.6	5.3	7.6	7.8	11.7	− 3.5
II	57.0	22.0	54.3	28.4	7.4	8.3	8.0	7.9	0.1
III	35.0	17.1	32.6	22.4	7.8	8.4	7.7	3.3	4.2
IV	14.5	11.6	15.8	15.8	3.7	7.9	6.9	2.1	4.7
1981 I	− 3.2	4.1	− 1.5	6.0	5.6	6.6	5.6	0.3	5.3
II	1.7	0.4	2.0	− 1.8	3.1	4.9	4.9	− 0.3	5.2

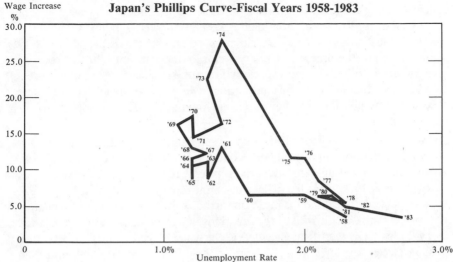

Unemployment Rate

were far smaller, compared with the previous experience, 28.4 percent and 7.4 percent at their respective peaks. Thus the initial effect of import-price increases was contained successfully in 1979-1980 without causing spiral repercussions on the price of products at the later stages of production.

The favorable price performance in the wake of the 1979-1980 round of oil-price increases was caused largely by the rapid increase in labor productivity attained during the economic recovery that began after the middle of 1977. In contrast to the first oil shock, which took place at a time when the Japanese economy was near its cyclical peak, the economy was still in the early stages of a cyclical upturn when it was hit by the second oil shock. The existence of considerable slack in the economy enabled manufacturing productivity to rise by 12.1 percent in 1979 and 9.1 percent in 1980. Wage demands by trade unions were also moderate, which reflected both the lessons learned from the bitter experience of the inflationary flare-up of 1973-1974 and generally easy labor-market conditions. With wage increases held below 7 percent, manufacturing unit labor costs fell both in 1979 and 1980.

Chart 1 plots Japan's Phillips curve (showing the relationship between inflation rates and unemployment rates) for the period from 1956 to 1982. The curve sloped down to the right in the 1956-1971 period, as envisaged by theory, but turned upward from 1972 to 1974. Since 1979, it appears that the relationship between wage increases and the unemployment rate has returned to the normal downward slope that existed prior to 1972. With the unemployment rate still standing at what are historically high levels for the Japanese economy, wage increases moderated considerably after 1979.

The 1981 Economic White Paper, prepared by the Economic Planning Agency, cites a number of factors responsible for the moderate wage development seen since 1979. First, inflationary expectations were subdued sufficiently, thanks to the firm anti-inflation policies pursued on both the fiscal and monetary fronts. Second, the practice of lifelong employment meant that job security was preferred to high wages, especially at a time of general economic uncertainty. Third, there was no wage indexation in Japan; and, finally, considerable flexibility was provided by the practice of paying significant portions of income as bonuses.

Much credit for the successful containment of imported inflation after 1979 should be given to the government's conduct of monetary and fiscal policies. At the first signs of upward pressure on prices, monetary policy tightened as early as April, 1979, when the official discount rate was raised from 3.5 percent to 4.25 percent. The discount rate was further raised in four steps, ultimately to 9 percent in 1980. Growth of the broad measure of money supply, measured as M-2 plus CD's (certificates of deposits), was reduced from 13.1 percent a year in December, 1978, to 9.1 percent a year by the end of 1979, and then to 7.2 percent by the end of 1980. Fiscal policy, which was quite expansionary in 1977 and 1978, turned neutral in early 1979, and then became restrictive when it was decided to postpone a part of the budgeted public-works program until the following fiscal year. Fiscal austerity was maintained in the 1980 budget, which allowed for only a 10 percent increase in general account spending with virtually no increase in public-works spending.

After a sustained climb in 1977 and 1978 to a peak of 178 yen to a dollar, the yen exchange rate weakened considerably after October, 1978. It fell to 264 yen to a U.S. dollar in April, 1980, down by 33 percent from the peak reached in the Autumn of 1978. Nearly 70 percent of Japan's imports consists of energy and raw materials. When their prices rise sharply—as they did both in 1973-1974 and 1979—Japan's trade balance deteriorates quickly, mostly on the import side. Huge current account deficits emerge, which lead to sharp depreciations of the yen that magnify the effect of the rise in the price of oil and raw materials.

From late 1978 to March, 1980, the yen import-price index rose 110 percent, nearly a quarter of which was explained by the yen's depreciation during the same period. The pattern was reversed, however, when the yen recovered from 264 yen to a U.S. dollar in April, 1980, to 200 yen to a dollar at the end of the same year. The 32 percent appreciation of the yen during this time undoubtedly made a significant contribution to a 7 percent fall in the yen import-price index over the same period. Since more than 95 percent of Japan's imports are still denominated in the U.S. dollar, the key variable in these calculations remains the dollar/yen exchange rate. Under the floating exchange-rate regime, the current Japanese import composition means that fluctuations in the price of energy and raw materials exert powerful effects on Japanese prices.

The Response of Monetary Policy

After the mad inflation of 1973-1974 and the recession that followed it, the deepest in the postwar period, the Bank of Japan decided in the mid-1970's to introduce a major change of emphasis in the conduct of its monetary policy. The change of emphasis can be summarized as follows:

(1) Achievement of price stability became the single most important objective of monetary policy.
(2) Control of the money supply (defined as M-2 plus CD's) was emphasized as an important intermediate target.
(3) Efforts were made to increase the effectiveness of interest rates in implementing monetary policy.

That a central bank should have cited the achievement of price stability as one of its most important policy objectives was nothing new. Nevertheless, it represented a significant departure from the basic position taken during the 1960's for the Bank of Japan to declare officially that price stability should henceforth be given the highest priority in the conduct of its monetary policy against all other competing objectives.

Until the end of the 1960's, it was generally believed, at least within the Bank of Japan, that there were trade-off relationships among price, employment and balance-of-payments objectives, and that the ultimate objective of monetary policy was to strike a proper balance among the three objectives of price stability, full employment, and external equilibrium. Life was fairly simple for the Bank of Japan during the 1960's because conflicts among these objectives were relatively minor. When the economy was near or at its cyclical peaks, prices would begin to rise and the balance of payments usually moved into the red. The Bank of Japan would then tighten credit severely, prices would stabilize after a short time lag, and a surplus would emerge in the balance of payments. The key variable for monetary policy was the movement of the trade balance, and monetary policy was generally effective in keeping the economy on a high noninflationary growth path.

Matters became far more complicated with the coming of the 1970's. The easy monetary policy that was pursued at the beginning of the decade in an attempt to defend the yen's parities in order to fend off the potentially defla-tionary effect of a rising yen resulted in a disastrous inflationary spiral followed by a deep recession. The 1960's policy that attempted to strike a balance among prices, employment and the balance of payments was discredited by the mid-1970's. The Bank of Japan restated its official position as follows: Only through the attainment of price stability could both economic growth and ex-ternal equilibrium be sustained. For its intermediate target, the Bank placed increased importance on control of the money supply. This change in emphasis reflected the profound change that took place in the structure of the flow of funds in Japan that accompanied the considerable slowdown in Japan's basic growth rate. During the 1960's, when rapid economic growth was led by the investment and export sectors, many Japanese companies were in significantly overborrowed positions. Their heavy indebtedness meant that the strength of their business activities was reflected directly in their loan demands at banks, especially at city banks. Under these circumstances monetary policy could be effective in controlling business activity. The amount of increase in lending by city banks was used as an intermediate target by the Bank of Japan in effecting its monetary policy. Interest rates were tightly regulated at artificially low levels and, therefore, were not suitable for use as an intermediate target by the central bank.

With the substantial deceleration of economic growth that emerged in the early 1970's, corporate liquidity improved because capital spending was reduced. This, in turn, weakened the direct link that had existed previously between business activity and loan demand at city banks. With the increased liquidity of corporations now serving as a cushion between the two variables, the Bank of Japan recognized by the middle of the decade that control of the flow of bank lending was no longer a sufficient guide for monetary policy. It decided to pay more attention to the level of total liquidity in the economy and, hence, to growth in the stock of money. The bitter experience of inflation in 1973 and 1974, which was fueled by the earlier explosion of the money supply, also played a large part in prompting the Bank of Japan to adopt control of the growth of the money supply as an intermediate target.

An article, entitled "The Importance of Money Supply in Japan," which appeared in the July, 1975, issue of the Bank of Japan's *Monthly Report*, marked the beginning of a new orientation to its monetary policy. In July, 1978, the Bank began to announce at the beginning of each quarter its estimate of the daily average of the money stock (M-2 plus CD's) during the ensuing quarter as a percentage increase over the corresponding quarter of the previous year. As a targeting method, the practice adopted is far less strict or mechanical than in the United States. The principal monetary target in the United States, M-1 (currency plus demand deposits), is published weekly. In Japan, only monthly statistics are available for the various monetary aggregates, and these are published only after a six-week lag. In addition, targeting does not focus exclusively on money supply; due consideration is given to the movement of short-term interbank money rates.

Once control of the growth of the money supply is adopted as the main intermediate target, it follows automatically that interest rates must be allowed to fluctuate freely. The underlying rationale is that as the level of liquidity in the economy is raised, the effectiveness of monetary policy can be secured only if the opportunity costs of physical investment are influenced sufficiently by changes in the returns available on financial assets. In addition, further pressures toward the freeing of interest rates in Japan arose from the growing volume of government bonds issued and the increasing influence of international monetary developments on Japan's financial markets.

Table 4
Table 4
Liberalization of Money and Bond Markets Since 1977

	Money Markets			Bond Market	
Call Market	Bill Market	"Gensaki," CD's		Secondary Market	Primary Market
1977				(Apr.) Liberalization of the sale of govt bonds held by financial institutions (after a grace period of a year). (Dec.) BOJ's market operations to be based on subscriptions instead of fixed allocations to financial Institutions.	(Jan.) The first issue of 5-year gov't medium-term discount notes.
1978 (Jun.) Flexible changes in call rates. (Oct.) Introduction of 7-day call loans with rates freely determined by markets.	(Jun.) Liberalization of secondary market trading and rates for bills one month after issue. (Nov.) 1-month bills with no restrictions on rates. Liberalization of rates on over 3- and 4-month ends bills.			(Jan.) Competitive bidding to be used for BOJ's market operations in govt bonds. (Jan.) The first sales of gov't bonds from Treasury Fund Bureau on the basis of competitive bidding. (Jun.) The first "buy" operations by BOJ on a competitive bidding basis.	(Jun.) The first issue of 3-year medium-term coupon notes on the basis of competitive bidding.
1979 (Apr.) Abolition of daily fixing of call rates.	(Dec.) Liberalization of bill rates.	(Apr.) Easing of restrictions on dealing in GENSAKI market by banks.[1] (May) The first issue of CDs with no restrictions on interest rates. (May) Liberalization of trading in GENSAKI by nonresidents.		(May) Easing of restriction on the sale of gov't bonds by financial institutions (the grace period: 7-9 months).	(Jun.) The first issue of 2-year medium-term Coupon Notes.
1980 (Dec.) Easing of restrictions on borrowing by securities companies.		(Mar.) Liberalization of interest rates on non-resident free yen deposits by foreign official institutions.			(Jun.) The first issue of 4-year medium-term coupon notes.
1981 (Apr.) Easing of restrictions on lending by city banks.				(Apr.) Easing of restrictions on the sale of gov't bonds by financial institutions (the grace period: 3 months). (May) BOJ's selling operations in TBs on the basis of prevailing bills rates.	

[1]GENSAKI literally means present (Gen) and forward (SAKI).

Sources: "Review of Financial Developments in 1981." The Bank of Japan, *Monthly Report*, May 1981.

Table 4 provides a chronological list of measures that have been taken in the direction of interest-rate deregulation. In the interbank markets, daily fixing of call rates and bill rates was abolished in several steps between June, 1978, and October, 1979. In the open money markets, bank CD's, for which banks are free to offer any competitive rates, were first introduced in May, 1979. In May, 1981, the Bank of Japan began to conduct selling operations in Treasury bills on the basis of prevailing market rates. In the bond market, June, 1978, marked the first public issue on the basis of competitive bidding on medium-term government notes with maturities of two, three and four years; competitive bidding also began to be used for the Bank of Japan's market operations in long-term government bonds in June, 1978. In addition, control on interest rates paid on nonresident yen deposits by foreign governments, central banks, and international organizations were freed in March, 1980. The move was followed in December, 1980, by the deregulation of interest rates paid on foreign-currency deposits held at Japanese banks by Japanese residents.

Fiscal Policy and Debt Management

The sharp increase in government bond issues since the middle of the 1970's is undoubtedly one of the most important factors contributing to major changes in Japan's financial landscape. Although government bonds were first issued in fiscal year 1965, Japan's fiscal position during the decade of the 1960's was basically in equilibrium—supported by rapidly increasing tax revenues that were more than sufficient to finance growing government spending. This happy combination of rapid economic growth and a fiscal surplus came abruptly to a halt in the early 1970's. Although tax revenues began to fall short of earlier expectations owing to the slowdown of economic growth, the expansion of government spending continued unarrested. As a consequence, huge deficits emerged in government budgets.

Table 5 shows the major items of government revenues and expenditures for fiscal years 1966 to 1981. After increasing at an annual rate of 18.7 percent between fiscal years 1966 and 1973, central government general account expenditures continued to expand at a slightly slower rate of 15.6 percent from fiscal years 1974 to 1981. By contrast, the growth rate of tax revenues was nearly halved in the second period, compared with the first, from 21.7 percent to 11.3 percent a year. As a result, government bond issues increased to 14.3 trillion yen in fiscal year 1980, which represented 5.9 percent of nominal GNP, and financed 32.7 percent of total government expenditures in that year.

The emergence of the widening fiscal gap as a major economic issue in the 1970's was caused by a rapid deceleration in the growth of tax revenues. As can be seen in Table 5, one of the important characteristics of the Japanese revenue structure is its high dependence on direct taxes, such as personal and corporate income taxes, which accounted for 81.3 percent of total tax revenues in fiscal year 1973. In particular, the 40 percent share taken by corporate taxes is exceptionally high compared with the rate imposed in other advanced countries. Given the steep progression of marginal tax rates for personal income taxes and the high volatility of corporate profits, this tax mix means that tax revenues are highly procyclical: rising fast when the economy grows fast but decelerating sharply once economic growth slows down.

The wage explosion in 1973 and 1974 in the midst of spiraling inflation in those years dealt a major blow to a fiscal structure based on corporate tax revenues, which declined by as much as 29 percent in fiscal year 1975, reflecting the sharp setback in corporate profits. This development resulted in an unexpectedly large revenue shortfall, and government bond issues had to be increased significantly. Although tax revenues recovered in the following years, the difficulty reemerged in fiscal years 1981 and 1982, when the economy was hit by

Table 5
Central Government Revenues and Expenditure

	Billions of Yen					Annual Rate of Increase				
	FY 1966	FY 1973	FY 1975	FY 1978	FY 1981	FY 1966-FY 1973	FY 1974-FY 1981	FY 1974-FY 1975	FY 1976-FY 1978	FY 1978-FY 1981
Revenues	4,552	16,762	21,473	34,907	47,125	20.5%	13.8%	13.2%	17.6%	10.5%
Tax Revenues	3,370	13,302	13,689	21,734	31,298	21.7	11.3	1.4	16.7	12.9
Income Tax	1,084	5,332	5,482	7,753	12,941	25.6	11.7	12.2	18.6	1.4
Corporate Tax	1,032	4,518	4,128	7,913	10,352	23.5	10.9	-4.5	24.2	9.4
Other Taxes	1,254	3,452	4,079	6,068	8,005	15.6	11.1	8.7	14.2	9.7
Nontax Revenues	516	1,694	2,503	2,499	2,927	18.5	7.1	21.6	-0.1	5.4
Borrowings	666	1,766	5,281	10,674	12,900	14.9	28.2	72.9	26.4	6.5
Expenditure	4,459	14,778	20,861	34,096	47,125	18.7	15.6	18.8	17.8	11.4
Social Security	629	2,220	4,136	6,735	8,868	19.7	18.9	36.5	17.6	9.6
Education and Science	564	1,643	2,707	3,881	4,822	16.5	14.4	28.4	12.8	7.5
Debt Service	42	685	1,102	3,232	6,654	49.0	32.9	26.8	43.1	27.2
Pensions	195	471	759	1,332	1,803	13.4	18.3	26.9	20.6	10.6
Local Government Finance	830	3,244	3,351	5,741	8,723	21.5	13.2	1.6	19.7	15.0
Defense	346	953	1,386	1,863	2,429	15.6	12.4	20.6	10.4	9.2
Public Works	910	2,560	3,487	5,797	7,001	15.9	13.4	16.7	18.4	6.5
Economic Cooperation	29	123	168	260	425	22.9	16.8	16.9	15.7	17.8
Others	914	2,879	3,765	5,255	6,400	17.8	10.5	14.4	11.8	6.8

the second oil shock and subsequent stagnation. The revenue shortfall alone amounted to 1.2 percent of nominal GNP in fiscal year 1981.

On the expenditure side, notable increases occurred in spending for social security and debt service. Provisions for social security in Japan were raised rapidly in the early part of the 1970's, to a level comparable with those of most advanced Western countries, on the assumption that rapid economic growth would continue to generate sufficient tax revenues. With the expenditure level thus raised, it remained on a strong upward trend because of inflation and the rapid aging of the population.

Spending on public works also increased considerably in fiscal years 1978 and 1979 as the government attempted to reflate the economy out of the prolonged recession that followed the inflation of 1973-1974. As a consequence, government deficits continued to expand and so, too, the expenditure on debt service. With the rapid increase in debt service, which in the initial budget for fiscal year 1982 amounted to 15.8 percent of the total central government general account spending, a vicious circle began in which the government was forced to borrow in order to pay interest on its past debt.

Faced with these daunting fiscal prospects, the late Prime Minister, Mr. Masayoshi Ohira, proposed the introduction of a general consumer tax in 1979, but was defeated badly in the general elections held at the end of the year. Mr. Zenko Suzuki, who took over from Mr. Ohira in 1980, changed the course toward budgetary balance and sought a remedy in administrative reforms aimed at spending cuts. The budgets for both fiscal years 1980 and 1981 were highly deflationary, with no increases allowed for public-works spending. The deflationary backlash of this restrictive fiscal stance proved unexpectedly severe. Consequently, the budget deficit increased because of the slow growth in tax revenues.

When government bonds were first issued in fiscal year 1965, the Japanese bond market was still immature and constrained by a policy of regulated and artificially low interest rates. The terms of issue were negotiated between the Ministry of Finance and the subscribing syndicate group at below-market rates, with the bulk of issues directly purchased by the numbers of the syndicate. Only one type of government bond existed: seven-year coupon bonds (the maturity of which was later extended to ten years). Financial institutions included in the syndicate were prohibited from selling their holdings of government bonds in the secondary market. No problem arose at that time because the volume of new issues was small. The Bank of Japan was able to absorb almost all of the issues (after the expiration of a grace period of a year) from the subscribing financial institutions through the normal buying operation required by Japanese monetary policy.

The large increases in government bond issues since fiscal year 1975 have made this funding arrangement impossible to operate. The problem has become acute, especially since fiscal year 1979 when monetary policy was tightened and bond prices fell sharply in the wake of emerging inflationary pressures caused by the second oil-price upheaval. The situation for city banks, which still held

Table 6
Maturity Structure of Government Bond Market
(as of March, 1983)

Years to Maturity	Amount (trillion yen)	Percent	Cumulative Percent
14 to 15 years	0.3	0.3	0.3
9 to 10	12.8	13.3	13.6
8 to 9	9.9	10.3	23.9
7 to 8	12.1	12.6	36.5
6 to 7	11.1	11.5	48.0
5 to 6	9.8	10.2	58.2
4 to 5	11.1	11.5	69.7
3 to 4	8.6	8.9	78.6
2 to 3	9.3	9.6	88.2
1 to 2	6.2	6.4	94.6
Less than 1 year	5.2	5.4	100.0
Total	96.4	100.0	—

a nearly 40-percent share in the buying-syndicate group, became untenable; by 1979 their increased subscription to new government bond issues amounted to more than 80 percent of the increase in their deposits in that year.

Against this background, the restrictions on the sale of government bonds by financial institutions had to be eased considerably. Prohibition on resales was reduced to the first three months after the initial issue. Activity in the secondary market expanded significantly, and this was inevitably accompanied by the emergence of a considerable gap between regulated yields in the new-issue market and freely determined yields in the secondary market. During the period of tight credit in 1979 and 1980, secondary market yields rose to 200 basis points above issuing yields, resulting in large capital losses on bank holdings, which put their capital position in serious jeopardy. In the early 1980's, changes in the issuing terms of government bonds have become more frequent than they were before. Terms were changed three times in 1981 and five times in 1982. Nonetheless they still tended to lag behind market trends, creating such serious difficulties in July and August of 1981 that the new-issue calendar had to be suspended.

Under pressure of its ever-growing funding requirements, the government also took steps to diversify its methods of financing. January, 1977, marked the first issuance of five-year discount government notes, which became popular with individual investors because of the tax advantages they offered. Medium-term government notes began to be issued in 1978 with maturities of two, three and four years, with issuing yields determined by the market through public auctions.

Table 6 shows that at the end of March, 1983, nearly 60 percent of the outstanding volume of government bonds and notes issued in the market had more than five years to final maturity. This clearly contradicts the general preference of Japanese investors for financial assets with maturities of less than five years. The government had forced itself out of the shorter-term market by the fear that its presence might jeopardize the funding abilities of private financial institutions. Two-year time deposits are a major source of funds for city banks, whereas long-term credit banks and trust banks rely heavily on five-year bank debentures and five-year loan-trust certificates respectively. Since interest rates paid on bank debentures and loan-trust certificates are strictly regulated, it was and is feared that more competitive funding by the government through medium-term notes would greatly upset the existing order and structure of the Japanese financial market, and seriously undermine the very foundation on which many financial institutions operate at present.

Nevertheless, given the prospects of a continuing large-scale government funding requirement, it is inevitable that the government will increasingly resort to medium-term note financing, which will lead to a fundamental rethinking of the present regulated interest-rate structure imposed on government bonds, bank debentures, loan certificates, and bank deposits. In addition, the increasing volumes of government bonds which have been issued since fiscal year 1975 are beginning to fall within the maturity range of less than five years. Since these bonds are traded freely in the secondary market, pressures for further liberalization of the interest-rate structure in Japan became uncontainable.

Progress Toward a Freer Financial System

The most conspicuous development in the Japanese financial scene in recent years is the progress that has been made toward the liberalization of financial markets. The underlying reason for this liberalization is the profound change that is taking place in the fundamental structure and nature of the Japanese economy—namely, a significant slowdown of the secular growth rate, major changes in the pattern of the flow of funds, the rapid accumulation of financial assets, and the increasing sensitivity of market participants to financial costs and returns available on different financial instruments. The progress of financial market liberalization has further been accelerated by two additional developments that will have significant implications for the future of the financial system. First is the massive increase in government bonds now being traded in open markets. With the total amount of government bonds outstanding having exceeded 100 trillion yen, this massive increase has shifted the center of gravity in the Japanese financial system from negotiated transactions to market-based transactions. The second development is the growing pressure of internationalization, which requires that rules and practices in Japanese markets become more compatible with those in the rest of the world.

The question of the extent to which the inflation experienced in the 1970's is responsible for these developments is difficult to answer, except to note that the impact of inflation in Japan probably has been less direct and dramatic

Table 7
Personal Financial Assets

	Billion yen (Percent) At the end of March			
	_1971_	_1976_	_1981_	_1982*_
Cash	3,981	9,142	13,425	17,167
	(5.3)	(5.0)	(3.8)	(4.0)
Demand Deposits	8,035	19,433	26,728	32,628
	(10.7)	(10.6)	(7.6)	(7.6)
Time Deposits	32,802	87,389	181,575	218,808
	(43.9)	(47.7)	(51.4)	(51.0)
Private Institutions	25,058	62,826	119,625	142,586
	(33.5)	(34.3)	(33.9)	(33.2)
Post Office Savings	7,744	24,563	61,950	76,222
	(10.4)	(13.4)	(17.5)	(17.8)
Trust	4,139	10,824	21,016	28,347
	(5.5)	(5.9)	(6.0)	(6.6)
Insurance	9,552	22,534	47,108	59,633
	(12.8)	(12.3)	(13.3)	(13.9)
Bank Debentures	2,436	7,250	12,610	15,016
	(3.3)	(4.0)	(3.6)	(3.5)
Securities	12,317	25,440	47,658	56,115
	(16.5)	(13.9)	(13.5)	(13.1)
Bonds	1,822	5,578	16,574	19,231
	(2.4)	(3.0)	(4.7)	(4.5)
Equities	9,229	16,893	25,956	29,072
	(12.3)	(9.2)	(7.4)	(6.8)
Investment Trust	1,266	2,969	5,128	7,812
	(1.7)	(1.6)	(1.5)	(1.8)
Others	1,515	1,019	2,984	1,518
	(2.0)	(0.6)	(0.8)	(0.4)
Total	74,777	183,031	353,104	429,231
	(100.0)	(100.0)	(100.0)	(100.0)

Source: The Bank of Japan: Flow of Funds Account Equities are valued at market prices.
*End of December, 1982.

than in the United States. Although the experience of inflation in 1973-1974 was traumatic, inflation itself was contained and reversed before it caused lasting damage or engendered inflationary expectations in the public. The imported inflation of 1979-1980 was basically a one-time phenomenon, which subsided once the initial effect was absorbed. Nevertheless, the experience of inflation has profoundly influenced the process of financial evolution. First, the inflationary experience of 1973-1974 was the most important trigger for the change in the orientation of monetary policy that has taken place since 1975. The importance of controlling the money supply was officially recognized, and measures were taken to allow interest rates to fluctuate more flexibly than before in order to enhance the effectiveness of monetary policy.

Table 8
Uses of Corporate Surplus Funds

		Percent composition of net increases			
	1965-1975	1976-1981	1979	1980	1981
	(Average)	(Average)			
Currency and Deposits	91.9	71.5	64.3	54.2	57.8
Cash and Demand Deposits	43.4	16.9	5.0	− 24.3	− 1.6
Time Deposits	48.5	48.4	41.9	69.1	48.8
CD's	—	6.2	17.4	9.4	10.6
Fixed Interest Rate Securities	4.5	21.6	27.0	38.9	36.9
Trust	3.5	6.9	8.8	6.8	5.3
Total	100.0	100.0	100.0	100.0	100.0
(Unregulated Financial Assets)	4.5	27.8	44.4	50.5	49.6

Source: Review of Financial Development, 1981: Monthly Report of The Bank of Japan May, 1982.

Second, the fear of rekindling inflation has led to adherence to the principle that market pressures should be reflected sufficiently in the issuing terms of government bonds. The secondary market for government bonds was allowed to develop freely and the issuing terms of these bonds, though still negotiated between the Ministry of Finance and the syndicate group, began to change frequently.

Third, the 1973-1974 period saw a major public protest against the erosion of the real value of savings. Legal actions were taken, although lost in the courts, and a considerable shift has since taken place in the composition of personal financial assets—away from monetary assets to higher yielding assets (as shown in Table 7). Table 8 shows that nearly 50 percent of corporate surplus funds are now placed in assets whose yields are determined by free-market forces.

Finally, to the extent that inflation is an international issue, the Japanese financial market cannot remain immune to the changes taking place in U.S. financial markets in response to inflation. Violent fluctuations in U.S. interest rates are transmitted to Japan via exchange-rate movements, and in order to moderate exchange rates, Japanese rates have had to move freely as well.

With the considerable progress so far achieved in the direction of interest-rate liberalization, the Japanese financial market is now divided into two major segments: One in which interest rates are allowed to move freely and the other in which interest rates are still largely regulated. The former segment consists of the short-term money market and the secondary bond market. The latter is represented by the primary bond market, the deposits market, and the loan market in which both short-term and long-term prime rates are regulated. Chart 2 provides an outline of the interest-rate structure as it existed in the Summer of 1983.

With the rapid growth of unregulated markets, the total financial structure in Japan has become highly unstable. The constant shift of funds from the

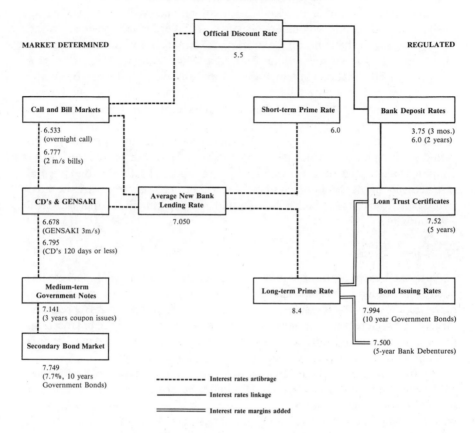

Chart 2:
Interest Rate Structure in Japan

MARKET DETERMINED   **REGULATED**

Official Discount Rate
5.5

Call and Bill Markets
6.533
(overnight call)
6.777
(2 m/s bills)

Short-term Prime Rate
6.0

Bank Deposit Rates
3.75 (3 mos.)
6.0 (2 years)

CD's & GENSAKI
6.678
(GENSAKI 3m/s)
6.795
(CD's 120 days or less)

Average New Bank Lending Rate
7.050

Loan Trust Certificates
7.52
(5 years)

Medium-term Government Notes
7.141
(3 years coupon issues)

Long-term Prime Rate
8.4

Bond Issuing Rates
7.994
(10 year Government Bonds)

Secondary Bond Market
7.749
(7.7%, 10 years Government Bonds)

7.500
(5-year Bank Debentures)

-------------- Interest rates artibrage
—————— Interest rates linkage
═══════ Interest rate margins added

The Size of the Representation Money and Capital Markets
End of August, 1983

	Billion Yen
Call Market	4,675
Bill Market	4,977
CD Market	5,984
GENSAKI Market	3,743
Medium-term Government Notes	10,998
10-year Government Bonds	90,945
Total Bank Deposits	183,867
of which	
Time Deposits	113,461
Loan Trust Certificates	24,066
5-year Bank Debentures	22,687

regulated to unregulated markets is causing considerable strain on the traditional boundaries among different categories of financial institutions and their respective functions. Pressures on the existing regulatory framework, which still places the highest priority on the maintenance of financial order and the preservation of the status quo, have become enormous. As market forces have begun to play a more important role in allocating financial resources, the need to provide for special situations in which these forces alone do not work optimally has been recognized—especially in such areas as housing finance, the financing of small- and medium-sized firms, as well as large-scale project finance in the fields of energy, high technology, and so on.

The liberalization of the Japanese financial market has now probably completed its first phase, in which developments were largely driven by the uncontainable forces of the market. In the next phase of liberalization, a fundamental restructuring of the regulatory system itself will be necessary to ensure the maximum benefit in terms of both efficiency and equity within the changing overall environment.

Short-term Money Markets

As in the United States, the liberalization of Japan's financial markets has been spearheaded by a rapid expansion of the short-term money markets. Until the middle of the 1970's, short-term money markets in Japan were represented largely by two interbank markets, namely the call market and the bill discount market, where interest rates were fixed, based on the consensus of market participants and under strong guidance from the Bank of Japan.

The first move toward the deregulation of interest rates took place in June, 1978, when the authorities began to eliminate the practice of a daily fixing of interest rates in the call market. By October, 1979, the deregulatory process was completed, both in the call and the bill markets. This move was paralleled by the rapid growth of open markets in which nonbanks are allowed to participate. Prior to the introduction of CD's in May, 1979, on which issuing banks are free to offer any competitive rates, the only open market was the GENSAKI market, the market for trading in bonds on the basis of repurchase agreements, used primarily for financing the bond holdings of securities dealers with the surplus funds of corporations.[2] The opening of the CD market provided an important impetus to the growth of open money markets, and active arbitrage transactions between the interbank and the open markets brought interest rates in both markets closer together.

Table 9 shows the rapid growth in Japan's money markets. By the end of 1982, the total size of the four money markets had grown to more than 18 trillion yen, more than double their size five years earlier. In addition, after the new Foreign Exchange Law (FOREX) came into effect in December, 1980, foreign-

---

[1]GENSAKI literally means present (GEN) and forward (SAKI).

Table 9
Size of Money Markets

Year	Call Market	Bill Market	GENSAKI Market	End of the Year (billion yen)	
				CD Market	Total
1970	1,817	—	635	—	2,452
1975	2,332	2,080	1,835	—	6,246
1976	2,567	2,591	2,084	—	7,242
1977	2,617	3,084	3,136	—	8,837
1978	2,326	3,740	4,207	—	10,273
1979	3,473	2,777	3,960	1,812	12,022
1980	4,133	2,538	4,507	2,358	13,536
1981	4,699	3,116	4,481	3,291	15,586
1982	4,494	5,413	4,304	4,342	18,553

currency deposits held by Japanese residents at Japanese banks were freed completely. At the end of 1982, these deposits amounted to 1.6 trillion yen, or nearly $7.2 billion. Furthermore, there was a rapid expansion of the dollar call market, which reached 7.5 trillion yen at the end of that year.

One missing element in the Japanese short-term money market is the absence of a Treasury bill market. At present, Treasury bills (T-bills) are issued at a fixed discount rate, below the official discount rate; therefore, most of the new issues are subscribed to and held only by the Bank of Japan. In May, 1981, however, the Bank of Japan began to use its holdings of T-bills for selling operations at market rates, and this has led to active open-market trading in T-bills. The total amount of selling operations in T-bills in 1981 reached 3 trillion yen, and the practice was continued in 1982 and 1983. Although it will still be some time before the Ministry of Finance will agree to a complete liberalization of the issuing terms for T-bills, the recent actions by the Bank of Japan clearly indicate the mounting pressure in this direction.

Another factor favoring the further development of the short-term money market in the near future is the growing volume of long-term government bonds now approaching maturity. As discussed earlier, the issuance of ten-year government bonds increased sharply after 1975. It is now estimated that the amount of government bonds with less than a year to maturity will rise to 2 trillion yen, 3.3 trillion yen, 6.6 trillion yen, and 7.6 trillion yen, respectively, at the end of fiscal years 1982, 1983, 1984, and 1985. These near-maturing bonds will begin to be traded as an equivalent of short-term money-market paper; when they actually mature, the government will be forced to refund them by issuing short-term government securities, thus making it just a matter of time for an active, free, short-term government-securities market to evolve in Japan. (See Table 10.)

Table 10
Maturing Government Bonds

Time to Maturity	March 1983	March 1984	March 1985	March 1986
		Trillion Yen		
Less than 3 years........	11.1	16.8	24.1	31.0
Less than 2 years........	5.3	9.8	14.1	18.2
Less than 1 year	2.0	3.3	6.6	7.6

Estimated by Nomura Securities Company
KINYU ZAISEI JIJO, July 19, 1982.

New Saving Instruments

The progress in the money markets is also matched at the retail level by the introduction of a number of new savings instruments designed to attract personal savings, the flow of which has become increasingly yield-sensitive. Although the speed and extent of financial innovation so far represented by these instruments are not as dramatic as in the United States, partly because of the continuing regulations on the introduction of new financial products, the implications of these new savings instruments for the future financial structure in Japan are considerable.

Broadly speaking, new instruments that have so far appeared can be divided into two categories. The first group came at the initiative of the securities industries; the basic idea here is to add easy cashing facilities to high returns available in the securities market. The idea materialized in the form of medium-term government bond funds (MGF), which were first introduced in January, 1980. Funds are invested in medium-term government notes with a maturity of two to four years and in the call and the bill markets; they are cashable after a grace period of a month with just an overnight notice, and offer a return of 5.69 percent, compared with 1.75 percent for ordinary deposits and 3.75 percent for three-month time deposits at banks. Public reception has been enthusiastic and the total size of MGF exceeded 3.5 trillion yen at the end of September, 1983.

The second category includes those instruments (or packages) that offer improved final returns to savers within the existing framework of regulated interest rates via a formula of compound interest rates and reinvestment of interest incomes. In addition, the limit of tax exemption for interest income (at present, interest income on savings of up to 3 million yen is exempted from income tax) is applicable only with respect to the initial amount of savings, even though interest income may be reinvested. Maturity Designated Time Deposits (MDD's) are a modified version of existing time deposits offered by commercial banks.

The depositor designates a specific maturity date between one and three years, but MDD's can be cashed after a grace period of a year with one-month's notice. The final return on three-year MDD's thus rises to 6.367 percent, compared with 6 percent for ordinary two-year time deposits.

A package known as "Wides" is a modified version of the existing five-year bank debentures offered by long-term credit banks. Although cashable at any time at the expense of a redemption fee, the final return, if held for five years, goes up to 9.606 percent, compared with a straight 8 percent yield on existing bank debentures. The trust bank's version of the similar modification is called "Big." "Big's" yield 9.63 percent if held for five years, compared with 8.02 percent available on existing loan-trust certificates.

Some observers are now beginning to express concern over the implications of the intensified competition among borrowing institutions for the future structure of the Japanese financial industry. Given the existing tight controls on interest that banks can pay, banks are always at the losing end of competition. At the same time, the increased cost of obtaining funds is biting into profit margins of nearly all financial institutions. With a further expansion of short-term money markets clearly in sight, the position of commercial banks is made especially vulnerable because companies are likely to continue switching the investment of their surplus funds away from bank deposits into money-market instuments. Under these circumstances, liberalization of interest rates paid on banks deposits, especially in large accounts, now seems inevitable, and with this a new round of competition among financial institutions will probably lead to yet another wave of financial innovation.

High International Interest Rates

High interest rates in the United States, a response of U.S. financial markets to persistent inflationary pressure, have provided attractive investment opportunities to Japanese financial institutions as well as to individuals, and thus have indirectly influenced their financial behavior. The most immediate effect of the magnetic attraction of high U.S. interest rates can be seen in the massive increase of Japanese investment in foreign bonds, notably U.S. bonds, which amounted on a net basis to $5.8 billion in 1981 and $6.1 billion in 1982.

Life insurance companies were the leading force in this development. Their investment in foreign bonds amounted to 68.7 billion yen in the year ending March, 1983 ($2.7 billion at the average exchange rate for the period), raising total holding of foreign bonds to 2,053 billion yen ($8.6 billion). In fact, investment in foreign bonds during the fiscal year that ended March, 1983, amounted to 13 percent of the net increment of their total assets; and 6.3 percent of their total assets were held in foreign bonds, at the end of March, 1983.

Pension funds managed by trust banks have also started to invest in foreign bonds. In the 18 months from January, 1981, to June, 1982, their foreign bond investments amounted to ¹62 billion yen ($0.72 billion), representing slightly more than 10 percent of the increase in their total assets. Having fallen somewhat behind life insurance companies in foreign investment, trust banks are stepping up their efforts in this direction. It is estimated that as much as 20 percent of the increase in their total assets in fiscal 1982 went into foreign bonds.

This surge of foreign investment by Japanese financial institutions has been underpinned by two factors: The first is the high yields available on foreign bonds. In the past few years, yield differentials between Japanese bonds and foreign bonds widened at times to as much as 7 to 8 percentage points. Although exchange-rate risks had to be reckoned with, yield differentials of this magnitude were often considered sufficient to cover possible exchange losses over the medium term. In addition, exchange risks were reduced by the increasing diversification of the currency mix. The market distributions of Japanese investment in foreign securities in 1982 was: United States, 31.4 percent; United Kingdom, 20.8 percent; Luxembourg, 25.9 percent; Australia, 10.5 percent; and Canada, 6.5 percent. Moreover, in some cases investment was covered by forward exchange contracts over a period of more than one year.

The second factor responsible for the growth of foreign investment by Japanese institutions is the increasing shortage of investment opportunities at home. Both life insurance companies and trust banks traditionally invested major portions of their assets in loans to domestic companies. At the end of March, 1973, 62 percent of the total assets of life insurance companies were represented by loans to domestic companies, but this proportion was reduced to only 37 percent by the end of September, 1982. With the considerable slowdown of domestic economic growth, domestic loan demand is unlikely to grow significantly, and investment opportunities outside Japan will be sought eagerly by these financial institutions.

The enthusiasm for foreign investment was shared by individuals, as demonstrated by the rush into dollar-denominated zero-coupon bonds in January and February of 1982. The episode was caused partly by fears that were aroused at that time over the introduction of the Green Card System, a system designed to close tax loopholes by identifying all tax-exempt savings accounts. However, the episode also served to demonstrate how responsive Japanese individuals can be once they are informed sufficiently of alternative investment opportunities. On a net payment basis, Japanese investment in zero-coupon bonds amounted to $1.12 billion, of which $0.78 billion took place in February, 1982, alone.

The FOREX law, which became effective in December, 1980, allows Japanese residents to open foreign-currency deposit accounts with Japanese banks without restrictions, thereby enabling domestic companies and individuals to participate indirectly in overseas deposit markets. The important development is the prospect of an introduction of overseas CD's and commercial paper to domestic investors. The initial plan was to liberalize their domestic sales starting in April, 1982, but was deferred because of the unexpected weakening of the yen in that year.

Attractive investment opportunities presented by historically high interest rates abroad have been combined with the substantial progress toward liberalizing foreign-exchange control in Japan. The exposure of Japanese investors and savers to the ebbs and flows of international financial developments has increased greatly. Pressures for a freer and more liberal financial system in Japan are now firmly in place.

UNITED KINGDOM

Alan Budd* and Geoffrey Dicks**

WE BEGIN with a brief survey of developments over the past two decades. The sections following then divide the history of inflation into four subperiods which correspond to successive Labour and Conservative administrations. Those divisions emphasize the most interesting developments during these years: namely, the changing directions of economic policy, particularly in relation to the control of inflation. Within each section, we examine developments under three headings: The first describes what happened to prices and other key economic indicators; the second describes the policy responses; and the third, with all the benefits of hindsight, appraises the events and the policy decisions

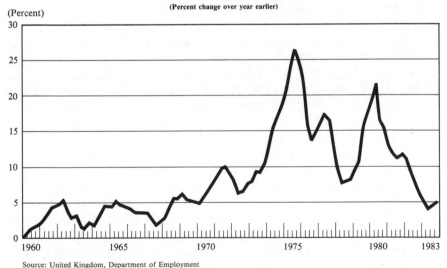

Chart 1:
Retail Prices, 1960-1983
(Percent change over year earlier)

Source: United Kingdom, Department of Employment

*Professor of Economics and Director, Centre for Economic Forecasting, London Business School.
**Senior Research Officer, Centre for Economic Forecasting, London Business School.

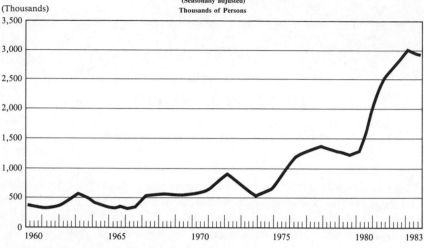

Chart 2:
Unemployment, 1960-1983
(Seasonally adjusted)
Thousands of Persons

(Thousands)

Source: United Kingdom, Department of Employment (excludes school leavers)

taken at the time. The account of the responses of the financial sector is less readily divided into these subperiods, and we report it in a separate section. The final section provides a general summary.

Charts 1 and 2 summarize the record. Inflation, measured by retail prices, averaged about 3½ percent a year between 1960 and 1965. From the mid-1960's, inflation started its acceleration and reached a peak rate of 25 percent in 1975. Since then, there was a second, but lower, peak in 1980, followed thereafter by a fairly steady reduction in inflation. At the same time, unemployment has moved relentlessly upward, with a rapid increase in the years following 1979. It is a depressing picture. The acceleration of inflation in the late 1960's and in the 1970's brought no benefits in terms of reduced unemployment (quite the contrary), and a very high cost has been paid to bring inflation back to its former rate.

Certain events stand out as landmarks in the history of inflation during these years. The first is the devaluation of the pound in 1967; the second is the change in banking arrangements—generally known as Competition and Credit Control—in 1971, and the monetary explosion that followed it; the third is the floating of sterling in 1972; the fourth is the more than quadrupling of oil prices in 1973-1974; and the fifth is the doubling of oil prices in 1979-1980. The first three of these landmarks represent actions taken by governments; the last two were external shocks. However, as we shall see, the policy response to the first oil price shock was very different from the policy response to the second.

Policies toward inflation have, in general, followed three phases. In the first phase, in the United Kingdom it was still recognized that at least a short-term choice had to be made between inflation and unemployment (though the most evident choice was that between a satisfactory balance of payments and unemployment). During that phase, which lasted until 1970 or 1971, one aim of policy was to improve the terms of the choice, particularly through the use of prices and incomes policies.

In the second phase, which ran from about 1971 to 1975, inflation was regarded as a social rather than an economic phenomenon. Therefore, there seemed to be no conflict between a rapid expansion of demand and attempts to reduce inflation; in fact, it was often argued that rapid growth would cure inflation. That phase ended with the inflationary explosion—and recession—of 1975.

The final phase has recognized the part played by the money supply in generating inflation. From about 1975 to 1978 the monetary approach was buttressed by incomes policies of one type or another. Since 1979 counterinflationary policy has relied on the control of the money supply, supported by fiscal policy.

The Inflationary Experience: 1964-1970

Economic Developments

The incoming Labour government of Prime Minister Harold Wilson in October, 1964, inherited an inflation rate of 4 percent; wages were rising at an annual rate of 5.2 percent. The deflationary measures taken to protect the exchange rate during 1965 and 1966 brought the inflation rate down so that by November, 1967, retail price inflation was below 2 percent, and producer price inflation was only 1.7 percent. This success in reducing inflation was helped by a favorable movement in world prices, which caused a fall in import prices.

Following the Labour government's devaluation of November, 1967, wages and prices were caught between the conflicting pressures of the lower exchange rate—tending to raise prices and wages—and the severe deflationary policies adopted by the government—tending to lower them. In the year immediately following devaluation, retail prices rose by 6 percent and wage rates in manufacturing rose by about 9 percent. Import prices rose by 14 percent; export prices rose by about 9 percent. These developments showed that there was at least some short-term gain in competitiveness from the devaluation. Under the pressure of the tight budgets of 1968 and 1969, these gains were held for an additional year. During 1969, retail prices rose by only 5 percent and wage inflation slowed to 6 percent. Producer prices rose by only 3 percent. By the time of the election of June, 1970, however, inflation had started to accelerate. Retail price inflation was 6 percent and wages were rising by 10 percent.

Output grew rapidly in 1964 in response to the expansionary budget of 1963, put forth by the Conservative government under Prime Minister Harold

Macmillan. Gross Domestic Product (GDP) grew by over 5½ percent. The growth rate slowed to 3 percent in 1965. The National Plan of 1965 promised growth at an annual average rate of 4 percent but achievement fell some way short, with growth at 1.8 percent in 1966 and 2 percent in 1967. In 1968, export growth of over 20 percent helped produce a GDP growth of about 4½ percent, but in the following two years output growth fell back to 2½ and 2 percent.

In delayed response to the 1964 boom, unemployment continued to fall until the beginning of 1966, when it was about 1 percent of the working population. Thereafter, unemployment climbed steadily until mid-1968, when it reached a rate of 2.3 percent. The more rapid growth of output in 1968 produced a small reduction, but by late 1969 unemployment was rising again, and it reached 2.4 percent by mid-1970. In June of 1970, the Conservatives under Prime Minister Edward Heath thus inherited a combination of rising unemployment and accelerating inflation.

The Policy Response

The policy measures of 1964 to 1970 were dominated by two problems: first the attempt to avoid devaluation and then, after 1967, the attempt to make devaluation work. The other major aim of policy—the attempt to achieve a faster rate of growth—was soon subordinated to those problems. At the time, inflation was not regarded as a major problem; the main objective of counterinflationary policy was to relieve the balance-of-payments problem by helping to improve competitiveness. The main weapon—incomes policies— also reflected a command-and-control approach to wage and price setting that was motivated by the aim of achieving equity in income distribution as much as by any feeling that inflation was undesirable.

The crucial policy issue in the early days of Wilson's new Labour administration in October, 1964, was whether to devalue the pound. The Labour government inherited a sterling crisis that, in turn, could be related to the previous government's attempt to make "a dash for growth." The Conservatives under Macmillan had introduced an expansionary budget in 1963 in the hope that a sustained expansion of demand would allow output to break through the short-term constraints on the economy, particularly that presented by the balance-of-payments deficits. At the same time, Macmillan's government tried to combine rapid growth with price stability by buying the approval of the unions for an incomes policy. The attempt failed, partly because the unions did not wish to cooperate with the Conservatives prior to an election the unions expected the Conservatives to lose. It is possible to date the history of accelerating inflation in Britain from that expansionary budget of 1963. It established the precedent for the attempt—to be repeated many times—to solve all Britain's economic problems at once by a rapid expansion of demand.

Having decided not to devalue sterling, Wilson's incoming Labour government took a number of steps to protect the exchange rate, including the imposition of a 15 percent surcharge on imports of manufactured and semimanufactured goods. It also started discussions with the International Monetary Fund (IMF) about the use of international credits to finance the deficit. In November, 1964, Bank Rate, the discount rate on central bank credits, was raised from 5 percent to 7 percent; devaluation was avoided only by the Bank of England's announcement of its receipt of credits of £3 billion from foreign central banks and from the Bank for International Settlements (BIS).

The sterling crises kept recurring. In July, 1965, a crisis budget was introduced to deflate the home economy, to reduce import finance, and to tighten exchange controls. The budget of May, 1966, which followed a second general election victory for the Labour party under Harold Wilson, was again deflationary. The final attempt to avoid a devaluation was made in a package of deflationary measures introduced in July, 1966. In spite of those measures, a continued loss of international reserves eventually forced a devaluation on the Wilson government in November, 1967. The exchange rate was cut from $2.80 to $2.40 to the pound.

At the same time, the Labour government introduced a number of deflationary measures, which were further strengthened in the extremely severe budget of the following March. Finally, following renewed speculation against sterling in November, 1968, the Labour government introduced an import deposit scheme that required importers to deposit 50 percent of the value of imported goods with a bank for six months before obtaining customs release. The overall effect of fiscal policy was to reduce the budget deficit significantly. In 1968-1969, the deficit was down to only 1.3 percent of GDP (from 3.6 percent in 1966), and in 1969-1970 there was actually a budget surplus.

Monetary policy under Wilson's Labour government was used to reinforce the deflationary measures introduced before and after devaluation. However, monetary policy was not seen as a direct means of controlling inflation, and no consideration was given to setting quantitative targets for the growth of the money supply. Calls for special deposits and directives about the growth of bank lending were seen as a means of controlling credit, and thereby expenditure, rather than as a means of controlling the money supply. Interest-rate policy was viewed as a tool for regulating domestic demand and influencing short-term capital flows. The various instruments of monetary policy tended to be used in conjunction as, for example, in November, 1965; July 1966; and November, 1967. Bank Rate tended to be raised by 1 to 2 percent, and then lowered subsequently in steps of ½ percent.

Apart from the targets for bank lending, the only occasion on which a general target for monetary policy was set was in June, 1969, when Mr. Roy Jenkins, then chancellor of the exchequer, agreed to a limit for domestic credit expansion of £400 million for the financial year 1969-1970 in a Letter of Intent to the IMF. That target was met, and monetary growth was kept down to 2 percent in that year, after increases of 9½ percent in 1967-1968, and 10.7 percent in 1968-1969. Edward Heath's Conservative government, which came to power in June, 1970, thus inherited a position in which fiscal and monetary policy were both exceptionally tight.

Alongside fiscal and monetary policy, Wilson's Labour government tried to control inflation by a succession of incomes policies. These policies were intended not only to control the general rate of inflation but also to impose central direction over movements in relative pay and prices. General directives on wages and prices were, therefore, accompanied by considerable monitoring and attempted control of individual pay settlements and price increases. The main objectives of the incomes policies were to improve competitiveness (particularly before devaluation) and to achieve an equitable distribution of incomes.

The government's hope was that compliance with its incomes policy would be voluntary, and the Trades Union Congress (TUC) did cooperate in the early stages by establishing its own procedures for examining wage claims. There were three elements to the prices and incomes policies: a series of statements about pay and price norms over particular periods; legislation that empowered the government to enforce pay and price limits; and the establishment of the National Board for Prices and Incomes (NBPI), to which pay and price increases could be referred. The stages of the policy were:

July to December, 1966: a pay and price freeze;
January to June, 1967: a period of severe restraint;
July, 1967, to March, 1968: a zero norm with a limited number of exceptions;
March, 1968, to December, 1969: a 3½ percent limit on wage and salary increases;
and, in 1970, a limit of 2½ to 4½ percent for wage and salary increases.

The accompanying Prices and Incomes Acts gave the government power to freeze pay and prices if they broke the guidelines. At the same time, the government could refer increases to the National Board for Prices and Incomes and could order a standstill for the period of the reference. It could also suspend a pay or price increase which the NBPI had rejected. Subsequent studies suggest that the policies had a temporary effect in slowing down the rate of wage increase.

Policy Appraisal

In retrospect it can be seen that the policies of 1965 to 1970 were based on a wholly mistaken diagnosis of the United Kingdom's economic problems. At the time, it appeared that the exchange rate of $2.80 to the pound was at the heart of those problems. The loss of competitiveness was said to be the prime cause of the nation's poor growth performance and the deteriorating trade-off between unemployment and an adequate balance of payments. Defense of the exchange rate, it was argued, was preventing the cure of the problem. Behind those arguments lay the view that wage inflation was endemic to Britain. Since

Britain also had a low growth of productivity, the country was bound to lose competitiveness under a regime of fixed exchange rates.

It was true that Britain was losing competitiveness, but this had little to do with the fixed exchange rate. What had happened was that the large devaluation of the pound in 1949 had given Britain a considerable competitive advantage. This advantage had allowed the British economy to operate at exceptionally low levels of unemployment during the 1950's. At the same time, competitiveness was eroded by a relative acceleration of U.K. wages and prices. By the end of the 1950's, Britain's competitive advantage had been wholly erased; thereafter any attempt to return to low levels of unemployment caused ever more serious balance-of-payments problems. The balance-of-payments crises were not caused by the fixed exchange rate; rather, they showed that demand was excessive. A devaluation could improve matters only if it permanently reduced the real exchange rate and cut real wages. In retrospect, one can recognize that labor was not in excess supply in the U.K. labor market. Devaluation was, therefore, likely only to raise U.K. prices while leaving real wages and the real exchange rate unchanged.

The attempts to avoid devaluation by tightening fiscal and monetary policy might have worked if they had been maintained with persistence, but such persistence was unlikely in a new government that had pledged to produce rapid economic growth. Instead the government tried to bolster its policies by considerable intervention in price and wage setting. The original hope was that a voluntary policy for prices and incomes would be agreed upon by the government, the employers, and the unions. The reward for cooperation was to be the faster economic growth promised in the National Plan. Again, the policies could have improved competitiveness only if employees had been prepared to accept a cut in real wages; the prices and incomes policies also would have had to be backed by consistent monetary and fiscal policies. The policies themselves veered between voluntarism and compulsion.

Alongside the overall attempts to control inflation by general policies, the Labour government relied on the Prices and Incomes Board, set up in 1965. The Board reviewed an extraordinary selection of pay and price increases, including: road haulage rates; prices of bread and flour; prices of soap and detergents; electricity prices; wages, costs and prices in the printing industry; electricity supply industry clerical and administrative workers' pay; salaries of the Midland Bank staff; gas tariffs; laundry and drycleaning prices; rail pay; bakery pay; pithead coal prices; beer prices; Scottish teachers' pay; busmen's pay; industrial civil servants' pay; productivity agreements by British Oxygen, Esso and Imperial Chemical; cost and profit margins in the wholesale and retail fruit and vegetable trade; building society interest rates; pay of local authority manual workers in Scotland; newsprint prices; and compound fertilizer prices. That selection covers only the period to the end of 1966. It reveals the extent to which the government adopted a command-and-control approach to prices and rejected the idea that the setting of relative prices and wages could readily be left to market forces.

Wilson's Labour government attempted to control prices and wages by direct techniques. It also used direct intervention in its attempts to control monetary growth and relied on directives from the Bank of England to limit the growth of bank lending.

Once the decision to devalue had been taken, the government adopted orthodox fiscal and monetary policies to hold down domestic demand in order to stimulate exports. Again, however, unless employees had been prepared to accept the accompanying cut in real wages, which they were not, the policy of devaluation was bound to fail.

The Inflationary Experience: 1970-1974

Economic Developments

Inflation accelerated during the first year of Edward Heath's Conservative government, which took office in June of 1970. By the end of 1970, retail price inflation was about 7 percent, and it was approaching 10 percent by mid-1971. The rate slowed slightly during 1972, and moved down toward 7 percent. Wages, however, continued to accelerate. By the end of 1971, they were rising at a rate of 9½ percent and, by the end of 1972, they were rising at a rate of 15½ percent.

After 1972, the falling exchange rate of the pound was accompanied by a rapid increase in prices. Retail prices rose by 10½ percent during 1973 and accelerated to 18 percent during 1974. However, the incomes policies as administered by the Heath government appeared to have had some success in restraining wage increases, at least in 1973, when the rise in earnings abated to about 12½ percent.

In 1970 and 1971, world price movements generally helped to hold down the U.K. inflation rate. Import prices rose by only 2 percent during 1970 and 5 percent in 1971. During 1972, the rise in import prices accelerated to over 9 percent, partly because the exchange rate fell by about 10 percent in the second half of the year. World commodity prices rose sharply during 1973. This development, along with a 7 percent decline in the exchange rate, drove import prices up by almost 40 percent in that year.

The Wilson government's final budget in 1969 deflated the economy and produced two years of slow growth, 2 percent in 1970 and 1.4 percent in 1971. Unemployment, which had been rising after mid-1969, started to rise rapidly in the early months of 1971. By the beginning of 1972, it had reached 3½ percent of the work force. The Heath government's expansionary budget, which was introduced in 1972 in response to the rise in unemployment, produced a growth of GDP of 2.7 percent in 1972 and of 7.2 percent in 1973. (The extraordinary growth of 1973 coincided with, and was helped by, a worldwide economic boom. Exports rose by 11½ percent.) Unemployment fell from early 1972 onward, and was down to 2 percent of the work force by the end of 1973.

The Policy Response

In 1970, it was widely believed that the incoming Conservative government led by Mr. Heath would rely much more heavily on market forces than had the preceding Labour administration. This was rapidly shown to be wrong, however. Although Mr. Heath had been responsible, under the previous Conservative government of Mr. Macmillan, for introducing the legislation to abolish resale price maintenance, he was by nature an interventionist with a strong belief in administrative solutions to economic problems.

The electoral success of the Conservatives had no doubt been partly brought about by the severity of the Labour government's fiscal policy, but it was also a result of anxieties about inflation. In a much-quoted phrase, Mr. Heath had promised to cut inflation "at a stroke." This was to be achieved by cutting indirect taxes, which would in turn, it was hoped, cut the rate of wage increase and set up a virtuous circle of lower inflation and more rapid growth. Mr. Heath did not follow this line of action, but the Conservative government soon found itself embarked on a course of rapid fiscal expansion. The cause of this expansion, which gained momentum from about mid-1971, was the combination of rising inflation and rising unemployment, which transformed the Heath government's view about the inflationary process.

The preceding Labour administration of Mr. Wilson had adopted the orthodox post-World War II view that inflation and unemployment were inversely related. This view was embodied in the Phillips curve (first presented in 1958), which demonstrated a fairly stable inverse relationship between the rate of wage increases and unemployment. The Labour government tried to achieve a more favorable trade-off between the two through its reliance on incomes policies. Although it attained some temporary success, it also had to rely heavily on conventional deflationary policies. In response to those deflationary policies, unemployment started to rise in mid-1969. Inflation started to rise at the same time. The conclusion was that the Phillips curve was dead.

The view emerged that British inflation had social rather than economic causes. A number of such social explanations were put forward: the breakdown of order reflected in the student riots of 1968, the takeover of major trade unions by left-wingers, and so on. Given this new explanation for inflation, the government concluded that the uncomfortable choice between full employment and price stability no longer had to be made; the government could, therefore, embark on an expansionary policy to reduce unemployment. This might even help reduce inflation. If inflation threatened to accelerate, it could be addressed by persuasion or, that failing, by compulsion.

This transformed view of inflation and the consequent change in policy approach were accompanied by the Bank of England's announcement of a fundamental change in the monetary system known as "Competition and Credit Control" (the title of the Bank of England paper, published in April, 1971). Competition and Credit Control was one of the few actions of Mr. Heath's

Conservative government that reflected a market-oriented approach to economic policy. It had two central ideas: The first "competition," was intended to end the cartel arrangements in relation to borrowing and lending rates operated by the London clearing banks; the second idea, "credit control," was to end the previous techniques of direct controls over bank lending, which had relied on quantitative instructions to the clearing banks from the Bank of England.

These moves were partly a recognition of the inevitable. As will be described below, the Bank of England's use of direct controls over the clearing banks and their inability to compete for funds at market rates had led to an expansion of a parallel money market that was not only frustrating the government's monetary policy but was also taking business away from the clearing banks. Thus the clearing banks welcomed the new arrangements.

It was not clear to what extent the government intended Competition and Credit Control to herald a new era of monetary policy, either in the sense of new techniques of monetary control or in the use of monetary policy to combat inflation. The Bank of England suggested that it intended to rely less on interest rates as an instrument and indicator of monetary policy in the future; it also warned that much wider fluctuations in interest rates might occur. It was not obvious that the government or the Bank of England intended to adopt a more monetarist approach to counterinflationary policy. One important change was that banks were to be given much greater freedom in choosing the composition of their assets. This change, together with the relaxation of reserve requirements, laid the foundation for the monetary explosion of 1971-1973. The broadly defined money supply (M-3) rose by 12 percent during 1971 and by 25 percent and 23 percent in the subsequent two years, largely because of the rapid increase in bank lending.

The monetary expansion was accompanied by a significant relaxation of fiscal policy. There were major tax cuts in the budget of 1972, and public expenditure was allowed to expand rapidly. In June, 1972, the decision was taken to float sterling as a "temporary measure" in response to continued losses of reserves. Many hoped that the move would be permanent and that it would finally remove the balance-of-payments constraint from U.K. economic development and policymaking.

At the same time, the government was becoming alarmed by the rise in wage rates, which by mid-1972 were 12 percent higher than a year earlier and accelerating. An attempt was made to achieve a voluntary agreement among the unions, the employers, and the government. The so-called Chequers arithmetic promised to deliver 5 percent per annum growth of output for two years in exchange for pay increase limits of £2 per week and a limit of 5 percent for price increases. When the proposal was rejected, the government introduced statutory controls on prices and pay in November, 1972. There was a 90-day statutory standstill with provision for an additional 60-days if necessary.

Having started with a price and pay freeze, Mr. Heath's Conservative government soon adopted the full apparatus of an incomes policy. The 90-day standstill was extended for 60 days, and the government proposed that the second stage of the pay policy should restrict pay increases to £1 per week plus 4 percent. A Pay Board and a Price Commission were established to regulate pay and prices.

Stage Three of the incomes policy was announced in October, 1973, and introduced in November. It proposed a pay limit of 10 percent, with the agreement that pay could be increased by 1 percent when the retail price index rose by 7 percent from its level of November, 1973. The system, known as the Threshold Pay Agreement, therefore appeared to offer a guaranteed real increase of pay of at least 3 percent. At the time, the rate of inflation was above 10 percent and rising, and it looked as if pay claims would be running at the rate of 13 percent or more. Believing that the inflation rate would fall, the government hoped that the threshold system would hold down wage settlements while satisfying the unions' aspirations for increases in real incomes.

Between the announcement of the proposals for Stage Three and their introduction, the price of oil rose by 66 percent. That was only the first large step toward the quadrupling of oil prices that took place within the next three months. Originally it was thought that the threshold payments system might be triggered once during the year from November, 1973. In fact, it was triggered eleven times. Meanwhile, the mineworkers rejected a 7 percent Stage-Three pay award and instituted a ban on overtime. This became a full-scale strike in February, 1974. The Heath government had been forced to introduce a temporary three-day workweek at the beginning of the year in order to save energy; in response to the strike, the government called a general election in defense of its incomes policy. It lost.

Policy Appraisal

The Conservative government's attempt to combine rapid growth with low inflation achieved a record combination, for the postwar period, of high unemployment and high inflation. The prime cause of the inflation was the fiscal expansion and monetary explosion of the years 1971-1973, although the quadrupling of oil prices in 1973-1974 and the ill-fated threshold payments system added to the problems.

The errors in policymaking were partly an extension of the errors made by the previous administration. The Labour government had hoped that devaluation would achieve a permanent reduction in the real exchange rate; Mr. Heath's Conservative government hoped that a flexible exchange rate would remove the major constraint on sustained economic growth. Each government tried to control inflation through a series of incomes policies. Whereas the Labour government reinforced those policies by exceptionally tight fiscal policy, the Conservative government embarked on a major fiscal expansion.

Although Mr. Wilson's Labour government recognized that devaluation needed to be supported by tight fiscal policy, Mr. Heath's Conservative government failed to understand the significance of the move from fixed exchange rates. It regarded the fall in the exchange rate after 1972 as a misfortune that was harming an otherwise successful counterinflationary policy. It did not recognize that the fall in the exchange rate was a consequence of its own policies. Its view of the inflationary process is well illustrated by its "Consultative Document: The Price and Pay Code for Stage 3," published in October, 1973:

> In Stages 1 and 2 we have succeeded in restraining the domestic causes of inflation. But we have had to face a surge in world prices of a kind which has not struck the United Kingdom for over 20 years. World price increases have pressed on the prices in our shops, both directly and through the sterling exchange rate. They have turned the terms of trade sharply against us at heavy cost to the balance of payments, and the effect of this on the exchange rate has added to the pressure on prices.

This was written at the end of two years in which the money supply had risen by over 50 percent.

The final folly of the Conservative government was the introduction of the threshold payments system. It was based on the view that the Treasury was better at forecasting inflation than were the employers or the unions. It also included a promise of a real growth of incomes of 3 percent, something that the government does not have the power to bestow. In fact, GDP *fell* during the period of Stage Three. The attempt to get a quart out of a pint pot was bound to cause a wage and price explosion, which rapidly absorbed the excessive monetary growth of the previous two years. It was ironic that the Conservative government lost an election fought over the question of its right to impose a Stage Three settlement on the miners.

The Inflationary Experience: 1974-1979

Economic Developments

In March, 1974, the new Labour government, under Prime Minister Harold Wilson, inherited accelerating inflation, a three-day workweek, and a potential crisis from oil shortages as OPEC threatened to cut supplies. Inflation accelerated during most of 1974 and 1975 in delayed response to the policies of the previous Conservative administration. At the beginning of 1974, inflation ran about 12½ percent; it worsened during the year, reaching over 18 percent despite measures introduced in the July budget to cut prices. Retail price inflation reached a peak of just under 27 percent in mid-1975. Thereafter, progress in reducing inflation was rather erratic. Retail price inflation slowed to about 13 percent in 1976; rose again temporarily, partly in response to the rapid fall in the exchange rate; and then fell fairly rapidly to below 8 percent in 1978. It then began yet another rise and was back in double figures by the time the Conservatives won the election of May, 1979.

Wage rates also accelerated through mid-1975, fueled by the threshold payments system. By mid-1975, wage rates were 33 percent higher than a year earlier. Thereafter, wage inflation abated: By the end of 1976 it was 12 percent; by the end of 1977 it was about 10 percent. The collapse of incomes policies during 1978, however, brought a renewed acceleration of wage inflation; by year end, wage rates were 18 percent higher than they had been a year earlier. Average earnings for the whole economy were rising at an annual rate of 14 percent.

The exchange rate, which had fallen by nearly 10 percent in 1973, was stronger in 1974. It rose against the yen and held its value against the dollar. This stability can be explained largely by the investment of the OPEC surpluses in sterling. During 1975, the exchange rate fell; it continued to fall during most of 1976. The final blow was a newspaper report that the International Monetary Fund believed that sterling should be valued at about $1.50. That report brought the rate down to $1.55 and brought about a package of deflationary policies that ended, and then reversed, the fall.

During 1977, the government started by trying to prevent an appreciation of sterling against the dollar. It then switched its target to trying to hold the value of the effective exchange rate of sterling. Finally, in November, it ceased intervening to hold the currency. The exchange rate rose in the first quarter of 1978 and then fell to a slightly lower level, which was sustained during most of the rest of the year. The rate started to rise again in the first quarter of 1979, possibly in anticipation of a Conservative victory.

Since 1974 had started with the three-day workweek, which resulted in a 2½ percent fall in total output between the fourth quarter of 1973 and the first quarter of 1974, and since output in 1973 had been at an unsustainably high level, it was hardly surprising that output fell in 1974. GDP fell by about 1½ percent. Many people—including almost all economic forecasters—were surprised, however, by the further fall of output in 1975. GDP fell by about 1 percent. The fall can be explained partly by the world recession. In expenditure terms, the main source of the recession was a rapid reduction in inventories and a rise in the household savings rate. In the United Kingdom, as in the rest of the world, it is possible to relate these changes in expenditures to the reduction in the real money supply in the previous year.

There was a renewed growth of output after 1975. GDP rose by 2.8 percent in 1976 and by 2.1 percent in 1977. The growth in 1977 was particularly welcome because it accompanied a tightening of fiscal policy. GDP grew by over 3 percent in 1978, spurred by an expansionary budget and a rapid rise in real incomes as accelerating wages accompanied decelerating prices.

Unemployment was starting to rise when Mr. Wilson's Labour government came to power in March, 1974. It rose steadily, from about 2½ percent to about 5.3 percent, between the beginning of 1974 and the end of 1977. The reasonable growth rates of 1976 to 1978 brought unemployment down so that it stood at about 5 percent by the end of 1978—still a very high rate by postwar standards.

The Policy Response

The general tone of the inflation policies adopted by Mr. Wilson's 1974-1979 Labour government was not unlike that of his previous Labour administration of 1964-1970. The approach attempted to combine fiscal stringency with price and incomes policies. The fiscal stringency was effective for only about one year, and the incomes policies eventually failed. Still, it is possible to date the use of monetary policy as a direct means of controlling inflation from this period.

While a member of the opposition, Mr. Denis Healey, the new chancellor of the exchequer, had criticized the Conservative government's loss of control of the money supply and the rapid growth of the Public Sector Borrowing Requirement (PSBR). Mr. Healey therefore had to be seen to be doing something about it. In his first (March, 1974) budget, his policy measures were intended to reduce the PSBR while leaving the net effect on demand neutral. This was to be achieved partly by raising corporate taxes which, it was assumed, would have no impact on aggregate demand and expenditures.

The Labour government elected in February, 1974, barely had a working majority. Mr. Healey introduced a second budget in July that was undoubtedly designed to help achieve victory in a subsequent election. The budget was mainly directed at reducing inflation. The value-added tax (VAT) was cut from 10 to 8 percent, and subsidies on bread were increased. It was estimated that the measures would eventually cut retail prices by 2½ percent. Apart from their electoral popularity, measures to cut inflation were thought to be particularly desirable, since the threshold payments system was magnifying any price increases via the rapid feedthrough from prices to wages and back to prices.

In October, 1974, the Labour Party, under Mr. Wilson's leadership, called a new election, which it won with an increased majority. In then introduced the third budget of the year in November. The main objective was to provide generous tax relief to the corporate sector (thereby reversing the policies of the March budget). It also sought to reduce the PSBR by £800 million, but this was a case of running very fast and failing to stay in the same place because the PSBR was far above its original target. This overshooting was partly the result of the fall in output and partly the result of the open-ended commitment to food subsidies. There were also exceptionally large forecasting errors. The PSBR for 1974-1975 turned out to be almost £8 billion, compared with the original estimate of 2.7 billion pounds.

The budget of April, 1975, again attempted to reduce the PSBR by over £1 billion and promised further cuts of £3 billion in the following financial year. As a reversal of earlier policies, the measures were expected to add 2¾ percent to retail prices. In fact, the PSBR again exceeded the budget estimates but by a narrower margin than in 1974-1975.

Some moderate reflation through relaxation of hire purchase (installment credit) regulations was introduced in December, 1975. The budget of April, 1976, was described as "conditional," since it attempted to buy consent to an incomes policy by offering tax cuts of £1.3 billion in exchange for the Trade Unions Congress' (TUC) agreement on a 3 percent pay round. The PSBR was expected to rise to £12 billion. (In fact, it was below £9 billion.) The most important change in fiscal policy was forced on the Wilson government by the collapse of the exchange rate in October, 1976. As part of the conditions of a $3.9 billion loan from the IMF, the government announced cuts in public expenditure for 1977-1978 and 1978-1979, and also announced targets for domestic credit expansion. As a result, the PSBR in 1977-1978 was reduced to £5½ billion.

The April, 1978, budget was expansionary and allowed a PSBR of £8.2 billion. The outcome was £9.4 billion and marked a sharp reversal of the earlier move toward fiscal moderation.

The Labour government inherited a minimum lending rate (MLR) of 12½ percent, only ½ percent below the record level of 13 percent.[1] It also inherited controls, known as the "Corset," which the Heath government had imposed on bank lending. During its first year in office, the Labour government permitted a slow but steady relaxation of monetary policy and allowed MLR to fall in small steps to 9¾ percent. At the same time, it progressively released special deposits, a form of reserve requirement. The growth of the money supply (M-3) fell to 10½ percent in 1974-1975, compared with 25 percent in 1973-1974. It was held at about 10 percent for the following two years, with MLR averaging about 11 percent. In the exchange-rate crisis of October, 1976, MLR was raised to 15 percent in order to support the pound. At the same time, the government announced a target for domestic credit expansion. In the budget of March, 1977, Mr. Healey announced a target for monetary growth in the range of 9 to 13 percent for the financial year 1977-1978.

In the course of 1977, MLR was reduced rapidly from 14½ percent to 5 percent. The main reason for this move was the attempt to prevent the exchange rate from rising, especially against the U.S. dollar. The government also had to intervene in foreign-exchange markets on a massive scale. Although the exchange-rate policy was changed again in November, 1977, the change came too late to prevent a rapid growth of the money supply, and the outcome was monetary growth of 16 percent. The expansionary budget of 1978 put further pressure on the money supply. Money-supply growth was held within its limits only by an increase in MLR to 14 percent in the course of the year and by the reimposition of the Corset.

Mr. Wilson's Labour government came to power while Stage Three of the Conservative government's incomes policy was in operation. The new government quickly settled the miners' strike, but otherwise tried to enforce Stage Three. The price regulations were tightened. After the expiration of Stage Three in November, 1974, the government and the TUC agreed to a "social contract"

---

[1] The minimum lending rate of the Bank of England to the money market, which replaced Bank Rate. MLR itself was subsequently abandoned in August, 1981.

under which pay moderation would be rewarded by expanded social expenditure. The result was a rapid acceleration of wage increases to about 30 percent per year by the end of 1975.

In March, 1976, Mr. Wilson announced his retirement and was succeeded in office by James Callaghan, who launched a new series of incomes policies. The first set a limit of £6 per week for all pay increases. The limit was generally held, and wage inflation fell to about 12 percent by the end of 1976. Phase Two of the incomes policy, announced in June, 1976, limited wage and salary increases to £2.5 for those earning up to £50 per week, to 5 percent for those earning between £50 and £80, and to a maximum of £4 per week at all higher levels of earnings. (This was equivalent to an overall increase of about 4½ percent on average wages and salaries.) Some elements of the price code were relaxed at the same time. After Phase Two, the government was unable to get TUC agreement to a new stage of the incomes policy and it limited itself to issuing a 10 percent "guideline" with a threat of sanctions against those firms that exceeded it. Wage increases accelerated during 1978 as employees restored pay levels that had been suppressed by the first two stages of the pay policy.

As its final effort, the Callaghan government published a white paper, "Winning the Battle Against Inflation," in July, 1978. Its main proposal was a limit of 5 percent for pay settlements, which could be increased by "self-financing" productivity deals. Again the government could use sanctions against firms that exceeded the limit. The limits, however, had little effect, except in the public sector. The government applied sanctions to Ford U.K. after it had breached the 5 percent pay guidelines, but the government was subsequently defeated in a House of Commons vote and had to lift the sanctions.

Policy Appraisal

If Mr. Heath's Conservative government of 1970-1974 deserves zero marks out of 100 for its counterinflationary record, the 1974-1979 Labour governments of Mr. Wilson and Mr. Callaghan can perhaps be awarded a score of 50. Mr. Wilson's government inherited an accelerating rate of price increases, and little could have been done to avoid inflation approaching 30 percent. The government's early measures tried to control inflation by cutting indirect taxes and increasing subsidies. It thereby postponed, but did not avoid, the final burst of inflation in 1975. It was also reluctant to deflate the economy, even though it had criticized the monetary and fiscal excesses of the previous Conservative government. This reluctance was partly a result of its interpretation of the effects of the 1973-1974 quadrupling of oil prices. The Labour government assumed that the sudden transfer of wealth to the oil producers would increase the world's savings ratio and thereby reduce demand and output. It believed, therefore, that the oil importers should offset this contraction by expanding domestic demand. This argument was, at best, only half correct, but it meant that the necessary adjustment of policy in the United Kingdom was postponed. (Since the United Kingdom was the only industrial economy that attempted to put such expansionary policies into effect, it incidentally acquired an exceptional share of the West's balance-of-payments deficit.)

Acceptance of a more orthodox approach to economic policy was enshrined in a speech by the Prime Minister, Mr. Callaghan, in September, 1976:

> "We used to think that you could just spend your way out of a recession and increase employment by cutting taxes and boosting government spending. I tell you in all candour that that option no longer exists, and that insofar as it ever did exist, it worked by injecting inflation into the economy. And each time that happened the average level of unemployment has risen. Higher inflation, followed by higher unemployment. That is the history of the last twenty years."

Although that statement seemed to recognize the limitations of government policy, Mr. Callaghan's Labour government made two important errors after 1976. The first was that it held down the exchange rate during 1977. This had two consequences: The first was that it blocked one of the major mechanisms by which tighter monetary and fiscal policies can reduce inflation. If the exchange rate had risen (as it clearly would have done without massive government intervention and a rapid reduction in interest rates), import prices would have been lower. In fact, the prices of all tradeable goods would have been lower because of the effects of international competition. The second consequence was that exchange rate intervention fed reserves into the banking system. The monetary consequences were not apparent for a time as investors were willing to buy government debt as interest rates fell; but the effects became clear by the beginning of 1978.

The other major policy error was the overexpansionary budget of 1978. The immediate consequences for the money supply were suppressed, but inflation started to accelerate. The full consequences for the money supply were revealed in 1979 and 1980.

The government's attempts to implement incomes policies did little to control inflation in the longer term, and by 1978 they were virtually ineffective, except in the public sector. The 5 percent target set for the 1978-1979 pay round was unrealistic since it was inconsistent with the government's monetary policy. The "winter of discontent" of 1978-1979, caused by the government's attempts to impose the target, must have contributed to the Labour Party's electoral defeat in May, 1979. However, it passed on to Prime Minister Margaret Thatcher's incoming Conservative government—as it had itself inherited from the previous Conservative government—accelerating inflation and serious potential problems in pay settlements. The Labour government had also paid a high price to the unions for their consent to incomes policies and had thereby increased the difficulties of defeating inflation.

The Inflationary Experience: 1979-1983

Economic Developments

Mrs. Thatcher's Conservative government, which took office in May, 1979, inherited an accelerating inflation rate that had again broken into double digits. More serious, possibly, was the problem of wage inflation. The Labour government's attempts to control wage increases by incomes policies had largely collapsed, at least in the private sector, but public-sector wages had been kept artificially low. Before the election, the Conservatives had agreed to accept the recommendations of the Clegg Committee on public-sector pay, which had suggested pay increases of between 25 and 30 percent for public-sector employees. Although this was described as "catching up," there was always the risk that pay increases of that magnitude would be copied by the private sector.

The Thatcher government's first budget, introduced, in June, 1979, increased the value-added tax (VAT) from 8 percent to 15 percent, which added about 4 percent to prices. That move and the sharp rise in oil prices that followed the second oil shock produced a rapid acceleration of inflation. By the end of 1979, the inflation rate was over 17 percent; it had reached a peak of 22 percent by mid-1980. Once the initial effect of the increase in VAT had dropped out of the figures, the inflation rate started to fall slowly. By the end of 1980, inflation was down to 15 percent, and by the end of 1981 to 12 percent. (There had been a slight acceleration of inflation in the latter part of 1981 in response to the fall in the exchange rate.) Progress continued during 1982; inflation was only 6 percent by the end of the year. By the time of the general election of June, 1983, it was down to 4 percent.

Wage inflation followed a similar path. The trend of pay increases was set in the engineering industry after a prolonged strike during 1979. By the end of 1979, wage rates were 15 percent higher than a year earlier; during the 1979-1980 pay round, wage rates rose by about 20 percent. Thereafter, there was a steady slowdown in the rate of increase. Average earnings rose by only 12 percent during the 1980-1981 pay round, and by about 10 percent in the following year. Pay settlements averaged about 6 to 7 percent.

In spite of the rapid increase in wages in 1979 and 1980, one source of more stable prices was the rise in the exchange rate during those two years. The effective weighted-average exchange rate of the pound rose by 10 percent during 1979 and by a further 13 percent during 1980. In early 1981, the rate started to fall and ended the year 10 percent lower than it had started. It then stayed remarkably stable at between 90 and 92 (compared with an average value of 100 in 1975) for most of 1982. However, in the last two months of 1982, the rate started to fall rapidly, and it ended the year at 84, with a dollar exchange rate of $1.63. The rate continued to fall during the early months of 1983, reaching a low point in March of $1.45. (The effective rate fell to 78.1.) Much of this decline could be attributed to worries about the possibility of a fall in oil prices and to fears of electoral defeat for the Conservatives. Confidence about the OPEC price agreement and large leads in the polls for the Conservatives helped to bring about a strong recovery of sterling. By election day in June, 1983, the rate was $1.58, with a weighted index of 87.0. By an extraordinary coincidence, that was the level of the effective exchange rate when the Conservatives had come to power under Mrs. Thatcher four years earlier.

During 1979 and 1980, the combination of rapid wage increases, high interest rates, and a rising exchange rate was almost lethal for the corporate sector, particularly in manufacturing. Probably because it did not anticipate the fall in demand during 1979, industry ended the year with excessive inventories. The rapid reduction in inventories was the main single element of the decline in output in 1980. By the end of 1980, manufacturing output was 16 percent lower than it had been in the second quarter of 1979. Output then hovered at roughly the same level throughout 1981 and 1982. The drop in total industrial production was slightly less severe, thanks to North Sea oil. GDP also reached a plateau about 5 percent below its early 1979 level by the end of 1980, and showed little or no signs of recovery during 1981 even though May, 1981, was officially designated as the trough of the recession. Output remained fairly flat during 1982, although the recovery produced a growth of GDP of about 1 percent in the year as a whole. Signs of a recovery in manufacturing output eventually appeared in early 1983.

Unemployment started to rise in the second half of 1979 and rose very rapidly during 1980 and 1981. The rate more than doubled from 5.3 percent in December, 1979, to 11.6 percent in December, 1981. A further 300,000 became unemployed during 1982. Although the rate of increase had abated, partly because of special employment schemes for young workers, there were no signs of the rise in unemployment coming to an end.

The Policy Response

The Conservative government elected under Mrs. Thatcher was clearly identified with a new approach to economic policy. In fact, its hallmark was the utter rejection of the policies of the Conservative Heath government of 1970-1974; in many ways it continued the policies of the 1974-1979 Labour administrations of Mr. Wilson and Mr. Callaghan. The Conservative party had made a clear promise in its election campaign to cut income tax, and had also claimed that it would reduce inflation. Promises about the overall performance of the economy were less clear. The general idea was that government intervention (and public expenditure) would be reduced and that market forces would be allowed to operate more freely. These changes were expected to improve the performance of the economy. It was implied that one result would be a decrease in unemployment. One widely used Conservative election poster showed a long queue of unemployed with the slogan "Labour isn't working."

Having won the election in May, 1979, Mrs. Thatcher's Conservative government presented its first budget in the following month. It cut income taxes as it had promised, but it had to find additional revenue from other sources in order to meet its promise to reduce the PSBR. As mentioned previously, it chose to increase the VAT rate from 8 to 15 percent, thereby adding about 4 percent to retail prices. At the same time, it encouraged the public corporations (including gas, electricity and telephones) to raise their charges. This was a risky strategy at a time when the government was embarking on a counterinflationary policy. The policy itself consisted of the reduction in the PSBR and the extension of the Labour government's target for monetary growth of 9 percent for the remainder of the financial year. The Conservative government retained the Corset as a means of controlling monetary growth, but it also raised the minimum lending rate (MLR) by 2 percent.

By November, 1979, there were serious worries that monetary policy was too lax; the MLR was raised from 14 to 17 percent. The budget of March, 1980, was again deflationary, aiming to reduce the PSBR by about £800 million, even though output was expected to fall by over 2 percent in 1980. At the same time, the Thatcher government announced a "Medium-Term Financial Strategy," which presented figures for the growth of the money supply and the PSBR for the years to 1983-1984. This strategy provided the framework for the Thatcher government's counterinflationary policy. The provision of monetary targets was expected to influence expectations about the inflation rate, and the provision of figures for the PSBR was intended to reassure financial markets that the monetary targets could be achieved at reasonable rates of interest. The money supply target for 1980-1981 was presented as a range of 7 to 11 percent for sterling M-3 (the broad definition of the money supply). The figure for the PSBR for 1980-1981 was £8½ billion.

The money supply, in fact, rose at an annual rate of nearly 20 percent in 1980-1981, and the PSBR was £13 billion. The excessive growth of the money supply was partly caused by the removal, in June, 1980, of the Corset, which resulted in considerable reintermediation of funds through the banks. The overshooting of the PSBR can partly be explained by the unexpectedly large fall in output and rise in unemployment. The government chose to allow the overshooting of the money supply rather than see interest rates rise further and, in fact, reduced MLR to 16 percent in July, 1980, and to 14 percent in November. The reluctance to raise interest rates stemmed partly from fears about the survival of the corporate sector and partly from the continued rise in the exchange rate, which suggested that monetary policy was possibly tighter than the figures for sterling M-3 suggested.

The budget of March, 1981 saw a further tightening of fiscal policy at a time when the United Kingdom was already experiencing its deepest post-World War II recession. The budget measures were intended to reduce the PSBR by £3.3 billion. The estimate for the PSBR was £10½ billion, approximately 4½ percent of GDP. This was higher than the ratio of 3 percent for 1981-1982, proposed in the 1980 version of the medium-term financial strategy, but it was nevertheless an exceptional move in postwar experience. The target for the money supply for 1981-1982 was set in the range of 8 to 10 percent. When the budget was introduced, the chancellor of the exchequer cut MLR by 2 percent to 12 percent.

The minimum lending rate was suspended in August, 1981, and the base rate charged by the clearing banks became the important interest-rate indicator. Under guidance from the Bank of England, this rate was raised from 12 percent to 14 percent in September, 1981, and then to 16 percent in the following month. This move matched rises in U.S. interest rates.

In relation to the medium-term financial strategy, 1981-1982 was far closer to the targets than 1980-1981 had been. The PSBR was only £8.7 billion, and the money supply grew by about 15 percent. The budget of March, 1982, saw a further confirmation of the fiscal aspect of the medium-term financial strategy. The PSBR was set at £9½ billion (3½ percent of GDP). However, the monetary targets were relaxed to a range of 8 to 12 percent for 1982-1983, compared with the 5 to 9 percent originally envisaged. At the same time, the targets were extended, in an undefined way, to include a narrow M-1 and PSL2, a broader measure of private-sector liquidity.

For most of 1982, the Thatcher government encouraged reductions in interest rates. The clearing banks' base lending rate fell from 14½ percent at the beginning of the year to 9 percent by November. However, the fall in the exchange rate in that month led to an increase in the base rate to 10 percent.

The Thatcher government has generally refused to countenance incomes policies of any kind. However, it announced pay assumptions for public-sector employees in calculating its cash limits for public expenditure. These assumptions have tended to be lower than the going rate of earnings increases in the private sector, and the government no doubt hoped to provide some guidance on private-sector pay by this means. The government has been prepared to face strikes in the public sector (civil servants in 1981, health workers in 1982) to enforce these pay limits and has usually won.

Policy Appraisal

The period since May, 1979 has witnessed the most sustained effort since World War II to use fiscal and monetary policy to reduce inflation. The policies were introduced under extremely unfavorable conditions. The inflation rate was already accelerating in 1979, partly because of the excessive fiscal expansion in the 1978 budget and partly because wages were rising rapidly following the collapse of the Labour party's incomes policies. The money supply was being kept under control only by a combination of the Corset and rising interest rates. Adding to these problems, oil prices doubled in 1979-1980.

Thus far the Thatcher government's policies have seen the inflation rate rise to a peak of 22 percent then fall, by the middle of 1983, to 4 percent. At the same time, GDP has fallen by about 6 percent from its level in the second quarter of 1979, and unemployment has more than doubled. That is a mixed record, and it is difficult to appraise whether the decline in the inflation rate could have been achieved at a lower cost in terms of unemployment. The most questionable policy action was the increase of VAT in 1979. Although it was offset by a simultaneous cut in income tax, the resulting rise in retail prices undoubtedly contributed to the disastrous wage increases of 1979-1980. The potential supply-side benefits of such a shift from direct to indirect taxes were likely to be small. One must conclude that the action significantly increased the costs of reducing inflation.

Other doubts about policy actions can be raised in retrospect. One concerns the choice of sterling M-3 as the single indicator of monetary policy. It was a misleading indicator in the conditions of 1980, particularly since a large part of sterling M-3 bears interest. With the relative return on money exceptionally high, what appeared to be a condition of excess money supply was, in fact, a condition of excess demand for money. One consequence was the rise in the exchange rate, which greatly added to the problems of industry even if it simultaneously helped to control inflation. Another doubt concerns the budget of 1981. It can be argued that its psychological effect on industry dampened any hopes of recovery. A similar criticism can be made of the raising of interest rates in the Autumn of 1982 when a tenuous recovery was once again just beginning.

These questions and criticisms are directed toward the tactics of the counterinflationary policy rather than toward its strategy. The strategy appears to offer excellent hopes of a permanent reduction in inflation. The final and crucial question, however, is whether inflationary expectations have adjusted sufficiently that it will be possible to see a recovery of output without a resurgence of inflation. That question cannot yet be answered.

In June, 1983, Mrs. Thatcher became the first Conservative prime minister in this century to win a second successive term of office. The large Conservative majority will encourage a continuation of the counterinflationary policy launched in 1979. The Conservative election manifesto promised to produce price stability "ultimately." Many of the questions about the longer-term costs and benefits of the policies should be answered in the next four years.

General Appraisal

The period of our study has seen inflation rise from below 4 percent prior to 1965 to nearly 27 percent, and then fall back to 4 percent by mid-1983. The start of the period saw increasingly desperate attempts to prevent the devaluation of sterling. When the exchange rate was eventually devalued in 1967, most commentators saw the move as providing a great opportunity for a better economic performance; few recognized that the most important consequence was to be higher inflation. In his broadcast announcing the devaluation, Prime Minister Wilson said, "The pound in your pocket has not been devalued." He was quite wrong: U.K. prices soon reflected the total effect of the devaluation.

After 1967 came a succession of different policies. Tight fiscal policies and a series of incomes policies were employed until 1971. They were followed, after 1971, by an unprecedented fiscal and monetary expansion, resulting in further attempts to control inflation by price and incomes policies. Although the fiscal and monetary policies were somewhat reversed from late 1973 onward, it was impossible to avoid the consequences of the earlier extravagance, and inflation came close to 30 percent. The quadrupling of oil prices in 1973-1974 did not help, and the threshold payment system made it inevitable that a swift rise in wages would result. However, some other European economies, notably West Germany, were able to cope with the oil price shock with far less impact on domestic inflation.

The significant change in policy was imposed on Britain by the International Monetary Fund in 1976. There was a large reduction in public expenditure in 1977 and an attempt to observe monetary (or at least domestic credit expansion) limits. Unfortunately, the potential benefits were wasted by the Labour government's attempts to prevent a rise in the exchange rate. In 1978, the counterinflationary policies were effectively abandoned by the adoption of an overexpansionary budget. The Labour government attempted to disguise this by reimposing limits on monetary growth (through the use of the Corset) and by proposing ever more unrealistic targets for incomes policies. As noted previously, by the time Mrs. Thatcher's government was elected in 1979, inflation was again on the rise.

The policies pursued since 1979 have had some extraordinary features. For example, the Thatcher government simultaneously embarked on a campaign to cut inflation and introduced policies that added 4 percent to prices. The result was a rapid rise in inflation to over 20 percent. Also, the government adopted monetary targets at the same time that it greatly reduced its ability to control the money supply directly. For example, from May, 1979 onward, it successively: removed the Corset; abolished exchange controls; abandoned first Bank Rate and then minimum lending rate; and abolished the reserve assets requirement.

The common element in what may seem bold, if not foolhardy, steps has been the belief that it is possible and desirable to control inflation within free-market conditions. This approach represents an important act of self-denial, since it means that the task of reducing inflation and controlling the money supply has to be solved by consistent developments in other policies, especially fiscal policy. Another element of this approach has been a refusal to consider the use of incomes policies even when, as in 1979-1980, wage increases were disastrously high. In the case of incomes policies, there has also been some desire to encourage both employers and employees to understand the consequences of excessive wage settlements.

Inevitably, mistakes were made, particularly in the early stages of the policy.

However, each successive year has seen not only a progressive fall in inflation but also a more comprehensible balance of fiscal and monetary policy, with each falling within the government's targets.

It would be pleasant to believe that this story of inflation in Britain ends in 1983, with inflation firmly under control and on its way to a complete disappearance. Unfortunately, there is not, as yet, a consensus either about the priority to be attached to price stability or about the means of achieving it. The Labour Party's proposed economic policies, for example, deny the existence of any relationship between fiscal policy or monetary growth and inflation and also assume that a cut in the exchange rate is a successful way of permanently improving competitiveness.

The history of this period suggests that attempts at rapid expansion of the economy, combined with incomes policies to prevent inflation, fail to achieve either growth or price stability. The Thatcher government's response has been to concentrate on what it believes are the fundamental causes of inflation—excessive fiscal deficits and monetary growth—and it has been prepared to accept the consequences of a severe fall in output and a rapid rise in unemployment. The opposition parties have reacted by proposing intervention (the reintroduction of exchange controls, for example), by investigating more elaborate forms of incomes policies, or by offering the solution of "planning agreements."

The sweeping victory of Mrs. Thatcher's Conservative government in the 1983 general election showed that the electorate was unwilling to accept the alternative policies offered either by the Labour Party or by the Social Democrat-Liberal alliance. There should, therefore, be a period of at least another four years during which the Conservative government's policy experiment is continued. The Thatcher government promises a further steady reduction in monetary growth. It has also reduced the fiscal deficit to about the same percentage of GDP as it was in the 1960's, a period of generally low inflation and low unemployment. It will now be possible to see whether the policies can restore that kind of performance.

Response of the Financial Sector

A number of themes can be emphasized in recording the performance of the financial sector during the 1965-1983 period. The dominant theme is that of the response to accelerating inflation. The rise of inflation was accompanied by a major shift in the nature of financial flows. The striking feature, until recent years, was the rise in the public-sector deficit, largely matched by a rise in the household-sector's surplus. (One can argue that the rise in the public-sector deficit was itself a prime cause of the rise in inflation.) The financing needs of the public sector presented a challenge to the financial intermediaries, and certain institutions saw a massive increase in the value and the volume of their business. At the same time, the financial position of the corporate sector tended to deteriorate.

In addition to these background trends there were also shocks to the system. The 1960's saw considerable reliance on direct controls over the clearing banks as an instrument of monetary policy. One consequence was the rise of the parallel money market, that is, markets outside the traditional clearing banks. The introduction of Competition and Credit Control in 1971 marked a major institutional change and ushered in rapid growth of the money supply. Two years later, attempts to control monetary growth led to a banking crisis. After 1975, the banking sector, in particular, had to cope with specific targets for monetary growth. Since 1979, the financial sector has progressively been freed from official controls, but the Bank of England has by no means abandoned its use of powers of persuasion to direct the actions of the banks.

The Flow of Funds

Table 1 shows the broad picture of financial developments over the period. We can distinguish among three periods.

Until about 1972, the public sector's financial deficit was kept within a range from a surplus of about 1½ percent in 1969-1970 to a deficit of about 4½ percent in 1967. Over the period of the Labour administration, the average value of the deficit was 2 percent of GDP. The second period, from 1973 to 1980, saw public deficits generally above 4 percent of GDP, with a peak ratio of 8 percent in 1975. The third period, since 1981, has seen a reduction in the ratio in spite of the economic recession.

During the first period, the main counterpart to changes in the public-sector's deficit were changes in the overseas sector's surplus (i.e., the balance-of-payments deficit). Thus, the counterpart of the rise in the public deficit in 1967 was a large balance-of-payments deficit on current account and the counterpart of the budget surplus in 1969-1970 was a large balance-of-payments surplus on current account.

The apparent stability of the total private-sector surplus prior to 1972 provided the basis for the development in 1974 of "New Cambridge" economics, which argued that attempts to increase demand through fiscal expansion simply result in an increase in the balance-of-payments deficit, with little or no effect on domestic output. However, this idea was being proved wrong even as it was being expounded. It was true that a rapid increase in the balance-of-payments deficit in 1974 accompanied the increase in the public-sector deficit. But in 1975 and 1976, further increases in the public-sector deficit were accompanied by significant improvements in the balance of payments. The main offset to the rise in the public-sector deficit was a rise in the personal-sector surplus.

During the third period, the fall in the public-sector deficit has been accompanied by a fall in the personal-sector surplus.

It is possible to link these developments through a theory of the inflationary process. According to this theory, the main force sustaining inflation during the 1970's, after the initial monetary explosion of 1971-1973, was the large

Table 1
Net Acquisition of Financial Assets by Sector
(as percent of nominal GDP)[1]

	Private Sector		Public	Overseas
	Personal Sector	Company Sector	Public Sector	Overseas Sector
1964	2.1	−0.6	−3.2	1.2
1965	3.1	−0.5	−2.6	0.1
1966	3.4	−0.8	−2.6	−0.4
1967	2.6	−0.1	−4.2	0.8
1968	1.5	−0.6	−2.5	0.7
1969	1.9	−1.0	1.2	−1.3
1970	3.4	−1.9	1.5	−1.9
1971	0.9	1.1	−0.6	−2.3
1972	2.5	2.0	−2.8	−0.4
1973	4.5	−0.2	−4.2	1.6
1974	5.7	−4.2	−6.3	4.5
1975	6.1	−0.0	−8.1	1.6
1976	5.4	−0.5	−7.6	0.8
1977	4.3	0.8	−4.7	0.0
1978	6.3	−0.6	−5.4	−0.7
1979	7.7	−2.1	−4.9	0.5
1980	9.5	−1.8	−5.0	−1.5
1981	7.7	−0.5	−3.4	−2.8
1982	3.8	0.8	−2.6	−1.9
1983 (est.)	1.9	2.4	−3.6	−0.5

Source: *Economic Trends* and London Business School calculations.

[1]Sectors do not sum to zero because of residual error in national accounts.

public-sector deficit. The resulting inflation raised the personal-sector savings ratio as individuals sought to maintain the real value of their financial assets. Thus, the counterpart to the rise in the public-sector deficit was a rise in the personal-sector surplus, and the process is being reversed as the public-sector deficit and inflation are being reduced.

The Financial Sector and the Money Supply

If, for the moment, we concentrate on the broad definition of the money supply (sterling M-3), we can consider the pressures on the money supply and the role of the financial sector in terms of the conventional monetary identity:

Growth of money supply equals:
Public Sector Borrowing Requirement (PSBR)
plus bank advances to the non bank private sector
minus purchases of public-sector debt by the nonbank private
sector
minus external finance.
(All those categories are defined as flows.)

For much of the first period, with public-sector deficits on a moderate scale, the main pressures on the money supply came from fluctuations in the scale of bank lending to the private sector. Bank lending was particularly high in 1964, but was subsequently reduced virtually to zero in 1966. In 1969, the public sector made a negative contribution to monetary growth. From the end of 1963 to the end of 1969, the average growth of sterling M-3 was below 6 percent a year.

As described previously (in the section outlining the policy actions of the Labour administration between 1964 and 1970), the main means of controlling the money supply during that time was through policies directed at the clearing banks (including actual instructions about the growth of bank loans and advances). One result of these controls was the expansion of the secondary banking system and the rise of a parallel money market.

The conventional techniques of monetary policy operated through the discount market. The discount houses, by convention, agreed to cover the weekly issue of Treasury bills, and the finance for this operation was provided by overnight money from the London clearing banks. In the official money market, the Bank of England simultaneously held interest rates below market levels and rationed lending by the clearing banks. In response, the secondary banks developed certificates of deposit, interbank lending, and a greatly increased trade in local authority debt. They also successfully competed away wholesale money from the clearing banks, as did the finance houses. The result was that the clearing banks saw their share of sterling bank business fall. (At the same time, they could play little direct part in the booming Eurocurrency business.) In that sense Competition and Credit Control was a de facto recognition of the ability of the financial sector to circumvent attempts to restrain its activities.

Between 1963 and 1970, the deposit banks (the merchant banks, the overseas banks, etc.) grew rapidly relative to the clearing banks. The clearing banks lost their share of U.K. resident deposits (which fell from 92 percent in 1963 to 78 percent in 1970). They also lost their share of bank lending to the U.K. private sector. The remarkable development, however, was the growth of the total business of the deposit banks. Whereas total deposits at clearing banks grew by just 29 percent from 1963 to 1970 (from £7.9 billion to £10.2 billion), total deposits at deposit banks grew by 650 percent (from £3.7 billion to £27.5).

The rapid growth of the deposit banks' total business was in forms of financial assets—certificates of deposit, interbank lending, and so on—which virtually excluded the clearing banks. The rapid growth also reflected the development of the Eurodollar market. Although the clearing banks had become involved in these activities by buying merchant banks, they welcomed the opportunity to enter these markets in their own right.

During the years prior to 1971, when the clearing banks as a cartel maintained control over each of their lending and borrowing rates and the Bank of England exercised direct restraints on bank lending, the clearing banks could compete for business only in other ways. For example, Barclaycard (the first major credit card in the United Kingdom) was introduced in June, 1965, and the Westminster Bank opened the first 24-hour cash machine in 1965. Individual banks sought to provide a larger network of branches through merger. Barclays acquired Martins Bank in 1968, and the National Provincial and the Westminster Bank merged in 1969.

The introduction of Competition and Credit Control in 1971 not only allowed the clearing banks to compete for the funds that were being traded in the parallel money market but also allowed all banks considerable freedom to rearrange their assets in favor of the most profitable line, namely bank loans and advances. Not only was this rearrangement possible, the whole level of assets (and liabilities) could be increased through a relaxation of the reserve assets requirement. The result, not surprisingly, was a rapid rise in bank lending. The annual flow of bank lending rose from £800 million in 1970 to £1600 million in 1971, and to over £5,500 million in both 1972 and 1973. This increase in bank advances accounted for almost all of the growth of the money supply between 1971 and 1973. The public sector (net of sales of debt) made only a small contribution to monetary growth. It was clear that there had been a suppressed demand for bank advances prior to 1971 and also that the private sector readjusted the structure of its liabilities when it was free to do so.

In all the excitement, some financial institutions made unwise loans, particularly to the real estate sector, which experienced a spectacular boom. When the government eventually tried to slow down the growth of the money supply in the latter part of 1973, the banks incurred serious losses. The governor of the Bank of England referred to the newer institutions as "deposit-taking institutions on the fringe of the banking system": Some of these so-called fringe banks collapsed, but the clearing banks did not escape unharmed.

The growth of the money supply in the years immediately following the introduction of Competition and Credit Control was thus largely a matter of portfolio rearrangement, but the financial sector later had to deal with the problem of a rapidly increasing public-sector deficit, and, in some years, with the problem of a large corporate-sector deficit. Table 2 illustrates the pressures on the money supply.

In 1972 and 1973, the growth of bank advances accompanied a comfortable surplus or approximate balance for the industrial and commercial companies. The problem of financing the public-sector borrowing requirement (PSBR) became increasingly severe after 1972, and control of the money supply required large sales of public-sector debt to the nonbank private sector. Much of this was intermediated through the rest of the financial sector. In 1977, fiscal restraint

Table 2
Money Supply in the 1970's

	PSBR (£ billion)	Sales of debt to nonbank private sector (£ billion)	Bank advances to private sector (£ billion)	Corporate sector surplus (£ billion)	Growth of money supply (percent)
1971	1.4	2.1	1.6	0.8	11.8
1972	2.1	1.0	5.5	1.3	23.4
1973	4.2	2.3	6.0	−0.1	25.5
1974	6.4	3.2	3.4	−2.9	15.6
1975	10.5	5.6	−0.4	0.0	8.8
1976	9.2	5.8	3.4	−0.8	8.3
1977	5.9	8.5	3.2	.0	8.0
1978	8.3	6.0	4.7	1.0	15.3
1979	12.6	10.9	8.6	−1.6	12.6

Source: *Economic Trends* annual supplement, 1984.

greatly eased the financing problem, but this was also a year in which large sales of public-sector debt were possible because of the prospect of falling interest rates. The most difficult years for the corporate sector were 1974 and 1979. In the latter year, the deficit was accompanied by a rapid growth of bank advances.

The importance of the nonbank financial sector can be indicated by adding together the PSBR and the corporate-sector deficit. Apart from external financing items and in the absense of direct lending by the household sector to the public sector or to companies, the nonbank financial sector has to provide the means of intermediation if a rapid growth of the money supply is to be avoided. Table 3 shows the acquisition of public-sector debt and the lending to the corporate sector by the nonbank financial sector.

The first column of Table 3 shows the importance of the nonbank financial sector in acting as an intermediary for financing the growing PSBR. Its role in corporate finance has been less significant, and the industrial and commercial companies have had to turn to the banks to finance their exceptional deficits.

The years 1980-1982 again saw pressures on the financial sector. In 1980, there was a high PSBR and also very high borrowing by the company sector. The banking sector had to cope with a large share of the intermediation and, at the same time, there was significant reintermediation following the removal of the Corset. The Thatcher government chose to allow the money supply to rise by 22 percent, compared with its target range of 9 to 11 percent. The reduction in the PSBR since 1980 has helped but the corporate sector, under considerable pressure, continued to rely on the banks. Thus, not until 1982 was the Thatcher government able to achieve its targets for monetary growth.

Table 3: The Nonbank Financial Sector
(Billions of Pounds)

Year	Acquisition of Public-Sector Debt	Acquisition of Company Securities	Total
1971	1.4	1.1	2.5
1972	.6	.9	1.5
1973	1.1	.3	1.4
1974	2.1	−0.2	1.9
1975	4.1	1.7	5.8
1976	3.1	1.2	4.3
1977	6.3	1.9	8.2
1978	4.4	1.8	6.2
1979	7.4	1.9	9.3
1980	5.8	2.3	8.1
1981	5.4	2.2	7.6
1982	5.1	2.9	8.0

Source: National Income and Expenditure (Blue Book), 1983, Table 13-6.

Although direct quantitative controls on bank lending have generally been ruled out since the introduction of Competition and Credit Control, the tradition of guidance by the Bank of England has not been completely abandoned. In some cases the guidance has, reportedly, encouraged the banks to continue lending beyond their normal prudent limits. One such case was during the great financial pressures on companies in 1980. (Having responded to this guidance, the banks were understandably annoyed at having a special tax levied on them in the budget of 1981.)

The other method of controlling bank lending, first introduced by Mr. Heath's Conservative government in 1973, was officially called the Supplementary Special Deposits Scheme, generally known as "the Corset." The Corset imposed a limit on the size of certain bank liabilities (interest-bearing eligible liabilities.) If the limit was exceeded, noninterest-bearing deposits had to be made with the Bank of England. This requirement progressively became a serious penalty, and it effectively controlled bank lending. In 1973, bank lending was slowing down of its own accord and the measures imposed by the Corset were redundant, but the position was very different when the scheme was reintroduced by Mr. Healey, the Labour government's chancellor of the exchequer, in 1978. The fiscal expansion was exerting considerable pressure on the money supply. The banks found many ways to avoid the constraints of the Corset and the growth of the measured money supply was thus kept artificially low. Reintermediation (the resumption of funds flows through deposits at banks) following the removal of the Corset in 1980 may have accounted for 5 or more percent of the growth of the money supply in that year.

Table 4
The Household Sector:
Main Financial Uses and Sources of Funds
(1971-1980—Cumulative)

Financial assets acquired by households	*Billion pounds*
Bank deposits	28.2
Building society* deposits	39.5
Life insurance and pension funds	58.5
Total	126.2
Financial sources of funds	
Bank loans and advances	11.6
Sales of corporate securities	14.9
Borrowing from building societies	33.9
Total	60.4
Cumulative surplus (increase in *net* financial assets)	66.0

*Institutions similar to U.S. savings and loan associations

Source: National Income and Expenditures (Blue Book) various issues.

The Household Sector's Surplus

As discussed earlier, the main counterpart of the rise in the public-sector deficit during the 1970's was the rise in the household-sector surplus. This development provided the financial sector with an unprecedented opportunity to expand its role as an intermediary. We have already discussed its role in financing the public-sector deficit. In this section, we examine how well the financial sector met the needs of the household sector.

If the financial sector was to operate effectively, it had to perform three tasks. The first was to cope with the rapid growth of personal savings; the second was to provide savers with some form of protection against inflation; the third was to take the best possible advantage of the incentives offered by the tax system. Table 4 shows the broad developments.

The banking sector found it hardest to meet the challenge posed by the growing flow of savings by individuals and households. It was able to retain its near monopoly of the provision of the means of payment, but this was not an unmixed blessing because the costs of handling transaction accounts rose rapidly and the banking sector found it hard to bid for the balances that would have helped offset these costs. This was particularly true of the clearing banks, which provide almost all the checking facilities for the private sector. As described earlier, they were unable, before 1971, to bid for or lend funds at market rates, and although they expanded their money-market business during the 1970's, they did not compete actively for the deposits of the household sector.

A more important development in the relationship between the banks and the household sector was the growth of bank lending. The flexible overdraft system remained the main way of lending to companies, but banks extended two forms of lending to the personal sector through personal loans and credit cards. Personal loans were for fixed sums with agreed repayment schedules. Credit cards provided a far more flexible loan system, subject to prearranged limits. The credit-card system grew rapidly but was vulnerable to fraud and, in times of recession, to considerable problems of bad debts.

In their attempts to attract funds, the banks were at a disadvantage compared with other institutions because interest paid on bank deposits is fully taxable. It is, however, paid without any deduction for taxes due by the recipient, thus providing a timing advantage to those who later pay taxes and an appeal to those who do not pay income tax. (But those who do not pay tax are unlikely to have large bank accounts.) In more recent years, the clearing banks have made a more serious attempt to attract funds from the household sector by offering special returns to those who agree to save regularly and by offering money-market rates for sums as small as £2,000.

The building societies were far more successful in acquiring short-term funds from individuals. They have a slight tax advantage in that they pay interest *net* of tax. The tax is deemed to have been paid at the standard rate. However, the rate of tax paid by the building societies (the so-called composite rate) is slightly less than the standard rate because not all investors would, in fact, be liable for taxes. All other things being equal, this allows the building societies to offer a more attractive net interest rate than the banks. The building societies are an unusual part of the financial sector, since they act almost entirely as a financial intermediary *within* the household sector; they do not make a major contribution to financing flows between the household sector and other sectors. One needs, therefore, to explain both the growth in building-society deposits and the growth in lending for purchases of homes.

For most of this period, loans for home purchases were the only variety of loan for which interest was tax deductible for the household sector. After tax relief was taken into account, the rate of interest paid on home loans was generally far below the rate of appreciation of home prices. Home purchases financed by loans thus became an attractive form of investment for the household sector with occasional boom periods, as in the early 1970's. To meet a constant high level of demand for home loans, the building societies were able to attract deposits by offering competitive rates, by greatly expanding the number of branches, and by staying open on Saturdays, when the banks were closed.

The lion's share of the household sector's surplus was placed through life insurance companies and pension funds (Table 4). The relative size and the rapid growth of these funds during the 1970's is shown in Table 5.

Table 5
Total Assets of Insurance Companies and Pension Funds
(£ billion)

	Insurance companies	Pension funds
1965	9.8	5.3
1970	15.5	7.8
1980	65.2	53.9

The pension funds receive particularly favorable tax treatment. The funds themselves do not pay income tax or capital gains tax. For approved pension schemes, employees' contributions receive full tax relief, and no tax is paid on employers' contributions. This favorable treatment makes pension schemes a tax-efficient way of compensating workers. That is not to argue that, even with their favorable tax treatment, pension contributions are necessarily preferable to wages. There can be serious penalties to those who leave jobs, and younger employees may find themselves paying very high rates of interest if they have to borrow. However, the figures show how popular this form of saving became in the course of the 1970's. (It should be noted that the conventions of national income accounting treat both employers' and employees' contributions to pension funds as part of disposable income.) The growth of pension funds was given a further boost in 1978 by regulations setting higher standards for private pension schemes.

The insurance companies continued to provide their traditional function of insurance against risks, but during this period they also became the major vehicle for those seeking a medium- to long-term savings instrument. They thus filled the gap between the banks and the building societies (that offered short-term investments) and the pension funds (that offered very long-term outlets for contractual savings). In addition, the insurance companies themselves act as managers for pension funds, so that part of their growth can be explained by the growth of pension plans.

The insurance companies enjoy the same tax advantages in relation to their managed funds as do the pension funds; they pay neither income tax nor capital gains tax. The tax position of the personal saver is also favorable as compared with other forms of savings, though not as favorable (for employees) as contributions to pension funds. Personal contributions to life insurance funds carry tax relief at approximately one-half of the standard rate of income tax.[2] In other words, at the current time, the net cost of contributions is 85 percent of the gross cost. (There is an upper limit as a proportion of total income.) That 15 percent advantage provides the insurance companies with a significant edge in bidding for the household-sector's funds and the companies have stressed it, with considerable success.

[2]Tax relief on new life assurance policies was removed in the Budget of March, 1984.

131

The acceleration of inflation meant that investors sought some means of preserving the real value of their savings. One result was a shift from nonprofit policies (which guaranteed a fixed return) to alternative policies which include a smaller guaranteed return plus bonuses based on profits. Provided that the companies, in turn, have been able to hedge against inflation, the latter policies provide a better hedge against inflation.

As an extension of the idea of profit-participating policies, the life insurance companies developed a very wide range of savings instruments. An important example was unit-linked life insurance, which in theory linked life insurance with the purchase of unit trusts (mutual funds). In practice the pure insurance element in these policies was small but it qualified them for tax relief so that unit-linked policies, in effect, provided the public with a means of buying unit trusts at a discount. Insurance companies also offered investment in a variety of funds including property, equity, fixed interest, and cash funds. At times during the 1960's and 1970's, the insurance companies were able to offer exceptionally valuable short-term returns, since it was possible both to use the tax benefit and to cash in the policy within a short period. The tax laws have been subsequently changed to try to ensure that the tax relief provisions to life insurance are not used simply as a means of avoiding tax for short-term investments.

Insurance companies have offered both contractual savings plans and single-premium bonds. The single premium provides some insurance, but otherwise it is invested in a preferred form of financial asset and again provides a form of investment at a discount compared with other assets available to the household sector. Because the funds are readily marketable, the single-premium bonds have provided a flexible and relatively tax-efficient means of saving. Yet another class of investment offered by the insurance companies has included the income and growth bonds that are lump-sum investments providing a return over a fixed period (e.g. five or ten years). The income bonds pay out regular income; the growth bonds accumulate the interest.

The general picture of developments in the insurance industry has been one of the creation of a very wide variety of schemes to meet the needs of the household sector. While the investors have sought to protect themselves from inflation, the companies have had to adjust their assets to meet the changing nature of their liabilities. Table 6 shows how the total funds of the industry have moved.

If one considers real estate as an equity-type investment, inasmuch as it offers some protection against inflation, then we see that the total investment in corporate securities and real estate has stayed fairly constant as a share of total investment. However, within the total, the weight of property has doubled. This has consisted partly of new property developments and partly of sale-and-lease-back arrangements that have provided a source of funds for the corporate sector.

As stressed previously, the financial sector had to act as an intermediary in financing the large public-sector deficits of the 1970's. Since inflation was

Table 6
Composition of Insurance Company Funds
(Percent of total)

	U.K. Corporate Securities	Real Estate and related	Total
1965	40.8	9.7	50.5
1970	39.4	11.6	51.0
1980	29.8	21.0	50.8

generally higher than expected, the government was able to finance its deficit at the expense of its creditors, including the insurance funds. Because there was also a sharp deterioration in company profitability, the financial institutions found it hard to maintain the real value of their funds.

By 1983, the position seemed to have been reversed. Inflation had fallen more rapidly than expected and government securities therefore, offered exceptional real returns. (This has partly reflected worldwide developments.) At the same time, the government has issued index-linked securities which, by definition, remove the risk of unexpected inflation. Ironically, it has done so at the same time that it has conducted policies that themselves should greatly reduce the risk of further bouts of accelerating inflation. In addition, expectations of restored corporate profitability have raised common stock prices to record levels. As a final point, the abolition of exchange controls in 1980 greatly increased the freedom of the financial sector to acquire overseas assets, which has resulted in a considerable shift in portfolios.

To summarize, the 1970's saw a considerable expansion of the financial sector's business, particularly that of insurance funds. However, this increase in business was itself part of the story of rising inflation. In spite of the ingenuity they showed, the financial intermediaries were not able fully to protect their investors from the effects of inflation. If, in the future, inflation is controlled, the flow of funds through the financial sector will grow much less rapidly, but it will be easier to offer adequate *real* returns to investors. The optimal outcome for the future would be for personal savings to continue to grow and be translated into tangible investment by a profitable corporate sector. To judge from the evidence, in the United Kingdom, the probability of such an outcome is certainly higher in 1983 than it was just a few years ago.

CANADA

Carl E. Beigie*

Introduction

ALTHOUGH the outside world generally views the Canadian economy as a "tail" wagged by the United States, the period since the mid-1960's witnessed a number of Federal Government policy initiatives aimed at reducing the involuntary dimensions of this linkage. The resulting policy experimentation was intellectually interesting, but its practical results were bitterly disappointing. After sliding through the 1970's on a modestly less volatile economic course than that of the United States, Canada entered the 1980's with deeply embedded inflationary forces. In the end, Canadian officials decided they had no effective alternative to following the United States into a severe monetary policy crunch.

From mid-1981 to the end of 1982, the Canadian economy went through an exceptionally harsh downturn—much deeper than a traditional recession, but not quite bad enough to be labeled a full-scale depression—in which output, employment and capacity utilization fell much more sharply than at any time since the 1930's. The question that continues to plague the Canadian economy, as it does that of the United States, is how long the recovery that started in 1983 can be sustained, thereby bringing down a high unemployment rate, without rekindling inflation. It is a question that remains a source of confusion and erratic speculation among Canadian opinion leaders.

Characteristics of the Country

Canada's recent experience with inflation can be viewed as verging on the unique, primarily in the efforts that were made to decouple its economy from the global, and more particularly the U.S., inflation experience. In pursuing, and then essentially failing to achieve this objective, certain of Canada's economic and political characteristics set it apart, at least to a degree, from other industrialized nations. The manner in which political choice within the

*Professor of Management, University of Toronto and McGill University. The author wishes to thank James K. Stewart of Dominion Securities Ames for his comments and assistance.

environment created by these characteristics converted inflation that initially was externally generated into inflation that ultimately became internally generated, makes Canada an especially interesting case study.

Unique Characteristics

Economic

Canada has a very open economy, with total receipts and expenditures in international current account transactions running at somewhat greater than a quarter of the value of its gross national product. This openness is particularly pronounced in Canada's trade relations with the United States, which account for roughly 70 percent of its merchandise exports and a comparable percentage of its imports from all sources. As a result, fluctuations in the U.S. economy have a pronounced effect on the level of effective demand experienced in the Canadian economy.

The vulnerability of interdependence through trade is made even greater by the degree to which Canada's economic structure is focused on production and trade in resource commodities. Exceptionally dramatic world commodity-price movements during the 1970's showed up in significant fluctuations in Canada's terms of trade. On the whole, these terms-of-trade effects were favorable, but international price movements were reflected quickly in domestic inflation rates and in the profit performances of firms in the resource sector. As profits rose, so did demands for wage increases by workers in this sector, and these demands spread through the entire economy. Granting them caused additional cost pressures that later fueled inflation. Furthermore, an economy that concentrates on resource production is especially vulnerable to large multiplier effects arising from an expansion of investment to meet perceived long-term shortages of world supplies. Such a perception swept across the country during the early 1970's and again in the early 1980's, feeding an attitude that the country was uniquely positioned to isolate itself from the main consequences of global economic distress.

Another distinguishing feature of the Canadian economy emerges from a legacy of deficits in its international current account transactions. As a result of these deficits, Canada's net international indebtedness position had reached nearly $100 billion by the end of 1981. (Because of a sharp decline in imports resulting from recessionary conditions, Canada recorded current account surpluses in 1982 and 1983.) During much of its history, Canada was able to finance all, or at least a large portion, of its trade deficits with net long-term equity capital inflows. It could, therefore, be argued with reason that the current account deficits served to accommodate a real transfer into Canada arising from autonomous foreign direct investment.

In the 1970's, Canada experienced a shift in long-term equity capital flows. Policies affecting foreign direct investment generally, and foreign ownership in the energy sector specifically, cut down on inflows. At the same time, Canadian investors were expanding their direct investment outflows. This meant that continuing current account deficits had to be financed increasingly through induced net inflows of debt capital. Therefore, Canadian interest rates had to be kept at levels that would attract such debt movements, which meant, in effect, that Canadian rates had to be above those generally available in the United States. (This conclusion applies even with regard to current account surpluses so long as a significant portion of Canada's large net international indebtedness has to be refinanced on a continuing basis.) In short, Canadian monetary policy was constrained to follow U.S. monetary policy quite closely. (This constraint became binding given Canadian exchange-rate policy, which is described below.

Political

A noteworthy factor on the political side, especially in an era when policy matters figure so crucially in the economic environment, is that the same man, Pierre Trudeau, was the country's Prime Minister between 1968 and 1984. Except for a brief but important period of minority government (1972-1974), and an even briefer period as leader of the official opposition (1979), this man, who is commonly acknowledged to be "bored" by economic matters, skillfully combined the traits of intellectual brilliance, exceptional style, and organizational discipline within his party (Liberal) to dominate the Canadian national scene.

Although there is heated debate on the point, in my view Mr. Trudeau and his governments displayed pragmatism rather than any clear and consistent philosophical ideology in approaching the economic challenges and opportunities the country faced. The course taken reflected certain biases: a modest amount of egalitarianism; some centralism even to the point of statism; a large dose of technocratic elitism; and a degree of what is commonly referred to as nationalism. To anyone who is impatient with the time it takes economic reality to be reflected in political decisions, Trudeau's pragmatism often comes to light only after a very long lag.

The only consistent theme in Canadian economic policy over the past 15 years, at least prior to the 1981-1982 recession, is a striving for control over the consequences of externally generated, and largely unpredictable, events. Pursuit of this objective has involved experimentation with policy, sometimes to the point of adventurism. It has resulted in sudden about-faces in matters such as controls on incomes and prices, energy policy, and foreign investment, as well as in relations with business, labor and the United States. Most of all— although this would come as something of a surprise to observers of most of Canada's mainline economic forecasters—this pursuit has meant that the direction, even though certainly not the exact timing, of Canadian policy could be largely anticipated. Economic logic eventually catches up with political adventurism in Canada, at least sufficiently to show the broad limits on independent action in the increasingly homogenized, interdependent world of the advanced industrial nations.

A second important factor on the political side has been Canada's unique brand of federalism. The special problems of Quebec and its needs for linguistic and cultural defense mechanisms are well known. A far broader constraint on effective central government action in economic matters has been the amount of power possessed by the provinces to pursue their own courses, with Ottawa largely being left a residual role for achieving national policy goals. Examples include the provincial debt issues in foreign capital markets which—because they are carried on without coordination regarding either amounts or timing— have occasionally disrupted Bank of Canada efforts to stabilize the external value of the Canadian dollar and the spending policies of the provinces which— because they account for roughly half of total government expenditures in Canada—make it all that more difficult for Ottawa to achieve its stabilization intentions.

Provinces have the power not merely to operate at cross-purposes with the central government, but also to block Ottawa's initiatives in important areas. Attempts to implement a national energy policy were hampered throughout the 1970's by the demands of Alberta, which produces the bulk of Canada's oil and a large share of its natural gas. Ottawa's objectives were heavily weighted in favor of consumers, reflecting the fact that seats in the House of Commons are proportioned on the basis of population. Alberta, with the bulk of energy production and a modest population base, naturally placed priority on pro- ducer interests. The outcome on prices was a compromise that served reasonably well the political purpose of the contending levels of government; the objective of economic efficiency, however, was not very well reflected in the negotiation process, as will be seen later.

If one views incomes policies as having any potential viability as an anti- inflation tactic, the division of powers in Canada limits severely the prospects for their implementation. A federal program was introduced throughout the country from late 1975 to early 1978, but the constitutional basis on which Ot- tawa justified this initiative was so shaky that it was forced to apply a far more restricted restraint package when it moved into this area again in mid-1982.

A third feature of the Canadian political scene is unique not in kind but in degree, at least in comparison with the situation in the United States. All economies in the so-called free world are mixed, combining public initiatives with private enterprise. In Canada, the mix is skewed increasingly toward public- sector involvement. Government enterprises, or Crown corporations, figure dominantly in a host of transportation and other service industries, and this organizational form has been spreading into a wider range of industrial activities (for example, aircraft production, energy production and distribution, and chemicals). Moreover, both federal and provincial governments have become highly active in bailing out some private-sector firms in distress, and in selecting others to serve as chosen instruments for the pursuit of policy objectives.

The expanded scope of government in Canada has had two particularly important impacts on the country's inflationary experience: The more direct has been the influence of government-administered price movements on the timing of changes in the broad price indicators. During the early phases of inflationary pressures, administered price lags held down the recorded rate of price advance; when these pressures eased, the lag operated to keep up the recorded rate of inflation. The resulting distortion in the ability to see true turning points contributed to misreadings of the impacts of policy among the general public and fueled demands by labor for wage gains to protect real incomes against inaccurately anticipated inflationary erosion.

A second impact of a growing role of government is more philosphical in nature but, in my judgment, it lies at the heart of the politics of inflation in Canada. In contrast to the United States, where distrust of government is traditional, Canadians generally have a deeply felt suspicion of the marketplace, which they view as being heavily influenced by external forces. Government is looked upon as a protector by the majority of Canadians. During the period under review, the Federal Government, under Pierre Trudeau, actively encouraged that view. As a result, Canadians turned to government to protect them against inflation, and this protection came to be looked upon as a "right." Throughout most of the 1970's, this expectation was met to a significant degree, but in ways that were building up problems that finally had to be dealt with in the 1980's.

With this background, I turn to a description of the major factors influencing the Canadian experience with inflation.

Major Elements in the Canadian Inflation Process

An effective description of a country's experience with inflation requires a reasonably accurate analysis of why the general level of prices begins, and then continues, to rise. An excessive rate of growth in the supply of money will cause inflation, but acknowledging that near-tautology does not carry us very far in understanding why a government allows the money supply to grow too fast at the cost of a departure from the politically attractive situation of stable prices. Any simple explanation is almost certainly misleading in the case of Canada.

The standard explanation of how inflation began in Canada lies largely in external forces. When the United States decided to expand its military operations in Vietnam in the mid-1960's, it did so by adding a large dose of deficit spending to an economy that had reached effective full employment. The resulting excess demand spilled over into Canada, which was also near its effective production capacity limits. An improved balance of trade crowded out domestic demand, so that Canada imported inflationary pressures.

During the late 1960's and early 1970's the United States, as well as Canada, pursued a vacillating policy course in an effort, on the one hand, to keep inflation within what subsequently would appear to be quite low limits, and, on the other hand, to keep unemployment from rising above what would also seem, in the light of later developments, too low a ceiling. As the political cost of unemployment was perceived to have grown too great, however, the entire industrial world, including Canada and the United States, embarked simultaneously on an expansionary course that globalized inflationary pressures. As was the case in the mid-1960's, Canadians were again easily persuaded that these later inflationary forces had little to do with their own country's actions.

The problem of imported inflation can be serious for a relatively small, highly open economy. That vulnerability can be reduced, though for reasons explained later not completely eliminated, by allowing the national currency to float in foreign-exchange markets. Canada, acting sooner than other nations and despite some pressure from the United States to hold the Bretton Woods-line, abandoned the pegged relationship with the U.S. dollar in the late Spring of 1970.

Having "depegged" the Canadian dollar, however, the government was reluctant to let it float freely. The currency moved up toward parity with the U.S. dollar fairly quickly, generating nervousness that export- and import-competing industries, and the jobs they generated, would be in serious jeopardy if the Canadian dollar rose further. To hold the Canadian dollar down, the authorities allowed international reserves to rise sharply over the next several years. A much more important response in the context of inflation, however, was that the Bank of Canada permitted a rapid expansion of the money supply, thereby allowing potential inflation to be converted into actual inflation. The Bank's logic was that interest rates had to be kept down sufficiently to prevent net capital flows from pushing the exchange rate upward. Largely for this reason, M-1 growth averaged roughly 14 percent annually in the period 1971-1973.

It should be recognized that a flexible exchange rate can go only so far in isolating a country from externally generated inflation. If, as was the case during the early 1970's, a sharp running up of world commodity *and* natural resources prices figure strongly in a nation's economic activity, major microeconomic pressures will be exerted on that nation, irrespective of the exchange-rate regime. Commodity prices will rise internally, as they will in all countries, unless price and export controls are adopted. More important, higher world prices mean higher profits for domestic producers, and these higher profits serve as an inducement to increased wage demands. In a highly competitive labor market, these demands would not have to be met. A condition of such a market, however, would be that sales prospects—and profits—would deteriorate in sectors not producing natural resources.

Canada could not quickly expand capacity in its resource industries and, even if it could have, the result would have been inconsistent with the country's desire to reduce the degree of its reliance on this sector. There was a widespread sense in the nation that other sectors would continue to receive support so that reasonably full employment would be sustained. This sense, combined with the buoyancy in resource exports, created a psychology of abundance in the early 1970's. Such a psychology, together with good profits and a government-supported notion that inflation was not Canada's fault, led to an environment in which labor throughout the economy demanded, and usually received, gains in wages and salaries that more than kept up with price advances.

Another aspect of Canada's inflation that has external roots arises from the country's closeness to the United States both in geography and in consumer tastes. Moreover, U.S. companies figure significantly in the operations of the Canadian economy through their numerous Canadian subsidiaries. As a result of these tight linkages, price movements in the United States tend to be paralleled quite closely in Canada, even when economic conditions in the two countries differ.

Acknowledging the existence of strong external forces affecting Canada's inflation experience, clearly additional factors of internal origin were also present. Monetary policy, both with respect to the behavior of the exchange rate and to the lack of discipline regarding rates of growth in money supply aggregates, was certainly a key consideration. So too was fiscal policy, but in a manner that requires careful elaboration.

The argument made here is that significant changes in the allocation of a nation's output over time are a major factor influencing the evolution of economic policy problems, including the problem of inflation. Between 1960 and 1972, total expenditures by governments in Canada rose as a share of gross national expenditure (GNE) by about 6 percentage points, from 18 percent to 24 percent. This means that governments—federal, provincial and municipal—increased their share in the economy by roughly a third. (The level, share and rate of growth of total government spending, inclusive of transfer payments, were much greater, but this raises a different and more complex set of analytical problems.)

In light of much contemporary comment on fiscal policy, it is interesting that this increasing government share—which came during peacetime—was accompanied by a shift from a modest deficit to a modest surplus in the total government budgetary position. Moreover, the increased share did not come at the expense of a crowding out of business investment (which fluctuated around a nearly constant share of GNE in the period) or of net exports (which actually improved during the period). Instead, the increase came exclusively from a fall in the personal consumption component of GNE.

To put the increased government share of GNE into perspective, it should be noted that 6 percentage points is more than twice the impact of higher energy prices on this component of total national spending. Its effects have been of two types. One arises from the fact that, in a cyclical sense, government demand is more stable than other spending components. Therefore, the cycle was subject to less fluctuation, reinforcing the notion among labor that the risks of downturns had been reduced. Fear of softness in labor markets is a source of discipline on wage demands.

A second effect of a rising government expenditure share, especially when it is accompanied by an improving budgetary position, is that the tax take of governments must be rising. Tax rates did not have to rise by much in the 1960's— there were increased taxes to finance various social programs such as medicare and unemployment insurance—because Canada's progressive personal income-tax system was so robust. Steep progressivity in schedules meant that tax revenues rose much faster than did total incomes.

Even though the share of GNE going to personal consumption fell during the 1960's, family consumption rose in absolute terms because real income per family unit registered healthy gains. Thus, the increased share accounted for by government came from extracting a high proportion of national economic growth, not at the expense of a decline in real disposable income per family unit.

Government's share of gross national expenditure moved up very modestly in the 1970's, but a decline in 1979 and 1980 put the figure almost exactly where it had been in 1972. During the decade of the 1970's, however, two new factors entered the scene. One was that Canadian productivity improvements virtually stopped. Declines in performance on this measure were universal throughout the industrial world, but in Canada the deterioration was particularly notable.

Without productivity growth, average per capita, or per family unit, real incomes cannot improve (apart from increases in participation rates), and in Canada they did not during the second half of the 1970's. As a result, peoples' sensitivity to the impact of a bigger government share in the economy was heightened, thereby contributing to a shift in perceptions about the basic causes of Canadian inflation.

The second new factor that emerged was a decision by Ottawa and all the provinces other than Quebec to index the personal income-tax system to the rate of inflation, beginning in 1975. This policy initiative will be discussed more fully in a later section, but it is important to note here that this action essentially removed government's ability to finance an increased share in the economy without raising tax rates. Prior to indexation, they had even been able to reduce some taxes.

Canada, like the United States, experienced a significant increase in the level and share of government spending during the second half of the 1960's. Unlike the U.S. experience, which was related to expenditures for the Vietnam War, the increase in Canada was almost entirely for programs for which expenditure growth took on a life of its own. Financing for these programs came fairly easily until the mid-1970's because of strong growth in taxable incomes and a progressivity in tax schedules that was steep enough to reward government treasuries in periods of high inflation. With the onset of very slow real-income growth and the introduction of personal income-tax indexing, however, tax-revenue growth fell off sharply and a mounting budgetary deficit emerged. Canadians began to realize that excesses of complacency were eroding the country's economic performance.

Another broad internal dimension of Canada's inflation experience arose from a failure to grasp quickly the impact of structural developments that were eroding the indicative value for policy purposes of traditional economic benchmarks. Major changes in labor-market conditions that reduced significantly the ability of the economy to reach conventional targets for full employment were especially important in this respect. In the middle of the 1960's, the newly created Economic Council of Canada, a federal agency, put forward the notion that the country should seek to achieve an unemployment rate of about 3 percent. Four factors, at least, made this a completely unrealistic target for the 1970's and the 1980's.

First, the recorded unemployment rate reflects both the frequency and the average duration of unemployment. Institutional changes, specifically in the operations of the national unemployment insurance program, were designed expressly for the purpose of tiding people over periods of unemployment so they could be more relaxed as they engaged in a search for the "right" next job. The intended impact was achieved in an extension of the average duration of reported unemployment. Therefore, a rise in reported unemployment of as much as 1 to 1½ percent, it has been variously estimated, would not cause a rise in the pain traditionally associated with unemployment.

Second, Canada experienced an exceptionally rapid growth in the labor force during the latter part of the 1960's and throughout the 1970's. The baby boom following World War II was even more pronounced in Canada than in the United States, as was Canada's immigration experience. The two forces combined to produce very large demographic changes. Both were supplemented by a surge in the participation rate of women in the labor force.

These influences from the labor force were felt most significantly in a reduction in the average length of job experience of workers. The logic of the "learning curve" would indicate that productivity, on average, would be lowered, at least temporarily, because of this factor. Moreover, finding jobs for all of these new workers would mean that aggregate demand in the economy would have to grow quite rapidly, creating an environment in which experienced employees could be expected to ask for, and to receive, generous increases in compensation. In short, this meant a rise in inflationary cost pressures at any particular level of overall unemployment, which can be described as a deterioration in the short-term trade-off between inflation and unemployment.

Third, several factors relating to the union movement in Canada almost certainly served to aggravate further the deterioration in the trade-off. A much higher percentage of the labor force is unionized in Canada than in the United States, and organization among public-sector employees is particularly widespread. Many of these public-sector unions were relatively new and had only recently been given the right to strike. Determined to close, and in some cases to try to reverse, a traditional gap with workers in the private sector, the leadership of these unions bargained aggressively for sharply higher benefits. In the period of peak settlements during 1975, just prior to the introduction of price and wage controls in Canada, wages in the noncommercial sector (mainly public-service employees) were rising roughly twice as fast as in the commercial sector.

Fourth, Canada is especially vulnerable in the face of structural changes working their way through the world economy. Canada's secondary manufacturing industries grew up behind relatively high tariff walls but in an environment of openness to foreign direct investment. As a result, Canada's fairly small internal market was carved up by too many firms producing too broad a range of products for efficiency, by international standards, to be achieved. Tariffs created a margin for inefficiency that, in most cases, was fully used. As international competition intensified, and continues to do so because tariffs are scheduled to decrease further through the 1980's as the GATT Tokyo round of negotiations is implemented, many of Canada's manufacturers are under serious pressure. This pressure can be met effectively only through some combination of reduced rates of wage increase, a further decline in the relative value of the Canadian dollar, and/or a major initiative to improve productivity performance. A long legacy of protection from international reality makes such adjustments difficult to achieve and adds to the problems associated with attaining low unemployment simultaneously with reasonable price stability.

Government Policy Responses

Prior to the 1973-1974 OPEC oil price shock, the general course of the Canadian economy closely paralleled that of the United States. The first half of the 1960's saw a steady improvement in output and employment without serious inflation, similar to that achieved in the United States during the brief Kennedy era. From 1966 to late 1973, the erratic ups and downs that reflected U.S. experience during the Vietnam buildup of inflation and subsequent efforts to correct them were also accepted in a fairly passive manner by the Federal Government.

As noted earlier, three Canadian initiatives in the 1960's and early 1970's added to problems experienced later. Government spending on goods and services increased steadily as a share of gross national expenditure. The power of unions was augmented, especially by granting public-sector workers the right to strike. Thirdly, toward the end of the period, the Canadian dollar was allowed to float upward to moderate the pressure of imported inflation; but, at the same time, monetary policy became excessively loose in an effort to keep the Canadian dollar from rising too much relative to the U.S. dollar.

One other development in the policy area during this period merits brief attention. In an effort to improve the deteriorating prospects of its automotive sector, the Canadian government launched a duty-remission scheme to encourage large-scale, specialized production for export markets in 1963. U.S. trade law threatened the viability of this unilateral scheme. In an effort to avoid a serious conflict in bilateral trade relations, Canada and the United States negotiated a conditional free-trade pact for this sector in 1965. One key result of the auto pact was that productivity improved dramatically in the Canadian sector of the industry. Because of this improvement, demands were made by labor in both countries that Canadian workers' wages should rise to nominal (with respect to each nation's currency) parity with those of U.S. workers. The industry could not deny this demand.

The problem was that the granting of wage parity in the key automotive sector unleashed similar demands in other industries that did not have the benefit of a free-trade deal to boost their productivity performance. These demands were resisted, but strong markets and good profit pictures encouraged labor to keep up the pressure. As a result, during the 1970's Canadian wage parity with the United States became a far more common phenomenon than productivity parity in manufacturing industries.

The OPEC price shock of 1973-1974 created an exceptionally awkward political challenge for the Canadian Federal Government. Whereas most other industrial countries were net importers of oil and had little choice but to raise domestic prices sharply and quickly, Canada was enjoying what turned out to be a short-lived status as a net exporter of oil. (It was importing large amounts to supply eastern markets, but exporting even more to the United States from the western producing region in a pattern determined by transportation economies.)

Pressure from consuming provinces—especially the politically central Ontario and the left-leaning New Democratic Party (NDP) that held the balance in a minority Liberal Federal Government—produced an oil-pricing policy that brought about a rate of increase in oil prices that was slower than anywhere else in the industrial world. There was heated debate about the wisdom of this approach, the hottest being generated by producing provinces and firms. What won the day was the claim that since OPEC was not pricing on market economics but rather on the basis of pure power, a country with large internal oil supplies relative to its needs did not have to suffer the trauma of a sharp rise in the domestic price of such a key commodity. Therefore, Canada's internal oil price lagged behind the world oil price and continues to do so, although the gap has narrowed significantly.

From the perspective of Canada's inflation experience, Canadian pricing policy has had four important consequences (ignoring impacts on the supply side that might affect Canada's ability to respond effectively to future world oil-price shocks). *First,* this policy launched the country on a course of seeking to differentiate itself from global economic forces. (Its earlier decision to float the currency was a return to a policy that it had followed in the 1950's.) Nothing, in my opinion, had a more dramatic psychological effect than did the Canadian oil-pricing policy in terms of instilling a notion among the public that Canadians could, and should, receive special treatment in the face of world economic distress.

Second, by holding down the rate of oil price advance after the 1973-1974 and 1978-1979 world price increases, Canada got a badly distorted view of its comparative inflation performance. Canadians were not relaxed about inflation, but they tended to take misplaced satisfaction from comparing their country's consumer price index, which included relatively low energy-price increases, with the CPI's in other countries, which included relatively high energy-price increases. Throughout the period the Federal Government would point with pride to this false indicator of relatively superior performance.

Third, because the Canadian oil price was scheduled to rise in steps over many years, some future inflation could be fairly easily predicted. Anticipating this inflation, income demands were scaled upward accordingly, and the process took on the characteristics of a self-fulfilling prophesy. The Federal Government simply gave no credence to the notion that a price shock, if inevitable, should be taken quickly in order to minimize the cumulative inflationary consequences.

Fourth, the large gap between the domestic and world price for oil proved an irresistible lure to revenue-hungry governments, federal and provincial. New taxes were tacked onto energy consumption and added to the ultimate rise in final prices in this sector. By mid-1983, even though the price of gasoline to motorists reflected a lower average price to producers than the world price, Canadians generally paid more at the pump (adjusting for differences in currencies and the size of the gallon) than did most drivers in the United States.

The 1973-1974 oil-price surge spurred inflation and also dampened global demand because oil exporters did not spend all their increased revenues immediately. Most industrial countries chose not to offset lower nonenergy purchasing power with stimulus, and a sharp recession resulted. Canada experienced a downturn in its economy, but it was not deep enough to meet the technical definition of a recession. Government spending rose, both in real terms and to offset inflation, and taxes were cut, especially through programs aimed at encouraging saving. Also, as noted earlier, in 1974 Canadians were informed that beginning in 1975, the personal income tax system would be indexed for inflation by annual adjustments in the key exemptions and in brackets for computing marginal rates. All provinces except Quebec are tied to the federal personal income-tax collection system, and they simply acquiesced to this initiative.

The general recession in most industrial countries in 1974-1975 produced some slowing in inflationary forces in late 1975 and 1976. Although Canada narrowly avoided this recession, it benefited from a spillover of moderating inflation in the United States. The problem was that by the Summer of 1975 Canadian wages were still rising rapidly. Of particular concern was the fact that wages in Canada were going up roughly twice as fast as those in the United States. Business and government were rightly concerned that with the Canadian dollar remaining near parity against the U.S. dollar and with significantly lower productivity in most manufacturing industries, this differential wage escalation, if it persisted, signaled very serious problems for the future.

Since the late 1960's, the Canadian Federal Government had toyed with the notion of formal restraints on incomes. In the late Winter and Spring of 1975, the government held discussions with business and labor in an effort to obtain their support for a restraint package. These efforts failed, however, largely because the government proved too inflexible in the face of counterdemands from the other parties. As the Summer of 1975 came to a close, with the economy strengthening and wage increases remaining high, the Federal Government decided it had to act decisively (later statistics suggest that the rate of wage increase had peaked even before any special measures were taken).

The course adopted was a strategy of gradualism. It consisted of four tactical initiatives, not all of which were applied gradually. The four were in the areas of monetary, fiscal, wage-and-price, and structural policies. As an intellectual exercise, the package Canada introduced in the Fall of 1975 was soundly reasoned. In practice, however, the result was a bitter disappointment. An examination of the difference between theory and practice is important because such an examination shows clearly that the problems Canada has encountered must be laid at the feet of its politicians, not its economists.

Monetary Policy

The growth in monetary aggregates was allowed to surge upward in 1971, 1972, and 1973, in large part because of a desire to prevent the exchange rate from rising further than it had after the decision to allow the Canadian dollar to float. Monetary growth eased in 1974, but roared upward again in the first half of 1975. During the Summer of that year, the Bank of Canada became converted to monetarism. Control of inflation, the Governor of the Bank, Gerald Bouey, declared, required discipline to be exercised over the rate of money-supply growth. But the monetary rule could not be imposed immediately, it was decided, without causing a severe short-term recession with high levels of unemployment. Therefore, the central bank committed itself to a moderate but steady path of year-by-year reductions in the rate of growth of M-1 (the bank's preferred monetary indicator). It was the approach that led to the term *gradualism* being applied to the government's overall policy course, and it also described its vision as to the future path of inflation.

The Bank of Canada stuck with its intention in 1976, when all measures of the money supply (except M-3) recorded a marked reduction in rate of growth compared with 1975. Moreover, the Canadian dollar was allowed to fall sharply late in that year. Although the decline was attributed to Quebec's election of a government whose leadership was dedicated to seeking separation, subsequent events belie this federalist interpretation. Although the timing and initial pace of the decline were undoubtedly influenced by the election of the Parti Quebecois, the previous, and continuing, deterioration of the country's unit labor costs relative to those in the United States dictated a major adjustment in the level of the currency's international value.

As it turned out, however, the Canadian central bank did not stay the course it had set for itself. Although the picture varies somewhat, depending on the monetary aggregate employed (for example, M-3 recorded an increased rate of growth in 1976 but then fell off in 1977 and 1978), the bank's preferred indicator, M-1, showed an increase in the rate of growth in 1977 and 1978. Using the monetary base as the indicator, no significant further easing of monetary growth after 1976 could be observed until 1980.

The central bank's conversion to monetarism was thus a selective one, and public debate focused more on what the bank said it was doing than on what it actually did. The bank was somewhat misled by the decline in reported inflation in 1976 and 1977, on the one hand, and overly concerned to prevent too weak a performance in terms of output growth and unemployment, on the other hand. It was also slow to recognize structural changes that produced an upward shift in the velocity of M-1. Moreover, and crucially important, the central bank was anxious about the exchange-rate consequences of too large a positive differential emerging between Canadian and U.S. interest rates. Real rates were too low in both countries in this period. The United States, under President Carter, encouraged rapid GNP growth to bring down unemployment, and Canada, acting through the bank's policies, was unwilling to buck the trend. A premature return to rapid demand growth largely wiped out the progress made on inflation following from the 1974-1975 recession (and, in the case of Canada, the brief flirtation with strict monetary discipline).

Fiscal Policy

In an effort to obtain business and general public support for its overall policy package, the Federal Government pledged that it would keep its expenditure growth at no more than the trend rate of growth in the economy. This was, in effect, a pledge to stop the increase in the government share. This pledge was to be carried out immediately—no gradualism here. Government kept its word, but it is not clear that its commitment was sufficiently strong for the task.

Throughout this episode in policymaking, remarkably little attention was paid to the question of whether the government had frozen its share—which, as noted earlier, had increased significantly in the 1960's, at too high a level given its revenue base. If this was in fact the case, government was faced with an emerging squeeze on two counts. One was that real growth in the economy, measured on a per capita basis, was showing signs of slowing, and this weak performance continued for the rest of the 1970's and the early 1980's. The second factor was personal income-tax indexing.

The strongest argument for tax indexation is that it serves as a brake on government spending, which might otherwise be financed by inflationary windfalls rather than by formally legislated, and politically unpopular, tax increases.

The only problem with this logic is that it ignores the use of deficit financing to cover any revenue shortfall. Government budgetary deficits had become a major problem in Canada by the early 1980's and merit separate attention later. The point to note here is that the Federal Government's pledge in late 1975 represented no more than a commitment to prevent the existing situation from deteriorating further. If that existing situation represented a state of dynamic disequilibrium, the government did little that would restore fundamental balance.

Wage and Price Controls

In practice, controls on wages and prices, at least in peacetime, have failed to perform up to the promises of their designers and implementers. What almost always happens is that the controls are used as a substitute for sound monetary and fiscal policy. If there is any chance that they will work, that chance requires they be used to complement other policy tools used in an integrated manner to restore equilibrium in a disoriented economy. No way has been found to stop inflation without some pain, but, in theory, controls might ease the transition and its attendant costs in lost output and unemployment.

Such thoughts were very much on the mind of the Canadian Federal Government as it devised the policy package introduced in the Fall of 1975. The authorities knew they had to get monetary and fiscal policies "right" and thought they had the correct approaches for doing so. As already noted, monetary policy changes started off on the right foot, but the Bank of Canada failed to stay its stated course. Fiscal policy was conceived as having been put right, although limiting the growth in government spending—a reasonably tough political move—was not the same thing as reversing the impact of past trends toward excess.

The third part of the government's package was the introduction of a controls program administered by the newly created Anti-Inflation Board (AIB). Given the complexity of controlling costs and prices in a modern economy, the staff of the AIB was quite modestly small. As will always happen with any controls program, the AIB was plagued with claims of unfairness by specific groups of workers and firms. There have subsequently been many commentaries on the performance of AIB, with background analytical support cited spanning the entire gamut of sophistication. A consensus has emerged from these commentaries that the AIB produced quite limited results, and these results were more pronounced in their impact on wages than on prices.

My own assessment, which must be based on hypothesis rather than on careful empirical testing, is that the AIB was a failure for the simple reason that it was based on a set of general rules that did not address—in fact that made worse—the psychological dimensions of Canada's economic difficulties. Simply put, the rules the AIB administered were far too generous in the income gains they allowed. By trying to appear fair and logical, the government was largely ineffective.

The heart of the controls program lay in the calculation of allowable earnings increases for workers. This calculation was to consist of three factors. One was geared to meeting specific inflation targets in the future: 8 percent in 1976, 6 percent in 1977, and 4 percent in 1978, after which the program was scheduled to terminate. Wages were allowed to rise by these target amounts. If actual inflation exceeded the target, workers could make up the difference in the next year. If actual inflation fell below the target (as it did largely for fortuitous reasons in the first year of the program), however, workers were allowed to pocket the difference. This one-way process was subsequently altered in practice, but by then the damage had already been done.

A second feature of the basic AIB rules was that wages would be allowed to rise by up to 2 percentage points to reflect productivity gains. This figure was derived by taking the average economywide experience over the previous 20 years. Although the trend had deteriorated in the years immediately preceding the creation of the AIB, it was incompatible with the government's view of fairness to forecast that this break in trend would persist.

The third general provision was allowance of up to another 2 percentage points for workers whose past wage-increase experience had been to fall behind inflation. This allowance was applied on a selective basis, but it was completely at variance with the economic logic of differential wage adjustments as a mechanism for achieving microeconomic transitions.

Other features of the program involved maximum and minimum wage adjustments for which the general rules would be overridden. Rules on prices, which quickly replaced unworkable rules on profits, were aimed at allowing only "legitimate" cost pass-throughs. (We will not discuss these complex mechanics further because the focus of any effective controls program must be on the income side.) Dividend payments were strictly controlled by the AIB, but other forms of "unearned" income were not.

As was the case with the indexing of the personal income tax, the AIB rules were constructed using the CPI as the policy base. Both initiatives created the notion in the minds of average Canadians that they had acquired a "right" to be fully protected from all forms of inflation, regardless of source. This was in keeping with the notion, previously discussed, that inflation in Canada came from external, not internal, causes. The policy actions by the government, which culminated in the AIB, were fully consistent with this politically self-serving belief.

Full indexation of wages is incompatible with an effective anti-inflation strategy. It is impossible to offset three types of price increases that are recorded in the CPI: (1) prices that rise because real costs rise, as in the case of energy costs that go up because lower-cost sources are depleted; (2) rises in import costs owing to a depreciation of the national currency; and (3) the impact of indirect taxes that are raised to pay for increased government expenditures. All three types of CPI-inflating factors were present in Canada during the mid-to-late 1970's, and the protective influence of the AIB rules seriously impeded the process of adjustment to their effects that market forces would otherwise have encouraged.

It is highly instructive that when the AIB program was phased out several months ahead of schedule because of pressure from both business and labor, average income gains almost immediately fell below the levels that the AIB rules would have judged allowable. Indeed, labor generally was more successful in achieving real wage improvement during the AIB period than it has been subsequently.

Structural Policies

Determined to cover all bases, the Canadian Federal Government included a fourth area in its Fall, 1975 package: policies aimed at improving the microeconomic performance of the economy. The government failed miserably in this area for reasons that can be traced to the political pressures that microeconomic initiatives inevitably provoke.

The benefits of specific initiatives are generally widely spread and small in terms of per capita impacts; costs, in contrast, are borne by a relatively small number of individuals who have economic motivation to mobilize to fight them. Failing to accept that many small benefits add up to a large total when specific micro initiatives are cumulated, the government protected special interests and even took new actions to satisfy particular demands that were pressed with sufficient zeal. Examples of the process just described are legion: Marketing boards that sheltered inefficient producers were put in place or maintained. Public-service unions were granted benefits, the costs of which could not be met except through inflation in prices charged (a prime example being in the postal system). And firms that got into trouble through sloppy management were bailed out or bought up and placed on publicly funded welfare.

Going even further, the government enacted a series of legislative measures (at both the federal and provincial levels) that imposed new costs on the public and on the economy's performance. These measures included restrictions on foreign direct investments that have brought jobs, access to new technologies, and a more competitive managerial spirit to the Canadianization provisions of the National Energy Program (NEP).

It is not surprising, based on this review, that the package of policies adopted in the Fall of 1975 did not work. Following a marked drop in inflation as recorded in the CPI in 1976, price rises regained momentum and were higher in each subsequent year through 1981.

Stopping Inflation: Strategic Unemployment

The strategy of gradualism preoccupied Canada from late 1975 through early 1978, at which point the AIB controls program was terminated. Looking back over that period, one is struck by how little this conceptually integrated—and even innovative—strategic package actually accomplished. The Bank of Canada did stay the course, moving progressively toward lower and lower rates of M-1 growth until the strict monetary rule was being applied in the early 1980's. Nevertheless, inflation remained high until 1982. The Federal Government, sticking to its word, applied tough discipline on expenditure growth and, were it not for the impact of higher interest rates on the cost of carrying the national debt, did not increase its share of the country's total economic activity. Even so, the federal deficit increased massively, reaching about $30 billion in 1982-1983.

During the second half of the 1970's and until approximately the middle of 1981, Canada was put on hold until the imminent battle was joined. A deeply entrenched psychology of inflation could not be stopped until the full dimensions of a policy of tight monetary restraint were implemented completely. This began to happen only in late 1980, and even then it took time for the actors in the economy to become aware that this was not just another false start.

The so-called holding period was frustrating in the sense that inflation and unemployment fluctuated around a rising trend and the Canadian dollar fell significantly, if erratically, reaching the level of roughly $0.80 to the U.S. dollar (although it fell even lower for a brief period). However, nominal wage gains moved up almost in line with inflation for those still working and real output kept rising. (The real GNP rose by less than the expansion in potential GNP, reflecting the eroding effect of inflation on the gradually slowing growth in money supply.)

At one level, the actions regarding the NEP and the Foreign Investment Review Act (FIRA) provoked a sharply hostile response from foreign business interests and, with somewhat more moderation, certain foreign government officials. At another level, these actions produced massive shifts in capital flows into and out of Canada. The result of a major net outflow of capital was both a further, although only temporary drop, in the external value of the Canadian dollar (to $0.77 to the U.S. dollar), and upward pressure on Canadian interest rates (together with some strong warnings by the Bank of Canada regarding commercial bank lending to finance Canadian acquisition of assets held outside the country) to stem the tide.

The administration of FIRA has now been greatly eased, and it is unlikely that it will swing back again for many years. The NEP remains a major irritant internationally, but its main consequences in terms of Canada's inflation experience lies in its erroneous forecasts, a point to which we shall turn shortly.

The final level on which to discuss the NEP and FIRA is their impact on Canadian psychology. Although the West, specifically, and large segments of the Canadian business community, generally, reacted very negatively to these initiatives, the broad public strongly supported them. Such actions showed assertiveness and a determination to reshape the economic future of the country. They bought the government time in the face of mounting economic distress.

Canadian economic policy had begun a significant and dramatic shift by 1981. The strategy of gradualism had played itself out, and the country had moved to a new approach to stopping inflation: the strategy of unemployment. There were three main dimensions to this shift.

First in importance, the Bank of Canada, even though its actions had been slow and erratic, stayed with a course of bringing down money-supply growth. A move toward more monetarist policies in the United States seemed to help strengthen the Bank's resolve. It was determined not to pump up money-supply growth, even in the face of the slowing of real-output growth that followed inevitably when cost-induced inflation ate up the bulk of available money expansion.

Second, just before Ronald Reagan's election, the U.S. Federal Reserve Board moved decisively—no "gradualism" there—to adopt a significant tightening of monetary policy. The most immediate result was a sharp increase in interest rates, and Canada could not avoid a parallel increase in its rates. Thus, the Bank of Canada—and the government generally—could claim rates were high because of U.S. actions, thereby covering over the consequences of what it had much earlier decided was the only course for its own monetary policy.

The lesson here is important. Having a small, very open economy, Canada cannot control inflation through monetary policy alone—no matter how sound it might be—if the United States follows a basically different monetary-policy course. If the United States follows a similar sound course, however, then Canadian monetary policy operating in parallel can have a major anti-inflationary impact.

The third dimension of the shift was unintentional, but it is central to the explanation of why Canada experienced such a sharp recession in 1981-1982. The NEP would have made far more economic sense, although it would also have provoked far more external criticism, if world energy prices had continued the rapid increase the Canadian government had forecast. When these prices stabilized and then fell, the resource-abundance-induced complacency in Canada collapsed. By the end of 1983, the costs of the NEP to Canada had become monumental. Casting our focus more broadly, the general erosion in 1982 of commodity prices around the world hurt investment in Canadian resource industries profoundly. It has also reversed the situation Canada experienced during much of the 1970's, when commodity-price movements yielded a positive terms-of-trade effect for Canadian real incomes.

The sudden end to Canadian complacency was beyond the ability of government to alter through activism. Its massive deficits prevented it from introducing significant new fiscal stimulus. Investment fell sharply as new markets dried up for what Canada thought foreign buyers would always pay dearly to obtain. Consumers, worried about their futures, turned toward protection via personal saving, with the rate of personal saving rising from 10 percent to just over 15 percent of disposable income. The only expanding component of demand was an improvement in the country's current account balance. Import demand fell sharply, but exports (70 percent going to the United States) remained steady in dollar terms.

Beginning in the middle of 1981, Canada went through by far its worst post-World War II recession. From its prerecession peak, real GNP fell by 6 percent through the end of 1982. Unemployment rose to just under 13 percent of the labor force. But even though unemployment averaged 11 percent in 1982, the rate of inflation measured by the CPI still averaged 10.8 percent that year. Even so, the inflationary psychology had been reversed dramatically; by December, 1983, the CPI was only 4.2 percent higher than it had been a year earlier.

A development to note with respect to the rapid decline in Canadian inflation over the period since roughly the middle of 1982 is the government's "6 & 5" program. This federal initiative had two major components. The first, and more controversial, applied the limits of 6 percent and 5 percent to wage increases for federal and parafederal employees in the first two years following the termination of existing contracts. Most of the provinces eventually adopted their own versions of public-sector controls, broadly similar to the federal program.

A nation's economy can be divided into three segments. One is the market segment, in which prices and wages respond reasonably flexibly and quickly to changes in demand for its output. Even a mild recession has a rapid impact on this segment.

The second segment is the private "power" portion in which prices are administered by oligopoly-dominated firms, and wages are set in negotiations with generally powerful unions. Once a strong inflationary trend is established in this segment, it takes a fairly strong recession to brake that momentum. By the middle of 1982, Canada's recession was more than deep enough to stop inflation in these two parts of the economy. Prices were no longer rising rapidly, and gains in wages (and especially in salaries) were down sharply when new contracts were signed.

The problem lay in the third segment: the public "power" portion. As noted earlier, this had become a very big slice of the Canadian economy, and it was the slowest reacting to recessionary conditions (although it, too, did respond eventually). The "6 & 5" program was a politically astute way to speed that reaction.

The second component of "6 & 5" applied these limits to certain transfer payments and to the indexing applied to personal income taxation. Because inflation came down so dramatically in 1983, these limits have involved little real cost. From a psychological perspective, however, the limits signaled a toughness in government resolve that was totally lacking in the earlier AIB program.

Is it really fair to speak of a "strategy of unemployment" in Canada? This is not what the government overtly set out to achieve, but it is what its anti-inflationary policy approach has, in effect, become. By the end of 1983, real output had more than regained its prerecession peak. As already noted, inflation had come down to just over 4 percent. But unemployment was still at 11.1

percent of the labor force in December, 1983, unchanged from October and November. The United States, by contrast, closed the year at 8.2 percent unemployment, and this differential relative to Canada was large in comparison with historical norms.

The problem is that the government concluded that it had almost no room to move to bring the unemployment rate down faster. Its deficit was a problem, especially in the view of a business community the government was trying to cultivate. Its interest-rate policy was dictated by U.S. policy in this area. The Bank of Canada recognized the probability of a very large, and potentially inflation-generating, fall in the Canadian dollar if it pushed interest rates in Canada noticeably below those in the United States.

If the government faced a public that understood economics better, it might stimulate the economy by underwriting a variety of output-expanding investments without incurring permanent increases in its deficits or any significant rise in domestic investment rates. As it is, however, the government is taking the path of least resistance on the unemployment problem, just as it did earlier on the inflation problem. That path involves arguments that unemployment has structural dimensions that cannot be responded to quickly. Meanwhile, having had these arguments accepted by the 89 percent of the labor force that is working and enjoying the benefits of a much lower inflation rate, the government takes credit for devising a successful strategy as growth moderates the slack in labor markets.

Several other factors help to explain public tolerance for the lackluster performance of the Canadian economy in this period. One key factor was that the U.S. economy was doing poorly in many respects at this time as well. For a while, U.S. inflation climbed noticeably higher than did Canadian inflation, and U.S. unemployment was also well above that country's earlier experience. Canadians use the United States as a reference point, and when they see their neighbor in economic distress—and wandering around in search of effective solutions—they tend to relax at least somewhat their criticisms—and their expectations—of their own leaders.

Another, and very important, factor was a continuing activism on the part of the Federal Government. The Canadian people did show their displeasure with the Trudeau government by electing a minority Progressive Conservative government in May, 1979. But that government blundered into another election a few months later when a moderately tough, but quite realistic, budget was defeated in Parliament. The Liberals swept back into power with deceptive treatment of the energy pricing issue and, more importantly, in my judgment, promises that only they could take control over the country's destiny through firm Canada-first actions that blunted foreign influences.

The 1980 federal election and the policy action that followed were fed by sentiments referred to earlier: that the nation's economic problems were largely of external origin and that Canada had the internal wherewithal to shield itself if only it exercised its sovereignty more firmly. Following their return to office, the Liberals set about devising a dramatic new initiative to increase domestic control of Canada's oil and gas industry. This initiative was brought forward in October, 1980, with the announcement of the National Energy Program (NEP). Also in this period the government made life more difficult for potential foreign investors in Canada through changes in the administration of the Foreign Investment Review Act (FIRA), and with threats of even tougher measures on the near horizon.

Quite apart from the political persuasiveness of this approach, its economic logic is shaky. On the one hand, if current unemployment can be explained on structural grounds, then it is hard to understand why inflation continues to decline. If this anomaly can be rationalized, on the other hand, one has to wonder what types of structural policy initiatives the government has in mind for dealing with the problem. There are high costs arising from unemployment, but the debate in Canada has not yet begun to address them, possibly because of relief that the inflation-braking deep recession of 1981-1982 appears over.

Canada's inflation experience appears to be largely ended, at least for now. The importance of monetary discipline has been well learned and well implemented. The need to restrain government expenditures on consumption-augmenting programs has also been fairly well recognized. In 1984, the country will go to the polls to elect a new Federal Government. The contest to assume the prime ministership will not include Pierre Trudeau, and the odds currently favor two men, Brian Mulroney and John Turner, both of whom will carry on with determination the effort to keep inflation down.

Looking to the future, however, Canada's economic prospects are unclear. My assessment is that Canada will continue to follow a monetary policy that keeps its inflation roughly in line with U.S. inflation. If U.S. inflation stays down, however, monetary policy alone cannot solve Canada's unemployment difficulties. Unless one or more of the following three steps is taken, the Canadian economy is likely to operate well below its potential for many years into the future:

(1) Stop worrying about the government deficit and take whatever initiatives are necessary to acquire net foreign financial inflows to help pay for it. (Any further increase in the government deficit would hurt business confidence, however, and the probability of a steady depreciation in the currency would add to the inflation-unemployment trade-off-problem.)

(2) Undertake efforts to reduce the power concentrations within the Canadian economy, beginning, most probably, in the unionized sector. The problem, however, is that government has had a large hand either in creating power bases or in allowing these bases to be used to increase pressures on prices and costs.

(3) Launch a comprehensive economic strategy to focus on two supply-side initiatives: One would involve major efforts to rationalize Canadian industry to adjust to the combination of reduced tariff barriers under GATT

and much more intense competition for markets from newly industrialized players in the international arena; the other would involve a massive commitment to changing and increasing the skill levels and improving the geographic mobility of the Canadian labor force. A strategic initiative of the required magnitude would run into many problems. It would cost a great deal of money, raising government deficits over a long period. The high degree of government involvement in the restructuring would raise business fears and would involve very tricky negotiations at both the federal-provincial and the Canada-United States levels. Nevertheless, many thoughful—as well as many not-so-thoughful—observers of the Canadian economic scene have concluded that the dimensions of the tasks facing the country require initiatives on this grand scale.

Thus, there can in truth be no conclusion to this Canadian story. Inflation got out of hand, but pragmatic responses after a number of false starts brought it down to manageable proportions. Bringing unemployment down as well will be a far more difficult task. If unemployment remains high, there is always the lurking danger that, in the future, a government will come along with a strong bias for sacrificing price stability for a better near-term growth performance. Living with that danger has forced adjustments in the operations of Canadian financial institutions so that business can carry on.

Responses in the Financial Sector

As was the case in other countries, in Canada high inflation led to high interest rates. Moreover, periodic changes in the government's approach to inflation produced wide swings in both nominal and real interest rates. The nation's financial institutions and practices, which had matured during a period of relatively low and stable rates, were forced to change markedly in response to lender and borrower reactions to this new inflationary environment.

For the commercial banking system, rising and erratic interest rates resulted in a shortening of the average maturity of its term deposits. Greatly increased interest-rate sensitivity came to characterize bank liabilities as these term deposits, together with the banks' notice deposits, constituted a growing proportion of total claims on the system. Since bank assets had a longer maturity structure and were thus less capable of being altered quickly to reflect changing monetary conditions, the increased interest-rate sensitivity of liabilities squeezed bank earnings.

To protect themselves, banks and other financial intermediaries made growing use of relatively new loan instruments that incorporated variable rates and variable terms. Although business loans had been at the prime rate or prime plus before, the practice was extended and variations were applied increasingly to residential mortgage loans during the 1970's. By 1982, it is estimated, roughly half the business loans made in Canada, and approximately one-third of new mortgages, had adjustable interest-rate features. Variable-term mortgages are not yet common in Canada, as they are in some other countries, but variability in terms for business financing has increased through the greater use of bonds and debentures with retractable (or callable) and extendable features, and through the incorporation of convertibility provisions in the debt instruments brought to market.

The introduction of loans with greater variability in interest-rate terms was a natural outgrowth of the increased interest-rate sensitivity of bank liabilities. This had the effect of shifting much of the interest-rate risk from banks to corporate and household borrowers. Although this change in the loan-making process allowed the banks to serve their primary function—financial intermediation—more efficiently and effectively, the banks have been caught in a negative publicity trap when interest rates declined sharply in a short time span. The press can be relied upon to report on stories of mortgage holders who bet wrong and took mortgage renewals for three or five years at rates they thought would be lower than they could get in the future—only to see rates drop, locking them in to exceedingly burdensome mortgage payments for several years. The issue of the banks' responsibility to allow for refinancing in such circumstances is extremely complicated and remains to be resolved.

For the corporate sector, flexibility in bank loans provided a welcome alternative to financing through the issuance of long-term debt at the high rates purchasers of bonds and debentures demanded. Although this reliance on bank loans creates potentially serious problems for corporate treasurers and makes companies much more vulnerable during cyclical downturns, firms were often faced with no other effective choice. Corporate borrowing by nonfinancial institutions was supplied by banks to the extent of only 12 percent of the total in 1967, but that figure has risen to about 40 percent more recently. What choices did exist came from favorable tax treatment of dividends that increased the attractiveness of preferred share issues; from the use of extendables, retractables, and convertibles, noted earlier; and from the possibility of borrowing in the United States when interest-rate differentials widened sufficiently, as in 1975, 1977, and 1981.

Another impact of the high interest rates that accompany inflationary economic conditions has been a concerted effort by corporations to maximize the return on their short-term assets. In response, Canadian banks have provided concentration accounts, whereby corporate funds are consolidated into a pooled holding and managed on a daily basis. These funds are then either invested in short-term money instruments or, when in excess of near-term needs, targeted to pay down outstanding bank loans. This service is now provided to both large and small business customers. The results of this innovation are seen in a shift in corporate deposits with banks from the demand to the nonpersonal term and notice categories. The split was about 65 percent to 35 percent in 1967, but has shifted more recently to about 20 percent as against 80 percent.

Several other changes arising in the banking sector can be noted more briefly:

(1) Beginning in the mid-1970's, banks began to eliminate the use of compensating balances. This provision had enabled businesses to borrow at preferred rates if they kept a portion of the loan receipts in demand deposits at the lending bank. Banks decided to make loan terms more straightforward by phasing out this practice and raising the interest rates on loans to reflect their true cost.

(2) About the same time, banks moved to make greater use of marginal costing for their services. The resulting unbundling meant that a package of services was no longer provided to clients without charge or at a nominal fee in return for maintaining a set level of demand deposits.

(3) In May, 1967, noncheckable savings accounts were introduced, bearing a higher rate of interest than checking accounts. Rates paid on fixed-term deposits were also increased in an effort to lengthen the maturity of the banks' liabilities.

(4) In September, 1979, daily interest noncheckable savings accounts were introduced, reflecting the impact of the computerization of accounts on the trend away from demand deposits. (Since 1981, daily interest checkable accounts have also existed in Canada.)

Government borrowers have been hit by the same forces as corporate and mortgage borrowers and have responded in a similar manner. One of the more interesting features of Federal Government financing is the degree of reliance placed on Canadian Savings Bonds (CSB's). The first CSB issue in 1946 replaced wartime bonds sold to Canadians to help finance the war effort. That first issue raised just under $500 million, but subsequent annual issues have increased steadily in size. Following the 1983 campaign, CSB's outstanding amounted to over $33 billion, just under a third of total Federal Government debt outstanding.

CSB's are the nearest thing Canada has to an indexed bond. They can be converted to cash, plus accrued interest, at any time, but they are nonmarketable. The rates are set to be attractive in relation to alternative short-term interest rates at the time of issue, which they have to be because of the large turnover that has to be refinanced each year. More importantly, because of the exceptionally high liquidity of CSB's, the government is faced with a constant problem of cashing in during periods of rising rates. As a result, ingenious bonus provisions have been made over the past decade, with the bonus payments being eligible for treatment as capital gains upon receipt, in an effort to restrict withdrawals.

During the 1970's, the Federal Government and most of the provincial governments saw a marked shrinking in the terms structure of debt outstanding because costs for long-term bond financing became prohibitive. As a result, much greater reliance was placed on the use of Treasury bills and shorter-term bonds. One outcome was a feeding of the supply side of the money market, which helped this relatively new element of the Canadian financial market expand rapidly. Regardless of what happens to the rate of inflation in the future, the money market will stay very active, now that it has matured, because it is responsive to so many needs.

The impact of inflation on Canadian financial markets has been negative in a number of respects, including: the virtual disappearance of the market for corporate long-term debt issues; a wave of mergers and acquisitions as corporations became convinced that buying was a superior alternative to building; and an overemphasis on acquiring nonoutput-generating assets as inflation hedges. On the positive side, financial markets became far more flexible and efficient as inflation left participants with no other choice. Now that Canadian inflation is down, the country's financial structure will help keep it down. If inflation surges again in the future, however, it will not catch the financial system unprepared.

SWITZERLAND

Nicolas Krul*

"BUT SWITZERLAND is unique"—is a not infrequent reflection by outsiders on the Swiss economy. This attitude fails to recognize that the country's sound performance in economic matters has as often been achieved *despite* its unique features as *because* of them. Superficially, the Swiss experience may appear to some to lack the flesh and blood of real political and economic life, and may seem to fail to provide credible guidance for the economic policies of others. Nonetheless, there are several aspects of policymaking worth noting, not the least of which is an unflagging propensity to do what is possible, prudent and intelligent, and to reject doctrinaire, a priori reasoning. In this respect, the dogged struggle against inflation has been no exception.

The Struggle Against Inflation: Pressures and Contradictions

After a decade of growth and stability, the 1960's saw the Swiss economy bump up against suddenly accelerating prices. To be sure, Switzerland had experienced inflationary bouts in the past, and was keenly sensitive to the instability that had bedeviled the countries around her for quite some time. Nevertheless, the return of Europe to the discipline of external convertibility at the end of 1958, and an average annual price increase of around 1 percent during the easy 1950's, fed the idea that preceding inflations had been associated with particular, noneconomic disturbances, and that the menace was now safely laid to rest. When prices started to accelerate to an annual rate of 4.2 percent in the second half of 1962, complacency was, therefore, rudely shattered—all the more so because no external forces could be incriminated. At the same time that the country was confronted with a deterioration of its relative price performance, there was a singular paucity of policy instruments to remedy the situation.

The Swiss National Bank (SNB) alone had remained alert to the dangers of domestic inflation. In 1956, the SNB had warned that large and recurring inflows of capital were fomenting an excessive domestic expansion of credit and

*General Manager, Gulf and Occidental Investment Company S.A., Geneva, Switzerland.

demand. Over the next several years it stressed that low interest rates, while failing to stem such inflows, were financing an investment boom critically dependent upon a rapid increase in foreign labor (then representing some 25 percent of the total labor force). Even earlier, in 1952, the SNB had unsuccessfully sought to have a minimum reserve requirement incorporated into the revised law governing its powers.

That episode, and subsequent events, lay bare the three perennial problems of Swiss anti-inflationary policy. The first difficulty is fairly universal. The basic theory of inflation and its control are fragile and, therefore, spawn a controversial variety of policy prescriptions. In the case of Switzerland, such difficulties were further compounded because the newly regained prosperity had not entirely eradicated the fear of an unavoidable deflationary transition from war to peace (or from postwar reconstruction to normal times). That fear had been explicitly translated into the somewhat one-sidedly Keynesian guidance to policy that was incorporated into the "economic articles" of the Swiss Constitution in 1947.

The second difficulty, which Switzerland shares with other small European countries, is the openness of its economy. Switzerland's total population approximates that of a modern metropolis. Its economy is dependent on exports and imports of goods and services to the tune of 35.4 percent and 35.1 percent, respectively, of its gross domestic product (1982). Nonetheless, the trade flows are small in comparison to the capital flows associated with Switzerland's role as an international financial center. In the view of many, the fact that Swiss financial institutions serve as intermediaries to world capital flows and the consequent obligation that fact imposes on the country to peg its exchange rate precluded an effective Swiss business-cycle policy.

The third problem, however, is peculiar to Switzerland itself: the confederal structure of government and the strict application of direct democracy within that confederal framework. First, the Swiss confederal structure vests sovereignty in the cantons, which only partially delegate power to the central government. Fiscal sovereignty is thus mainly exercised by the cantons, which control 86 percent of total revenue and 84 percent of total expenditure, leaving the central government with a negligible policy base that is almost 70 percent reliant on indirect taxation. Further, the cantons apply their fiscal policies without any regard to macroeconomic national considerations or monetary policy links. Finally, both cantonal and federal tax laws are subject to compulsory electoral approval and/or a referendum organized at the initiative of the voters.

In practice, the political system provides for explicit tax-to-expenditure trade-offs under direct electoral control in the context of an ingrained resistance to any increase in the nominal rates of taxation. On two occasions, in 1970 and in 1977, the Federal Council (the Swiss Cabinet) and the majority of the political parties proposed new constitutional articles to improve the confederation's financial balance and the flexibility of its fiscal policy. The proposals were twice rejected by the voters.

The inculcated notion that centralized policymaking would automatically weaken the confederal political structure has fortified ideological resistance to an active economic policy at the national level. For example, in 1962, when new policy measures were discussed to correct a situation of patent overheating of the economy, a member of the seven-person Federal Council attacked such views as being "in direct contradiction with the principles which govern our economic system. . . and most likely to introduce a counterproductive element in the precision mechanism of our complex market economy." And the chairman of the Swiss Banking Corporation expressed the bankers' view that cyclical policies "the relevance and efficacy of which are contested by a large part of the population. . .would introduce a measure of legal uncertainty and inequality in a way incompatible with the traditional structure of responsibilities."

The combination of a confederal structure—that is, a widely dispersed decision-making process—with a deeply embedded political laissez-faire preference exposes the Swiss economy to private or semiofficial economic pressure groups with the power to influence pricing and policymaking. Almost 30 years ago, a former member of the cabinet pointed out that "it is no exaggeration to state that the central government consults, in virtually all important matters of policy, with all kinds of organizations, whether their objectives are oriented toward the public good or purely self-serving. Consultation with the professional bodies has become the backbone of the system and, one can say, its normal foundation."[1]

In Switzerland, more than in any other Western industrial country, the pricing and policymaking record demonstrates that when professional organizations become an integral component of decision making in a political system that lacks the capacity to constrain or to compensate, the economy as a whole risks domination by contradictory claims, rather than dominating those contradictions. Thus, by March, 1964, the pressures and contradictions of its own system submerged the Swiss economy. Both the cantons and the private economy were finally forced to concede that centralized direct intervention could no longer be postponed. Despite violent opposition, the Federal Council imposed a sweeping stabilization program through an emergency procedure provided for by the constitution. Switzerland was thus launched onto the troubled waters of inflation and of anti-inflation policy.

The Shoals of Inflation: 1964-1973

The decrees of March, 1964, which covered monetary policy, the construction industry, and the labor market, were initially conceived as transitory measures. Domestic forces continued to thwart more systematic endeavors that

---

[1] P. Rubatel, "Les relations confederation-groupements interesses." 64th supplement to *la vie economique,* Bern, 1957.

might have reformed the fiscal structure; enhanced the Swiss National Bank's authority to make policy; and attenuated the distortive influences of existing institutional income-distribution arrangements. Opposition to centralized policy remained strong, even though, as the *Economist* observed in 1964: "The healthy refusal of the Swiss to hold Bern in awed respect is not matched by a willingness to do all those rather troublesome and expensive things that would make it unnecessary for Bern to extend its authority." To make matters worse, external events offered little respite. The West German revaluation of 1961, although very small, ushered in the era of currency crises that culminated in the 1971 breakdown of the Bretton Woods system.

Currency unrest, which began with the events of May, 1968, in France, destabilized capital flows and threatened the European payments system. The 1964-1973 phase of Swiss policy became a bewildering succession of stop-gap measures aimed at containing external disturbances and, at the same time, laboriously defusing domestic demand pressures. With hindsight, however, the policy interventions of 1964 to 1973 can reasonably be credited as having had both a measure of strategic unity and a favorable longer-term impact.

The Shift to Policy Activism After 1964

The tenacious efforts of the Federal Council and the Swiss National Bank to establish at least the principle of a national monetary policy gradually succeeded. Beginning in 1964, from decree to decree and one gentleman's agreement to another, Parliament and the banking industry were grudgingly prodded into acceptance of an active monetary policy. The 1970 report of the Bank for International Settlements (BIS) noted revealingly: "At the beginning of September the [Swiss] monetary authorities reached a gentleman's agreement with the major banks on the principles on which credit ceilings and marginal minimum reserve requirements could be applied if necessary. Simultaneously a ceiling was imposed on total domestic lending. . .In the circumstances it was decided not to proceed with legislative proposals to widen the scope of the National Bank's policy instruments."

Similarly, although successive initiatives to rationalize fiscal policy continued to be shipwrecked on the shoals of cantonal and taxpayer opposition, efforts to regain financial balance began to receive a more tolerant reception. The legal (but vague) stipulations concerning compensation for income tax "bracket creep" were quietly shelved and federal indirect taxes were regularly increased, with the result that the Swiss income elasticity of taxation came to stand at 1.21 between 1960 and 1970, compared with 1.06 in West Germany and 1.15 for the OECD nations as a whole.

On the other hand, the growth of public expenditure slowed from nearly 11 percent per annum to a still excessive 9 percent. The public sector remained a procyclical element, but it was at least able to avoid the outlandish deficits incurred in other countries and to confound the worst of the domestic extrapolations that the early 1960's had inspired.

A policy-induced shift of the industrial structure from labor-intensive industry to industries that were skill and capital intensive was an important strategic gain. The main instrument for effecting these policies was a strict application of the immigration law of 1931. Between 1956 and 1964, the non-Swiss segment of the labor force had increased by about 50,000 workers a year, or at an annual rate of 1.7 percent of the active population. This influx raised the foreign component of Swiss civilian employment from 8 percent in 1950 to a peak of 30 percent in 1964. Subsequently, the new regulations reduced the number of foreign workers by 28,000 a year between 1965 and 1978, thus diminishing the foreign component to 23 percent by 1980. The diminution of labor supply stimulated two shifts: from labor-intensive to skill-and-capital-intensive industry; and from investment in infrastructure to investment in the higher-technology industries. It also revived the extensive emphasis on vocational training (through traditional apprenticeship programs and compulsory attendance at trade schools) that Switzerland had originally developed in the nineteenth century in order to catch up with England and France, and later systematized in the 1978 Vocational Training Act.

Labor productivity (defined as real GDP per person employed) increased from the 1 to 2 percent range that prevailed in the early 1960's to a 4 to 5 percent range by the end of the decade. Furthermore, trade policies (tariff reductions) put specific pressure on labor-intensive industries and such uneconomic lines of production as footwear, clock and watchmaking, textiles, clothing, bulk chemicals, and simple machinery. Another positive longer-term development was the overdue discovery of, and subsequent efforts to remedy, the statistical and analytical precariousness of Swiss economic policymaking.

Nonetheless, the cyclical results of the 1964 switch to policy activism were disappointing. The shift did initially succeed in reducing demand—but at the expense of intensifying cost pressures. Labor-market policy increased pressures on wages by tightening supply and slowing the promotion of Swiss workers. Hourly earnings in industry, which had risen at an annual rate of around 4.5 percent between 1959 and 1962, climbed sharply at around 8 percent a year between 1963 and 1966. Between 1960 and 1973, real wage growth was 5.2 percent annually, compared with a "warranted" real wage growth of 3.4 percent. Reactivation of interest-rate policy, while endeavoring to minimize the incentive for a repatriation of Swiss capital that had been invested abroad (over which no controls could be exercised), also pumped up interest costs, which were then transmitted to the cost of living via the large Swiss mortgage market.

Last, but not least, indexation of agricultural incomes, coupled with price and market guarantees plus protection against foreign competition, transformed the agricultural sector into a source of chronic inflation with adverse consequences well beyond the food sector.

The Reappearance of Demand Inflation: 1969-1972

Against this background, the old bogey of demand inflation reappeared in the wake of the worldwide recovery from the 1967-1968 slowdown and the capital inflows triggered by speculation on the possible revaluation of the deutsche mark in 1969. Swiss exports, which had grown at an average rate of 4.4 percent per year in 1966 and 1967, increased by 9.7 percent in 1968 and 13 percent in 1969. A sharp rise in private consumption and investment followed in 1970 and 1971, lifting the rate of growth of the domestic product well above the normal growth rate of the economy.

Aided by a substantial deterioration in the terms of trade resulting from a strong rise in import prices, the domestic upswing induced an adverse swing in current account equal to about 3 percent of GNP. However, the liquidity effect of the external current account deficit was more than recouped by a sudden reversal in asset preferences of both domestic and foreign investors, who became increasingly convinced that a devaluation of the dollar and a concomitant appreciation of the Swiss franc were inevitable. Their convictions were amply vindicated in May, 1971, when the Bundesbank, followed by the central banks of Austria, Belgium, the Netherlands and Switzerland, suspended official exchange operations—and when subsequent events in August and December of 1971 resulted in a 13.9 percent upvaluation of the Swiss franc vis-a-vis the U.S. dollar.

Capital inflows slowed during a short period after the Smithsonian Agreement of December, 1971, that reset exchange parities. But, within months, the inflows again became a flood, totally swamping domestic liquidity ratios. Serious steps were taken to dampen capital inflows. On February 14, 1972, the SNB imposed a compulsory foreign-exchange conversion program on the commercial banks. In March, minimum reserve requirements on bank liabilities to nonresidents were increased to 100 percent. In June, a referendum approved and prolonged the urgent federal decree "to safeguard the currency." Thereafter, until January, 1973, when the Swiss National Bank finally allowed the Swiss franc to float, twelve additional policy measures were introduced in a vain struggle to regain control over the creation of domestic liquidity.

In short, starting in 1969, Switzerland had become an economy caught between domestic and foreign exchange policies. A climax was reached in the twelve months between March, 1971 and March, 1972, when official intervention in the foreign-exchange market caused the Swiss monetary base (deposits of the Swiss private sector with, and notes issued by, the Swiss National Bank) to rise by 47 percent a year, and M-1 (currency and demand deposits in the hands of the nonbank public) to increase by 26 percent a year. Not surprisingly, inflation—propelled both by rising costs and by the creation of excess liquidity—accelerated from 4.7 percent a year (as measured by the consumer price index) during the 1964-1970 period, to 6.6 percent in 1971, 6.7 percent in 1972, 8.7 percent in 1973, and 9.8 percent in 1974. By that time, however, inflation had become endemic in all OECD nations. Although it deteriorated

Table 1

Swiss Price Indexes[1]

Export Prices	1960-1967	1967-1973
OECD Countries	200	78
Major Countries	200	82
Smaller European Countries	177	77
West Germany	228	129
Swiss Index (absolute annual change)	3.2 percent	3.6 percent
Import Prices		
OECD Countries	160	71
Major Countries	178	68
Smaller European Countries	133	79
West Germany	267	155
Swiss Index (absolute annual change)	1.6 percent	3.4 percent
Consumer Price Index		
OECD Countries	133	94
Major Countries	144	96
Smaller European Countries	84	82
West Germany	133	119
Swiss Index (absolute annual change)	4.7 percent	6.2 percent
Implicit GNP Deflator		
OECD Countries	157	111
Major Countries	168	115
Smaller European Countries	102	93
West Germany	142	117
Swiss Index (absolute annual change)	4.7 percent	6.2 percent

[1]Swiss Indexes expressed as a percent of other indexes.

in absolute terms, Switzerland's price performance improved relative to that of most other industrial countries. (See Table 1.)

The Floating Rate Regime

The Swiss decision in January, 1973, to allow the franc to float—like the subsequent dollar devaluation of February 12, 1973, and the March decision of the EEC countries to manage a joint float—occurred against a background of rampant chaos in the exchange markets and with the belief that the convulsion would turn out to be the last major tribulation in the quest for a new set of stable exchange-rate relationships among the major countries. Indeed, in its communique of March 27, 1973, the Committee of Twenty of the IMF

167

recognized that "floating rates could provide a useful technique in particular situations but that a reformed system exchange rate regime should once again be based on stable but adjustable par values."

In the initial phases, the floating Swiss franc was considered to be a temporary by-product of the contradictions that then assailed an economy that was monetarily integrated with the U.S. dollar zone but commercially integrated with Europe. Gradually, however, as the prospect of international monetary reform receded, the float of the Swiss franc came to be viewed as a significant domestic policy event that provided an opportunity for regaining national monetary authority. Indeed, it was no coincidence that the Swiss National Bank was among the first (in 1974) to specify a declared target for the growth rate of monetary aggregates as a means of firmly signaling its intention to limit the rate of monetary expansion, while at the same time emphasizing its responsibility so to do. In a sense, the acceptance of a floating exchange rate put the Swiss National Bank firmly in control of the Swiss money stock and thereby considerably strengthened its ability to wage an effective war on inflation.

Developments from 1973-1979

As matters turned out, the distress that began to engulf the world through volatile exchange rates, erratic capital flows, and steeply rising energy costs overwhelmed the theoretical autonomy of Swiss monetary policy. External uncertainties and domestic responses generated an opportunistic mix of ad hoc adjustments that at one point included broad capital controls; a prohibition on payment of interest on existing nonresident bank deposits; negative interest (at an annual rate of 40 percent per annum on new nonresident deposits); limits on forward operations and foreign borrowings; selective credit ceilings; quantitative domestic liquidity measures; restrictive regulations aimed at public issues in the financial markets; building restrictions; wage, price and profit guidelines; and new limitations on the inflow of foreign labor.

Gradually, the overly formidable policy assault, the steep appreciation of the Swiss franc, and the recessionary impact of higher energy costs jointly exerted a draconian squeeze on economic activity. Real GNP, which had decelerated from an annual average rate of growth of over 4.1 percent between 1969 and 1973 to a 1.7 percent growth rate in 1974, fell by more than 7 percent in 1975. As a consequence, the consumer price index, which rose at a 6.7 percent rate in 1975, slowed to 1.7 percent in 1976.

The very success of the Swiss domestic adjustment, which was accompanied by current account surpluses of $2.6 billion in 1975 and $3.5 billion (nearly 6 percent of GNP) in 1976, revived strong upward pressures on the exchange rate of the Swiss franc. Starting in 1975, intervention in the exchange market was required to hold down the franc. The lesson was clear: A free-floating exchange rate allowed Switzerland to regain control of its domestic monetary policy, but it posed enormous problems for a small industrial country that also has a very large financial sector.

In 1976, the volume of uncontrolled Swiss-franc-denominated deposits in the Eurocurrency markets amounted to 53 percent of the domestic Swiss franc money supply (M-2). This ratio rose to 84 percent by 1980. For the overall period 1973-1980, the average ratio of Euro-Swiss francs to domestic Swiss francs was 65 percent, compared with 46 percent for deutsche marks and 22 percent for the U.S. dollar.

In 1978, a further appreciation of the Swiss franc, by more than 20 percent between March and September of that year, led to intense pressure from exporting industries. Therefore, the tight money-supply target was abandoned; controls over capital exports were relaxed; and the central bank engaged in massive purchases of foreign currency. As a result, M-1 increased over the year by 16.6 percent instead of by the originally targeted 5 percent, and rose at a 32.5-percent annual rate during the six months prior to March, 1979. As a consequence of these changes in policy, the exchange rate of the Swiss franc (adjusted for relative inflation) dropped by 13 percent between the second quarter of 1979 and the second quarter of 1981. In part this fall reflected the opposite shift in U.S. monetary policy, which was tightened in 1979 in order to correct the previous fall in the exchange rate of the dollar.

One more lesson was learned from the experience of 1978-1979: For an export-dependent economy like Switzerland, both the stability of the real exchange rate and the stability of its general price level are indispensible conditions for balanced growth. Because it is difficult simultaneously to achieve exchange-rate stability and money-stock targets, the central bank has to reserve its right to depart temporarily from one of the targets if the Swiss economy is seriously disrupted by movements in the other. The Swiss authorities temporarily abandoned their monetary-growth target in 1978. The hope that a temporary rise in the money stock would not provoke price consequences proved to be ill founded. The rise in consumer prices, quiescent at a 1.1 percent rate in 1978, ineluctably accelerated to 3.6 percent in 1979, 4 percent in 1980, and to around 6.5 percent in 1981 and 1982. In part, the rise was caused by the second oil-price shock. Nevertheless, the acceleration also demonstrated once again that the simultaneous pursuit of both exchange-rate and money-supply (or interest rate) targets is illusory.

Monetary Policy Reactivated

Persistent weakness of the Swiss franc (which fell from a high of 1.45 francs per dollar in the third quarter of 1979 to around 2.15 in the middle of 1982), coupled with the reversal of capital flows induced by exchange-rate depreciation, presented Swiss monetary policy with an opportunity to come into its own once more. In January, 1979, the Swiss National Bank started to dismantle its impressive array of direct intervention measures, notably by repealing (1) the decrees prohibiting the purchase by nonresidents of Swiss portfolio securities; (2) the negative rate of interest imposed on new foreign inflows; and (3) the ban on interest payments to nonresident holdings.

By early 1980, most of the emergency measures had been abolished or rendered dormant (i.e., incorporated in the now partially revised federal law concerning the SNB). At the same time, the SNB was able to resume a more traditional monetary policy. Firstly, it was allowed to set a target for the monetary base rather than as before for M-1; secondly, it was allowed to broaden the method of monetary-base control to include not just direct intervention but also minimum reserve requirements, the sale of so-called sterilization rescriptions (short-term notes), and foreign-exchange interventions and swaps; thirdly, because the authorities reluctantly acknowledged that the Swiss franc had become an international currency, the SNB was allowed to undertake forward operations of up to two years in order to influence the premium or discount on forward exchange rates when the currency tended to overshoot or undershoot.

This time, again, the change of policy was pragmatic rather than ideological or analytical. It was the recognition that foreign demand for Swiss francs would be largely satisfied—one way or another. If Swiss capital controls could be imposed, the supply could and would occur through money creation in the Eurocurrency markets. This would further reduce the scope for action by the Swiss authorities. The revised thinking of the authorities was that if the Swiss franc was in fact being used as an international asset, it would be better to conduct business in a way that enabled them to be informed on, and more in control of, current developments. Accordingly, an attempt was made to bring back some of the Swiss franc business that had flowed to financial centers outside of Switzerland, though it was realized that such a process of reversal would be protracted in any case.

Fiscal Policy

While monetary policy eventually recovered lost ground, in its habitual mode fiscal policy continued to plod along between grudging parliamentary concessions and a staunch resistance both to higher taxation and to higher public outlays. (In May, 1979, a second referendum on the Federal Council's proposal to introduce a national value added tax failed to gain a majority.) In the meantime, however, two factors transformed attitudes toward fiscal policy. First, the fiscal-policy experiences of other countries reinforced the overall skepticism with which activist budgetary policies have been traditionally viewed in Switzerland. In his speech to the general assembly of shareholders of the Swiss National Bank in April, 1982, Dr. Fritz Leutwiler summed up a general feeling when he said: "In Switzerland, the fiscal sovereignty of the cantons and the municipalities has fortunately preserved the national economy from [fiscal] experiments."

Second, the efforts to rebalance public-sector finances started to bear fruit.

Between 1972 and 1981, public expenditures increased from 23 percent to slightly more than 27 percent of GNP. At the same time, however, revenue increased from 21 percent to 26.5 percent of GNP, thanks to regular upward revisions of the rates of sales tax and other federal indirect taxes (tobacco, energy, etc.).

As intended by the federal act on financial planning, passed in 1979, a reduction of expenditure and the gradual improvement of revenue produced a balance in the 1981-1982 budget. For the 1979-1982 period, the consolidated government's consolidated account showed an average annual deficit equal to 0.6 percent of GNP, a small fraction when compared with a gross savings rate of around 27 percent of GNP. To be sure, enduring longer-term balance is not yet secure. The financial plan for 1983 continued to press for further reductions of expenditure coupled with more taxation (on energy, certain banking transactions, heavy goods vehicles, and motorway users). Overall, however, the public sector has at least ceased to be a conduit of inflation.

Labor Market and Industrial Policies

Alongside monetary and fiscal policy, policies that actively promote structural changes in the industrial sectors of the economy have become important ancillary weapons in the anti-inflation arsenal. The principal labor-market policies that were applied were constraints on foreign migrant workers, vocational training or respecialization programs, and the strict application of the "Industrial Peace Agreement" of 1937. (Before 1937, labor relations in Switzerland were strained; conflicts numerous; and the trade-union movement revolutionary in character. In 1937, after a particularly bitter conflict in the watch industry, employers and workers signed a general agreement pledging not to resort to strikes or lockouts and to settle labor disputes by arbitration. The agreement was later extended to the whole of the economy and has remained the guiding principle of Swiss industrial relations.)

The application of these labor-market policies succeeded in limiting the number of unemployed to 0.5 percent of the labor force without reducing the length of the work week. However, after 1971, the average length of the work week declined. In 1979, a proposal to reduce the official work week gradually to 40 hours was rejected by a referendum. Unit labor costs were also kept under control. Between 1960 and 1973, for instance, real wages increased at an annual average rate of 5.2 percent, as against an annual average increase of 3.4 percent warranted by expected increases in productivity. Between 1973 and 1980, both the warranted and actual real wages rose at an annual average rate of 1.3 percent. The productivity effects of the labor-market policy cannot be gauged precisely because of the lack of accurate Swiss statistics on GNP produced per hour of work. It would appear, however, that gains in labor productivity declined significantly, although productivity in the industrial sector rose at the 1¾ percent per annum rate characteristic of most EEC countries.

Industrial policy, by contrast, has been applied for the most part by indirect means. It endeavors to stress—often quite brutally—the inevitable competitive consequences of the massive appreciation of the Swiss franc, the worldwide proliferation of production centers, and the crumbling of tariff barriers. Only limited official financial and technical assistance is available to bolster a process of adjustment largely initiated by business itself. For the time being, attempts to analyze the effects of industrial restructuring in terms of supply flexibility, output costs, and other inflationary factors remains incomplete because of gaps in the statistical system. However, several studies—and some sectoral indicators of production, productivity, exports and import substitution—indicate that profound sectoral shifts have taken place. In all probability, these shifts have contributed to a more efficient use of resources and to an overall attenuation of cost pressures.

Discretionary Adaptation: 1973-1982

Since 1973, the strategy of adaptation via the discretionary use of several instruments in an economy willing—and able—to endorse the cost of adjustment has resulted in an outcome that must be assessed as remarkable both in absolute terms and in comparison with other OECD countries: From 1976, real GDP in Switzerland grew annually by some 20 percent above the European average; unemployment has remained negligible; the average current account surplus for the period 1973 to 1981 was larger than it had been in the preceding six years; total official reserves (including gold at its pre-1971 value) were maintained at some 55 percent of annual imports; the social-security system has remained in substantial surplus; and budgets have been in near balance. Above all, Switzerland's price performance improved markedly relative to most major nations. (See Table 2.)

Deteriorating Export Performance

Both in official and private sectors there is little complacency, however. The steady deterioration of Switzerland's manufacturing export performance (shown in Table 2), caused by the real effective appreciation of the Swiss franc, is troubling. Estimates of market gains and losses are to be interpreted with caution because of the statistical uncertainties in the price/volume breakdown of foreign trade data. Even so, the data clearly show that Switzerland suffered a significant loss in its manufacturing competitiveness. Between 1970 and 1982, measured in terms of a common currency, unit labor costs in Swiss manufacturing and export prices of Swiss manufactures rose relative to those of its principal competitors, namely West Germany, Japan and the United States.

To be sure, continuing efforts to lower the price elasticity of foreign demand for Swiss exports through increased use of high technology have started to

Table 2

Relative Performance of Swiss Indexes[1]

Rise in Implicit GNP Deflator	1960-1980	1960-1967	1967-1973	1973-1980
OECD Countries	77	157	111	37
Major Countries	84	168	115	40
West Germany	109	142	117	77
Smaller European Countries	57	102	93	26
Rise in Consumer Prices				
OECD Countries	69	133	94	38
Major Countries	72	144	96	41
West Germany	108	133	119	83
Smaller European Countries	53	84	82	30
Rise in Imports				
OECD Countries	42	160	71	25
Major Countries	42	178	68	25
West Germany	90	267	155	54
Smaller European Countries	44	133	79	25
Rise in Exports				
OECD Countries	58	200	78	29
Major Countries	59	200	82	29
West Germany	103	228	129	60
Smaller European Countries	56	177	77	28

[1]Swiss Indexes as a percent of other indexes.

ameliorate the impact of the currency appreciation. There probably are limits, however, to any nation's export resilience in face of real exchange-rate appreciation. It is also worth noting that the deficit in the Swiss trade balance has been reduced by a sharp decline in energy inputs per unit of output, which fell 20 percent between 1973 and 1982.

Durability of Anti-Inflation Policy

A more pervasive concern relates to the durability of Swiss anti-inflation policy. There is no disputing the fact that the large decline in the foreign population and the impact of the Swiss franc's appreciation on import prices have exerted a strong downward pressure on inflation, a pressure that might prove to be temporary. The quota system brought about the departure of some 200,000 foreign workers (often accompanied by their families) out of a total civilian work force of three million, thereby substantially reducing demand. By 1982, the number of foreign workers had stabilized at around 700,000.

Table 3

Measures of Swiss Competitiveness in Manufacturing (1982)

	Switzerland	West Germany	Japan	United States
Unit labor costs (1970 = 100)	132	108	114	82
Export Prices (1970 = 100)	120	101	101	110

Source: OECD, *Economic Outlook,* July, 1983

As for imports, their modest price rise between 1970 and 1978 (a cumulative total of only 19 percent) is in sharp contrast to experience in other countries (e.g., 162 percent in the United States). However, since 1979 the average annual rise in the unit price of Swiss imports has risen to 8.5 percent per annum and is closer to the annual average of 16 percent experienced by OECD countries as a group. Beyond the impact of dollar appreciation, there is growing evidence of asymmetrical pricing responses to currency variations (cost savings from currency appreciation are retained by importers but cost increases resulting from currency depreciation are immediately transferred to the rest of the economy).

The burden of containing inflation is now virtually entirely assigned to monetary policy, with particular emphasis on the use of the monetary base as an intermediate target. However, the work of many scholars has cast strong doubts on the lasting viability of this approach, a fact also noted in the United States. The doubts about the efficacy of pure monetary control do not concern the controllability of the monetary base.

The Swiss National Bank maintains a flexible attitude and allows deviations whenever seasonal or exchange-rate developments induce reversible fluctuations. It is able, nonetheless, to control the longer-term trend of the monetary base through foreign exchange swaps (whose effects are similar to open-market operations in domestic securities), its application system for discount and lombard credits, and soon by a more extensive use of open-market operations in domestic securities. In addition, as the interest-rate reactions to the events of 1978 showed, the SNB enjoys a credibility that ensures rational market reactions to purely transitory shifts in its monetary policy; the market's assumption that deviations from announced trends are only transitory variations prevents portfolio restructuring that might otherwise have long-run implications for interest rates and money demand.

On the other hand, the greater control of its target by the SNB also entails a dilemma that has been well defined by Ralph Bryant: "The trade-off between reliability and controllability is especially acute for national economies significantly open to the rest of the world. If a definition of the national money stock is chosen to maximize the predictability and dependability of the relationships between money and national ultimate targets, the central bank may have very poor control over the money stock. If a definition is chosen to maximize the central bank's ability to control national money, the relationship linking that money to national ultimate targets may be weak and highly uncertain."[2]

The Swiss dilemma on this front has been theoretically and empirically verified by other authors. It seems to be substantially related to the impact of the exchange rate on the composition of the demand for money.

Three practical policy conclusions can be derived from the empirical evidence. The first is that central banks should keep far away from doctrinaire monetarism; they should set long-term targets for the monetary aggregates and abstain from fine-tuning. The second lesson is that policy should continue to stress the need for structural flexibility of the Swiss economy. Third, the constant threat of undesirable exchange-rate effects (notably from the external Swiss franc market where, for tax reasons, the bulk of financial innovation is occurring) requires the continued availability of adaptive, discretionary and flexible policy instruments.

On the whole, these three elements provide only limited scope for offsetting the potentially destabilizing effects inherent in the Swiss franc's growing role as an international currency, to say nothing of the pronounced swings that may occur in other major reserve currencies, especially the U.S. dollar. Nor is it certain that sufficient relief can be derived from such intangible factors as social consensus, industrial peace, and spontaneous structural adjustment. Confidence in such appropriate private-sector responses has been vindicated by past behavior. There is little historical reason to suspect that the Swiss rules of the game might someday become counterproductive. Nevertheless, vigilance, continuing efforts to discern pricing movements, and improvements in the ability of the nation to make policy decisions must remain as overriding imperatives in the years ahead.

Lessons from Swiss Stabilization Strategy

As stated at the beginning of this paper, because the Swiss experience seems to lack the flesh and blood of real political and economic strife to many foreign observers, any comparison of Swiss experience with other nations is not really valid. Yet, Switzerland's pragmatism—its capacity to adjust to the processes by which prices, costs and incomes are fixed or changed in detail by the volition and consent of individual and collective human agents—and its rejection of doctrinaire a priori reasoning do stand out as a guiding achievement. Switzerland started out by rejecting all interference with the principles of the market economy, but it rapidly accepted the view that: "There are certain ills you must try to cure by unfamiliar means when normal remedies fail."[3]

[2]Ralph C. Bryant. *Money and Monetary Policy in Interdependent Nations.* Washington D.C., The Brookings Institution, 1980, especially pages 485-501.

[3]Nello Celio, President of the Swiss Confederation, Opening Address to the First Conference of the International Center for Monetary and Banking Studies, Geneva, January, 1972.

The Swiss experience suggests that unfamiliar policy means will remain part and parcel of an overall stabilization strategy so long as the present international currency and financial systems remain fundamentally unreformed. Indeed, when exchange-rate expectations are so powerful or financial risks become so dominant as to render portfolio decisions unresponsive to the classic instruments of monetary policy, the authorities—recognizing that they are operating in a highly innovative and competitive financial environment—must perforce resort to administrative controls. It is the only way in which they can attenuate the distortions and promote the long-run good of their stabilization policy.

Swiss stabilization strategy illustrates the concept of a selective approach, one that encompasses not only monetary-fiscal demand management but active long-term income policies, manpower policies, foreign trade and exchange policies, and intense efforts to promote structural adaptation in industry. For some 20 years, Swiss stabilization policy has been conceived as a *structural* rather than as a *contracyclical* policy, inspired by the conviction that the greater the efficiency of the macro markets, the greater will be the relative price adjustments and the smaller the volume adjustments. In a sense, the Swiss experience strengthens the argument that money matters—but not so overwhelmingly that it can ensure balanced economic growth without adequate support from the other domains of policy. It also strengthens the case of those who argue that the solution to the difficulty of global policymaking lies not in abstracting economics even further from its social setting but, rather, in returning the subject from that abstraction to policies applied to human affairs.

FRANCE

Michel Develle*

FRANCE IS an inflationary society. Since the end of World War II, prices have risen faster in France than in most of its main trading partners. The rate of increase in consumer prices, which averaged 4.7 percent a year from 1963 to 1973, accelerated to 10.7 percent between 1973 and 1979, and to 13.8 percent between 1980 and 1981. This paper describes French price trends since the early 1960's; discusses the main causes of "French-style" inflation; looks at the changes that have taken place in the economy; and explains the various attempts that have been made to check this "veritable cancer" undermining France's economic development.

Price Trends in France

In describing the trend of prices over the past 20 years, three different but complementary measures may be used: the GDP (gross domestic product) price deflator, wholesale price indexes, and the consumer price index. French inflation is a rich and complex phenomenon and can be measured accurately only by viewing it from many different angles.

Changes in the GDP Deflator

The most comprehensive index for measuring the rise in prices in France is the GDP deflator. Six main periods may be identified:

Period	Average Annual Increase in GDP
1965-1968	3.4%
1968-1972	6.0%
1972-1975	10.7%
1975-1978	9.5%
1978-1980	11.1%
1980-1982	12.0%

*Director of Economic and Financial Studies, Banque Paribas, Paris.

France experienced an initial surge in inflation following the steep wage increases that accompanied the labor and student upheavals which began in the Spring of 1968. After previously being held at under 3½ percent, inflation suddenly climbed to a 6-percent rate. The first oil shock in 1973-1974 caused prices to accelerate sharply, raising the inflation rate to double figures. After this first shock, inflation was reduced only slowly in France. As a result of the combined effects of slower growth, inflationary pressures from social groups, and measures to counter inflation that were not vigorous enough, the rise in prices became locked in on an upward track of over 9 percent a year. In 1979, the second oil shock hit the French economy when inflation's roots were still very much alive, paving the way for further increases that pushed the GDP price index to over 12 percent, on average, for the period 1980-1982.

The Trend in Wholesale Prices: 1965-1982

The wholesale price series confirms the general thrust shown by GDP prices. These price trends also show how sensitive wholesale prices are to imported inflation caused by the oil shocks and by depreciation of the French franc over the period in question. This phenomenon will be discussed later, when we analyze the main components of the consumer price index. Four factors explain why French wholesale prices were so flexible during this period:

- the large and increasing proportion of raw materials and capital goods imported by French industry;
- the very rapid rise in French firms' wage costs and financial charges;
- the French firms' lack of capital, which means that all increases in costs have to be passed on in their selling prices;
- the weak influence of international competition—until 1974—because of the large sheltered sector in the national economy.

Increases in the Overall Consumer Price Index

Analysis of annual changes in consumer prices in France between 1965 and 1982 reveals that the period as a whole falls into a number of separate inflationary phases.

1965-1968: The average annual rise in consumer prices during this period was 3.1 percent, which was similar to increases in the other major industrial countries. It then accelerated very abruptly as a result of the political and social events of May, 1968, and climbed above 5 percent.

1969-1973: During this period, consumer prices continued to increase at well over 5 percent a year, pushed up by rising costs and demand pressure—the economic consequences of the political and social shocks of 1968. The international boom of 1969 then helped to accentuate inflationary pressures. French prices rose faster during this period than did those of its main trading partners, particularly West Germany. By the end of 1973, the inflation rate in France was again closer to the average for the major industrialized countries, which had also been overtaken by inflationary fever.

1974-1976: The raw materials crisis (agricultural and industrial) of late 1972 and the first oil shock accelerated French inflation to an annual rate of 15 percent at the end of 1974. It was in early 1974 that, for the second time, consumer prices in France rose much faster than in West Germany, and this gap between the two countries has persisted. During 1975, France's first serious recession since the end of World War II brought the rise in consumer prices down to 11.8 percent in the context of world disinflation. However, the sharp slowdown in inflation came to an end during the course of 1976 (9.6 percent), whereas disinflation continued in most other countries, particularly in West Germany.

1977-1978: Consumer prices rose at an annual rate of less than 10 percent over these two years (9.4 and 9.1), but there was no further deceleration despite world disinflationary influences and the energetic measures to counter inflation taken by Prime Minister Raymond Barre after September, 1976. It became clear during this period that there was an underlying rate of inflation below which it was difficult to go.

1979-1982: The rise in consumer prices accelerated as early as the Summer of 1979 under the twofold impact of the economic upturn in France (the GDP growth rate reaching 3.3 percent that year) and the second oil shock. In 1980, the effect of the second oil shock pushed the rate of increase in prices up to an annual 14 percent—close to the rate recorded at the end of 1974. Like the other major industrialized countries, France began to reduce inflation in early 1981, but this trend was halted by the spring elections, which brought into power a left-wing coalition of Socialists and Communists bent on boosting consumption and raising low wages and transfer payments. In Summer, 1982, the growing disparity between the rate of increase in prices in France and in the other major industrialized countries prompted the Mitterrand government to freeze prices and wages following devaluation of the French franc in June, 1982. In Autumn, 1982, the freeze caused the rise in prices to slow appreciably, and it was hoped that these measures would reduce the rate of rise of the consumer price index on a 12-month basis to 10 percent or below by the end of the year, a hope that was, in fact, realized only at the end of 1983.

Trends in the Components of the CPI

The overall consumer price index includes three main components—manufactures, services and food. Prices of manufactures played a leading role in the acceleration of prices at the retail stage in both 1974 and 1980. This was due mainly to the impact of the change in the relative prices of energy after the two oil shocks, magnified by the interaction of wage indexation and production costs. With two exceptions (1976 and 1977) the prices of manufactures were most sensitive to domestic and external inflationary pressures during the period 1965-1982.

Food prices rose more than the average for the total index twice: first in 1972-1973 as a result of the international crisis affecting agricultural commodities that preceded the first oil shock; then from the end of 1976 to mid-1977 because of the summer drought in France in 1976. They increased sharply again in 1981, following the decisions taken in Brussels (EEC) and France to improve farm incomes.

Service prices, which include directly controlled public-sector tariffs (electricity, gas, transport, etc.) rose faster than the average except for three short periods: 1974-1975, 1977-1978, and early 1980. The increase in service prices—whose share in GNP had grown substantially from 44.4 percent in 1965 to 52.2 percent in 1981—was primed by the rise in real wages, the growing share of public services, and the absence of any genuine international or domestic competition.

The Causes of French Inflation

In France, as elsewhere, inflation is a complex phenomenon in which monetary policies, budget policies, the behavior of wages, productivity and unit labor costs, import prices (particularly for energy and raw materials), as well as other factors, all play a part. The purpose of analysis is to disaggregate their influences on inflation.

Monetary Policy and the Rise in Prices

According to those who subscribe to the monetary theory of inflation, the main reason for the accelerating rise in prices in France between 1965 and 1982 was that the money supply grew faster than nominal GDP. It would seem, judging from a number of econometric studies covering the period 1959-1978, that money supply did, on the whole, grow faster than nominal output. The elasticity between the two variables is estimated to be 1.20, with monetary financing of the budget deficit, a big increase in bank lending, and inflows of short-term foreign capital being the principal causes of rapid money growth.

Quite a different argument is put forward, however, by those who are unconvinced that monetary factors are primarily responsible for French inflation. It is true, for example, that the tight credit restrictions introduced at the end of 1972 (quantitative credit policy) and the curbing of money-supply growth under Premier Raymond Barre's administration in 1977 did not significantly reduce the inflationary surge in French prices.

Nonetheless, in support of those who blame French inflation on excess liquidity, it must be noted that the development of a great many forms of credit not subject to quantitative ceilings (such as credits for exports, job creation, and energy saving) allowed domestic bank credit to grow very substantially over

Liquid Sources and Long-Term Capital, Selected Countries, 1973-1977
(Percent of total credit)

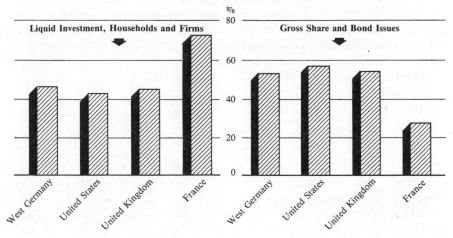

the period in question. Almost 45 percent of credit extension in France is on nonmarket terms.

Between 1965 and 1977, the broadly defined money supply (M-2) grew sharply in France. The borrowing requirement to sustain strong French growth could not be met by an adequate supply of long-term capital, and the use of short-term debt had to be accentuated in order to satisfy firms' requirements by tapping the substantial liquid deposits available. The structure of investments available in France is distinctly advantageous to liquid investments.

The very ease with which the adjustment to short-term financing was made contributed to the acceleration of inflation. After 1977, policy became restrictive and tighter credit controls were introduced, but without limiting the quantity of money to an extent likely to jeopardize the financing of final demand (exports, investment and household consumption). This tendency for the economy to become increasingly liquid is illustrated by the fact that the economy's liquidity ratio, the ratio of M-2 to GDP, rose from around 41 percent in 1970 to around 48 percent in 1980. To counter this trend, special emphasis was placed on increasing the supply of long-term capital. In some years, notably in 1978-1979, the current account balance put upward pressure on the French money supply, but from 1980-1983 it served to restrict the amount of liquidity in the economy.

In June, 1981, the annual money-supply growth target was raised from 10 percent to 12 percent, while credit restrictions were eased and compulsory reserve requirements were lowered. Analysis of the volume-price split in France also shows clearly that more and more liquidity had to be created in an effort to sustain the level of real growth. The rate of growth of production by volume slowed from 6.4 percent a year prior to 1967 to 2.2 percent between 1973 and 1978, so that inflation and growth were negatively correlated in the medium term.

Except for two years, 1977 and 1980, it can be argued that French monetary policy has not been really restrictive as regards the quantity of credit, despite an extensive system of regulations whose object since 1973 has been to check the excessive creation of money.

Budget Deficits and Inflation

Prior to 1968, fiscal policy was neutral vis-a-vis inflation. The reorganization of public finance under President Charles de Gaulle in the early 1960's, combined with strong economic growth, eliminated budget deficits and thus eliminated one source of inflation. The budget situation was, in fact, so healthy that the government was able to reduce the level of central government indebtedness. Serious thought was given to a constitutional act prohibiting the presentation of a budgeted deficit.

The student and labor disturbances of 1968 did lead to a substantial deficit; however, this was narrowed as a result of strong growth from 1969 to 1973. During the period 1965-1974 the rate of deduction from incomes (income tax and social-security contributions), expressed as a percentage of GDP, remained more or less constant at around 35.5 percent, thanks to the increase in budget revenues stemming from large increases in the value of output and its effect on revenue collections through the value added tax (VAT), and the relatively slow expansion of the welfare state in France.

After 1973, the oil levy on French wealth, the so-called oil tax, was paid by firms and by the government in the form of increased deficits, while households' real incomes continued to rise. The fall in budget revenues caused by the slowdown in economic growth and the simultaneous extension of welfare coverage (for the elderly, the unemployed, and families) led to a rise in the fiscal share from 35.5 percent in 1973 to 44 percent by 1982, and to a growing imbalance in public-finance budgets (state, local authorities, social security). The deficits had a threefold effect on inflation:

- Demand was stimulated excessively through large increases in public spending (especially 1968, 1975, and 1981).
- Between 1973 and 1982, regular steep increases in tax and quasi-tax pressures caused cost-push inflation to accelerate.
- In 1975-1976, and again in 1981-1982, excessive money creation was prompted by the fact that the budget deficit could not be financed out of savings.

In a country such as France, where money-supply growth is rapid for structural reasons, budgetary discipline is essential in order to prevent any acceleration of the rise in prices. The deterioration in public finance after 1975 is partly responsible for France's rapid inflation—notwithstanding the corrective measures introduced between 1977 and 1980.

Wages, Productivity, Unit Labor Costs

Cost inflation is one of the main reasons for the rise of prices in France. Such a price rise is due to independent increases in production costs or, via unit production costs, to declines in productivity and the rate of growth. It is likely that French inflation after 1974 was caused in large part by the slowdown in the rate of growth of the economy which, combined as it was with a slower increase in productivity, exerted upward pressure on costs.

There is considerable evidence that the wages and wage-linked social-security charges, together with a declining rate of productivity growth, have been a major vehicle for cost-push inflation in France. Productivity improvement fell from 4.4 percent a year prior to 1973 to 2.7 percent a year from 1974 to 1980. At the same time, the share of wages, including social costs in the value added by firms, rose from 62 percent in 1965 to an estimated 70 percent by 1982. Five percentage points of the rise represents the result of a rapid increase in wages proper; the other 3 percentage points reflects increases in social-security contributions payable by firms.

Comparing the increase in wages per employee with increase in labor productivity (total output/number of wage earners) shows the wage cost per unit of output, or unit labor cost. The effect on inflation of the slowdown in productivity has been heightened by the great uniformity of wage increases across all sectors in France. Sectors achieving productivity growth distribute this growth to workers because of the pressure applied by wage earners and unions. But comprehensive indexation means that these increases also spread to all sectors— including those with little or no productivity growth. This is a key factor in the mechanism both for French inflation and for the rise in unemployment. Sectors with low productivity levels become obliged to dismiss staff in order to contain rising production costs. After 1965, there were relatively big wage increases that were sometimes even larger in the very low-productivity sectors (such as the public sector and services.)

Chart 2 shows the extent to which wages were responsible for the acceleration of French inflation after 1973. Between 1960 and 1972, the spread was in the region of one point, but from 1972 to 1975, when French inflation moved into double figures under the initial impact of higher energy prices, the increase in the wage cost per unit of output was almost 3.5 points ahead of the rise in GDP prices.

The easing of consumer prices from 1975 to 1978 coincided with a more moderate average increase in the wage cost per unit of output: 9.6 percent, against 14.1 percent between 1972 and 1975. During the course of the second oil shock in 1978-1980, the spread in wage costs per unit of output was smaller— only 0.5 percent above GDP prices—but still very high. In 1981 and 1982, the rise in wage costs per unit of output accelerated slightly again despite the rapidly worsening labor market situation.

The trend in labor costs is one of the main reasons for the differing rates of inflation in France and West Germany. Between 1975 and 1978, unit wage

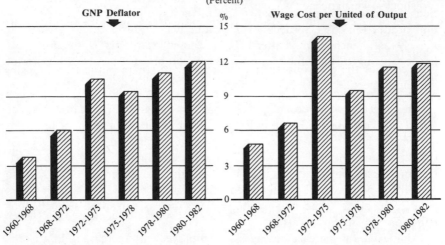

Chart 2:
Average Annual Change in General Prices and Wage Costs, 1960-1982
(Percent)

costs rose by 2.5 percent in Germany compared with 9.6 percent in France; and between 1978 and 1980 the rates of rise were 3.8 percent and 11.7 percent, respectively. The difference between the increase in GDP prices in the two countries during these two periods (i.e., 5.8 and 6.7 percent) is, therefore, easy to understand. Because productivity growth during the two periods in question was the same in both countries, the excessive increase of wages has been a key contributory factor in French inflation. This situation has been made worse by the absence in France of any German-style consensus between management and labor and by the unrealistic attitude of the French public authorities and firms toward the growth of wage earners' purchasing power.

Other labor-related factors have also tended to increase cost inflation in France. Contrary to what was done in West Germany, the United States, and Great Britain, French firms did not dismiss staff on a massive scale at the start of the 1973 oil crisis. The reasons for this lay in France's population structure, unions and management attitudes. The increase in the labor force, accentuated by the growing female participation rate, caused a substantial increase in the "natural" unemployment rate which, in turn, restricted the capacity of the economy to adjust. In 1965, unemployment totaled 156,000; by 1973, the number was 424,000; thereafter there was a steady rise, each year, to over 2 million in 1982. The situation was different in West Germany, which experienced almost zero labor-force growth and also pursued a much tougher policy vis-a-vis its migrant workers. The result was a sharper increase in the unit production costs of French enterprises and, therefore, in French wholesale prices.

Inflation caused by the rise in wage costs has been accentuated in France by the development of social benefits financed in large part by an increase in firms' social-security contributions. The surge in wage costs following the first oil shock—which pushed wage payments up from 64.4 percent of value added in 1973 to 69.2 percent in 1976—was due more to the rise in the relative share of employers' social-security contributions from 14.6 percent to 17.4 percent than to that of gross wages alone, which climbed from 49.8 to 50.6 percent. The costs of the generous unemployment benefits paid in the face of rising unemployment and irresponsible policy with regard to increased health spending were the primary causes of the surge in the social operating costs of the French economy. In this way, the economy was equipped with a mechanism that both fueled inflation and destroyed jobs. Financing the social-security deficit increased enterprises' costs; raised the inflation rate; and eroded firms' competitiveness; it thereby reduced their national and international market shares and ultimately produced increased unemployment which, in turn, brought further upward pressure to bear on the cost to firms of financing this unemployment.

After the second oil shock, the government sought to alleviate this vicious circle, taking steps to check the rise in prices and the worsening financial situation of firms by curbing the costs of the social-security system and raising the contribution that the beneficiaries (i.e., households) paid toward it. This policy was reintroduced in tougher form in the Summer of 1982, following the second devaluation of the French franc in that year.

Energy and Imported Raw Material Prices

The first oil shock almost doubled the rate of increase in consumer prices in France from 7.3 percent in 1973 to 13.7 percent in 1974. Between 1978 and 1983, the French inflationary cycle was touched off once again by the second oil shock, followed by a steep rise in the exchange rate of the dollar. Although oil prices rose at very much the same pace during both oil shocks, the second shock did not cause quite such a steep increase in consumer prices. Inflation increased from 9.1 percent in 1978 to 13.6 percent in 1980. However, the rate of French inflation relative to that of its trading partners deteriorated, particularly with respect to West Germany.

In addition to the effects of the oil shocks, which are further discussed below French inflation during this period can also be explained by the general worsening of France's terms of trade with all commodity producers. Between 1960 and 1972, increases in raw material import prices were small. Combined with the lowering of tariff barriers within the Common Market, this helped to moderate the pace of French inflation. From 1972 onward, on the other hand, the rise in raw material prices had a strong inflationary impact that spread to the whole of international trade, including manufactures. Only a policy of currency revaluation, coupled with strict regulation of domestic costs, might have kept imported inflation under control.

Import Prices and GDP Deflator, Selected Periods

(Percent per annum)

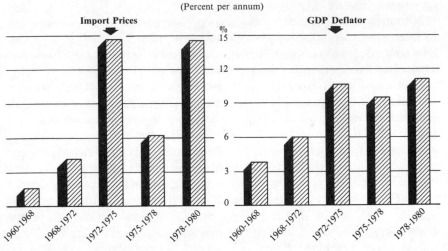

The Behavior of Exchange Rates

France is an open economy: It imports 80 percent of its raw materials, 73 percent of its energy needs, and 50 percent of its professional equipment. Imports accounted for 25 percent of GDP in 1982, against 11.6 percent in 1965. The combined impact of rising foreign prices and the French franc's weakening exchange rate play an important part in accentuating the rise in domestic prices. Alternatively, falling foreign prices and/or a rising French franc have the opposite effect. Chart 3 shows two periods when imported inflation increased domestic inflation pressure (1972-1975 and 1978-1980) and two periods when import prices had at least a relatively moderating effect (1968-1972 and 1975-1978). Comparing the trend in French import prices with the trend for the differential impact of import prices provides a second explanation for the inflation differential between France and West Germany. In Germany, for example, import prices rose by only 1.4 percent per year between 1975 and 1978 and by 8.5 percent per year between 1978 and 1980 against much higher rises of 6.1 percent 14.6 percent in France. The strength of the deutsche mark is the reason import prices rose so little in West Germany.

An examination of the French franc's exchange rate against the dollar and the deutsche mark over the period 1965-1982 confirms the influence of the exchange rate as a factor exacerbating French inflation. Econometric studies have demonstrated that the exchange rate exerts the least inflationary influence when the French franc is strong against the dollar but relatively weak against the deutsche mark (thus providing competitive advantages in the European and third-country markets). The depreciation of the European currencies against the dollar since 1980 is a factor that has done much to fuel recent inflationary pressures in France.

A country with a rate of inflation higher than that of its partners will see its international competitiveness diminish as its relative costs rise. To check this tendency, it will endeavor to offset its handicap by making export credits available at the lowest possible rates (there were no ceilings on export credits in France until 1982). Because of inflation, however, these rates will probably be well above those prevailing in countries with lower inflation, such as West Germany or Japan. Export growth will be made more difficult, and this will have a negative effect on the trade balance and, ultimately, on the exchange rate. The fall in the exchange rate will then cause domestic inflation to accelerate and push up interest rates as the monetary authorities take measures to counter the rise in prices and to defend the exchange rate. This is the vicious circle with which France has become very familiar since 1974.

Other Causes of French Inflation

Of the many other causes and factors of inflation that could be mentioned, three are noteworthy:

Price controls: Between 1965 and 1978—and again after 1982—France lived with price-control systems of varying severity that were not very effective in controlling inflation. It may even be said that price control was inflationary in some respects in that it allowed price rises without any reference to market conditions and competitiveness among firms. The decision to free industrial prices was taken in 1978, and some prices eased after an interim period dominated by the second oil shock. However, the freeing of certain service and food product prices resulted in some steep increases, while farm prices were subject to European Community (EEC) regulations and could not be closely controlled by the French authorities. The absence of real competition in many sectors of the French economy that are not exposed to international competition—such as the large service sector, cartels, monopolies, and the excessive indexation enjoyed by other sectors—makes true price freedom illusory but does not justify the imposition of mandatory price controls. Such controls, especially when applied blindly, cause serious miscalculations by industries on which they are imposed.

Inflation, profit margins, and financial costs: The steep rise in production costs in an economy faced with a slowdown in growth was bound to have an adverse impact on corporate profitability. We have already seen how the distribution of national income shifted in a direction favorable to wage earners. The net result on corporate savings is shown in Table 1.

The 1960-1974 investment boom came to an end because of the deterioration of enterprises' profit margins, the increase in their indebtedness (mainly short-term), and constantly declining demand expectations. The investment share of GNP was 19 percent in the early 1960's, 23.4 percent in 1970, and

Table 1

Table 1
Enterprises' Gross Trading Surplus as a
Percent of Value Added

	1965	1970	1973	1976	1980	1981	1982
Gross trading surplus	27.6	29.3	27.3	25.2	24.4	23.6	24.4
of which:							
• Corporation tax	3.2	3.2	3.4	3.4	3.2	3.2	—
• Interest payments	3.3	6.9	8.7	7.9	8.5	10.2	10.3
• Net distributed earnings....	—	4.3	4.4	4.4	5.3	5.4	—
• Gross savings[1]	16.7	15.4	11.1	11.4	11.4	9.0	9.7

[1]Gross savings = gross trading surplus-all taxes, interest payments, dividends and sundries.

Source: See statistical appendix.

24.3 percent at its high point in 1974. Because they had to cut down on their investment for lack of financial resources after 1974, French enterprises in effect ensured that their selling prices would increase in time as a result of their reduced competitiveness. Sacrificing first investment and then employment has not produced a sufficient upturn in enterprises' gross saving. The increased use of debt financing has, quite logically, increased inflationary pressure. In order to maintain an acceptable rate of return, enterprises have had to raise prices sharply, thereby stoking inflation at the retail stage.

Debt financing: The period of rising reliance on debt financing coincided with the emergence of positive real rates of interest. During the period under review, the measures taken by the monetary authorities to check the rise in prices, the fall in the exchange rate, and the increase in corporate indebtedness usually took the form of a steep hike in interest rates.

The combination of high interest rates (higher than inflation at the end of the period) and an economy based increasingly on debt can damage any economy. During an initial period, firms respond to the rise in their costs by increasing their debt and raising production prices—thereby accentuating both the problem and inflationary pressures. In France, this first phase gave way to a period during which sluggish demand and tighter monetary policy made it difficult to bet on inflation by contracting more debt simply to pay off earlier debts. The main features of this phase, which began immediately following the first oil shock, were numerous bankruptcies and the steady growth of unemployment, which made matters worse by restricting demand. Inflation was reduced only slightly from one cycle to the next, while factors of production were increasingly underutilized.

A Sociological Analysis of French Inflation

Since 1968, the rate of inflation in France has, on average, been well above that prevailing in the other major industrialized countries. This is not accidental. The year 1968 witnessed not just a students' revolt or an unplanned happening in an economy that had just experienced what was for it a period of unprecedented growth; 1968 was also a watershed in the behavior patterns of French citizens who from then on demanded that the benefits of growth be distributed more broadly. This marked the beginning of the end of the period of capital accumulation and, for many French, it meant access to the consumer society.

The period of capital accumulation that ended in 1968 was notable for:

- a very high rate of productive investment as a percentage of GDP (even if a substantial proportion of investment was in housing);
- a distribution of national income favorable to enterprises (until 1973); and
- a government with little debt.

The beginnings of mass consumption after 1968, on the other hand, were characterized by:

- an increased share of household consumption in GDP;
- a rapid rise in households' durable goods equipment;
- a widening budget deficit associated with rising social benefits.

This policy of rapid redistribution of national income in favor of households was called in question by the first oil shock. The political authorities were negligent in allowing the French population to believe that social benefits and energy could be paid for simultaneously. Self-interest prevailed and pressure groups increasingly quarreled over the distribution of a national income that was growing less and less rapidly. As a result, rising inflation and its corollary, rising unemployment, were inevitable. Inflation thus became endemic to French society, resting as it did on an economy in which growing indebtedness—of firms, the central government, and households—was causing increasingly serious weaknesses.

After 1973, French society was locked in on an inflationary course. With their hopes waning as a result of the oil shocks and the economic crisis, and with the increase in deductions from incomes (income tax and social-security contributions) caused by the government deficit, households and heads of businesses reacted by organizing themselves in such a way as to maintain—and, if possible, increase—their real incomes by strengthening indexation systems. An example is the perverse effect of wage indexation on consumer prices.

When external inflationary shocks (oil shocks or dollar shocks) occur, the price level of the country's expenditures (final demand) rises faster than the price level of the goods and services it produces. In short, the prices of consumer products grow most rapidly, and it is these prices that form the basis of wage indexation. If growth of GDP (i.e., production) is slow, indexing wages on consumer prices that are rising faster than the GDP deflator (the average price level for the production of the economy) results in overindexation. The effect is to increase the share of wages in national income. This is precisely what happened in France: Between 1965 and 1980 the share of wages in French GDP rose from 61.5 percent to 71.5 percent.

Policy Responses: An Evaluation

French inflation since 1965 has been a complex affair. Because the many varied causes have been affected by different economic policy responses, it is difficult to arrive at a clear picture. However, econometric studies carried out by the European Economic Community (EEC) and the French National Institute for Statistics and Economic Studies (INSEE) help to identify the factors responsible for the rise in prices.

The factors responsible for inflation of external origin (rise in import prices weighted by the share of imports in final uses) did play a part, but a much smaller one than that played by the factors responsible for internal inflation. From 1975 to 1980, the share of external inflation in the overall rate of inflation at no time exceeded 25 percent. From 1963 to 1968 and again from 1969 to 1974, French inflation accelerated rapidly. Investigations into the causes of French inflation, using the INSEE METRIC model, yield a ranking of the relative weights of the various aggravating factors:

	Percent of overall increase
• rise in wages	50
• imported inflation	25
• rise in social-security contributions	12
• economic policy effects	10
• other	3

The most striking feature of recent French experience is that between 1976 and 1982, in spite of the constraining policy pursued by the Barre government, the rate of inflation continued to be high against an international background that tended more to disinflation. The explanation must lie in the virulence of internal inflation in France, and in its resistance to the traditional methods of countering the rise in prices—fiscal and monetary policy. The sociological and cultural nature of French inflation (wage and income indexation without any reference to productivity) is thus confirmed.

Social and Incomes Policy

At a time when economic conditions in France were changing for the worse and prices were accelerating, French governments took upon themselves the responsibility of increasing the nation's social programs as if it were possible to share out something that did not exist.

The increase in tax pressures was too great by comparison with the economy's actual capacities. Compensation for unemployment was an understandable humanitarian concern, but it could be financed only for a short period. The economic crisis, which was wrongly believed to be cyclical in nature, was in fact a structural crisis. Inevitably it became impossible to finance a welfare state whose boundaries were continually being extended. The increase in social transfers against a background of much slower growth following the first oil shock deeply disrupted the productive system. It led to a loss of business competitiveness, and hence to worsening unemployment—which, in turn, threw public finance further off balance.

Such a situation could have been accommodated only by a stringent incomes policy. What should have been done—if the authorities and the country had so desired—was to finance unemployment and the rise in social transfers through a fall in primary incomes (wages, incomes, etc.) rather than through a drop in business competitiveness and investments. In some respects, the policies implemented after June, 1982, and reinforced in March, 1983, in an economic and social context that was even more difficult, appear to have been inspired by this line of reasoning.

Fiscal Policy

The strategy of a balanced budget was abandoned in 1974-1975. The authorities believed that the slowdown of growth could be checked through Keynesian measures at the cost of an increase in the general government's borrowing requirement. The decision was based on the gamble that the crisis would be short-lived. This economic philosophy rested on the erroneous belief that budget deficits were capable of reviving activity in an economy in which the decline in tax revenues and the burden of expenditures nonetheless made such a maneuver extremely risky. The outcome was a few short-lived recoveries in growth accompanied by very steep surges in inflation.

Until 1981 (1975 being an exception), the net general government budget deficit in France was significantly smaller than that in the other major industrial countries, such as West Germany. Starting in 1982, the budget deficit, expressed as a percentage of GDP, has been of the same order of magnitude as in West Germany and the United Kingdom, where very stringent policies of budget austerity have been applied. The inflationary impact of a budget deficit cannot be gauged from its relationship with GDP alone. Account must also be taken of the direction of budget spending—what the spending is used for, and the financial market's ability to provide the necessary long-term resources to prevent excessive money creation. In 1981, total gross bond issues placed on financial markets reached 120 billion francs compared with the 75 billion francs needed to finance the general government deficit. If one adds to this the considerable borrowing requirement of the public enterprises, the scope afforded to private enterprises to finance productive investments was indeed limited. One of the causes of French inflation is the coexistence of a tight financial market with a substantial budget deficit. This being so, the Treasury has had to resort to financing its deficit by monetary means, that is by issuing Treasury bills and placing them with banks.

Monetary Policy

Monetary policy in France since 1965 has been based on the theory that monetary management is necessary—but not in itself sufficient—to fight inflation. It has to be accompanied by a set of budgetary, fiscal and income policy measures. Also, monetary stringency can be applied only gradually to avoid the risk that business activity will fall too sharply. France has always resisted—and rightly so—hard-line monetarist doctrines.

French monetary policy is aimed at four things: the exchange rate, the inflation rate, the quantity of money, and the level of interest rates. Because the ultimate source of monetary growth is the growth of credit, it is on the counterparts of the money supply that control focuses, that is, on official foreign-exchange reserves, claims on the Treasury, and bank lending. Domestic bank lending—the most important counterpart of monetary growth—is controlled through growth targets. The effectiveness of such control is undermined by the existence of automatic refinancing privileges at fixed rates for certain credits such as medium-term export credits and at variable rates for Treasury bills. Adjustments in the compulsory reserve requirements imposed on banks and intervention by the Bank of France make it possible to control both the level of liquidity in the economy and interest rates.

French monetary policy until 1976 was subordinated mainly to the cycles of business activity; then from 1977 to 1980 to maintaining a strong franc; and from May, 1981, until March, 1983, once more—and with greater intensity— to the priority of financing the economy and fighting unemployment. The French economy's response to rises in interest rates is not large: The existence of automatic refinancing of credit and the partitioning of the various networks that engage in the collection and lending of funds negate monetary control. The monetary and financial networks enjoy various tax privileges and a quasi-monopoly position, which together make them relatively insensitive to variation in the cost of money. Nearly 45 percent of French credit is extended at administered rates that are different from the market rates.

Exchange-rate Policy

From 1959 to 1969, the prime objective of President de Gaulle's economic policy was to keep the French franc strong. From 1969 until the beginning of floating exchange rates in 1973, President Pompidou's government put forward a different approach, the idea being to build up a powerful export industry through a progressive but controlled weakening in the exchange value of the French franc. Since the first oil shock, French exchange-rate policy has been guided by the desire to shield the franc from erratic variations in the dollar, hence the erection of the more or less durable European monetary edifices (the Snake and the European Monetary System).

After September, 1976, under the direction of Premier Raymond Barre's government, the creation of the European Monetary System (EMS), which linked the French franc to the deutsche mark, was used to constrain French inflation. The increasing outward orientation of the French economy, the violence of the oil and dollar shocks, and the inflation differential among the member countries of the European Monetary System did not make the task an easy one. By the end of 1980, the French franc was already overvalued against the deutsche mark. The June, 1981, recovery policy, the widening general government deficits, and current payments deficits meant that a series of adjustments had to be made to the exchange rate of the French franc, relative to its partners within the European Monetary System. These adjustments took place in 1982 and 1983.

Financial Market and Credit Policies

French capital markets suffered from two basic weaknesses even before 1975. Although the rate of saving by households was high and rising (in spite of worsening inflation), a very large fraction of these savings was channeled into housing and real estate. Of the relatively small fraction that flowed into financial savings, the largest part was in highly liquid assets, such as deposits at banks and other financial intermediaries.

Prior to 1975, the relatively small flow of household saving into long-term securities (bonds and equities) of business enterprises did not present a major problem. Business in general was profitable and able to generate internal funds to finance its own growth. During most of this period the government sector was in comfortable surplus, and thus a net *source* of funds to the market. After 1975, both of these ameliorating factors changed adversely.

The slowing of economic growth after 1974 combined with a steady rise in the share of output claimed by wages and social-security taxes sharply reduced the self-financing ability of enterprises from nearly 62 percent of their total requirements in 1975 to 48 percent by 1982. At the same time, the government budget moved from surplus into serious deficit. Together with off-budget financing, including the financing of state enterprises, government became an increasingly large demander of funds in the financial market. As a result, the financial system as it existed was not able to achieve a smooth qualitative or quantitative matching of saving and borrowing. As business borrowing increased, much of it had to take the form of short-term debt.

The Barre government (1976-1981) introduced various measures to rectify the situation by improving the size and liquidity of the long-term capital market. Since 1981, the Socialist government has attempted to accelerate this development, principally by offering higher aftertax real rates of return on long-term bonds. These attempts have met with some success. The total annual volume of bond issues rose from around 2½ percent of GDP in 1975 to over 4 percent in 1982, and over 6 percent in 1983. Nonetheless, the total flow of savings into long-term instruments in France represents less than two-thirds of the corresponding volumes in West Germany or the United Kingdom. In the context of overall supply and demand, the French credit market continues to display two major weaknesses:

(1) Banks and financial intermediaries are forced to transform the essentially short-term deposits they receive into what are effectively long-term loans, a process that leaves them in a vulnerable position;
(2) To prevent the further worsening of such an unbalanced growth of credit extension, the government is forced into adopting a tight system of credit controls in spite of the drawbacks and perverse effects to which it gives rise.

The Barre Experience: 1976-1981

Like other major industrial nations, France suffered the twin shocks of worsening inflation and industrial recession after the oil shock and subsequent recession that occurred in 1973-1975. By 1976, it was clear that exchange-rate depreciation, fiscal reflation, and the increase in purchasing power and social benefits were aggravating basic economic problems. Another policy had to be found. This reaction on the part of the authorities was given the name "Barrism," after the policy's chief architect.

Taking office as prime minister in September, 1976, Raymond Barre decided to fight inflation, which was then still accelerating. Consumer prices were rising at over 10 percent at a time when the tendency in the United States and West Germany, in particular, was toward disinflation. The Barre government decided to tackle both the structural and cyclical components of inflation. Unfortunately the fight against the structural aspects was to remain a dead letter because of a lack of political resources and the very strong opposition to reform that was expressed in the most vigorous terms. Thus, only the measures against cyclical inflation were implemented. They met with a degree of success.

Beginning at the end of 1976, the government tightened the screws on parts of the inflationary mechanism by:

• Strictly controlling credit growth targets;
• Seeking to balance the general government account, and even to arrive at a surplus by end of the planning period (1980);
• Adjusting interest rates;
• Maintaining a strong French franc in order to reduce imported inflation.

However, by abandoning the fight against the basic structural causes of French inflation, the government reduced the chances of achieving its desired results. Thus, in early 1981, after four-and-a-half years of Barrism, French-style inflation was still running at nearly 12 percent a year.

The New Thrusts of 1981-1983

In May, 1981, a new Socialist government under President Francois Mitterrand took control. In its first year in office the government tried to combine a structural policy (the nationalization of banks and large industrial groups) with an attempt to boost consumption through an increase in social transfers and wage increases for lower-paid workers. The sluggishness of the international environment, the weakness of the French productive sector, the worsening of inflation, the widening of the foreign deficit, and two devaluations of the French franc led to a harrowing reappraisal of these policies.

In June, 1982, the thrust of policy was changed, with the highest priority given to fighting inflation through price controls, a stringent incomes policy, and budgetary austerity. These policies were combined with an unprecedented effort to spur industrial development.

Given a turn in the worldwide economic cycle from recession to recovery in 1983, these new initiatives should lead in the future both to a gradual expansion of the French economy and to a gradual reduction in France's rate of inflation.

Conclusions

With French business competitiveness considerably weakened, as witnessed by the decline in the self-financing ratio, and with France's internal and external indebtedness perhaps approaching its limits, the only thing to be done is to implement and maintain a genuine incomes policy that is not confined simply to the enforcement of wage norms.

If this absolute weapon against inflation is not accompanied by appropriate fiscal and monetary policies, however, its effectiveness will be blunted by two obstacles. The first is political: The fight against inflation in an economy of indebtedness takes time to produce results; however, in democracies the time available to the ruling team is dictated by elections. Second, in order to be effective, an incomes policy must not be confined solely to keeping a watch over wages; but this is the only element in the price structure that is known accurately.

Given the above, the mediocre record of the fight against inflation in France since 1965 is not surprising. Nevertheless, the fight against inflation is an essential condition for the revival of growth, fuller employment, and the restoration of the overall balance sheet of business. The fact that France is a member of a market-economy group of countries means that it is essential gradually to do away with the inflation differential between it and its partners that has been apparent since 1974. However, France's political and social system cannot withstand a sudden shift to deflation, because such a switch would have extremely destructive effects on employment in the short term. The growth of the labor force (by over 200,000 per year until 1985) will make it difficult, if not impossible, to take severely restrictive action. Disinflation in France will have to be gradual and progressive until 1985, by which time the employment constraint will begin to weigh less heavily.

Between now and then the fact that French inflation stems from multiple causes, such as:

- the system of incomes protection (social transfers as a share of household income has risen from 23.5 percent in 1965 to an estimated 35 percent in 1983);
- a financial mechanism biased toward debt, especially short-term debt;
- insufficient competition;
- too rapid growth of households' incomes;
- the weakness of productivity and investment;
- the inflationary behavior of government, businesses and households;

should encourage the authorities to make discriminating use of all of the different instruments—fiscal, monetary and incomes policy; incentives to saving; industrial development in the competitive sectors; adjustment of working hours; and so on—in order to reduce inflationary pressures without swinging into deflation. Although a severely deflationary policy would halt the rise in prices, it would probably also put an end to French democracy.

French society has lived too long in the Keynesian belief that inflation is less dangerous than unemployment. By following this doctrine, it ended up with both. France is now discovering a hard truth: Price rises do not produce additional real growth and they lead in the end to higher unemployment.

Inflation makes the financial situation of firms worse by introducing a hidden tax on production; with rising prices, the allowance for depreciation falls below the cost of replacing fixed assets. The rise in real interest rates, the eventual partner of inflation, discourages investment by making it difficult to incur additional indebtedness. Total economic growth declines as the difficulties of the productive system increase; employment suffers; and the nation's external trade position worsens because of the loss of competitiveness in both domestic and export markets. As a result, high inflation and high unemployment appear simultaneously. The error of economic policies over almost 20 years has been to try to fight first one and then the other without realizing this.

WEST GERMANY

Frank Wittendal*

ANY VISITOR to West Germany may read the word *Baukosten* (construction costs) on one of the small stone bridges, followed by a long number that takes up the entire length of the bridge. This is a reminder of the trauma provoked by the extraordinary post-World War I inflation that was experienced in Germany. It also explains today's consensus that inflation is one of the worst scourges a country can experience.

This consensus is now so deeply rooted in the everyday attitudes of people that it has become almost second nature in West Germany. As a result, behavior, clearly manifesting a will to fight inflation by all means, is not expressed as such. An illustration of this unconscious assumption is reflected clearly in a dialogue that took place on November 10, 1980, between members of the Treasury and Civil Service Committee of the British House of Commons and Dr. Hermann-Josef Dudler, a representative of the Deutsche Bundesbank:

Mr. Beaumont-Dark (member of the British Civil Service Committee): "When you say 'safeguard the currency' does [this] mean safeguarding the reserves or does it mean stopping it [from] rising too much? If you mean safeguarding the currency, does [this] mean you have to have a base rate for the currency as you see it against other people, otherwise is not the Government's economic policy then controlled by the Bundesbank? It would seem as though the Bundesbank controls everything, because they can say, 'We think the deutsche mark ought to be X'?"

Dr. Hermann-Josef Dudler (Deutsche Bundesbank): "It is safeguarding the currency. This translation from the German may be somewhat misleading. The way this term has been interpreted in Germany after the Bundesbank law had been enacted in 1957 is practically to preserve the internal value of the deutsche mark, not its external value."

Mr. Beaumont-Dark: "So you mean inflation, in other words?"

Dr. Dudler: "Inflation, yes. There is some ambiguity also as far as the meaning of the German term is concerned, but in practice, and with the full consent

*Senior Economist, The Conference Board, Inc. (Europe).

of the Government, this means nothing else than the internal stability of the deutsche mark."

Mr. Beaumont-Dark: "That is rather different."

Mr. Edward du Cann (chairman of the session): "What you have said, which is an amplification of the written evidence to us, I think will be of particular interest to the committee. Let me go on to ask you a different sort of question. Why do you think it is that Germany has been so successful in keeping close to the monetary targets which the Bundesbank has set?"

Dr. Dudler: "The basic reason, if you like, is probably beyond the control of the Bundesbank. It is the assumption from which the Bank can start that the German population is extremely sensitive to inflation and that the role of the Central Bank in public and in political terms and not just in legal terms is a very strong and autonomous one; so when we set out establishing a target and pursuing this we start from the assumption that the public at large is basically supporting the policy that lies behind it and we make sure that the economic developments as we forecast them or as the Government puts them into perspective in the form of a projection or objective, that these are broad objectives which by and large are fully supported, not only by the public but also by both sides of industry and also, of course, by the budgetary policies themselves."[1]

When reading the entire minutes of the hearings from which this text is excerpted, we find that the British representatives, who tended at times to explain the meaning of a monetarist policy to their German colleagues, did in fact discover that West Germany has been applying precisely such a policy with success. This was not because the control of monetary aggregates is sufficient to provide the control of domestic inflation, but because there is a basic agreement on the part of all economic partners to support any policy and measures adopted against inflation. From this viewpoint, the experience and response of the Federal Republic of Germany to inflation can be described, a priori, as a set of actions that are made both possible and successful because they express the fundamental willingness of all economic partners to refuse the internal depreciation of the currency.

This paper summarizes price movements in West Germany, and analyzes the basic factors generally acknowledged as having an impact on inflation: industrial relations and their effects on wages, external factors such as import prices, and government actions as expressed in the form of monetary, fiscal and budgetary policies. Unless otherwise stated, this essay deals with the period from 1965 to 1982.

Price Indexes and Price Movements

Inflation in West Germany is measured by a consumer price index (CPI) which is intended to represent the average change in a basket of goods and services

[1]House of Commons *Third Report from the Treasury and Civil Service Committee Session 1980-81. Monetary Policy* Vol. II. Minutes of evidence, pp. 298-99.

purchased by a private household. It is calculated for monthly expenses of approximately 2,300 deutsche marks (approximately $900).

The CPI is currently established with a base of 100 in 1976 and is weighted according to the results of a 1973 survey of household expenses. The collection of basic observations used for the calculation of the current index is large: 200,000 observations for 800 goods and services divided into nine categories, each divided into subcategories and groups.

The weighting of the components of the CPI can be summarized as follows:

- food at home 175.03
- beverages and tobacco 56.51
- restaurant 34.68
- clothing and shoes..................................... 87.46
- rent 133.27
- electricity, gas and domestic fuel......................... 49.13
- other household goods and services 100.10
  of which: furniture 28.97
- goods and services for transportation, information
  and communication.................................... 147.53
  of which: cars and bicycles 63.02
          gasoline and oil 27.04
          other goods and services for private cars...26.03
          foreign travel 13.82
          mail and telephone 17.62
- goods and services for skin and health care 43.16
- education and entertainment 78.73
- private foundation, other goods and services 94.40
  of which: business travel 38.20

                                                        ————
                                                    1,000.00

On the basis of the same collection of monthly observations, other specific indexes are published by the German Federal Statistical Office *(Statistisches Bundesamt):*

- Price index for a four-person household with high income;
- Price index for a two-person household: employee(s) with middle-range income;
- Price index for a two-person household: pensioners or those benefiting from social assistance.

Price Indicators Other than the CPI

West Germany publishes a full range of other statistical series on prices. They fall into seven categories:

(1) Price indexes for agricultural and forest products:
  • purchasing prices for the farming sector
  • agricultural production prices
  • production prices for the publicly owned forest sector
(2) Price indexes primarily concerning the manufacturing industry:
  • raw materials prices
  • production prices in the manufacturing sector
(3) Price index for the construction sector
(4) Wholesale price index
(5) Retail sales price index
(6) Import and export price indexes
(7) Indexes of mail and telephone communication prices.

Production price indexes are based on relatively large collections of observations— some 28,000 for the construction sector and some 15,000 in the manufacturing sector.

These indexes have to be considered in the light of the *Bundescartellamt* (the administration that deals with competition) action that prohibits cartel prices. The fact that, in general, there are few prices under control or administration (exceptions include steel and agriculture, which are subject to European Community regulations) gives particular relevance to production price indexes in West Germany, where these indexes represent effective market prices more objectively than they do in countries with directly controlled prices.

Long-term Price Movements

In the immediate post-World War II years, Germany experienced relatively high inflation: 9.3 percent in 1946, 6.9 percent in 1947, and 14.5 percent in 1948. However, currency reforms introduced by Professor Ludwig Erhard in June, 1948, marked the beginning of a long period of monetary stability and an economic evolution that raised the living standard of the German worker from a near starvation level to that of the best-paid worker in the world within a period of 30 years.

On June 21, 1948, in his speech marking the introduction of the new currency system, Professor Erhard stated quite unambiguously that: "Nothing will endanger the stability of the new currency if we take the pain of keeping our open household in order, and conduct our money and credit policy in a manner that guarantees harmony between the production of goods and the development of the purchasing power."

Between 1949 and 1982, the inflation rate was below 3 percent a year. This rate, however, covers seven periods, each characterized by average annual inflation at different rates:

- 1949 to 1955: zero inflation,
- 1956 to 1961: 2 percent,
- 1962 to 1966: 3 percent,
- 1967 to 1970: 4.3 percent,
- 1971 to 1975: 6 percent,
- 1976 to 1979: 3.6 percent,
- 1980 to 1982: 5.4 percent.

Inflation started to become a problem only at the end of the 1960's.

Taking the year 1970 as a reference point and dividing the 12-year period 1970 to 1982 into two equal segments (in 1976 the weighting system of the CPI was changed), we can summarize the behavior of prices as follows: Electricity, oil and gas, because of the two oil shocks, increased at a rate of 10 percent in the first period and 12 percent in the second; apart from this acceleration, the period 1976 to 1982 was characterized by lower inflation for all other categories of goods and services that comprise the CPI. That is, if electricity, oil and gas are excluded from the index, the average inflation rate would have been 5.7 percent per year during the period from 1970 to 1976 and only 4 percent a year during the period from 1976 to 1982.

Analyzing Inflation: Costs, Excess Demand, and Prices

In a book published in 1978, Wolfgang Sengebusch, a German econometrician, conducted a systematic analysis of the influence of costs (wage costs as well as costs of raw materials and imports) and of the overall inflationary environment that may result from permanent excess demand on producer prices.[2] Sengebusch studied these influences both at the aggregate level of the entire manufacturing sector and at the level of individual sectors of the industry. Quarterly data covering the period 1964-1974 were used for the estimates.

According to Sengebusch's model, changes in the CPI tend to reflect:

- one-fifth of production price movements in the food sector,
- one-fifth of production price movements in the consumer-durable goods sector,
- one-sixth of production price movements in the investment goods sector.

The impact of price changes in the construction sector on the CPI is relatively small; a 10 percent change in the price index of the construction sector generates less than a 1 percent change in the CPI.

Among the explanatory factors, there is a strong "autonomous" influence, representing an automatic upward drift in the CPI independent of the specific causal factors covered by the model. This autonomous influence is strong for almost every sector, even those in which the impact of wage movements are

[2]Wolfgang Sengebusch. *Ein Preismodell fur die Bundesrepublik Deutscheland.* Frankfurt am Main: Peter Lang Verlag; 1978.

important. For example, in the mining sector, where the ratio of wage costs to sales is the highest (42.1 percent), variations in these costs to sales account for only one-half of the variation in output prices.

This autonomous influence, however, is not positive for all sectors. In the case of the investment goods and food sectors, a "natural" downward trend in output prices has occurred. For the investment goods sector, such a tendency reflects a combination of productivity gains and the advantages of economies of scale that resulted from the opening of external markets to German goods; for the food sector, successive revaluations of the deutsche mark held down the rise in domestic prices for agricultural products.

Import prices are significant, not just for output prices of sectors such as the oil and mineral industries, but also for the CPI as a whole. However, according to the model, the influence of import prices on the CPI is delayed by two quarters.

Sengebusch's model has not escaped technical criticism. Nonetheless, given the statistical material available, it does provide a highly systematic explanation of the influence of identifiable costs and supply-demand market tensions on output prices. The significant finding of the model is that, even after all of these inflation-causing effects on the price level are taken into account, there remains an unexplained upward movement in the general price level. In short, in studying inflation itself it is not possible to distinguish clearly between the role of the mechanisms that transmit inflation (wage costs, import prices, supply-demand imbalances, etc.) from the role of forces that cause these factors to rise in the first place. For example, a rise in wage costs, as such, may not result in a general rise in prices—it does so only under certain conditions.

West German real wage costs, including social-security contributions, have risen at a faster pace than in the other major industrialized countries. Yet between 1965 and 1982, West Germany experienced a lower average rate of inflation in its CPI than did any other major economy. Nonetheless, the West German inflation rate from 1965-1982 averaged 4½ percent a year. Sengebusch's model does not in itself pretend to explain why prices in general rose at that rate. For an explanation, it is necessary to turn to the behavior of monetary policy.

Monetary Policy

Monetary policy in West Germany is conducted by the Deutsche Bundesbank, the central bank. The responsibility of the Bundesbank was clearly defined by legislation passed in 1957: *"the regulation of credit supply, with the target of safeguarding the currency."*

What is the practical meaning of the expression "safeguarding the currency" (in German: *die Wahrung sichern)?* In the hearings of the British Treasury and Civil Service Committee on Monetary Policy, quoted earlier in this essay, Dr. Dudler, the representative from the Bundesbank, explained that this expression meant "nothing else than preserving the internal value of the deutsche mark."

Otmar Emminger, former president of the Bundesbank, stated that, after 15 years, experience, the incompatibility of ensuring simultaneously the internal and the external value of the deutsche mark had been made clear; the deutsche mark has been revalued three times against the main external currencies and has also changed its value vis-a-vis gold. In addition, during three periods the deutsche mark has floated. The target of all 'these external changes has been to protect the internal purchasing power of the deutsche mark. According to Dr. Emminger, it is impossible to maintain indefinitely a fixed value of the currency when one is seeking stability of its internal purchasing power. The priority of internal price stability over external exchange-rate stability was also clear in the statement that stability of the internal purchasing power is of "primordial importance."

Safeguarding the Currency

The Bundesbank's role is to adjust the quantity of money in circulation to the needs of the economy, avoiding both an excess or shortage in the money supply. Such a definition, dating from 1957, belongs clearly to the monetarist school of thought, and affirms that "changes in the quantity of money available are the main determinant in the level of prices," and that "the control of the quantity of money available is the main instrument of any policy targeting price stability."[3]

This statement, by a former president of the Bundesbank, unambiguously shows the similarity between the views of the German Federal Bank and the monetarist school, even before such views became official doctrine elsewhere in the Western industrialized world. One may discuss at length whether such a coincidence simply reflects the fact that the monetarist approach is the proper one, or whether a monetarist doctrine expresses the natural and inevitable viewpoint of a central bank whose role is to regulate the money supply, and which has no other instrument for influencing the economy. Whatever the outcome of such a discussion, in practice West Germany has followed a relatively orthodox monetary policy for more than 20 years, and this policy has coincided with relative stability in West Germany's internal price level.

As is true in other countries, the application of a monetarist policy has not been without problems in West Germany. One problem is how to project changes in the velocity of circulation of money; that is, how to distinguish whether a change in velocity is primarily a short-term rather than a long-term problem.

The other main debate has concerned the reference figures to be used for targeting nominal growth in the money supply. Should the reference target be real income per capita, real GNP, or some other aggregate? And, after this reference target has been selected, what is the corresponding definition for the money supply that should be used to implement this growth target?

The Bundesbank has in practice been pragmatic. It has adopted the follow-

[3]Otmar Emminger, *Verteidegung der Deutschemark*. Fritz Knapp Verlag, 1980.

ing as a reasonable guideline for the medium term: "To let the volume of money available approximately increase with real [deflated] GNP plus an additional normative increase in the price level." (This has since been adopted as the target of the European Community, as a result of the September, 1972, economic guidelines adopted by the EC finance ministers.)

Economic Growth and the Money Supply: Maintaining Harmony

Using the criteria outlined above, how does the Bundesbank maintain harmony between economic growth and money supply? In practice, the Bundesbank cannot regulate the money supply directly, but only indirectly through its influence on commercial bank reserves—the main determinant of money creation. Its role is to establish a flexible range of variations for money-supply growth, and to assure that the money supply stays within this range.

Because of this flexibility and because the Bundesbank has only an indirect command over the money supply, central bank action always has uncertain effects in the short term, and these effects are subject to varying lags. Therefore, the timing of the Bundesbank's actions plays a determining role. As a result, the tools of monetary policy have been adapted in order to ensure that they have a rapid and proportionate effect on the money supply.

Until the early 1970's, the emphasis in monetary policy was essentially guided by the behavior of interest rates and money-market conditions. Only after the first oil shock (1973-1974) did the Bundesbank first place greater emphasis on monetary-growth targets and try to introduce a psychological—or anticipatory—factor into the system, independent of the handling of traditional elements such as the official discount rate or minimum reserve requirements. By so doing, the central bank has also signaled that it is now sharing the responsibility for safeguarding the currency with the government, labor and management.

The Bundesbank enforces its policy by a two-stage implementation procedure. It looks at a quantity target for monetary growth as an intermediate objective to be achieved in the long run, while, in the very short run—day-to-day operations or even over a month or two—it directs its actions in the light of money-market conditions, the liquidity position of the banking system, and key interest rates, in order to make them consistent with the long-run achievement of its basic monetary-growth target. Essentially the Bundesbank operates in the money market on a day-to-day basis to achieve the quantity objectives in the long-term, using a short-term policy that consists of a manipulation of money-market conditions.

Not until 1974, after the first oil crisis and after inflation had risen to over 7 percent per year, did the Bundesbank first publicly announce a target for monetary growth. At that stage, such an announcement was considered to be more an experiment than a change in monetary practice. The significance of this first official announcement of a monetary growth target was largely undermined by West German entrepreneurs and trade unions. At first they did not understand that the new attitude, in practice, implied more restrictive policies and actions to keep the money supply tight in order to reduce the pressure from increased costs and increased demand. Prior to 1974, entrepreneurs and trade unions had become accustomed to the Bundesbank's objectives being disregarded to a certain extent because they were too frequently contradicted by dollar inflows that were purchased by the central bank. By clearly announcing a monetary-growth target, however, the Bundesbank was publicly declaring that it would no longer accommodate inflows of foreign capital that would fuel the money supply, and that the effects of capital inflows would be offset in order to stay within the declared targets for monetary growth.

The intermediate target variable used by the Bundesbank, called the "central bank money stock," consists of currency in the hands of the nonbank public plus required minimum reserves on banks' domestic liabilities, calculated at a constant reserve ratio. The central bank money stock is the direct contribution of the Bundesbank to money creation. The choice of this indicator was based on the assumptions that it related well with the pace of monetary expansion and that its variations were similar to that of M-3 (the broadly defined money supply, currency in circulation, plus deposits of less than four years' maturity, plus savings deposits at statutory notice). However, in defining the money stock, the liquid assets of the nonbanking sector are given different weights according to their degree of liquidity: Experience has shown that the variation of the components of M-3 may diverge. In West Germany, for example, M-2 (which is equal to M-3 minus saving deposits at statutory notice) grew by 8½ percent in 1981, whereas M-3, the broader measure, increased by only 5 percent.

These divergent trends in the components of the money supply point to the shift in the distribution of monetary assets that resulted from high short-term interest rates. The owners of liquid assets tend to alter the composition of their holdings in order to maximize the income they produce. In 1981, for example, there was a shift in the growth rate of M-3 relative to M-2 because the three-month deposit was preferred to the short-term savings at statutory notice. Because of such shifts, the Bundesbank has elected not to adopt a narrow definition of money (M-1 in particular) as a criterion for action on monetary policy.

In spite of such refinements, monetary policy has to look beyond the increase in money aggregates alone. It is necessary also to consider the effects of monetary policies on nonmonetary assets. It is obvious, for example, that tight money-supply conditions encourage corporations to function with low inventories, which may result in bottlenecks and inflexibility in the production sector. It is also realistic to consider that high short-term interest rates, in a situation of an inverted yield curve (short-term interest rates being higher than long-term ones) are an incentive to deflect funds that would normally be channeled into long-term investments and to use them instead for short-term purposes. This leads to further rises in long-term rates which, in turn, make it necessary to employ still higher short-term interest rates to make money-supply control effective, thus dampening economic growth in the production sector.

At the end of each year, the Bundesbank announces its target for the growth of the central bank money stock for the coming year. The target is usually formulated as an average annual growth rate over four quarters, and is based on assumptions regarding the real growth of the GNP and on a normative inflation rate which is considered, ex ante, as unavoidable. In most recent years, because of uncertainties regarding both real growth and the impact of external events on domestic activity and finances, the Bundesbank has announced its target for the coming year in the form of a range. Furthermore, it has adapted this target range during the course of the year, announcing in June-July of each year that it was holding either to the upper or to the lower end of the previously announced range. In November, 1980, for example, the announced target range for 1981 was 4 to 7 percent. In the first two months of that year, however, the deutsche mark foreign-exchange rate weakened and came under pressure for devaluation, the current account position of West Germany was vulnerable, and the domestic inflation rate accelerated. As a consequence, in its report for the year 1981, the Bundesbank noted that it had to give a clear signal to strengthen confidence in the West German currency. The Bundesbank, therefore, raised the cost and cut the supply of liquidity to the banking system in late February. In addition, the Bank adjusted its target at midyear, announcing that monetary growth would be kept on the lower end of the initial range: between 4 and 5½ percent. This adjusted target was achieved: Between December, 1980, and December, 1981, the money stock did increase by 5 percent.

Regulating the Money Supply

The central bank uses four basic mechanisms to achieve its growth targets:

(1) It alters the discount and Lombard interest rates, which are the Bundesbank's own lending rates.

(2) It influences the liquidity position of banks: Under West German law, banks are required to maintain at the Bundesbank minimum noninterest-bearing reserve balances; these minimum reserves are determined in the form of a ratio of the bank's domestic and foreign liabilities and are calculated on a monthly average basis.

(3) It uses open-market policy (sales and purchase of Treasury bills).

(4) It regulates capital imports.

The scope and pragmatism of the central bank's actions cannot be better described than by referring to the memorandum prepared by the Bundesbank in answer to the questionnaire of the British Treasury and Civil Service Committee on monetary policy, referred to earlier in this chapter:

> "In the practical conduct of monetary policy in Germany it will hardly be possible to pursue monetary growth targets in the short or medium term and to link the use of the central bank's instruments in a 'quasi-automatic'

manner to changes in the money supply. In the short run, according to past experience, the money stock in Germany is often subject to considerable random fluctuations, and in the long run, too, it may move in ways that are not easy to explain on the basis of the observed relationships between the money supply and key macroeconomics variables (gross national product, domestic demand, prices, interest rates, exchange rate, methods of payment and cash-holding practices). Since the mid-seventies the economic and political disturbances have become more pronounced, and it is not impossible that attitudes in the financial, goods and labor markets have changed slightly. The Bundesbank has therefore tended not to counteract short-term—and possible reversible—departures of the central bank money stock from the target path (i.e., those of perhaps one to three months' duration) by immediately changing its interest rate and liquidity policy stance; first-of-all it must be clear that these departures are not of a very short-term nature. Furthermore, the Bundesbank is always guided in its decisions by the development of a large number of important monetary and general economic indicators.'' (pp. 294-295.)

Within the framework of such a pragmatic approach, there is no conflict between the internal and external stability of the deutsche mark. Since the ultimate goal is internal price stability, German authorities have accepted that an external appreciation of the currency is a price to be paid to achieve this goal. In addition, in recent years it has been recognized that the appreciation of the currency simply represents (with a lag) the fact that German prices did not rise as rapidly as those of its trading partners, and that, consequently, this was not a threat to the international competitive position of the country.

However, the sharp strengthening of the U.S. dollar in 1981, 1982, and 1983 vis-a-vis the deutsche mark led to serious questioning of this view. An additional surprise was that exchange rates were becoming increasingly volatile at a time when both inflation and inflation differentials had fallen throughout the world. In this regard, the Bundesbank's annual report for 1982 noted that "Most countries agree that interest rate induced deviations of the exchange rate from [the basic trend corresponding to the trend of international price and costs differentials] should be kept as low as possible."

Recent experience suggests that the classical argument, namely that exchange-rate trends reflect trends in relative prices and costs, had to be amended to show that exchange-rate variations also reflect anticipated changes in the relative rates of inflation.

Budgetary and Fiscal Policies

In West Germany, in contrast to other countries, the management of the public-sector deficit has not been a major problem for the monetary authorities until recently. However, this situation changed with the growth in the public-sector deficit to 4.5 percent of GNP in 1981. As a consequence, fiscal policy, which had been conceived principally as a countercyclical tool, is now principally aimed at bringing the level of the budget deficit down over the long term to less than 3 percent of GNP.

Trends in Revenues and Taxes

General government revenue can be divided into three main categories: indirect taxes, direct taxes, and social-security contributions.

The share of indirect taxes, which represented 35 to 40 percent of total government income in the 1960's, declined to less than 30 percent by the end of the 1970's. Simultaneously, the proportion of direct taxes increased from 28 percent in the 1960's to some 30 percent by the end of the 1970's. More substantially, the share of the social-security contribution rose from 26 to 33 percent. As a result of these developments, revenues today are derived almost equally from direct taxes, indirect taxes, and social-security contributions (approximately 30 percent each). The share of other receipts (between 7 and 8 percent of total government income) has not changed much over the past 20 years.

The structural change in government revenues, characterized by a long-term shift in the direction of more direct taxation, took place in several different stages. After 1968-1969 when a Value Added Tax (VAT) was introduced at a common rate of 11 percent and a special rate of 5½ percent for essential goods and services, the ratio of indirect taxes to GNP declined from 1970 to 1975, and rose in 1978-1979 partially because of increases in VAT rates. Conversely, the proportion of direct taxes rose during the period 1960-1975 (except for 1968-1969), and declined thereafter. The average rate of income tax on wages and salaries rose from about 7 percent in the early 1960's to 16 percent in the early 1980's—an increase resulting from the general rise in real income that moved an increasing proportion of taxpayers from the lower, flat-rate tax band into the middle progressive one.

Taxes on corporate profits experienced the most erratic changes because of swings in corporate profitability. Overall, however, a declining trend was observed for corporate taxes throughout the period 1960-1980, the decline being particularly pronounced after 1976, a result of the corporate tax reforms introduced in 1977 and of a more favorable fiscal treatment of depreciation allowances. Apart from these factors, however, the long-term reduction in the proportion of government revenues based on corporate profits is a result of the slow growth in corporate income and the absence of progressivity in corporate taxation.

The Federal Government's contribution to social-security funds was reduced from 45 percent in the mid-1960's to 40 percent in the mid-1970's, and has remained stable since then. To compensate for that reduction, the share of employee and employer contribution to the social-security funds was increased. This took place mainly in the period 1968-1976, as demographic pressures led to increased health expenses. For employees, contributions to social benefits rose from 11 percent of earnings to 16 percent between 1960 and 1980; for employers, in the same period, it rose from 17 to 32½ percent of the corporate operating surplus.

Trends in Expenditures

As a percentage of GNP, government income increased from 36 to 43 percent between the early 1960's and the early 1980's, and public expenditure (federal and local governments plus social-security funds) rose from 35 to 45 percent. Consequently, the share of the public sector in domestic consumption has increased substantially. To a lesser extent, the same development has occurred with regard to the proportion of public investment in total capital formation. In real terms both public-sector investment and public-sector consumption doubled between 1960 and 1980, which corresponds to a 3½ percent average annual growth.

With regard to current expenditure, growth was particularly rapid in the education sector in the decade 1965-1975. This growth resulted primarily from a rapid increase in the number of students, over 4½ percent per year on average in secondary schools and over 10 percent per year in universities. (These movements were only partially offset by a reduction in the number of teachers at the primary school level.) The annual growth rate of the number of students has dropped in recent years, to around 4 percent at the university level and 2 percent at the secondary level.

Also reflecting demographic trends, the growth in health expenditure was rapid during the 1970's because of the population was aging. These growth trends have been slowing in the 1980's. The opinion of the Organization for Economic Cooperation and Development (OECD) is that the natural growth (mainly explained by demographic developments) of education and health expenditures was supplemented by the faster rise in the cost of providing public rather than private goods and services, which itself is a function of the higher wage content of government activity.

Until the mid-1970's, the increase in the per capita pension rate was similar to the growth of per capita private consumption. The number of pensioners increased rapidly because of an aging population, so total outlays rose in real terms at an average annual rate of 10 percent between 1960 and 1974. Since 1975, the increase in the number of beneficiaries from pensions has been lower, and, in real terms, pensions grew at only 3 percent per year, made up of a 1½ percent annual growth in the number of beneficiaries and a 1½ percent annual growth (in real terms) in the rate of pensions per capita (over the same period the average annual increase in real private consumption per capita has been 3.3 percent).

Until 1965, child allowances increased rapidly in real terms but, thereafter, began to erode because of inflation. A change was made in the system of family support in 1975, and direct social-security payments replaced tax allowances. This modification resulted in an 11 billion deutsche mark rise in the yearly expenditure for child allowances. However, since 1975, the per capita allowance in real terms has not risen faster than per capita consumption and, because of a 3 percent per year reduction in the number of children under 15 (children over 15 do not benefit from the allowance), total family benefits have declined.

In 1980, unemployment benefits amounted to 18½ billion deutsche marks, or 8 percent of total transfer payments to households. Following the pattern of economic activity, unemployment benefits declined before the first oil crisis and started to rise sharply after 1975.

The doubling (in real terms) of government fixed investment between 1960 and 1980 occurred over several periods. Until 1963-1964 investment increased at a rapid pace, but this period was followed by a period of stagnation (1964-1965) and a decline (1966). Another period of rapid growth lasted until the end of the 1970's. The decade from 1970 to 1980 was also characterized by alternating periods of decline (1970-1972 and 1974-1977) and growth (1973-1974 and 1977-1978). However, the average annual increase of government investment was less than 1 percent in real terms during the decade 1970-1980, compared with 6 percent in the decade 1960-1970. This summary clearly indicates that the slowdown in public expenditure, resulting from policies aimed at reducing the public sector's expenditure in proportion to GNP, has been more pronounced with regard to investment than to current expenditure.

Housing was the predominant component in public investment in the initial post-World War II period, but was reduced in the 1960's as expenditures on transportation and communication—mainly road construction—became the most important item in public capital formation. The 1970's were characterized by a reversal of these trends and housing, once again, has tended to be more important.

Impact of the Budget Deficit

As described above, the public sector's finances have followed an expansionary trend over the past 20 years. Such an expansion is generally supposed to have a stimulatory effect. However, some debate has taken place in recent years in West Germany about whether a policy favoring the expansion of public finances always has a positive impact. The Council of Experts, which annually presents its report on economic conditions to the German government, pointed out in its December, 1981, report that in recent years, and especially in 1981, the economic environment had changed so that an expansion in the public deficit was no longer necessarily positive. According to the Council, as long as there is assurance that the external value of the currency will not be altered, government deficits do not lead to any significant increase in interest rates; indeed, the deficits in some cases may coincide with declining rates of interest. When such confidence in the future strength of the currency no longer exists, however, further increases in the public-sector deficit become harmful because interest rates rise, the exchange rate falls, inflation worsens, and the Bundesbank has to intervene with a tighter monetary policy, leading to further rises in interest rates. As a result, private investment falls and private consumption is reduced.

The deutsche mark has tended to rise through most of the post-World War II period. Thus, in fact, as opposed to theory, the main problem caused by the expansion in public spending in West Germany has had little to do with the hypothetical rise in interest rates such spending might have caused but rather from the fact that the quasi-permanent stimulation of domestic demand from government spending has distorted normal market mechanisms. Such distortion leads to difficulties when, for structural reasons, public spending can no longer play its stimulative role. Just such a difficulty occurred when public investment spending in the housing sector declined after the demographic expansion ended, and declined later in the transportation and communication sectors after both public roads and communication networks had been sufficiently developed. When that stage is reached, a government faces a temptation not to reduce its share of the economy and, hence, to shift its expenditures from capital formation to current expenditure. This was the case in West Germany.

At the beginning of the 1970's, gross fixed investment represented some 12 percent of general government spending. By the beginning of the 1980's, this proportion had fallen to less than 8 percent. At the same time, overall public-sector spending in proportion to GNP rose from 34 to 46 percent. The effects of such a change in the pattern of public spending are threefold: (1) The impetus given to the economy by government expenditures becomes weaker because a multiplier effect on the economy becomes smaller; (2) a long-term inflationary pressure is present because current expenditure contributes less than investment expenditures to the improvement of the long-run productivity of the country; and (3) the increase in current expenditure means that more of the budget is used for the remuneration of government employees, which tends to increase the proportion of statutory and inflexible expenses in contrast to public expenditures for investment. In this regard, it is significant to observe that the number of government employees in West Germany increased from 11 percent of total employees in the 1960's to 17 percent in 1980. Simultaneously, the proportion of government wage payments to total wage payments rose from 17 to 24 percent.

The progressive substitution of current public consumption for public investment reinforced the natural tendency of public expenditures to fluctuate less than public revenues because the latter reflect variations in the business cycle. As a result, public-sector expenditures tended to exert countercyclical effects, the public-sector deficit being higher during recessionary periods than in other periods.

In addition, in the Federal Republic of Germany, the structure of the public sector is characterized by the relatively small size of the central government's budget. The fact that the states and the local authorities determine their outlays in a rather independent manner creates yet another basis for inflexibility in the area of public spending. In 1967, however, a stabilization and growth law was passed that constrained the local administrations' budgets so that they conform better to the framework defined by the federal authorities.

Combined with the relative decline of investment in public spending, which itself is explained by the structural evolution just described, the overall increase of the public sector's share in the economy implied a significant reallocation of resources from the private to the public sector, where productivity is generally assumed to be lower. In 1980, the value added per person employed was estimated to be around 39,000 deutsche marks in the manufacturing sector and only 23,000 deutsche marks in the government sector. In addition, unit labor costs have been increasing faster in the public sector (on average by 6.5 percent a year in the 1960's and 7.1 percent in the 1970's) than in the private sector (on average, 3.6 percent a year and 5.3 percent a year, respectively, in the two decades).

During periods of high levels of capacity utilization (from the mid-1960's to the mid-1970's), both the private and the public sectors increased rapidly. Therefore, government's rising requirements, in terms of new employment and capital, tended to limit the possibilities —or to increase the costs—of private-sector growth. This occurred not only in the years when the public budget showed a deficit but also during periods of surplus, because the value added per person employed was always lower in the public sector than in the private sector and the government needed comparatively larger capital and labor inputs in order to generate the same additional cash flow as the private sector. Hence, the rechanneling of investment funds from the private sector to the public sector coincided with a decline in corporate-sector profitability, especially in the 1970's, for two reasons: (1) The government sector showed greater inertia than the private sector in periods of declining activity; (2) The same cost-advantage criteria that would lead to a favorable decision for new investment in the public sector might well have led to a rejection of the investment in the private sector, on the basis that the profitability it offered was too low.

Financial Market Responses to Inflation

The principal responses of the West Germany financial markets to inflation were:

(1) The proportion of corporate assets financed by equity capital declined sharply from 30 percent in 1965 to 20 percent by 1982.

(2) The savings share of the overall domestic sector was cut in half—from nearly 20 percent of annual net national product in the 1960's to 10 percent by 1981-1982.

(3) The volume of assets and liabilities of both banking and other financial intermediaries grew rapidly between 1960 and 1980, but relative market shares shifted away from commercial and mortgage banks into the cooperative banking sector.

Corporate Financing

It is frequently observed that West German industry is generally more highly leveraged than, for example, industry in the United Kingdom; that is, the equity of West German corporations in relation to their total assets is generally less than those of U.K. corporations. Different accounting practices may explain the apparent differences in the leverage or gearing ratio. For example, although U.K. accounting regulations allow revaluation of assets, in West Germany corporate assets usually have to be valued at historic costs. As a result, in a period of expansion such as 1971-1974, more than one-fifth of the net worth of U.K. companies was attributable to assets revaluation; such an adjustment did not appear in the balance sheets of West German companies.

However, the equity funds ratio (common stock and surplus as a percentage of balance sheet) did deteriorate in the period under review. It declined from 30 percent in 1965 to 27 percent in 1970 to 21 percent in 1980, and to about 20 percent in 1982. This movement was particularly pronounced in several consumer goods sectors. Between 1968 and 1980, for example, the ratio fell from 33 percent to 15 percent in the clothing industry, from 29 to 14 percent in the wood processing industry, and from 27 percent to 16 percent in retail trade. Structurally, the construction sector has always showed a relatively low ratio of equity funds, but this did not prevent it from deteriorating from 15 percent in 1965 to 6 percent in 1980.

The traditionally competitive West German industries, where the proportion of equity funds in the balance sheet is the highest, also experienced a decline in the equity funds ratio between 1965 and 1980. The chemical industry declined from 44 percent to 38 percent; iron and steel from 37 percent to 26 percent; and the automobile industry from 38 to 26 percent.

According to the Deutsche Bundesbank, the main cause of the persistent deterioration of the equity-capital base was the insufficient earning power of enterprises. The ratio of net cash flow (profit for the year plus depreciation) to sales declined irregularly from 7 percent in 1965 to 6 percent in 1980.

Nonetheless, the deterioration of the equity-capital base did not produce a significant change in the liquidity position of firms. Financial assets and inventories that represented more than 55 percent of total assets in the mid 1960's declined to 52 percent in 1970-1974, but recovered to 54 percent in 1975-1979 and 57 percent in 1981.

Short-term Versus Long-term Debt

The deterioration of the equity-capital base was accompanied by an increase in the proportion of short-term debts on the balance sheet. In 1966, short-term debts represented some 30 percent of the total balance sheet as against 18 percent for long-term debts. By the beginning of the 1980's, the share of short-term debts had risen to 45 percent.

The movement of inventories has been less pronouced in West Germany than in other countries with higher inflation. Periods of expansion were not accompanied by excessive stockbuilding because inflationary expectations did not rise as rapidly. However, inventory building did tend to accelerate during inflationary periods in West Germany, too. For example, when the consumer price index rose 7.8 percent between December, 1972, and December, 1973 (the maximum one-year rate for the period under review), the inventories of West German companies rose by 18.5 percent while sales increased by only 11.5 percent. By contrast, in 1976—another year of expansion but with much lower (4 percent) inflation—inventories rose by only 13 percent, with an 11 percent growth in sales.

These movements, combined with the deterioration of the equity-capital base and a decline in the willingness of the entrepreneur to provide risk capital, resulted in significant changes in capital structures. The proportion of tangible (or nonfinancial) assets taking the form of inventories increased from 30 percent in 1967 to 38 percent in 1970-1974 and to 45 percent in 1981. This trend led to an increased weight of inventories in the total assets of West German corporations (from 18 percent in 1967 to 24.5 percent in 1981), and, correspondingly, to the growing role of inventories as a counterpart of short-term indebtedness.

In short, changes in corporate financing over the past 20 years included:

- the diminishing role of companies' own funds;
- the increased share of short-term debt in financial assets, a share that rose faster than that of long-term debt (the ratio of short-term to long-term debt growing from 2 in 1967 to 2.5 in 1981);
- the rising role of inventories as a tangible asset.

It would, therefore, be legitimate to project an increasing sensitivity of industry pricing policies not only to long-term financing conditions, but also to short-term financing conditions. However, as stated before, German industry's constant exposure to international competition, both in domestic and foreign markets, prevented price increases that otherwise might have resulted from the increased cost of inventory financing. We have seen in the more recent period the limit and the danger of such a development—the recent recession has tended to provoke far more bankruptcies than occurred in the 1970's especially in the manufacturing sectors that are characterized by both a weak capital base and a high proportion of assets in the form of inventories: The industries most vulnerable in these respects are clothing (which had an equity to capital ratio of only 14.8 percent and which held 71 percent of its assets in the form of inventories), mechanical engineering (20.6 percent and 65 percent), electrical engineering (23.4 percent and 59 percent), and the textile industry (21.6 percent and 58 percent).

Consumer Savings

The overall savings ratio of the domestic sector—the proportion of the net (after-tax) national product available for capital formation—has been reduced dramatically in the last 20 years. In the 1960's, it was about 19.5 percent; it decreased steadily to 10.5 percent in 1981.

The deterioration of the savings propensity reflects principally the overall developments in the corporate sector outlined above, namely, the reduction in capital formation that resulted from shrinking cash flows and a weakening of the equity-capital base. By contrast, the savings ratio of households tended to increase. According to the Bundesbank's definition of savings, the savings ratio of households increased from 3 percent in the 1950's to 11 percent in the mid-1960's to 15 percent in the mid-1970's. Since then it has stabilized at between 14 and 15 percent.

An emerging characteristic of household savings in the 1970's was its tendency to rise in periods of recession and to fall in periods of expansion. For example, the savings ratio rose from 14 percent in 1973 to 15 percent in 1974 and to 16 percent in 1976. It then dropped when recovery began. A similar movement was observed in the more recent cycle: The ratio increased from 14.4 percent in 1979 to 15.3 percent in 1981.

Starting in 1949, the financial assets of German households grew from 19 billion deutsche marks (DM) to more than DM 404 billion in 1969—an average 16 percent growth per year. The increase was especially fast—21 percent per year—during the reconstruction phase of the 1950's, a result not only of the increase in the saving propensity itself, but also of policy measures taken by the authorities. Thereafter, the growth of household financial assets slowed to an average annual rate of 13 percent in the 1960's. In the 1970's, yearly growth was about 15 percent, and total financial assets of households for the year 1981 were estimated at about DM 1.6 trillion, of which 80 percent was in interest-bearing form. Thus, it is estimated that households received nearly DM 80 billion of interest and dividends in 1981, a substantial part of which was reinvested in new financial assets.

German households have tended to invest an increasing fraction of their annual disposable investment funds in bonds: 29 percent in 1981, compared with 10 percent in 1970 and 2 percent in 1949 just after the currency reform. By contrast, the proportion of funds allocated to the acquisition of shares (equities) has declined, from 26 percent in 1949 to 14 percent in the mid-1960's and 7 percent in 1978. In 1979, 1980, and 1981, the balance between acquisitions and sales of stocks was actually negative; in 1982 it was only DM 0.5 billion, as compared with a total of DM 156.7 billion of total household acquisition of financial assets.

Once monetary policy became more established (after the first official announcement in 1974 of a monetary target by the Bundesbank) and brought about higher interest rates, households tended to become even more sensitive to interest rates and less attracted by liquidity. The proportion of their financial assets invested in short-term savings accounts tended to decline, from 50 percent in the early 1970's to 37 percent by 1981. The higher level of interest rates also reduced the willingness of households to borrow for the purpose of consumption—one explanation for the higher savings ratio since 1980, a recessionary period characterized by tight money-supply conditions.

Financial Institutions and Markets

The two tendencies described above: (1) of West German corporations to require external financing in a larger proportion, and (2) of households to be more attracted by interest-bearing assets, coincided with a rapid expansion of the banking business.

In the 1950's, the volume of banking business—starting from the very low base of 1947, the year before the currency reform—was multiplied by a factor of about six; bank assets grew by 20 percent a year on average. Total assets reached DM 260 billion at the end of 1960.

During the 1960's and 1970's, the rapid expansion of the building and loan associations and insurance companies, whose volume of business grew by some 15 percent a year on average, dampened the increase of banking business. However, banking assets continued to rise to DM 817 billion by the end of 1970 (a 12 percent a year growth on average) and to DM 2,710 billion at the end of 1982 (an 11 percent a year growth).

Commercial banks represented about one-quarter of the total volume of banking business in 1970, about the same as in 1960. During the 1970's, this share was reduced to 22 percent. By contrast, the cooperative bank sector and the savings bank sector increased their market shares. This is especially true for credit cooperatives whose share increased from 5.8 percent in 1960 to 11.4 percent in 1982 (see Table 1).

Loans from all banking groups to domestic nonbanks was about DM 272 billion at the end of 1964. This increased to 513 billion (end 1970) to 804.5 billion (end 1974) and to 1,698 billion (end 1982). Thus, credit expansion was relatively faster before the first oil shock—and the coinciding surge in inflation—than it was after 1974. During these three periods, loans to the public authorities, which rose from DM 40.5 billion at the end of 1964 to DM 408.6 billion by the end of 1982, increased steadily at a faster rate than loans to domestic enterprises and households, which rose from DM 232 billion at the end of 1964 to DM 1,289 billion at the end of 1982.

In addition, the increase in loans to domestic public authorities tended to accelerate from an average yearly growth of 12.5 percent between 1964 and 1974 to 15 percent between 1974 and 1982. By contrast, loans to the private domestic agents grew at a slower pace after 1974 (8.4 percent a year on average) than prior to 1974 (11 percent a year). The rapidly rising volume of loans to domestic public authorities reflected the rapid rise in the public-sector deficit. Hence, during the most recent recessionary period, the annual amounts of new

Table 1
SHARES OF GERMAN BANKING GROUPS
IN THE TOTAL VOLUME OF BUSINESS
(percent)

Banking groups	1960	1970	1982
All banks	100.0	100.0	100.0
Commercial banks total	24.0	25.0	22.2
large banks	11.3	10.3	8.6
Regional banks and other commercial banks(including branches of foreign banks)...	10.4	12.2	12.2
Private bankers	2.7	2.5	1.4
Savings bank sector total ...,.	35.7	38.5	38.1
Central giro institutions and deutsche girozentrale	13.5	15.6	16.2
Savings banks	22.2	22.9	21.9
Cooperative bank sector total .	8.6	11.5	15.6
Central institutions of credit cooperatives	5.8	7.7	11.4
Credit cooperatives..........	5.8	7.7	11.4
Mortgage banks total.........	17.2	13.7	14.5
Private	5.8	6.6	8.9
Public	11.4	7.1	5.6
Installment sales financing institutions	1.5	1.1	1.2
Banks with special functions ..	10.2	8.4	6.8
Postal giro and postal savings bank offices................	2.4	1.8	1.6

Source: Deutsche Bundesbank, varies reports.

loans to households and private corporations dropped dramatically by 38 percent between 1979 and 1982, whereas funds destined for the government sector rose by a sharp 40 percent during the same period.

Such movements in the composition of credit flows illustrate the most controversial outcomes of monetary policies. They clearly demonstrate that a tightening in money-supply growth creates financing difficulties for the private and productive sector, while the government seems less affected. During a period of monetary stringency, the government does not immediately and directly have to face the sanction of high interest rates. (It can continue to borrow, and transfer the costs to the taxpayer.) However, the entrepreneur cannot avoid the constraints of minimum business profitability requirements and has to stop borrowing when the costs of borrowing exceed the marginal profitability of the capital invested. Consequently, it is not surprising that the most indisputable effect of the tightening of monetary policies in West Germany, as well as in other countries, since 1980, has been to depress investment severely.

Conclusions

This review of West Germany's experience and response to inflation has shown how difficult it is, when dealing with any factor, attitude or action that supposedly affects the level of inflation, to distinguish between its direct and indirect effects on the behavior of prices. The indirect effects may contradict the immediate effects over the long run. Economic mechanisms are complex; like biological organisms, they are built around local equilibria that are made to fit together via a constant flow of interactions, feedbacks and regulatory mechanisms. Therefore, the same factor or action may have contrasting effects in different environments.

We have seen, for example, that during the periods when the deutsche mark is strong and under pressure for upward revaluation (when Germany is attracting foreign capital), a large public-sector deficit does not seem to fuel inflation. This is true for the following reasons:

(1) West Germany is an open economy; a large share (30 percent) of German output is exported, and another large share (also about 30 percent) of demand is supplied by imports. When the deutsche mark rises, import prices fall. Thus foreign trade provides a steady brake on domestic prices.

(2) Because of the constant inflows of capital, interest rates remain low and the competition from public-sector borrowing does not lead to increases in the cost of financing for industry.

(3) The public-sector deficit itself (frequently considered to be inflationary because it has no corresponding counterpart of goods or services to be sold on the market and because the government sector is less productive than the private sector) is balanced by the inflow of foreign capital.

However, we have also seen that a large public-sector deficit can have negative (inflationary) effects when there is a weakening in the country's external position as occurred in 1980 and 1981, when the current transactions showed a deficit representing 1 to 2 percent of GNP. Thus the inflation rate rose from 4.8 percent in 1979 to 5.5 percent in 1980 and 5.9 percent in 1981.

Another example of complex interaction is found by comparing wage movements with inflation. Between 1960 and 1982, hourly wage rates increased (in nominal terms) by an average of 7.5 percent per year, yet inflation was, on average, only 4 percent. Consequently, in real terms, the hourly wage of the West German worker increased by 3.4 percent per year, an increase similar to that of French colleagues who experienced an average 7.4 percent inflation rate. However, the lower rate of growth of the nominal wage of the German worker gave an advantage over French counterparts, inasmuch as the appreciation of the former's currency enabled him to gain "international purchasing power." Still, it should not be forgotten that this is actually an advantage only under the condition that, in practice, the opportunity exists to purchase foreign goods or services.

This last observation leads to further comments on a circumstance that is not frequently examined in the theories or doctrines of inflation, namely the interface between the behavior of domestic prices and the structural developments in the country's participation in international trade. In order to clarify the matter, let us start from the hypothesis that a change in exchange rates may not result from inflation; that is, a change in exchange rates may differ from what would compensate for differences in national inflation rates, or it may be determined by anticipation of future inflation rates. We could also make the assumption that the oil shocks were not substantial causes of the inflationary trends that followed them. Possibly the sudden increases in oil prices actually manifested underlying inflationary tendencies.

For justification of these hypotheses let us look at past trends. The average inflation rate in Western industrialized countries was between 3 percent and 6 percent annually from 1950 to 1972. Only in 1973-1974 did inflation begin to take off. In the early 1960's, however, the value of the U.S. dollar began to erode relative to the currencies of the newly emerging trading giants, such as West Germany and Japan. During the 1960's, the U.S. dollar fell by 13 percent against the deutsche mark; in 1971 and 1972 it fell by another 13 percent. Although the Japanese yen did not appreciate significantly against the dollar until 1970, by the end of 1972 the dollar's purchasing power relative to the yen had fallen by 16 percent compared with 1960.

Yet, between 1960 and 1970, average annual inflation was 2.7 percent in the United States, 2.6 percent in West Germany, and 5.7 percent in Japan. In 1971 and 1972, average annual inflation was 3.8 percent in the United States, 5.4 percent in West Germany, and 5.2 percent in Japan. Thus even before the first oil shock and the subsequent surge in inflation, clear signs of disruption were present in the traditional international monetary system. Relative inflation rates did not lead to exchange-rate changes; indeed, the change in exchange rates has been in contradiction with inflation trends.

If inflation is not the causal factor, what then did bring about the disruption in the international monetary system? The modification of international trade patterns can be considered a possible cause of this disruption.

If we examine exports of the Western industrialized nations, it is apparent that West Germany's share increased from 7 percent in 1950 to 14 percent in 1960 and to 16 percent in 1970. Japan's share rose from 2 percent to 5 percent to 9 percent in corresponding years. In contrast, the share of U.S. exports declined from 30 percent in 1950 to 25 percent in 1960 and to 20 percent in 1970. By 1980, the shares of exports were 18 percent for the United States, 16 percent for West Germany, and 10 percent for Japan.

This summary of inflation vis-a-vis trade patterns points to quite a different explanation of exchange-rate variations and inflation than the generally accepted theories. The reduction in relative importance of the United States in international transactions has had two notable consequences:

First, the U.S. money supply, traditionally geared to the needs of the domestic economy, was insufficient to cover the new needs of international transactions. Another means had to be invented. The Eurodollar became the primary vehicle to take up the slack.

Second, other currencies began to compete with the dollar. This competition, together with the decline in the U.S. monetary leadership without a new emerging leader, sapped confidence in the international monetary system. Lack of confidence led to higher interest rates and inflationary behavior. Using such an explanatory scheme, the surge in commodity prices in 1972 and 1973 and the oil shock that followed can be viewed as an emerging manifestation of lack of trust and confidence—as the building of inflationary anticipations, rather than fundamental causes of inflation.

From this viewpoint, inflation results from the disruption of the monetary system and the floating of exchange rates. The rise in prices was a signal that following the changes in the relative trade strength of countries, the business world would no longer unconditionally accept the previous relations between major currencies.

The real question then follows: Is it possible and viable to reconstruct the international monetary system without the undisputed leadership of any one country, such as the United States possessed in the 1950's? Second, to what extent do the new trading giants participate effectively in the new system? That is, from a practical viewpoint, are these new trading giants willing to let their currencies play the role of an international reserve asset?

The answer from Germany has been clear thus far. The German authorities consider West Germany's economic and financial strength too narrow to enable Germany to accept the responsibility associated with having its national currency playing the role of an international currency. (To an even greater degree the same is true of Japan.)

Hence, the nature of the dilemma is clear. The rank of West Germany in international trade today is almost as important as that of the United States, but if one considers gross national product, Germany's GNP is only one-quarter that of the United States. It is, therefore, indisputable that if the West German currency were to play an international role equivalent to the dollar (and in relation to the West German share in international trade), this would endanger its internal stability.

Germany has had a successful policy of safeguarding its currency. This policy, aimed at "safeguarding the internal value of the currency," has relied in practice not only on the domestic consensus, but is also the result of a pragmatic approach to policies concerning competition that enabled the industrial structure to adapt to a world of increased free trade and interdependence. Together, these factors evolved to give West Germany a prominent role in world exports.

This evolution, in turn, coincided with the questioning of the traditional currency relationships among countries.

Germany today is, therefore, at a turning point. The acceptance of floating exchange rates—and the lack of reasonable prospects for a return to a fixed-rate system—may well give the wrong impression: that the burden of safeguarding the external stability of the currency has been alleviated. However, the recent proliferation of deflationary and protectionist policies also results from the attempts of various governments to control their external situation. At the same time, unemployment rates have risen sharply. These developments have made the transaction of international business in the free world more difficult than in the previous 20 years and will induce West Germany to refocus attention on its domestic economy; to reevaluate its public spending policy; and to develop concerted actions with its trading partners in order to avoid the adverse effects associated with the use of the deutsche mark as an international reserve currency. In short, the problems of developing a viable international monetary system in the context of disinflation have not yet been solved.

ITALY

J. Paul Horne*

IN 1960, the Italian lira was awarded the *Financial Times* of London's "Oscar of the Year" for being a strong and stable currency. In that year, consumer prices rose only 2.3 percent. Twenty-four years later, the lira had depreciated 61 percent on a trade-weighted basis; proposals for a "heavy lira" proliferated; and the inflation rate was at 16 percent.

A Country in Transition

A complex phenomenon under the best of circumstances, inflation is unusually so in Italy. The country has experienced a rapid and wrenching transition from being a semideveloped economy before World War II, to being the sixth industrial power in the West by the early 1980's. As large-scale demographic and occupational shifts occurred, the economy's structure changed remarkably. Social mores, work attitudes, and consumer habits changed radically as the far-flung collection of city-states that became Italy as recently as 1861 was consolidated and unified after World War II by *autostrade,* telephones and television.

Despite such changes, however, Italy's political institutions and the omnipotent Catholic Church remained surprisingly stable—so much so that "alternation" of left- and right-wing political parties in government still does not occur. The Church's party, the Christian Democrats (DC), has clung to power since 1945. But new power centers have developed in response to demographic, economic and social changes. These new power centers, notably the unions and the public sector (that is, the large group of state-controlled companies) have become major new influences on the economy—and especially on inflation.

To put the changes Italy has experienced since World War II into perspective and to provide a sense of some of the underlying noneconomic factors contributing to inflation, it is worth recalling a few of the country's basic characteristics.

*First Vice President and international economist, Smith Barney, Harris Upham & Co., Paris.

A 750-mile long and 155-mile wide peninsula between the Adriatic and Tyrrhenian seas, Italy is physically cut off from northern Europe by the Alps but is totally accessible from the Mediterranean. Because of the very length and diversity of the country, until recently Turin in the north was far closer to most North European cities, in terms of travel time, mentality and development, than to Palermo in the south. "Africa starts at Rome" was for a long time a popular, if unkind, expression of Italy's economic-social division into a poor South and a richer North.

Between 1945 and 1965, some one-third of Italy's population shifted from a rural life to an urban one. The main exodus was from the poverty of farms south of Rome to northern industrial cities and Rome, the seat of government and patronaged jobs. Internal immigration and emigration abroad remain, even today, important demographic safety valves for Italy's population, which grew at a net average 0.6 percent annual rate from 1971 to 1981, well below that of other Mediterranean countries.

A resource-poor country, Italy must import most raw materials, energy and a significant share of its foodstuffs. Economic development has boosted Italy's trade dependency. In 1960, imports accounted for 13.6 percent of Gross Domestic Product (GDP), but had risen to 24.1 percent of GDP by 1982. Exports rose from 10.5 percent of GDP in 1960 to 27.3 percent in 1982. Italy is among the most trade-dependent of the 24 industrialized member countries in the Organization for Economic Cooperation and Development (OECD), and is thus highly vulnerable to changes in international trade, import prices, raw material availability, and exchange rates.

Union power has grown rapidly since the immediate post-World War II period. Fifty percent of the Italian industrial work force is now unionized, the second highest proportion, after Sweden, in West Europe. Attracting the mass of new industrial and service employees in the 1950's and 1960's, union power peaked in 1969-1975, leading to large wage increases, a Charter of Workers' Rights, and Europe's most generous wage-indexation mechanism: the *scala mobile*. The three union confederations are closely allied with, but not dominated by, political parties.

The biggest of the confederations are the Confederazione Generale Italiana del Lavoro (CGIL), which is Communist-dominated (with a Socialist minority); the Confederazione Italiana Sindacati dei Laboratori (CISL), close to the Christian Democrats; and the left-of-center Unione Italiana del Lavoro (UIL), associated with the smaller lay parties. A joint federation of metalworkers' unions has become a new union power center. The rise of unions has been such that they now represent Italy's second most important political-economic power center, whose assent is required for virtually any economic or social policy change.

Another significant factor is the magnitude of Italy's "underground economy." A deep-rooted phenomenon among tax-allergic Italians, the *economia parallela* (representing perhaps 15 to 20 percent of GDP) was "discovered" by economists to be important only in the late 1970's. As growing unemployment coincided with a crackdown on tax evasion, the underground economy expanded until it has become an economic factor with major implications for productivity and prices.

The underground, or black-market, economy is a quintessential reflection of Italian traits: creativity, intelligence and a propensity to play games; an ability to render the simple byzantine; a respect for hard work and productivity; resourcefulness amid chaos; and a disdain for the herd instinct. These must be kept in mind when considering the theoretical and sometimes arid macroeconomic analysis of the history and structure of inflation, and policy reactions to it, in Italy since 1960.

Pre-1973: Inflation and Policy Responses

The Immediate Post-World War II Period and the 1950's

In the immediate postwar chaos, Italy experienced the hyperinflation common to war-destroyed economies. In 1946, wholesale prices were 25 times higher than they had been in 1938; and they doubled again in 1946-1947! The reasons were multiple: In 1945, indexation of industrial wages was adopted to protect workers' purchasing power. Monetary authorities permitted bank credit to expand 73 percent in 1947; in that year the state deficit amounted to or 15 percent of GDP. The consequent large increase in liquidity fueled demand for products that were in very limited supply, since reconstruction was just beginning. This caused sharply increased imports and a large trade deficit in 1947. The lira depreciated against the dollar from 568 lire in January, 1947, to over 900 lire by mid-1947.

The government reacted quickly. The Bank of Italy (BOI) restricted credit expansion by imposing required reserves of up to 40 percent on new deposits. An Interministerial Committee for Credit and Savings was created to supervise credit and monetary policy. The government cut the state deficit by reducing the growth of spending. Loans from the United States and other countries covered the balance-of-payments deficit. Measures were taken to reduce the effect of leads and lags.

In June, 1947, the Communists and Socialists were eliminated from the government after tense politicking and street demonstrations. The lira recovered to 575 lire to the dollar, remaining there until the sterling devaluation of 1949, when it was repegged at 625 lire to the dollar. (This rate was maintained until the dollar crisis began in 1971.) Wholesale and consumer price inflation slowed markedly.

The restrictive maneuver was so successful by mid-1948 that inflation was considered under control. The government and the Bank of Italy allowed bank credit to expand by 45 percent in 1948. The Marshall Plan—which underwrote

European reconstruction with over $20 billion between April 1, 1948, and June 20, 1952—provided Italy with $1.5 billion. This boosted official reserves, backed credit growth, and helped finance reconstruction and new industry.

The 1950's were halcyon years, from an economist's point of view: There was a near-perfect combination of high productivity, real growth, low inflation, and political stability. Such a performance was not to be repeated in the next two decades as the underlying circumstances and structures changed.

Gross national income rose by an average annual 5.8 percent (measured in constant prices) from 1951 to 1961. Inflation averaged 2.8 percent a year, measured by consumer prices; wholesale prices were virtually stable. From 1948 to 1960, industrial production rose at an average rate of 9.3 percent a year, while the output of investment goods rose by 11 percent a year.

Such low-inflation growth was made possible by sharply rising demand and a low-cost, mobile labor supply as rural inhabitants, especially from the South, flooded to higher-paying jobs in new industries in the central and northern cities. High unemployment kept the labor supply on the move and indexation of wages protected new industrial workers against inflation. The abundant labor supply and mobility were key factors in the virtuous circle in the 1950's. But the vocational and geographic immigration set in motion forces that later proved to be highly inflationary.

The primary policy objective of governments from 1948 to 1961 was to restrain domestic demand to a level consonant with growth of productivity and output, as well as to maintain equilibrium in the balance of payments. Italy's current account registered a surplus from 1948 to 1961, with very large surpluses in 1958 to 1961. Monetary and credit policy were expansionary as growth of total lending and deposits averaged 17.4 percent a year between 1948 and 1958, much of which financed capital spending.

The central bank's task of keeping interest rates low was made easier by the low growth of labor costs. While prices, measured by the GDP price deflator, rose at an average annual 2.5 percent rate from 1951 to 1961, unit labor costs in industry (excluding construction) rose by only 0.6 percent a year. This was a result of a slow rate of increase in wages for new industrial workers, even though productivity gains averaged 5.9 percent per year. Value added in the industrial sector rose by 8.1 percent annually in the 1951 to 1961 years. There was almost no upward pressure on output prices, and real disposable income increased regularly. (See Table 1.) Growth of productivity and value added in industry was so high that labor costs in services and the construction industry rose at significantly higher rates than in manufacturing without causing inflationary pressures on the economy as a whole.

The expression *il miracolo italiano* gained currency after 1955. Italian genius had apparently discovered the magic formula for satisfying rapidly expanding demand with rapidly rising output and productivity while maintaining very low inflation. At this time, virtually no other OECD country, except Japan, experienced a higher real growth rate with such low inflation. Moreover, the

Table 1
Industrial Output, Cost and Prices 1951 to 1979[1]
(average annual percentage change)

Year	Value added at constant prices	Per capita productivity	Per capita wages and salaries	Cost of labor per unit of output	Implicit price deflator for value added
1952	4.3	3.6	7.7	3.9	−1.7
53	7.5	5.3	7.9	2.4	−0.9
54	9.5	6.6	5.7	−0.8	−2.6
55	8.7	8.3	7.9	−0.3	--
56	7.9	5.3	7.4	1.8	−0.5
57	6.9	4.3	5.4	1.1	1.1
58	2.9	3.2	5.7	2.5	2.6
59	10.9	9.3	4.6	−4.4	−2.0
60	13.0	8.4	7.6	−0.6	--
61	10.3 11.3	5.3 8.8	6.6 9.8	1.3 0.9	1.8 −0.6
62	9.5	8.3	13.9	5.1	1.9
63	6.9	5.1	20.5	14.7	6.8
64	2.0	2.4	7.3	4.8	5.7
65	5.4	7.4	3.7	−3.5	1.5
66	9.6	10.2	7.3	−2.6	−0.3
67	10.2	7.7	11.5	3.4	1.8
68	9.7	7.9	6.6	−1.1	−1.4
69	7.3	5.5	8.9	3.1	2.5
70	8.2	5.3	18.9	13.0	7.5
71	0.9	0.9	10.9	10.0	6.6
72	4.4	5.6	11.3	5.5	4.7
73	10.4	8.7	21.8	12.0	10.5
74	5.2	2.7	22.5	19.3	20.3
75	−9.3	−9.2	22.3	34.7	21.0
76	12.3	11.9	23.6	10.4	16.6
77	1.6	1.5	19.8	18.0	18.2
78	2.7	3.1	14.4	11.0	13.1
79	6.3	6.5	17.9	10.8	14.4

Average annual rates of increase

Year	Value added at constant prices	Per capita productivity	Per capita wages and salaries	Cost of labor per unit of output	Implicit price deflator for value added
1951-1961	8.1	5.9	6.6	0.6	−0.2
1961-1969	5.5	6.8	9.9	2.8	2.3
1969-1979	4.1	3.6	17.9	14.2	13.2

[1]Excluding construction.

Source: Antonio Fazio, "Inflation and Wage Indexation in Italy," *Banca Nazionale del Lavoro Quarterly Review,* June, 1981, No. 127.

balance-of-payments surplus grew steadily, and exchange controls were eliminated. The lira was made fully convertible in June, 1958.

The Lira Loses its Luster: 1960-1965

The happy state of the Italian economy, outlined above, would apparently continue for much of the 1960's. However, even during these halcyon years, there were hints of problems.

A slowdown in international trade and domestic capital spending, for example, caused a hiccup in 1958. Real GDP growth slowed from a 5.4 percent rise in 1957 to 4.9 percent in 1958, and value added in industry rose by only 2.9 percent in 1958. The Bank of Italy quickly boosted liquidity, stimulating demand and capital spending. Liquidity was so plentiful that long-term interest rates dropped below 5 percent by 1961, even though real GDP rose an average 7 percent a year in 1959-1961.

Such a growth of liquidity, however, accelerated demand more rapidly than it did the increase in productive capacity. Moreover, most of the shift of low-cost agrarian labor to industry, construction and services had occurred by 1961. When unemployment dropped to 2.5 percent in 1961, Italy was as close to full employment as it has ever been. Indeed, 19 years elapsed before 20.2 million Italians were again employed.

It was inevitable that the Italian economy would show strains in the 1960's. In 1960-1962 real GDP rose an unprecedented 6.9 percent annually, and value added in industry grew at an equally remarkable 10.9 percent rate. But the rise in the cost-of-living index, which averaged 2.1 percent in 1957-1959, doubled to 4.6 percent in 1960-1963. The balance-of-payments surplus declined sharply in 1962, when Italy registered its first current account deficit since 1950, as import volume rose 37 percent in 1962-1963 and export volume growth slowed from 16 percent in 1961 to 7 percent in 1963. As demand outstripped supply, causing pressure on prices and external payments, it was clear that wages would be affected.

Workers' expectations had risen sharply in the 1950's. The initial "miracle" of the transition from subsistence farming to urban life—with shorter hours, cash in the pocket, electric lights, and maybe even a *frigo*—bred greater ambitions. Fiat's new "500" put what had been the greatest luxury of all within reach of the new proletariat. Demand for consumer goods rose dramatically.

A major political trend contributed greatly to an unprecedented wage escalation in the early 1960's. By 1961 it was evident that the Christian Democrats were losing power as their vote fell below 50 percent and negotiations to form center-right government coalitions grew more difficult. It was also evident that the Church's influence was weakening.

With the reluctant assent of the Vatican (where Pope John XXIII was preparing to modernize the Church with the Ecumenical Council that began in 1962) and the backing of key Italian business interests, notably Fiat, the Christian Democrats negotiated a new political arrangement with the Socialists. On June 21, 1963, an unprecedented center-left government took office. It included the Christian Democrats, the Socialists, the Social Democrats, and the Republicans. The *Centro-sinistra* was a watershed in Italian politics and for the Italian economy: Its program led the country to expect not only structural social-political reforms but also a continued economic miracle—especially in terms of income redistribution.

Unions, whose membership was swollen by the new industrial workers, began to exercise their power in wage negotiations. Per-capita wages and salaries in industry rose a record 14 percent in 1962 and 20 percent in 1963—omens of future wage growth. Agricultural wages rose 56 percent between 1962 and 1964; in construction the wage rise was 54 percent. This first post-World War II wage explosion was also caused by a tightening labor supply as the southern manpower pool began to dry up and demand for labor rose sharply.

A key reason for the surge in output, investment and employment was a cut in obligatory bank reserves in 1961. This allowed total domestic credit (TDC), defined as total lire and foreign currency financing to the public and private sectors, to rise to 15 percent of GDP in 1961 and 16.4 percent in 1962, having been under 10 percent throughout the 1950's.

This liquidity expansion boosted demand sharply and, in turn, caused prices to rise. Wholesale prices rose at an average annual 3.8 percent rate in 1962-1964, and retail prices, measured by the consumption component of GDP (the private consumption deflator), rose 5.6 percent annually in 1962-1965, compared with an average 2.5 percent in the 1950's. The volume of imports rose 37 percent in 1962-1963, and Italy's trade balance swung into deficit in 1962 for the first time since 1950.

The Bank of Italy moved to contain the inflationary surge by restricting money-supply growth in mid-1962 and by forbidding banks to maintain a net deficit position abroad. The government used taxation as an anti-inflation weapon for the first time, boosting taxes by 1 percent of GDP. To stabilize the exchange rate, the Bank of Italy arranged its first major swap line of credit with the U.S. Federal Reserve System, a mutual agreement for the two central banks to lend each other up to $1 billion in foreign exchange.

By 1964, these measures had slowed money-supply growth, cooled off demand, and moved the balance of payments back into surplus (where it remained until 1972). Consumer price inflation slowed from an average 6.1 percent in 1962-1963 to 5.2 percent in 1964-1965, and 2.3 percent in 1966. The cost of controlling inflation, however, was sharply reduced growth in industrial production, which slowed from an average 7.8 percent annual increase in 1962-1963 to 2.6 percent by 1964-1965.

Stop and Go Policies: 1965-1969

No sooner had the center-left government successfully controlled prices than it opted for reflation in 1964-1965. The public-sector deficit doubled in this period. Money-supply growth rose rapidly, boosted also by sharply rising credit demands from the private sector. The ratio of total credit demand to the GDP, which had dropped to 10 percent in 1964, rose to 15.2 percent in 1965 and 17 percent in 1966. Interest rates declined significantly, stimulating borrowing. The Bank of Italy authorized commercial and savings banks to invest part of their obligatory reserves in bonds—an action that was tantamount to reducing reserve requirements and that thus raised the credit multiplier. At the same time, monetary base creation was slowed as the central bank purchased fewer securities.

The stimulus was effective. Real GDP growth jumped from 3.3 percent in 1965 to an average annual 6.4 percent in 1966-1968. This last great surge of real postwar growth was caused in part by the liquidity increase engineered by the Bank of Italy. But it was also caused by formidable productivity growth as sharply increased domestic demand pushed capacity utilization to 90 percent. In 1966-1968, productivity in industry rose an average 8 percent per year and real GDP per person employed rose at a rate of 6.7 percent. One predictable result of this short-lived return to the virtuous circle was price stability: The cost-of-living index rose an average annual 2 percent in 1966-1969; interest rates were low as well.

To stabilize prices of securities issued by certain banks and by the government, the Bank of Italy initiated a new policy of buying and selling such securities in 1966. This action improved the bond market's liquidity, attracting far more investors (especially banks) and issuers. By 1967-1968, an estimated 20 percent of household savings was being invested in these long-term securities. The new policy stabilized interest rates even as bank deposits rose an annual rate of 15 percent in 1964-1968.

THE NEW EXTERNAL CONSTRAINT

The renewed period of high economic growth after 1965 was accompanied by a significant increase in Italy's dependence on foreign trade. Exports of goods and services as a proportion of Italian GDP rose from 11 percent in 1958 to 15.9 percent by 1970, while imports rose from 12 percent to 16.6 percent.

Italy's growing vulnerability to external developments was first exposed in the late 1960's. Increasing international liquidity (generated in part through the rapidly developing Eurodollar market) contributed to rising demand and trade, higher commodity prices, and balance-of-payments imbalances. When the U.S. economy began overheating with the Vietnam War, its rate of inflation and dollar interest rates both began to rise. High U.S. interest rates attracted capital out of Italy even though its own current account was in surplus in 1967-1968.

In 1969, international interest-rate differentials between Italy and other countries increased as most OECD nations tightened their monetary policies to control inflation while Italy's domestic economy was still accelerating, spurred by large public-sector deficits and a construction boom. Import prices and volumes rose sharply while higher foreign interest rates sucked out Italian capital. The Bank of Italy reacted quickly in mid-1969 to curb credit expansion.

More significantly, the central bank moved to gain greater control over the monetary base and independence from the government and its growing public-sector deficit. The rising deficit was itself provoked by the spending excesses of political forces in Parliament that had become increasingly hostage to the unions which demanded accelerating increases in real wages, enlarged rights for workers, and more social services and transfer payments.

In May, 1969, the Bank of Italy stopped buying and selling Treasury bills in unlimited quantities at a price equivalent to the official discount rate, as it had since 1962. It subsequently bought and sold Treasury bills at prices and in amounts consistent with its own objectives for overall liquidity growth. The Bank of Italy also raised the discount rate for the first time in 11 years and reduced intervention in the securities market. These actions led to disorderly conditions in a market already upset by the country's overall balance-of-payments deficit. Although the current account was in surplus, capital outflows amounted to 3.4 trillion lire in 1968-1969. Markets were also concerned by rising wholesale prices (which rose 3.9 percent in 1969 after virtually no change in 1966-1968) and a major upheaval in labor relations.

The Labor Revolution: 1969-1972

The Autumn of 1969 saw the first massive show of post-World War II labor solidarity, as unions called widespread strikes to achieve major wage gains and increased bargaining power in triennial wage negotiations. Industrial strikes resulted in 228 million manhours lost in 1969, four times the hours lost in 1968. Industrial production dropped 8 percent in the fourth quarter of 1969.

Labor unions had gained influence as membership rose sharply in the 1960's with the industrialization of northern Italy. The political environment created by the center-left government also encouraged the unions, whose militancy was spurred by rising unemployment as industrial employment ceased to grow. Although GDP rose by 27 percent between 1964 and 1968, industrial employment declined by 2.5 percent; total employment was down 4 percent; and total unemployment rose 35 percent in this period. It was evident that much capital spending by industry had been reoriented toward labor-saving after the wage flare-up in 1963.

The unions were also influenced by the wave of student demonstrations in Italy, France, West Germany, and the United States in 1967-1969, when student power was first dramatically exercised. Union tactics in Milan, Turin and

Bologna in 1969-1970 resembled the uninhibited student confrontations that were going on at the same time. This tumultuous period was called *l'Autunno caldo* (the hot Autumn) and the unions' gains were regarded as a key turning point for labor relations and the economy.

Labor advances in 1969-1970 were significant indeed. Hourly manufacturing wages increased 10 percent in the fourth quarter of 1969 compared with the fourth quarter of 1968, and by an unprecedented 21.7 percent for 1970 as a whole. Unit labor costs, which rose by an average annual 1.9 percent in 1966-1969, rose 26.4 percent in 1970-1971. The GDP price deflator, up an average annual 2.7 percent in 1966-1969, jumped 6.9 percent in 1970 and 7.2 percent in 1971.

A key reason for the reversal of Italy's traditional ability to absorb price and wage pressures was the *Autunno caldo's* impact on productivity. Productivity potential was reduced significantly by a new workers' rights statute, *Lo Statuto dei Laboratori*, proposed by the Socialist minister of labor, endorsed by the unions, and accepted (with reluctance) by private industry. The new statute, which covered all private firms with more than 20 workers, radically increased unions' and workers' rights. It established a juridical basis for protecting workers' rights, including the creation of a new magistrate who was empowered to rule on labor-relations disputes. Shop councils were given legal status. Union and nonunion representatives on the councils were empowered to decide numerous issues, including organizations of work and limitation of piecework overtime, a key source of productivity gains since 1945.

Another innovation was the creation of area councils representing shop councils of different industries in each geographic area. Not only did the unions control these councils, but political parties' representatives participated as well, politicizing what was originally intended to be a labor-relations forum.

Other legislation granted organized labor more transfer payments and social benefits. Pensions, for instance, were raised significantly and indexed to cover a larger share of inflation. Medical benefits were also improved.

The impact on productivity was startling. In 1966-1969, per capita productivity rose at an average annual rate of 7.8 percent. In 1970, the rate dropped to 5.3 percent, and in 1971 to 0.9 percent—a stunning reversal of the principal factor behind Italy's "miraculous" economic performance in the 1950's and 1960's.

The revolution for wage earners, 70 percent of whom are covered by triennial wage contracts, had a negative effect on capital spending. As relative prices shifted, with higher labor costs and lower capital costs, industry opted for more capital and less labor. The trend started in 1963 but accelerated in 1969 and thereafter. Despite this shift in the character of fixed investment, capital spending's share of GDP was maintained in the 1961 to 1975 period, except in regard to construction. (See Table 2.) The offset was a cutback in industrial employment and growing unemployment.

Table 2
Gross Fixed Investment[1]

Year	Machinery and Equipment	Transportation	Construction		TOTAL
			Housing	Total	
1961-63	6.9	1.9	7.4	15.2	24.0
1964-65	5.0	1.8	7.8	14.7	21.5
1966-69	5.1	1.8	7.2	13.9	20.8
1970	5.9	2.0	7.0	13.4	21.3
1971	6.0	2.0	6.0	12.3	20.3
1972	6.0	2.0	5.9	11.9	19.9
1973	6.8	2.0	5.7	11.4	20.2
1974	7.1	1.9	5.6	11.2	20.2
1975	5.9	1.8	5.3	10.6	18.3

[1]Percentage of gross domestic product at constant prices.

Source: Bank of Italy.

Monetary and Fiscal Policies: 1970-1973

The swift policy reaction to the *Autunno caldo* and the acceleration of wage-price pressures was decidedly restrictive. International factors contributed to this decision, including accelerating wage and price increases in other major countries, notably in the United States, and higher dollar interest rates. The government's measures in mid-1970 included tax and public tariff increases equal to 1 percent of GDP.

The dampening effect on prices was marked. Consumer prices, which rose 5 percent in 1970, increased 4.8 percent in 1971. Wholesale inflation was more than halved to 3.4 percent in 1971. The cost, however, was an economic slowdown, despite higher real incomes. A new phenomenon contributed to this: The household savings rate increased, a reaction to rising inflationary pressures that were to become more pronounced in the next decade of rising wages and prices. Industrial production slowed from a 6.4 percent increase in 1970 to a 0.5 percent decline in 1971. Capital spending in industry and construction slowed in 1971-1972 and capacity utilization dropped.

The slowdown meant that the balance of payments remained under control. Higher Italian interest rates reduced the interest differential with other major currencies, and the net outflow of capital—which had reached 2.3 trillion lire in 1969—slowed sharply in 1970-1971. The Bank of Italy was thus able to ease monetary policy in mid-1970. The monetary base, which rose at an average annual rate of 8.8 percent in 1966-1970, accelerated sharply, rising by 17.3 percent in 1971, 15.8 percent in 1972, and 19.3 percent in 1973.

Some of the rapid monetary growth was a result of the rising public-sector deficit caused by concessions granted in 1969-1970. The general government borrowing requirement rose from 2.6 percent of GDP in 1967-1970 to 4.6 percent in 1971 and 6.5 percent in 1972—a hint of things to come. With the Bank of Italy obliged to finance the deficit (and maintain a stable savings rate), the monetary aggregates accordingly rose sharply—M-2 rising 21.7 percent in 1971-1972 compared with an average 12.7 percent in 1966 to 1970. The TDC-to-GDP ratio climbed from 14 percent in 1966-1969 to 16.7 percent in 1970, and 23.8 percent in 1972.

Interest rates, which in 1966 to 1970 averaged 4.4 percent for six-month Treasury bills and 6.2 percent for long-term government bond yields, dropped in 1971, as economic activity declined and monetary policy was eased. This decline again led to a differential between Italian and foreign interest rates, causing the net capital outflow to quadruple to 2.0 trillion lire in 1972 (compared to 1970-1971).

For Italy, 1972 was a year in which the domestic economy performed well but the external balance worsened. Internally, greatly increased domestic liquidity and lower interest rates boosted private consumption and investment. Investment was helped by temporarily improved corporate profits as wholesale price inflation fell to an average 4 percent in 1971-1972; wage increases slowed to 10.4 percent in 1972, and productivity in industry rose by 5.6 percent in the same year. Unit labor costs rose only 6 percent in 1972, compared with an average 13.2 percent in 1970-1971. An international cyclical recovery in most OECD economies coincided with this 1971-1972 expansion, causing Italian exports to increase.

The balance-of-payments problem, however, grew increasingly acute, forcing the government to adopt a two-tier exchange market in January, 1973: The Bank of Italy intervened to stabilize the exchange rate for current transactions while allowing the rate for capital transactions to float. In February, 1973, the dollar was devalued for a second time; the world moved into a regime of floating exchange rates; and Italy abandoned the policy of pegging the lira to other European Common Market currencies. (Although the Common Market organized a new attempt to peg member currencies against each other in March, 1973, the lira, sterling and the Irish pound stayed out of the arrangement and floated independently.)

Another round of labor disputes, resulting in more concessions to the unions in the Spring of 1973, slowed industrial production and aggravated the capital flight while the current account deteriorated. The lira depreciated despite heavy intervention by the Bank of Italy; the rate of exchange relative to the U.S. dollar deteriorated from an average 582 lire in 1972 (its high since 1949) to 620 lire by mid-1973. (In February, 1973, the Bank of Italy began charting the lira's trade-weighted value, using February 9, the day before generalized floating, as base 100. In 1973, the lira fell 8.9 percent on this trade-weighted basis.)

The Bank of Italy forced most credit institutions to boost their holdings of medium- and long-term securities by 6 percent of total deposits in 1973. This move limited credit expansion and, at the same time, helped to finance the public deficit. The new policy aimed at a 15-percent nominal and 4.5-percent real increase in GDP; the reestablishment of payments equilibrium; and a Treasury deficit of no more than 5 trillion lire (8.5 percent of GDP). As interest rates rose, the Bank of Italy adjusted its policy to prevent large companies from monopolizing limited new credit at the expense of small companies. Nevertheless, overall liquidity increased, TDC-to-GDP rising to a post-World War II high of 26.2 percent in 1973.

The combined impact of monetary expansion, higher interest rates, and lira devaluation on inflation was dramatic. Consumer prices rose 10.8 percent in 1973, double the 1972 rise. Wholesale prices were up 17 percent, against a 4.6 percent rise in 1972. The GDP price deflator rose 11.6 percent, compared to 6.3 percent in 1972. Manufacturing wages were up 24.2 percent and, even though productivity rose 10.8 percent, unit labor costs jumped 12.9 percent, more than double the rise in 1972.

For the first time since the 1940's, the government tried to control some prices in mid-1973—an experiment that distorted relative price movements. The new controls were lifted in the Spring of 1974, and the government continued to use the system of administered prices in effect since the 1950's. The Interministerial Price Committee set (and continues to set) prices for electricity, fuel products, essential commodities, pharmaceuticals, rent and foodstuffs. Until 1974, the government kept these prices under tight control, usually allowing them to rise less than market prices. After 1974, however, administered prices and public tariffs were allowed to follow market prices more closely. By 1981, these administered prices accounted for 32 percent of the consumer price index (CPI). Because administered prices that are below market prices imply government subsidies (for example, for electricity) or lower corporate profits, the system distorts Italy's price structure and contributes to the state deficit.

In 1973, the economy responded to plentiful liquidity and rising demand. Corporate profits rose. Capital spending on plant and equipment rose 22 percent in real terms and construction was up 15 percent. Real GDP rose 7 percent in 1973—the last such surge the Italian economy was to enjoy to date. The next event was a traumatic external shock.

The Oil Shock and its Consequences: 1973-1979

The Arab oil embargo that followed the outbreak of the fourth Arab-Israeli War in October, 1973, led to a quadrupling of world oil prices by mid-1974. The impact on Italy was calamitous. The country had carried out reconstruction and built an industrial economy from 1945 to 1973 on the premise of low-cost labor, as well as low-cost oil and gas supplies. Labor costs had already risen sharply in 1969-1970, making Italy more vulnerable than any other large OECD country to the subsequent oil price shock of 1973-1974.

Italy's dependence on imported energy was very high because its small oil and gas reserves in the Po Valley and Sicily had already been depleted by 1974. Total energy consumption in 1960 was 38.1 million tons of oil equivalent (mtoe), 29.7 of which were imported. (Oil, including crude and oil products, accounted for 22.6 million tons.) By 1972, total energy consumption amounted to 114.7 mtoe—90 percent of which was imported (oil accounted for 88.9 million tons).

The first oil-price shock led to these consequences in 1974:

- Consumer prices rose 19.1 percent (25.7 percent on a fourth-quarter-over-fourth-quarter basis);
- Wholesale prices shot up 40.7 percent;
- Manufacturing wages rose 22.4 percent; unit labor costs in manufacturing rose 18.4 percent (34.6 percent in 1975) as productivity declined 9.7 percent—the only productivity decline in Italy in the post-World War II period; and
- The GDP price deflator rose 18.5 percent.
- The current account swung into deficit by 5.2 trillion lire.
- The exchange rate dropped from 607 lire per dollar at year-end 1973 to 650 lire at year-end 1974, losing 8.6 percent on a trade-weighted basis.
- Real GDP rose 4.1 percent in 1974, but the country moved into recession. By the fourth quarter of 1974, GDP had dropped 2.5 percent from the fourth quarter of 1973.

The immediate policy response was to borrow abroad to finance the deficit in the current account. Because the other oil-importing countries did the same thing and the recycling of OPEC's surplus had not yet commenced, interest rates rose and Italian access to the international capital market was restricted. Nevertheless, $1 billion was borrowed in the first half of 1974. At the same time, the Bank of Italy was spending an equivalent amount *each month* defending the lira!

Drastic action had to be taken. Early in 1974, the center-left government applied for a standby credit from the International Monetary Fund (IMF). Difficult negotiations with the IMF on economic and monetary policies caused the government to fall on March 2, 1974. Another center-left government was formed in time to sign the IMF letter of intent on March 27th.

The IMF program aimed to achieve equilibrium in the balance of payments; to restrain the Treasury deficit; and to slow credit expansion within 18 months. In the Italian negotiations, the IMF made an innovation in its customary practice of targeting Domestic Credit Expansion (DCE), focusing instead on Total Domestic Credit (TDC). Domestic Credit Expansion in Italy is the sum of total credit provided by the banking system to the private and public sectors (including lira loans, the issue of bonds and Treasury bills, and financing of the Treasury by the Bank of Italy). Total Domestic Credit, however, is the total flow of credit in lire and foreign exchange to all domestic sectors, including the nonfinancial sectors' net purchases of bonds and bills but excluding equity issues.

This focus on TDC represented a key change in Italy's monetary policy. The Bank of Italy had focused on the monetary base for controlling bank liquidity until 1973. But large swings in foreign external payments and the rapidly growing public-sector deficit made such an approach difficult. Moreover, controlling the monetary base alone meant volatile bond yields, hence difficulty in financing the public-sector deficit—as is again the case in aggravated form today. The new policy meant more reliance on ceilings on bank loans and banks' portfolio requirements, with limits set for individual banks. This practice had the advantage that additional bank liquidity does not mean more lending because of the loan ceilings and, hence, can be used to buy state bonds. Foreign currency loans were excluded, meaning that the banks could borrow abroad and thus boost reserves.

Planned TDC expansion was limited to 22.4 trillion lire for the year ending March 31, 1975—the credit increase judged necessary for a 15-percent nominal GDP growth and 4 percent real growth. (A 22-percent increase in gross fixed investment in nominal terms was implied.) A ceiling of 9.2 trillion lire, equal to 9 percent of GDP, was put on the Treasury deficit in 1974 (against 7.5 trillion lire in 1973).

The balance-of-payments objective was to achieve approximate balance in nonoil trade by reestablishing equilibrium between domestic demand and supply, reducing imports, and boosting exports. The additional oil bill would be paid by reduced real income and increased productivity. Exchange-rate policy was premised on the hope that the 17 percent traded-weighted devaluation of the floating lira since February, 1973, would maintain competitiveness. Floating would continue. To slow the capital outflow, interest rates would be allowed to rise to reduce the differential against interest in other currencies. Finally, capital controls would be imposed.

The implementation of the IMF program and the oil shock both had major consequences. The first was political. Refusing the cut in workers' real income, implied by the IMF-government measures, the Italian Socialist party withdrew from the government in October, 1974, terminating the center-left coalition that had endured for 11 years. This forced the Christian Democrats to govern with minority coalitions until 1980, when the center-left coalition was resurrected.

In effect, the Socialist party's withdrawal in 1974 ended any hopes of restraining the unions. It is worth noting that the center-left was a major factor in the rise of union power and of the sharp shift of national income to the working class. This redistribution of income raised labor costs, created new labor rigidities, and increased Italy's vulnerability to external shocks.

The Scala Mobile

The second major consequence of the IMF program and the oil shock occurred in January of 1975, when the Confederation of Italian Industry *(Confindustria)* reluctantly agreed to the union confederations' demand that the automatic wage indexation mechanism, the *scala mobile*, be altered to increase the degree of indexation. The new system proved to be one of three elements that caused a new quantum jump in Italy's structural inflation, the other two being higher energy costs and the public-sector deficit.

The first *scala mobile* in 1945 covered only northern Italy, but coverage was extended to the whole country in 1946. The *scala mobile* provided equal lire increases for *each point* of increase in the cost-of-living index for all industrial workers, regardless of wage levels. In 1950, differentiated lira values were introduced for different wage levels and geographic regions. The lira values for each point were raised in 1957 and 1963; territorial differences were eliminated in 1969.

The 1975 agreement, however, returned to an indexation method of uniform lire increases (as opposited to percentage increases) for *all* categories of workers covered by national contracts at all wage levels. Indexation was applied quarterly on the basis of accumulated increases in the monthly cost-of-living index. Moreover, the *scala mobile* was extended to all agricultural and service workers and to some government workers. The effect on wage indexation was significant. The Bank of Italy calculated that the previous *scala mobile* had accounted for 3 percent a year (of an average 20 percent annual wage increase up to 1972) and 6.5 percent a year in 1972-1974. The degree to which inflation was offset by indexation adjustments averaged 50 percent up to 1975. The new system raised the inflation offset to 75 percent in 1976-1977 and to around 80 percent since then.

The coincidence of the new *scala mobile's* with the energy shock was unfortunate. It became virtually impossible to force Italian wage earners to absorb the higher energy costs without, in turn, affecting wages and exacerbating the underlying rate of inflation. The degree of imported inflation associated with the rise in energy prices was thus magnified in Italy by the sliding scale.

Despite a 1974 reform making the income-tax structure substantially more progressive, the government has since failed to adjust tax brackets adequately for inflation. As a result, fiscal drag eroded much of the income increase for wage earners generated by the 1975 *scala mobile* system. (Fiscal drag had the perverse effect of reducing the progressiveness of the 1974 income-tax structure.) Moreover, the fixed lire-per-point wage-adjustment system flattened wage differentials. It also cost the unions bargaining power in wage negotiations. But these drawbacks did not prevent the unions from fiercely resisting any change in the mechanism between 1975 and early 1983, when the first significant change was made.

The third major consequence of the IMF-government measures in 1974-1975 was Italy's first post-World War II recession. The IMF program reduced money-supply growth and interest rates rose rapidly as the banking and corporate sectors became illiquid. Private consumption growth declined and import growth shrank quickly. The slump in worldwide import demand cut back on Italy's export growth.

Real GDP growth shrank 2.5 percent in the fourth quarter of 1974 compared with fourth quarter 1973; it dropped 3.6 percent on average in 1975 and industrial production declined 8.8 percent. Gross fixed investment fell 14.6 percent in volume in 1974-1975. Productivity fell 9.7 percent, the largest decline in postwar history. The current account registered a $8 billion deficit in 1974. But as the recession cut imports, the deficit shrank to $581 million in 1975. The lira depreciated slightly against the dollar in 1975 and fell 3.7 percent on a trade-weighted basis.

Inflationary pressures were pronounced: Consumer prices rose 25.7 percent in 1974 on a fourth-quarter to fourth-quarter basis (19.1 percent for the year) and a further 17 percent in 1975. Wholesale prices rose an average 40.7 percent in 1974, but only 8.6 percent in 1975. The GDP price deflator moved up by 23.8 percent on a fourth-quarter to fourth-quarter basis in 1974, and 17.5 percent on average in 1975. As hourly wage increases in manufacturing of 22.4 percent in 1974 and 26.7 percent in 1975 were aggravated by a productivity decline, unit labor costs rose 34.6 percent in 1975, the biggest one-year increase ever.

The recession's severity led to stop-and-go policies that failed to stabilize the economy. The Italian government was not solely to blame. In the Summer of 1975, the European Economic Community (EEC) finance ministers and the EEC Commission recommended stimulus for Italy. In late 1975, the Bank of Italy lowered bank rates and the discount rate; limits on bank borrowing abroad were removed; bank reserve requirements were cut by one-third; government spending was boosted 23 percent; and the public-sector deficit was doubled to 13 percent of GDP. Higher pensions accelerated public disbursement; reduced personal income taxes and inflation-adjustment of corporate assets also stimulated an economic rebound.

Total domestic demand rose at a 12-percent annual rate by the end of 1975, and business inventory accumulation also rose. However, prices accelerated; the external account deteriorated badly; the lira depreciated; and foreign-exchange reserves dropped to $600 million by year end. Pressure on the lira was so intense that the foreign-exchange market was closed for 40 days on January 20, 1976. Authorities put on the brakes again; raised the discount rate; eliminated automatic financing of export credits; and boosted reserve requirements. In 1975-1976, Italy also borrowed $500 million from the U.S. Federal Reserve, $1.5 billion from the Bundesbank (for which it pledged some gold reserves—an unprecedented ignominy), $1 billion from the EEC, and about the same amount from the IMF.

The Second IMF Program

The situation required new IMF negotiations for additional standby credit by late 1976. A new stabilization program was agreed upon, although the government's conflicting policy moves in 1974-1976 were criticized. The new 20-month program was even tougher than that in 1974, focusing now on the Treasury deficit, inconsistent monetary policies, and excessive wage indexation. The IMF emphasized the need for a reduction in the public-sector deficit, control of inflation through lower wage increases, and stabilization of the exchange rate.

Specific measures implemented in response to the IMF included increased taxes and public tariffs, equivalent to 3.3 percent of GDP in 1977; subsidized corporate social-security contributions; higher interest rates; renewed limits on lira bank lending; and changes in labor relations. Under growing public pressure, the unions made their first concessions since 1975, agreeing to increase productivity; to eliminate indexation systems more generous than industry's *scala mobile;* to abolish indexation of severance pay reserves; to improve labor mobility; and to reduce the weight of public-utility tariffs in the *scala mobile* index.

The measures produced dramatic results. The lira stabilized, thanks to high interest rates and massive foreign borrowing by firms and banks. Bank of Italy exchange policy was aimed at appreciation against the dollar (since some 35 percent of imports were dollar priced) and depreciation against European currencies. Foreign-exchange reserves rose by $6.8 billion in 1977, and the current account showed a $2.1 billion surplus. The weaker lira and improved productivity boosted export growth, while a two-quarter recession reduced domestic demand and imports.

The inflationary situation improved; the rise in consumer prices slowed to a 15.7-percent annual rate by the fourth quarter of 1977 (from 21 percent in the fourth quarter of 1976); wholesale prices slowed to a 10.6-percent annual rate in the fourth quarter, from a 31 percent rate in the previous fourth quarter; the GDP price deflator also dropped—from a 21.9-percent rate to a 15.9-percent rate in the fourth quarter of 1977; and the rise in unit labor costs declined to 17.5 percent.

The 1977 IMF program was a success: External stabilization was achieved and inflation was slowed. The IMF standby credit was never drawn. Stable international raw material and fuel prices and OECD economic recovery helped. But a key explanation was offered by Luigi Spaventa, a leading economist. "The Government measures were drastic enough," he said, "that public opinion could immediately perceive [them] as implying a change of regime. A tough fiscal policy gave a sense of urgent need for stabilizaton which monetary policy alone could not have provided.... This sense of urgency was of utmost importance in inducing the unions to adopt a new and cooperative attitude and to accept officially that they should make concessions [on]...productivity and labor costs.... Expectations and confidence were restored."[1]

Unfortunately, this spirit of national emergency evaporated by 1979-1980, making it even more difficult to establish a consensus on key anti-inflationary policies aimed at reining in excessive public spending, cutting back the *scala mobile*, and improving the quality of public administration.

From Historic Compromise to Center-left

A major new political development contributed to the sense of national purpose in 1976-1977. National elections in June, 1976, saw the Communist party vote rise to 34.4 percent, while the Christian Democrats dropped to 38.8 percent and the Socialists to 9.8 percent. Negotiations to form a government were stymied by the Socialist refusal to form a new center-left coalition without the Communists. The Christian Democrats, traumatized by electoral losses and a possible Socialist-Communist alliance, accepted tacit Communist support for a minority Christian Democratic government. The Communists agreed to abstain in Parliament on government legislation. In return, the Christian Democrats consulted the Communists on major policies.

The Communist party took its role seriously, encouraging the CGIL, the Communist-dominated union confederation, to be more cooperative on labor costs. This led to the "Lama line," named for Communist labor leader Luciano Lama, which resulted in the major unions making concessions in 1977.

The Communists also pushed the Christian Democrats to restrain government spending, control the Treasury deficit, restructure Italian industry, revise the national accounting system, reform local-government finance, implement a general agricultural reform, and restructure the medical welfare system. To everybody's astonishment, a number of new reform laws were approved by Parliament in 1977-1978 with Communist support.

Communist party cooperation was so positive, and so needed by the weakened Christian Democrats, that the Communists joined the parliamentary majority in 1978, actually voting for the government. This was as close as the Italian Communist party ever got to party secretary Enrico Berlinguer's goal of a *compromesso storico* (or historic compromise) to govern Italy in coalition with the Christian Democrats and Socialists. Nonetheless, the party's cooperation produced few tangible benefits despite vigorous economic recovery from late 1977 to 1979. And the Christian Democrats stalled on implementing the new reform laws. The Communist party's rank and file began to rebel against what many called Berlinguer's "revisionist line" of collaborating with the old Christian Democratic enemy.

---

[1]Luigi Spaventa, "Two letters of intent: external crises and stabilization policies in Italy 1973-1977," *Conference on IMF Conditionality,* Institute for International Economics, March, 1982.

In early 1979, Berlinguer's demand for full Communist party participation in the cabinet was refused by the Christian Democrats. This led to an early national election in June, 1979, in which the Communists' vote dropped to 30 percent, while the Christian Democrats won 39 percent. By this time a new Socialist personality, Bettino Craxi, had succeeded in dominating the Socialist party with a program unabashedly pro-NATO, anti-Moscow, and strongly in favor of structural economic and social reforms by a center-left coalition. In early 1980, Craxi and the Christian Democrats agreed on a new *Centro-sinistra* coalition with the Social Democrats, Republicans and Liberals. The Socialists gained key cabinet posts—defense, finance and foreign trade—but Craxi's request to be prime minister was rejected by the Christian Democrats.

The political situation thus changed drastically from 1976 to 1980, just as the economic situation shifted remarkably. In late 1977, the economy moved into high gear, albeit with some serious problems. Industrial production rose 9.6 percent in 1978 (through the fourth quarter) and 6.7 percent in 1979, as domestic demand responded to easier monetary policy and lower interest rates. An international cyclical recovery led to a 10.1 percent increase in the volume of exports. Real GDP rose 5.6 percent in 1978 (to the fourth quarter) and 4.9 percent in 1979. Capital spending on machinery and equipment surged by 9.6 percent in 1979.

Inflationary pressures alternated in 1977-1979. Consumer prices rose 12.1 percent in 1978, less than the 18.4 rise in 1977, but edged up again in 1979 to 14.8 percent. Wholesale prices, which rose 16.6 percent in 1977, were up 8.4 percent in 1978, accelerated by 15.5 percent in 1979. The GDP price deflator rose 14.1 percent in 1978, against 19.1 percent in 1977, but moved up 15.2 percent in 1979. The rise in manufacturing wages accelerated from 16.2 percent in 1978 to 19 percent the following year. Productivity rose only 2.3 percent in 1978 and 3.7 percent in 1979, resulting in a rise in unit labor costs of 11.2 percent in 1978 and 9.6 percent in 1979. It was clear by 1979 that structural inflation in Italy had roughly tripled in 1974-1979 from the 1969-1973 period.

In effect, monetary and fiscal policies had contributed both to good economic growth and to inflationary pressures. The monetary base rose an average annual 20.6 percent in 1976-1978 and was accelerating. The broader measure of the money supply, M-2, averaged a 23.7 percent annual growth rate, compared with a 13.9-percent average annual nominal GDP growth. Much of the fault lay with the government, rather than with the Bank of Italy, because the government was politically unable to restrain public spending. The public deficit averaged 9.5 percent of GDP annually in 1976-1979.

External accounts were, however, a bright spot in 1977-1979. Export volume rose 10.1 percent in 1978 and 8.9 percent in 1979, while import growth accelerated from 8 percent in 1978 to 14 percent in 1979. Terms of trade improved by 4 percent in 1976-1979. The current account registered surpluses of $2.5 billion in 1977, $6.2 billion in 1978, and $5.5 billion in 1979. Stabilization of commodity prices and oil imports in 1976-1978 helped the trade account before economic recovery again boosted fuel imports in 1979.

The lira strengthened against the dollar from an average 875 lire in 1976 to 804 lire in 1979; however, the lira's trade-weighted exchange rate fell. Total reserves, excluding gold, rose dramatically from $3.3 billion at year-end 1976 to $18.2 billion in 1979. The payments and lira performance in 1976-1979 were the most remarkable since the 1950's. Nevertheless, the government and the Bank of Italy prudently insisted on fluctuation margins of plus or minus 6 percent for the lira when it joined the new European Monetary System (EMS) on March 13, 1979. Other EMS currencies were allowed a margin of only plus or minus 2.25 percent.

Part of this success is attributed by the Bank of Italy's Antonio Fazio to the relatively restrained economic growth in 1974-1977 when real GDP grew in aggregate only 7 percent, domestic consumption rose 7.4 percent, and total investment volume dropped 11.3 percent. This slow growth limited total import growth to only 13 percent in 1974-1978, while export volume rose 39 percent and terms of trade improved by about 10 percent.

External and Domestic Deficits: 1980-1983

As the resuscitated Center-left government took over in early 1980, however, a major new economic crisis was already developing. Deficits were the problem: both the external deficit—caused by the 1979-1980 oil shock and the strengthening dollar—and a domestic public deficit that was growing out of control. These problems persist despite efforts by the government and the Bank of Italy to restore equilibrium.

The External Deficit

Although prices, wages and the price of oil accelerated again in late 1979, fiscal policy in 1979 and early 1980 aimed to sustain demand through personal income-tax cuts, an expanded housing program, and absorption of corporate social contributions by the government. The Bank of Italy, however, leaned against inflationary pressures in late 1979, raising the discount rate to 15 percent; the prime rate reached 20 percent. In spite of these increases, interest rates were below the rate of price increases. Bank credit ceilings were tightened, as were penalties for exceeding the limits. Additional measures were taken against capital outflows. TDC expansion was targeted at 15.7 percent, compared with a 16-18 percent growth in nominal GDP.

Tax and public tariff increases, however, were again weakened by Parliament, raising questions about the new coalition government's unity. Public spending was restricted but the public-sector deficit, targeted at 10 percent of GDP, was expansionary despite the government's intent to cool off the economy. This contradictory policy stance left Italy vulnerable to the oil shock that lay ahead.

The oil price rise in 1979-1980 dampened international trade, causing Italian exports to stagnate while domestic demand, output and anticipatory stockpiling kept imports rising well into 1980. Terms of trade deteriorated; a $16 billion trade deficit resulted.

The current account plunged to a deficit of $9.7 billion in 1980, the largest in Italy's history. The adverse $15.2 billion swing from the $5.5 billion surplus in 1979 to the 1980 deficit was one of the largest such payments shifts ever for any OECD country. The lira depreciated from 804 lire to the dollar at year-end 1979 to 935 lire by year-end 1980, and its trade-weighted depreciation rose from 44 percent to 48.5 percent.

The major factor behind the dramatic trade deterioration was the increased cost of oil imports. The volume of net oil imports rose only slightly to 95.7 million tons in 1980, but the cost jumped from $8.8 billion in 1978 to $20.6 billion in 1980, as the average OPEC price rose from $12.95 per barrel at year-end 1978 to $33 by year-end 1980.

The second oil price shock produced some positive action by the government, whose ministerial ranks included for the first time some talented young technocrats. An ambitious energy program (prepared in 1976-1979) and approved by Parliament in early 1982, aimed to reduce dependence on oil and other energy imports. As the International Energy Agency noted: "Breaking the mold of oil dependence represents a physical task of enormous proportions and the marshalling of huge resources."

The plan calls for expanded nuclear power, increased energy conservation, and faster development of coal and gas. The aim is to stabilize the volume of oil consumption by 1990, reducing oil's share in total primary energy (TPE) consumption from 68 percent in 1980 to 50 percent in 1990. TPE itself is to be reduced by 7 percent. A 62 percent increase in electricity use (with increased coal and nuclear production), a 50 percent increase in the use of gas, and a decrease in the use of heating oil are also planned.

According to the International Energy Agency, the most serious obstacle is that 90 percent of electricity is sold at "social prices" set by the government below world energy prices, making it difficult to use the price incentive to improve consumer conservation. Financing of new nonoil electricity capacity, estimated at 38 trillion lire, will be difficult for the electricity authority that has huge deficits and a large outstanding debt because of its unrealistic pricing.

Italy has, however, reduced its total energy/GDP ratio by 17 percent since 1973, much of this achieved in 1979-1981, when primary energy demand fell 0.5 percent. Dependence on oil also declined from 75 percent of domestic energy requirements in 1973 to 65 percent in 1982, and oil consumption dropped 29 percent in the same period.

Also exacerbating the external deficit was a loss of competitiveness dating from the 1969 labor revolution and the 1975 *scala mobile* agreement, aggravated further by the external payments crisis of 1974-1975. The impact of declining productivity and rising unit labor costs on Italy's competitiveness far offset the lira devaluation. (Productivity, or real GDP per employed person, rose only 6.8 percent in 1977-1979 while unit labor costs jumped 38.3 percent.)

Italian competitiveness against its major trading partners—West Germany, France and the United States—has been calculated by the Banca Nazionale del Lavoro for the period 1973 to mid-1982, based on wholesale prices and exchange-rate fluctuations. The study shows that Italy gained competitiveness against West Germany in 1974-1979 but lost it again in 1980-1981. Competitiveness against France declined from 1976 to mid-1982. Italy lost to the United States from 1976 to 1980, after which the sharp dollar rise caused the United States to lose competitiveness.

Corporate profitability deteriorated significantly during the 1973-1982 period. As national income shares shifted to wages and the public sector, profitability fell, and private-sector capital spending declined as a proportion of GDP. A study by Dr. Brovedani of the Banca Nazionale del Lavoro points out that even though Italian corporate balance sheets tend to minimize stated profits, their real situation deteriorated sharply nonetheless. Using data from more than 1,000 publicly held companies, in no year between 1974 and 1980 were companies profitable in the aggregate, though much of the total loss was concentrated in a few industries, such as steel and chemicals. Net losses (after interest and taxes), which peaked in 1975 and 1977, still amounted to 3 trillion lire in 1980. A vicious circle of low profitability, increased external financing, rising interest rates, and operating losses explains the situation. The net result is an average annual debt ratio (debt as a percent of total assets) of 80 percent since 1975-1977. The government's failure to permit revaluation of fixed assets and inventories with inflation adjustments has contributed to corporate debt problems.

Privately held Italian companies reacted to these pressures in 1981-1983 by significantly reducing inventories, improving management of increased financial assets (e.g., holdings of high-yielding Treasury bills rose), and by boosting debt financing from 2.1 percent of total long-term financing in 1981 to over 15 percent by year-end 1983. Increased foreign financing at lower interest rates and reduced domestic bank borrowing also helped to improve the corporate debt situation in relative terms. The Bank of Italy reported in mid-1983: "In the 1976-1982 period the imbalance in the corporate financial structure improved. Measured in constant prices the operating margin was better and total debt tended to decline."

The Domestic Deficit

Although the IMF agreements emphasized control of the public-sector deficit, successive governments failed to check public spending. This has produced a rising public deficit, which has become an increasingly important factor in inflation. General government borrowing (meaning government, social security, and local authorities) rose from an average 3.7 percent of GDP in 1967-1974 to 8.3 percent of GDP in 1974-1980. The 1980 restrictive program caused the deficit to drop, but it reaccelerated in late 1980 with the state subsidy of corporate social contributions, measures to aid earthquake victims, and slower tax-revenue growth.

In 1980, fiscal revenues rose 42 percent (as the result of tougher measures for advance tax payments and a crackdown on payment of the value-added tax), but total disbursements were also up 42 percent because of increased wages and pensions. The 1980 government deficit (cash basis) totaled 31 trillion lire. The total borrowing requirement of the "enlarged public sector" (central government, social security, local authorities, the railways and highway agencies, the postal administration, and municipal companies, but *not* including the deficit-ridden state industrial and service groups) amounted to 40.7 trillion lire. A key reason for the increased public-sector deficit was progressive loss of control over expenditure as a growing share of GDP kept shifting to the public sector. Moreover, the Italian government was partially decentralized in the early 1970's, although control over taxation remained in Rome—a combination that resulted in rising local deficits.

The few reforms undertaken were slowly and ineffectively implemented. In 1977, local authorities were forbidden to borrow from banks for current operations and were put on a cash basis. In 1980, financing of capital transactions by local authorities was limited to the government's central deposits bank. Since 1979, a national cash budget and financial authorization bill have been mandatory; so has a ceiling on the public deficit.

Despite such efforts, spending continued to rise unchecked in 1981 as government parties failed to curb patronage spending at all levels, refused to cut social spending, and balked at raising taxes. While revenues rose 22 percent in 1981, government wages and pensions rose 30 percent and interest payments jumped by 40 percent.

In June, 1981, the Bank of Italy was freed of its obligation (dating from a 1975 Interministerial Committee for Credit and Savings ruling) to finance the Treasury whenever public demand for Treasury debt fell short of the amount offered. This requirement had forced the Bank of Italy to finance the Treasury, and had thus reduced its ability to conduct an autonomous monetary policy. Since the "divorce," the Bank of Italy refused several times to finance the Treasury, forcing a rise in Treasury bond yields in order to sell the additional debt. This rise provoked a reaction from the political parties and unions that urged restoration of the central bank's obligation to finance the Treasury. Recent governments have, however, had the courage to keep the divorce in effect. As a result, the Treasury must tap more national savings to finance public spending, rather than monetizing new debt.

By year-end 1981, the enlarged public-sector borrowing requirement rose to 55 trillion lire, equal to 12.5 percent of GDP, and up from 31 trillion lire in 1980. The economic cycle and higher interest rates contributed to the increase.

The external deficit remained very high because of the continued rise in energy prices, aggravated by the lira's sharp depreciation against the dollar, which amounted to 29.8 percent between the end of 1980 and year-end 1981. Trade-weighted depreciation rose from 44 percent in January, 1980, to 55 percent by year-end 1981. Even though import volume dropped 9.6 percent, the trade deficit rose to $10.4 billion and the current account deficit totaled $8 billion in 1981.

Problems Worsen: 1980-1983

External and public-sector deficits continued to characterize the economy through 1983, despite efforts by increasingly alarmed governments. The current account deficit declined somewhat but still totaled $5.5 billion in 1982. However, the recession in 1981-1983 sharply reduced import volume, helping to produce an estimated current account surplus of $1.5 billion in 1983.

In the 1980-1982 period, the cumulative deficit was $23.2 billion, most of which was financed by capital inflows. Given that the international economic shifts and domestic economic recovery that jointly cured the external deficit in 1976-1979 are not likely to be repeated, current account deficits will have to be financed externally, or with reserves, until export competitiveness can be improved and imports restrained to restore balance. The continuing lira depreciation makes the situation more difficult. By January, 1984, the lira had fallen to 1,713 lire per dollar, and its trade-weighted depreciation stood at 61 percent.

Financing the current account deficit has boosted Italy's external debt sharply. Private and public debt (excluding short-term bank debt) totaled 23 trillion lire at year-end 1980 ($24.6 billion at year-end 1980 exchange rates); by December 31, 1982, the total amounted to $40 billion. In 1981, a "queuing" system was instituted by the Bank of Italy to discipline borrowing in foreign markets. Debt servicing costs are expected to peak in the 1985-1987 period. As Bank of Italy governor Carlo Azeglio Ciampi warned, gross foreign debt (including short-term bank debt) totaled $51 billion at year-end 1982, equal to 128 percent of total reserves (including gold reserves at the end of March, 1983), and to 16 percent of GDP. Since 1980, external debt in Italy had increased faster than in any other major OECD country. Unless the current account deficit and the public deficit (much of which is financed abroad) were controlled, Italy's credit rating would be so impaired, he said, that Italy would find it increasingly difficult to obtain new credit.

The public-sector deficit emerged as the critical problem of the 1980's, despite the efforts of an unusual politician, Giovanni Spadolini, leader of the tiny Republican party (PRI). Spadolini became Italy's first non-Christian Democratic prime minister in July, 1981, on a platform of unprecedented reforms to cut spending at all levels and to raise revenues. A total public-sector deficit target of 50 trillion lire was set for 1982. However, Parliament refused to approve the required spending cuts and tax-and-tariff increases, and the recession boosted social spending and cut revenues. The result was a 1982 public-sector deficit of 79.6 trillion lire, equal to 17 percent of GDP. Spadolini, although respected, could not fight the political maneuvers of the Christian Democrats and the Socialists, whose leader (Bettino Craxi) was ambitious to be prime minister. In November, 1982, old-time Christian Democratic politician Amintore Fanfani became prime minister of a five-party Center-left coalition government whose subsequent collapse led to the June, 1983, national election.

The Fanfani government targeted the 1983 public deficit at 71 trillion lire, but the Treasury minister forecast in July, 1983, that it would reach 100 trillion lire—or 17 to 18 percent of GDP—unless drastic action was taken. By 1982, interest on the public debt had also become a major problem: At 38 trillion lire a year, or 8.3 percent of GDP, interest alone accounted for 20 percent of total current state expenditure. Total public debt of 350 trillion lire at year-end 1982 equaled 74.5 percent of GDP. By mid-1983, public-sector spending, including interest on debt, absorbed 55 percent of GDP.

Stunned by an unprecedented 5.4 percent drop in its vote (to 32.9 percent in the June, 1983, election), the Christian Democrats finally caved in to Socialist pressure, and allowed Socialist leader Bettino Craxi to become prime minister of a four-party coalition including the Christian Democrats and Socialists. As Italy's first Socialist prime minister, Craxi obtained six Socialist cabinet posts, including the ministries of labor and foreign trade. The new government's top priority was to limit the public-sector deficit to 90 trillion lire in 1984 (compared to an estimated deficit of 87 trillion, or 16.7 percent of GDP, in 1983) by raising taxes sharply and limiting expenditure growth. Most observers considered this an impossible objective.

The Bank of Italy identified the main factors contributing to the extraordinary 1983 public deficit: Excessive state contributions to inefficient state companies; excessively rapid growth of public wages and of health and pension costs; a declining fraction of contributing workers as the population aged; pensions rising faster than inflation; and, finally, the government's failure to fix productivity standards for public service. (At year-end 1981, including the public services and state-controlled companies, the state employed 5.8 million people, or 28 percent of the employed work force.)

Policy instruments were themselves enfeebled by the crisis, and thus exacerbated it. The Bank of Italy's control over the monetary aggregates and credit diminished as the Treasury's requirements burgeoned. Although credit to the private sector in 1982 was restricted to a 13.5 percent rise (meaning a cut in real terms), Total Domestic Credit (TDC) rose 18.6 percent in 1981 and 21 percent in 1982 because of public-sector borrowing. The share of TDC controlled by Bank of Italy credit ceilings declined to about 20 percent by year-end 1982, and the private-sector's share of TDC declined from 83 percent in 1972 to 32 percent in 1982. Thus, the Bank of Italy controls the smaller proportion of total credit and Parliament the much larger share. This also means that the public sector crowds out the private sector.

Although the economy was in recession in 1981-1983, inflation was aggravated by the public-sector and external deficits. Consumer prices rose an average 21 percent in 1980, 19 percent in 1981, 16 percent in 1982, and 15 percent in 1983. They are forecast to rise 12-13 percent in 1984, well above the expected OECD average rise of 5-6 percent. Wholesale prices were also up in 1981-1983, even though declining oil and commodity prices should have helped. The GDP price deflator decelerated from 17.2 percent in 1981 to 14.7 percent in 1983, but is forecast to rise 2 percent in 1984. Productivity was down in 1981, was unchanged in 1982, down 1.2 percent in 1983, and is forecast to rise 2 percent in 1984. Units labor costs rose 21 percent in 1981, 16.5 percent in 1982, and 15.7 percent in 1983.

The Scala Mobile *Becomes Less Mobile*

A potentially important development for inflation occurred on January 22, 1983, when the unions, the Confederation of Industries (Confindustria), and the government signed a labor-cost agreement after 18 months of acrimonious talks. (In early 1982, the Confindustria had unilaterally abrogated the 1975 *scala mobile* agreement.) The new agreement reduced the degree of wage indexation for the first time since 1975, but the government had to make concessions that will boost the public deficit. Confindustria accepted shorter working hours.

The 1983 accord altered the *scala mobile* base index, reducing the point value (which remains equal for all workers). This effectively reduced the degree of indexation by 15 percent. Furthermore, future increases in value-added and other indirect taxes will not be taken into account in applying the adjustment. Limits were set on total monthly wage increases resulting from *both* the escalator and regular wage negotiations. These are based on inflation targets fixed jointly by all three parties. The initial targets were a 13 percent cost-of-living rate by year-end 1983 and 10 percent by year-end 1984. If inflation overshoots the target, however, a catch-up clause allows the parties to renegotiate on compensation—a major loophole. Total compensation increases were limited to 100,000 lire by year-end 1985. Together the changes effectively reduced overall indexation through the *scala mobile* by 18 percent, or to about 60 percent of inflation.

The government's concessions included adjustment of personal income-tax brackets for fiscal drag, increased absorption by government of corporate social-security contributions, a limit on public tariff and administered price increases to 13 percent, and better health insurance. These added at least 3.5 trillion lire to the public deficit in 1983. Confindustria's agreement to reduce the work year by 40 hours was not clearly defined and immediately led to disputes with some unions. All sides agreed to abide by three-year labor contracts.

Although billed as an historic change in labor relations, the January, 1983, agreement was riddled with ambiguities that caused 1982-1983 labor negotiations to drag on through 1983. Key problems included the mechanics of accumulating cost-of-living index decimal points; determining who is eligible for the 40-hour reduction in work time; and deciding which categories of workers are covered by the agreement. Nevertheless, a number of key unions, including state companies, signed contracts on the basis of the new pact. The critical importance of January 22, 1983, is that it marks the day when the unions acknowledged that they had to share responsibility for wage inflation. It was the first concession of union power since the 1969-1975 labor revolution. Early in 1984, Confindustria, the unions, and the government began negotiations on a catch-up for the 1983 inflation overrun, targets for 1984, and a continued reduction of the degree of wage and pension indexation.

Financial Market Responses to Inflation

In addition to official policy changes triggered by inflation and organized labor's efforts to protect real income, Italy's antiquated financial markets also began to respond to inflation, albeit slowly. Not surprisingly, individual and institutional investors moved in similar directions as they attempted to limit the erosion of incomes and profits. Given their long experience with war, political instability, and financial disaster (the savings system collapsed in the 1930's), Italians were diffident and cautious, disposed more toward conservation than innovation. Only after the 1973-1980 oil price increases and two recessions have investors taken a more aggressive approach toward management of their assets and businesses.

As the public sector increasingly monopolized the allocation of savings, the savings structure became distorted. Contrary to theoretical presumptions, household saving was stable or rose during inflationary periods because the public tried to maintain the purchasing power of its stock of financial capital. Total savings also seemed relatively unaffected by either nominal or real interest-rate levels. Diversification of savings abroad was blocked by exchange controls, an important limit to change.

A marked shift of savings toward government securities occurred after the 1973-1974 tax reform, which discriminated against private debt instruments (subjecting bonds to withholding tax for individuals but not for corporations). Treasury and other publicly issued bonds were exempt from the withholding tax. Although taxation subsequently changed several times, private bonds are still taxed, as are dividends. Other forms of investment income are exempted from income tax, including interest on bank deposits and Treasury instruments. After 1974, savings shifted toward bank deposits. Then, as Treasury yields began to rise as the government was forced to finance larger deficits, there was a pronounced shift to Treasury securities.

Household saving patterns changed markedly in the post-1973 period. Real estate became one of the few ways to keep abreast of inflation, resulting in a high proportion of family-owned dwellings. But a July, 1978, rent-control law made it virtually impossible for over 5.8 million owners to increase rents by more than 75 percent of inflation, or to evict tenants. This law led to a sharp drop in investment in rental housing and a housing market crisis that persists. In December, 1983, the *equo canone* law was modified slightly, giving owners larger rent increases under certain circumstances. Savings were accordingly channeled into other forms of investment. New investment instruments—such as funds in leasing certificates, discounted bonds, collectibles and directly managed real estate—were developed. The public also sharply increased its purchases of Treasury securities.

The most important shift in personal and institutional investing trends, however, occurred in 1979-1981, when the yields on tax-free Treasury bills *(buoni ordinari del Tesoro,* or BOT's) and Treasury certificates *(certificati di credito del Tesoro* or CCT's) rose. As Treasury requirements skyrocketed in 1979-1980, yields had to be raised to attract investors. The "divorce" between the Bank of Italy and the Treasury in mid-1981 loosened the link between the Treasury's borrowing needs and the Bank of Italy's monetary base, resulting in a faster reaction of money-market rates to the Treasury's requirements and the exchange rate. Elimination of discriminatory taxation on medium-term securities and certificates of deposit also encouraged use of those instruments. In 1981, Treasury security yields became positive (against inflation) for the first time, as the Bank of Italy tightened monetary policy and medium- and long-term interest rates rose by 5 to 6 percent.

Another significant development was the use of floating rate CCT's and bonds issued by the Treasury and special credit institutes. The CCT's, issued in maturities of two to five years, are indexed to the average yields of six-month BOT's plus about a ½ percent. A yield gap opened up between CCT's and other Treasury securities after year-end 1981. Another instrument, the ten-year "Real Treasury Certificate"—indexed to inflation plus a 2.5 percent interest rate—was introduced in mid-1983. By year-end 1983, CCT's were yielding 18-20 percent, but BOT's had dropped to 16.5-17.5 percent, and other rates were in the 15-16 percent range.

The reaction of individual and institutional investors was astonishing. In 1980, 25.5 trillion lire of fixed-rate BOT's were issued, compared with only 2.7 trillion lire of CCT's. By 1982, 27.4 trillion lire of CCT's were issued compared with 32.6 trillion lire of BOT's. Special credit institute securities more than doubled from 5.9 trillion lire in 1980 to 12.6 trillion in 1982. By year-end 1982, financial institutions held almost half of the total 348.7 trillion lire of outstanding Treasury and other government securities. In May, 1983, the Treasury inaugurated a competitive auction system for BOT's, aiming to reduce the cost and variability of Treasury yields.

In the 12-year period, 1971-1982, the share of total household financial savings invested in bank deposits rose from 36.8 percent to 50.9 percent, as bank interest ceilings were partially deregulated in the mid-1970's. Fixed-income bonds accounted for 18.1 percent in 1971, but dropped to 7.8 percent in 1980 before recovering back to 9 percent in 1982 with higher yields. Short-term instruments, such as T-bills, accounted for a negligible share in 1971 but rose to 13 percent by 1982. Equities dropped from 9.4 percent in 1971 to 6.9 percent in 1982. Investments abroad accounted for 9 percent of total financial savings in 1971 but declined to 2.3 percent in 1982 because of foreign-exchange controls.

Corporate Financing

Financing for Italian corporations has been very limited because of the distorted savings structure, which forced corporations to turn toward banks as their primary source of credit. This trend was strengthened as the energy crisis and two recessions chopped profits and internal financial resources. Italian companies now have the highest debt-to-equity ratios of any major OECD country.

The 1973-1974 tax reform enabled the special credit institutes (usually subsidiaries of the major commercial banks) to borrow on the open market, then use the proceeds to make long-term (up to nine years) loans to companies. Renewed in 1982, exemption from withholding taxes for the institutes strengthened their important intermediary role. Private debt issues stagnated because of the withholding tax on privately issued bonds.

Because of the limitations on private debt and the rapid rise of Italian interest rates, companies increasingly turned to foreign borrowing, interest on which is exempt from taxation. Foreign interest rates were usually lower, and the exchange-rate risk, although large, was quantifiable because of Italy's membership in the European Monetary System.

The Italian stock market is small—only 192 companies are listed on the Milan exchange—and total quoted company capitalization at year-end 1983 amounted to 37 trillion lire (or U.S.$22 billion). As a result, corporate financing through equity issues was lower than it should have been, though it rose significantly in 1971-1982. In 1983, a total of four trillion lire in new equity capital was issued—the largest amount in history.

Bank of Italy data illustrate private and public corporations' reliance on bank borrowing. (State-controlled firms are equally reliant on state subsidies or grants.) In the period 1971-1982, short-term bank debt of corporations rose from 22.7 trillion lire to 127.6 trillion lire. Medium-term debt (mostly from the special credit institutes) rose from 19.7 trillion lire to 109.5 trillion lire. Total bank debt declined from 61 percent of total corporate financing in 1971 to 50 percent in 1982.

A burst of inflation-fed speculation led to a 300 percent rise in Italian stock prices between 1978 and 1981. Equity financing flourished, although a Consob (the commission controlling the *borsa,* the Italian stock exchange) decision to require a cash deposit on all stock transactions caused a sharp setback after mid-1981. The rise in capitalization pushed the share of equity financing from 18.2 trillion lire, 26 percent of the total, in 1971 to 184 trillion lire, or 38 percent, by year-end 1982.

Reforms at Last

Although discussed for decades, key reforms to improve the financing situation usually fell victim to special interests, especially the banks, and to political parties' fears that reforms would affect their influence. But in March, 1983, a law was approved allowing corporations to revalue fixed assets in line with inflation after 1977, and to put part of the increased asset value into special reserves. The law also granted larger tax exemptions and accelerated depreciation on corporate capital investment. The immediate result was a spate of corporate reports for 1982 showing improved net worth, depreciation and increased dividends.

Bruno Visentini (finance minister and president of the Republican party), who authored the legislation, estimated that the change would boost aggregate corporate net worth by 35 trillion lire in the first year. It would also strengthen corporate balance sheets, improve profits and dividends, and thereby encourage greater stock-market participation.

Another reform, approved in the Spring of 1983, provided tax incentives for privately held companies to go public by listing their stock on Italian exchanges. A complementary—and perhaps more important—reform, approved in 1982, had authorized domestic investment in mutual funds. Such funds had operated in Italy since the mid-1960's. They were technically registered in Luxembourg, although they were regulated by the Bank of Italy and were managed by Italian companies. Numerous banks and financial institutions were ready to start funds when final regulations were issued in early 1984. Some experts forecast that 2 to 3 trillion lire, up to 2.7 percent of total 1982 household savings, may be invested in such funds. (Existing funds' net asset value was 1.8 trillion in late 1983.)

These three reforms could develop equity ownership in Italy. In the 1967-1977 period, private investors owned 27 percent of all equities; corporations 32 percent; public institutions 19.6 percent; and nonresidents 17 percent. By 1982, private shareholders' share had dropped to 12 percent; public institutions were down to 11.8 percent; and nonresidents were down to 8.2 percent. Companies, however, were up to 62 percent. The new funds are expected to attract individual investors back into equities.

Banking Modernizes Slowly

Italy's banking structure was fixed by the Banking Act of 1936, which limited commercial banks to short-term (up to 18 months) lending and created separate categories of savings banks, mutual banks, and "banks of national interest" (those owned by the state). Investment banks, as such, were not authorized. Commercial banks were specifically forbidden to engage in investment-banking activities. The special credit institutes were authorized for only medium- and long-term lending. The law has not been changed, and the banking structure has changed only slightly.

The state's role has become dominant. Eleven of the twelve major banks are now state controlled; the last to be nationalized was the Bank Ambrosiano, after its collapse in 1982. This means that most of the banking system's top management is politically nominated. In 1981 and 1982, under the Spadolini government, a number of technically competent bank managers were named for the first time. Nevertheless, the banking system remains highly politicized.

Banks are subject to myriad administrative controls and credit limits imposed by the Bank of Italy. The banking system was slow to adapt to the changing structure of the savings flows brought about by inflation. Disintermediation was caused by the Treasury's growing requirements and the rising yields it offered, which led to a shift from flows into deposits to flows into government securities. Deposit growth slowed from a 22 percent increase in 1977 to 9 percent in 1981. When deposit interest rates were raised in late 1981, the growth rate accelerated during 1982. The banks were similarly affected when the special credit institutes began issuing floating-rate securities in 1979. Investors and savers also shifted massively into BOT's and CCT's as the yields on these securities rose.

Yet another factor limited the banks: An "emergency ceiling," set in 1973, limited total bank loans to the private sector. This forced banks to place deposits in government securities. The change caused by the diversion of personal saving into Treasury securities and the lending ceiling imposed on banks was important. In 1972, time deposits represented 29 percent of total bank deposits; by 1982, they had shrunk to 15 percent as interest rates paid by banks lagged below Treasury yields. Demand deposits, however, rose from 15 percent of the total to 34 percent by 1982, as interest rates payable on them rose toward T-bill rates. In December, 1982, reserve requirements were adjusted to encourage banks to issue higher-yielding certificates of deposit (CD's). By mid-1983, CD's had attracted almost 1 trillion lire.

As savings shifted from institutions into the higher interest rates offered by the market, financial institutions also began to market higher-yielding instruments more aggressively. The banks publicized maximum lending rates for the first time in 1982. In February, 1983, Italian banks were free to set their own prime rates instead of using the prime rate fixed by the Italian Banking Association. In July, 1983, the Bank of Italy ended the official "emergency" ceiling on bank lending but an unofficial guideline of 14 percent was retained. All central bank limitations of credit were halted in January, 1984, but "coordination" was continued. One result of credit controls was the increased use of bankers, acceptances (a form of credit that developed because bankers, acceptances were not subject to the ceiling).

As the competitive spirit took hold with these modest steps toward deregulation, banks started offering wider financial services; securities transactions, leasing, and factoring of accounts receivable developed rapidly after 1980. (Banks still cannot enter insurance activities.) The share of banks' total margin represented by diversified financial services rose from 10 percent in 1974 to over 30 percent in 1982. International banking activities also burgeoned for the major banks, and total nonresident deposits rose by an average 25 percent annually between 1978 and 1982. (The Bank of Italy limited the use of foreign holding companies by Italian banks after the Banco Ambrosiano's Luxembourg company played a key role in that bank's collapse.)

The largest banks have tended to lose market share to the medium-sized banks, and especially to the 30 full-service foreign banks operating in Italy. This trend has been encouraged since 1980 by the central bank's more lenient branch-licensing policy. The major banks' share of deposits dropped from 54 percent of the total in 1978 to 49 percent in 1982, and their share of total loans declined from 56 percent to 49 percent. (These figures are somewhat diluted by the fact that major banks increased their takeovers of medium-sized institutions during this period.)

In mid-1983, Bank of Italy governor Ciampi announced that investment banks would be authorized and encouraged by the authorities. It is hoped that merchant banks will develop underwriting for Italian industry, help private companies to go public, and help expand the capital markets. But it is not clear whether enough nonbank capital and expertise exists to create an investment-banking structure independent of the major banks. New investment banks may simply be subsidiaries of the commercial banks, as are the special credit institutes, thereby extending the commercial banks' monopoly. Ciampi also warned that investment banking would not be the salvation of Italian industry, because financial costs are less important than are the unprofitable imbalances between costs and prices.

The investment banking initiative coincides with other reforms for investment funds and inflation accounting. Together with the growing competition for savings and profits caused by disintermediation and the introduction of floating-rate securities, the banking system is starting to change significantly. An improvement in the equity-capital markets would increase the amount of risk capital available to industry from national savings and thereby reduce dependence on bank credit.

Ciampi emphasized the need to make Italian banking more efficient and profitable. It was not until the late 1970's that electronic data-processing equipment was widely used by the major banks, and banks have always been overstaffed. Personnel costs in Italian banks account for 80 percent of total overhead whereas in other OECD countries the average is 60 to 70 percent. The Bank of Italy also criticizes the inadequate data on banks' own operations and their client companies, as well as excessive administrative controls. Nevertheless, Italian banks were ranked midway in terms of profitability among 16 OECD countries, with an interest margin equal to 2.8 percent of balance-sheet assets. (West Germany's interest margin is 2.1 percent.)

The Insurance Industry Adapts

Life insurance companies were as slow as the banking industry in reacting to inflation. Changes were made only after public pressure for protection of insurance against erosion by inflation led to disintermediation (i.e., a net withdrawal of funds into other investments). This slow change is surprising considering the large losses in purchasing power that holders of life insurance policies suffered first during World War II, and later through the early postwar policies that matured in the 1970's.

By the late 1970's, life insurance was not competitive as a savings vehicle. Life-insurance premium receipts dropped by 23 percent between 1970 and 1979. Savings were being directed toward higher-yielding securities that were indexed. In 1968, a first, modest effort was made to adjust insurance policies for inflation, with some large companies indexing policies for up to 3 percent annual inflation. But inflation accelerated rapidly to well above that rate in 1969. It was not until 1978 that the major companies offered a restricted number of clients indexation of 50 percent of the inflation rate, the extra costs being paid by the companies. But again inflation outran indexation, causing business to deteriorate still further.

Dr. Pietro Manes, economic adviser to the Riunione Adriatica di Sicurta, one of the largest insurance firms, reported that total life-insurance premiums grew 6.5 percent annually, in real terms, in 1948-1972 (while real GDP growth averaged 4.8 percent). The growth rate slumped in 1972-1981, *dropping* an average 2 percent a year even as GDP rose 3 percent.

As Treasury securities and indexed CCT's attracted a growing share of savings, the National Insurance Institute (INA) in 1979 offered policies indexed to 50 percent of inflation plus 3 percent. This formula was improved to 5.5 percent in 1981 and 6.5 percent (up to a ceiling of 21 percent) in 1982. It was an immediate success and the sale of INA policies began to rise. Other major firms offered another approach based on indexation of 50 percent of inflation plus 70-80 percent of the average yield earned on the invested premiums. The plan proved attractive, as some companies offered total yields competitive with BOT's and CCT's. The new policies boosted life-insurance premiums to 1.3 trillion lire in 1982, compared with 690 billion lire in 1978, for a real growth rate of 5 to 7 percent. Thus the decline in life insurance appears to have been reversed by adequate indexation.

Thus, Italian financial mechanisms, which had been notably backward during the noninflationary period of postwar growth, were forced to adapt when the investing public turned to new savings instruments to avoid erosion of its capital. Another influence was the inexorable competition from government borrowing, whose uncontrolled spending and financing requirements forced up Treasury securities yields, causing disintermediation from traditional instruments. Only then did banking, insurance and even Parliament begin to react with new instruments and reforms. The results, as seen from the changes between 1981 and 1983, suggest that modernization is occurring, albeit slowly.

The Underground Economy

Perhaps the most astonishing response to inflation in Italy has been the development of Western Europe's most elaborate underground economy.

Always allergic to paying taxes, Italians found the incentive to go underground sharply increased as inflation accelerated in the early 1970's. Many individuals and small firms of all types, engaged in virtually all activities, are paid without receipts and do not declare their moonlighting income. As inflation worsened and successive governments tightened tax discipline, the underground economy grew as rapidly as the fertile Italian imagination could adapt to the new rules and realities.

The magnitude of the *economia parallela* is, by definition, unknown but has been hotly debated since the mid-1970's. The Italian Statistical Institute (ISTAT) was so criticized that in 1978 it revised the national accounts by adding at one blow some 10 percent of total GDP. Estimates continue to proliferate about the underground economy's size, ranging up to 25 to 30 percent of GDP. But ISTAT observes, with some justification, that this valuation would make Italy's GDP larger than that of the United Kingdom, which seems improbable. A more likely figure is 15 percent of GDP.

The underground economy's real importance is greater than its simple incremental economic value. It is an important social safety valve, providing work for millions. Professor Luciano Gallino, who directed a National Research Council study on secondary employment, estimated in mid-1983 that some 5 to 7 million Italians work illegally *in addition* to the 20.4 million officially registered as employed. It is a moot question, then, just how serious "unemployment" is in Italy. Gallino noted that the black-market economy has been a powerful economic stabilizer since 1973, attenuating the sharp economic cycles and social tensions. Clearly, sociopolitical tensions would be much worse today without this safety valve.

The Future

Recent conversations with leading economists of different occupations and political persuasions reveal an apprehensive consensus. Despite scattered reforms instituted since the late 1970's, they fear that Italy's financial structure is under severe strain and that institutional controls are increasingly ineffectual. They point out that the central government's control over Parliament and the level of public spending, especially at the local level, is extremely weak. Taking an ever-greater share of national resources, the public sector grows more independent of institutional restraint. Organized labor's influence over wages, pensions and transfer payments remains crucial despite the concessions of January, 1983. The central bank's control of credit and monetary aggregates is shrinking as the Treasury's role grows. The checks and balances that would occur with alternation of governments of different political persuasion do not exist, since the country's second largest party (the Communist Party of Italy) is effectively excluded from power and the Christian Democrats' grip on power is perpetuated.

These factors mean that the low and controllable cost-push inflation that followed World War II has deteriorated into accelerating demand-pull inflation. Professor Giorgio Ruffolo, former head of the Ministry of Economic Planning and a Socialist economist, drew an analogy with "three rivers of demand that converged into a flood of inflation": labor costs, public spending (and deficit), and energy. He doubted that the state, whose principal role has been transformed into a transfer mechanism, could regain control soon enough to dam the flood.

The shift from a balanced "contributory" system in Italy to one based on increasingly unbalanced entitlements is fundamental, according to Dr. Antonio Martelli, director of economic studies of Confindustria. Until the mid-1960's, the social partners contributed equitably to maintain a highly productive economy in equilibrium. Since the reforms of 1967-1975 (of the *scala mobile*, education, health, unemployment benefits, social security, and pensions), however, the system is based on growing transfer payments not financed by increasing productivity. The *scala mobile* multiplies the impact of growing transfers, as well as of import prices, on the wage structure. Whereas the Japanese government obliged consumers to absorb the increased market price of oil in 1973-1980, Martelli noted that Italy's parties and unions protected the consumer from the full impact of price increases through government subsidies, transfer payments, the *scala mobile,* and lira devaluation. Today, Japan is competitive and Italy is not.

Several economists emphasized that tax reform cannot solve the public deficit-debt problem. Taxation and social payments presently account for 52 percent of GDP and should not be allowed to rise further. The most evident revenue sources have been exhausted by successive governments. Even tax evasion has been significantly reduced. Sen. Silvano Andrianni, director of the Communist party's economic studies center, noted that taxation falls disproportionately on wage earners, from whom it is easier to collect taxes. Independent income earners, such as small merchants, artisans and professionals, escape an equitable share of the tax load because the political parties are reluctant to crack down on collecting taxes from them. Recently, however, restaurant and hotel owners have been forced to provide "fiscal receipts" to customers, and electronic cash registers have been required since mid-1983 for all businesses with over 200 million lire of annual sales. Other tax reforms are needed to reach the incomes of professional people and to protect the progressive tax structure from the flattening effect of fiscal drag.

The proliferation since the 1960's of mechanisms that automatically transmit or magnify inflation was emphasized by Luigi Spaventa, an independent economist. The *scala mobile* is the worst of these mechanisms in his view, as it amplifies the inflationary effect of wages and import prices. In addition, other automatic mechanisms are pegged to the *scala mobile*. Still other inflation-perpetuating regulations include indexation of pensions and transfer payments; financing of local government spending; authorization of multiyear spending programs without appropriate revenue measures; and the central bank's financing of the Treasury.

The increasingly limited influence of monetary policy was singled out by the Bank of Italy's Antonio Fazio. He noted that excess liquidity has usually led to capital outflows, speculative inventory accumulation, lira depreciation, and higher inflation. Restrictive monetary policy was used in 1947, 1963, 1969, 1973-1974, 1977-1978, and since 1980—but with diminishing effect. The basic reason is that the Bank of Italy controls a declining share of total domestic credit because the uncontrollable public sector absorbs more and more credit and savings. Monetary policy is thus less effective in controlling total liquidity, even though it is increasingly restrictive toward private demand and private investment.

As the public sector has mushroomed, the savings structure has been distorted. Dr. Brovedani of the Banca Nazionale del Lavoro notes that although household savings were stable or rose during inflationary periods, corporate savings deteriorated after 1975. Total savings, relatively unaffected by real interest rates, rose in line with inflation, however, as the public's overriding need to restore its stock of savings made itself felt. There was a marked shift of savings toward higher-yielding government securities because of tax legislation and noncompetitive private bond and equity yields. The cost structure of banks is so high that deposit rates are not competitive, and the banks themselves are obliged to buy a growing share of government debt.

Most of these economists agree that a major public-finance crisis could occur in Italy in the mid-1980's. With a public deficit running at 13 to 17 percent of GDP, national savings will not suffice for both public- and private-sector requirements and, at the same time, finance the restructuring of Italian industry necessary to make it competitive externally. Among the fundamental remedies these economists recommend are reduced labor costs, diminished indexation of wages and entitlements, control of public spending, tax reform, and decreased dependence on imported energy. All agree that Italy's industry must rapidly improve its technological and productivity performance.

In November, 1983, the IMF formally warned the Italian government that it must take more vigorous action to cut the public deficit. Measures to date are inadequate to deal with the deficit, which the IMF likened to a "cancer" weakening "the productive potential of the economy." If no such drastic action is taken, Italy could find itself in an "unsustainable position."

If at least some of these reforms are not made, refinancing of the public debt may become a traumatic necessity, disrupting savers, industry, political parties, and the state alike. As this menace approaches, the "country can no longer afford to buy social consensus," Dr. Martelli warns. Reforms needed to avoid the crunch will require a degree of political will by political parties that has been conspicuously absent to date. Institutional reforms will be difficult but are essential.

Both Spadolini and Craxi, the two most recent prime ministers, have urged the need for more power for government to legislate, more centralized government control over state administration, and abolition of secret voting in Parliament. The first important step in this direction occurred in April, 1983, when a 40-man Parliamentary Commission for Constitutional Reform was approved overwhelmingly by government parties and the Communist party. This commission started work in January, 1984, to propose constitutional reforms in 1984 and 1985. These include increasing power for the prime minister's office; tying public spending to prior financial appropriations; limiting the right to strike; restricting the political affiliation and activity of magistrates, military officers, and the police; abolishing the provinces; and simplifying legislative processes.

Among the most important changes that could occur would be to end the proportional electoral system, in effect since 1919, that has perpetuated Italy's surfeit of political parties. This has forced governments to represent intricate coalitions and has enforced the influence of the small parties over government and the administration, while destabilizing the political situation. But it seems improbable that the small parties would vote for changes that would threaten their existence and power. Thus the fragmentation that rules Italy and the economy is likely to continue.

The electorate may, however, force change on the parties just as the nation's savers obliged the capital markets to change in response to inflation. The June, 1983, national election resulted in a historically large drop for the Christian Democrats, while the Communist party remained stable at 30 percent and the Socialists gained less than expected, rising to an 11 percent share of the vote. The Christian Democrats' influence and power have been rudely reduced. Whether or not the party can rejuvenate itself with younger leaders and more efficient policies remains to be seen. Whether or not Socialist Prime Minister Craxi can push through reforms quickly enough is also a question. But despite the electoral upheaval, a left-wing alternative of the Communist and Socialist parties still seems out of the question, although their influence on government policies may be enhanced.

Summary and Conclusion

Italy's inflation record is a sorry chronicle of a developing economy's evolution from a virtuous combination of low costs, high productivity, and appropriate government policies to a system vitiated by excessive social-labor costs and expectations, external vulnerability, and an uncontrollable public-sector deficit and debt. Weakened governmental institutions and powerful but fragmented political parties make the situation seem intractable.

Italy is far from the halcyon days of 1960 when the lira won its "Oscar." The 10,000-lire banknote is a symbol of the lire's decline and inflation's rise.

In 1960, it was a handsome, brown bill, so large it was nicknamed the "bed-sheet." By 1984, the lira had lost 61 percent of its value and the 10,000-lira bill was reduced to a dreary, small, green note less than half the size of its proud predecessor.

There have been some encouraging signs of structural changes since 1980, however: the Bank of Italy-Treasury "divorce," closer supervision of foreign borrowers, competitive bidding for Treasury securities, abolition of the ceiling on bank lending and more sophisticated reserve requirements, authorization of investment funds, inflation accounting, incentives to private companies to "go public," and the evolution toward indexed securities and insurance.

Moreover, Italy is blessed with economic-social shock absorbers that make an otherwise untenable situation workable. The underground economy is remarkably productive and a major social-employment safety valve, as well as an economic cushion. Even bureaucratic spending delays mean that not quite as much money is spent by the public sector. Finally, family and religious cohesiveness make the social fabric more resistant to the stresses generated by high unemployment and inflation.

Nevertheless, the structural changes that have led to sharply higher inflation and a large public-sector deficit are still at work. The wonderful synergy of low labor costs, high investment, rapid growth of demand and capacity, and balance-of-payments equilibrium is a thing of the past. The post-1973 combination of higher public spending, indexation, external deficit, and declining competitiveness, and lira depreciation has created an unhealthy instability. Inflation and the public deficit are the two key challenges to the country's current leaders.

The story of inflation in Italy may not have a happy ending. In early 1984, it is difficult to avoid a sense of impending crisis resulting from the public and external deficits and inflation. Will debt-ridden Italy prove, to be the Brazil or Mexico of Western Europe in the mid-1980's? We suspect that only when this danger is imminent and the alternatives sharply limited will the political determination be found to make the necessary and painful structural reforms to restore economic stability in Italy.

Part III

STATISTICAL APPENDIX
AND
NOTES

Table 1

Annual Growth Rates of Consumer Prices, 1965-1983[1]
(Percent)

	U.S.	Japan	W. Germany	France	U.K.	Italy	Canada	Switzerland
1965 IV Q	1.8	6.1	4.0	2.5	4.7	3.0	2.9	4.7
1966 IV Q	3.6	4.2	2.9	3.1	4.0	2.1	3.9	4.2
1967 IV Q	2.9	5.2	0.9	3.3	2.1	3.7	3.7	3.8
1968 IV Q	4.7	4.7	2.1	5.2	5.4	1.2	4.3	2.3
1969 IV Q	5.8	5.8	2.1	5.8	5.2	3.5	4.6	2.2
1970 IV Q	5.6	8.0	4.0	5.5	7.9	5.7	2.2	5.2
1971 IV Q	3.5	5.5	5.7	5.9	9.1	4.6	4.1	6.5
1972 IV Q	3.4	4.6	6.1	6.8	7.7	7.2	5.0	7.0
1973 IV Q	8.3	16.3	7.2	8.3	10.4	11.8	9.1	10.7
1974 IV Q	12.1	24.8	6.5	14.9	18.1	24.5	12.1	8.8
1975 IV Q	7.4	8.5	5.6	10.0	25.6	11.4	10.2	4.0
1976 IV Q	5.1	9.2	3.7	10.0	14.9	19.7	5.9	1.1
1977 IV Q	6.6	6.2	3.6	9.1	13.0	15.1	9.1	1.5
1978 IV Q	9.0	3.4	2.3	9.6	8.1	11.5	8.6	0.5
1979 IV Q	12.8	5.0	5.5	11.5	17.2	17.8	9.6	5.3
1980 IV Q	12.5	7.8	5.2	13.5	15.2	21.4	11.0	4.0
1981 IV Q	9.6	4.0	6.5	14.2	11.9	16.7	12.4	7.0
1982 IV Q	4.5	2.4	4.7	9.5	6.2	16.6	9.7	5.8
1983 IV Q*	3.3	1.7	2.6	9.8	5.1	12.8	4.6	1.7

*Preliminary
[1]From fourth quarter of the preceding year.

Notes to Statistical Tables

Table 1. Consumer Prices

Each of the eight countries measures its Consumer Price Index in somewhat different ways. The indexes reported in Table 1 vary with respect to the coverage of the index, the methods used to calculate the index and the frequency with which the relative weights within each country's index are updated. (For a detailed survey of these differences see C. Vannereau, "Comparibility of Consumer Price Indexes in OECD Countries," OECD *Economic Outlook—Occasional Studies,* July, 1975.) In addition, many countries calculate and publish more than one index.

The data shown in Table 1 refer in most cases to the official series entitled *Consumer Prices—all items.* The exceptions are:

Italy: Consumer Prices (wage and salary earners).
Japan: Consumer Prices (cities with populations of 50,000 or more).
United States: Consumer Prices (all urban consumers)—a series officially
designated as CPI-U.

In the United States, the Bureau of Labor Statistics calculates and publishes two CPI series, CPI-U and CPI-W. The CPI-W, the older index, covers urban wage earners and clerical workers, a group that comprises about 40 percent of the U.S. population. The CPI-U, published since January, 1978, covers *all* urban consumers, a group that comprises about 80 percent of the U.S. population.

The BLS continues to publish the CPI-W for legal reasons: It is the statistic used for indexing social-security payments and for measuring the esclator clauses (COLA's) in most collective-bargaining agreements.

In January, 1983, the BLS changed the way in which the CPI-U (the index in Table 1) is calculated: The pre-1983 method for calculating the home-owner component of the cost of living included the price of new homes, the rate of interest payable on mortgages, property taxes, property-insurance rates, and maintenance costs. The new component is simply the rental equivalent of the owner-occupied property. (In January, 1985, the CPI-W will also be shifted to the rental-equivalent basis for home-owner costs).

One reason for political opposition to the switch from the CPI-W to CPI-U was the expectation that CPI-U would show a *slower* rate of inflation. In fact, an opposite development has occurred. In December, 1983, the twelve-month rate of inflation, as measured by the CPI-U, was above the corresponding CPI-W measure—3.8 percent as against 3.3 percent.

For many countries, the long delays involved in adjusting the relative weights assigned to different components of the Consumer Price Index have led to the increasing use of the price index associated with the consumer expenditure component of the gross national or gross domestic product as a more up-to-date measure of the inflation that households confront. Because the "weights" in the personal consumer price deflator change continuously with changing patterns of consumption, such an index is automatically updated every year.

Table 2
Annual Growth Rates of Wholesale Prices, 1965-1983[1]
(Percent)

	U.S.	Japan	W. Germany	France	U.K.	Italy	Canada	Switzerland
1965 IV Q	2.7	1.2	2.0	0.5	4.6	1.9	2.3	0.6
1966 IV Q	2.8	3.0	0.9	1.5	2.2	0.0	2.5	1.1
1967 IV Q	1.3	1.8	-0.9	0.3	0.4	1.4	1.9	0.9
1968 IV Q	3.2	0.4	-0.4	0.3	3.9	-0.5	2.4	0.2
1969 IV Q	4.4	3.7	3.9	13.4	4.1	7.0	3.7	4.6
1970 IV Q	2.6	1.7	4.2	1.8	8.3	6.1	1.5	2.6
1971 IV Q	2.9	-1.2	3.6	4.2	6.2	2.9	3.0	2.2
1972 IV Q	3.5	4.4	3.8	7.4	8.3	6.4	5.1	5.6
1973 IV Q	11.6	23.9	8.0	19.8	9.6	24.0	14.6	13.9
1974 IV Q	18.7	23.3	13.5	19.6	27.6	38.4	20.4	12.7
1975 IV Q	7.0	0.7	2.2	-6.7	20.7	3.9	7.4	-5.6
1976 IV Q	3.2	6.3	4.2	12.6	17.7	30.7	4.2	1.0
1977 IV Q	7.1	-0.7	2.0	1.3	17.5	10.6	8.7	-1.1
1978 IV Q	8.7	-3.1	1.4	8.2	7.9	8.6	11.2	-3.1
1979 IV Q	12.8	16.1	6.7	13.4	15.5	20.2	15.2	6.9
1980 IV Q	12.4	11.1	7.1	8.0	13.3	16.9	12.4	4.4
1981 IV Q	7.3	1.4	8.7	12.8	11.1	17.9	8.5	6.0
1982 IV Q	3.7	1.7	4.1	8.5	7.8	12.4	4.4	1.4
1983 IV Q*	0.8	-3.2	1.5	14.4	5.6	9.1	3.6	0.9

*Preliminary
[1]From fourth quarter of the preceding year.

Table 2. The Producer (or Wholesale) Price Index

The wholesale (or producer) price indexes shown in Table 2 vary even more from country to country than do the CPI's in Table 1.

The French index measures the wholesale prices of industrial goods (tax included): the West German and United Kingdom indexes refer to industrial prices; the Italian index measures only the price of investment goods; the Swiss index measures the price of both home production and imports; finally, the United States index shown covers the producer prices of finished goods.

Table 3

Annual Growth Rates of GNP or GDP Deflator, 1965-1983[1]

(Percent)

	U.S.	Japan	W. Germany	France	U.K.	Italy	Canada	Switzerland
1965 IV Q	2.5	−1.2	3.5	.	4.7	3.0	3.5	.
1966 IV Q	3.7	6.7	3.0	5.1	4.4	1.9	4.3	.
1967 IV Q	3.1	7.2	0.9	2.6	2.3	2.5	3.9	.
1968 IV Q	4.8	5.1	3.2	6.7	5.7	1.8	3.2	.
1969 IV Q	5.5	4.8	5.5	4.7	5.5	5.8	4.7	.
1970 IV Q	5.0	9.2	7.1	6.2	8.1	6.7	4.9	.
1971 IV Q	4.7	3.7	7.7	5.9	9.2	7.4	3.5	.
1972 IV Q	4.3	6.8	5.1	6.7	7.9	6.7	5.5	.
1973 IV Q	7.1	16.3	7.3	9.0	8.9	13.1	11.6	.
1974 IV Q	10.2	19.1	7.6	12.2	19.5	23.8	15.1	.
1975 IV Q	7.7	4.3	3.8	11.5	24.9	13.0	10.2	.
1976 IV Q	4.7	5.9	3.8	10.6	12.6	21.9	8.7	.
1977 IV Q	6.1	5.4	3.7	8.5	13.2	15.9	6.1	.
1978 IV Q	8.5	3.9	4.3	10.0	10.6	13.7	6.7	1.9
1979 IV Q	8.2	1.5	3.9	10.5	18.4	17.6	11.9	3.7
1980 IV Q	10.2	4.1	4.2	11.8	17.4	20.2	10.4	3.1
1981 IV Q	8.7	2.0	4.6	13.1	9.5	17.5	11.1	6.7
1982 IV Q	4.4	1.2	4.8	9.6	7.1	17.2	10.4	7.8
1983 IV Q*	4.1	0.1	2.6	.	.	13.4†	3.8	.

*Preliminary
[1]From fourth quarter of the preceding year.   †To third quarter, 1983.
.Not available

Table 3. GNP or GDP Deflators

Although each country's system of national accounts differs somewhat from the others, the GNP or GDP deflator measure of price changes provides not only the broadest, but also the most uniformly calculated measure of relative price changes in the eight countries. The difference between the GNP and the GDP concept was covered in a note on p. 7.

Table 4
Annual Growth Rates of Industrial Production, 1965-1983[1]
(Percent)

	U.S.	Japan	W. Germany	France	U.K.	Italy	Canada	Switzerland
1965 IV Q	10.7	1.9	2.9	5.9	1.8	8.9	9.8	2.9
1966 IV Q	7.6	20.3	-1.4	2.9	-0.9	11.3	3.8	5.7
1967 IV Q	2.7	18.9	3.9	3.3	4.5	7.2	3.6	1.4
1968 IV Q	5.7	15.1	10.1	10.5	5.2	7.3	9.1	6.7
1969 IV Q	3.2	17.0	11.3	4.9	1.7	-6.1	3.5	8.8
1970 IV Q	-5.3	8.6	2.7	5.5	0.7	16.2	0.3	6.9
1971 IV Q	5.4	1.6	-0.8	5.2	-0.3	2.5	7.5	1.1
1972 IV Q	11.7	12.3	7.4	7.4	6.2	5.8	8.5	3.2
1973 IV Q	5.5	12.0	4.1	5.8	2.8	11.9	7.9	5.2
1974 IV Q	-5.2	-11.6	-6.0	-2.9	-5.1	-8.1	-0.8	-5.9
1975 IV Q	-1.0	-4.3	-0.7	-2.6	-3.8	-0.2	-3.2	-1.0
1976 IV Q	7.4	12.2	7.1	7.3	5.1	15.9	4.9	-5.3
1977 IV Q	5.9	2.4	1.6	0.0	1.4	-6.7	2.6	3.3
1978 IV Q	7.4	8.3	3.9	5.4	4.1	9.6	6.3	2.2
1979 IV Q	1.2	7.7	4.4	3.4	1.8	8.2	3.2	2.1
1980 IV Q	-2.5	0.5	-3.6	-3.6	-10.0	-2.2	0.0	1.0
1981 IV Q	-1.7	4.2	0.0	1.0	-0.1	-2.3	-3.5	-1.0
1982 IV Q	-7.5	-2.7	-6.2	-3.0	0.4	-5.9	-11.9	-8.1
1983 IV Q*	14.9	8.4	6.4	1.4	3.9	-2.7	16.8	0.0†

*Preliminary
[1]From fourth quarter of the preceding year.　　　†To third quarter 1983.

Table 4. Industrial Production

Industrial production is not an unambiguous concept. It can refer to the physical output of manufacturing industries, to manufacturing *plus* mining, to manufacturing *plus* mining and utilities, on in its broadest form to manufacturing, mining, utilities *plus* construction. Each country is free to choose its own limits.

The data shown in Table 4 generally refer to *total* industrial production (i.e., including manufacturing, mining and utilities but excluding construction).

Table 5
Annual Growth Rates of Real GNP/GDP, 1965-1983[1]
(Percent)

	U.S.	Japan	W. Germany	France	U.K.	Italy	Canada	Switzerland
1965 IV Q	7.9	10.0	4.8	.	1.7	6.3	7.7	.
1966 IV Q	4.2	12.6	−0.1	3.5	2.3	5.8	5.4	.
1967 IV Q	3.1	11.9	3.2	4.8	0.7	7.9	3.2	.
1968 IV Q	4.3	15.4	7.5	6.9	5.1	7.3	7.9	.
1969 IV Q	1.3	10.6	7.1	4.6	1.9	1.6	4.1	.
1970 IV Q	−0.1	6.9	4.3	6.1	3.1	7.4	0.9	.
1971 IV Q	4.7	4.4	1.6	5.7	2.8	2.3	9.4	.
1972 IV Q	7.0	10.7	5.5	5.9	3.4	4.8	5.8	.
1973 IV Q	4.2	5.5	3.0	4.3	3.7	7.9	7.8	.
1974 IV Q	−2.8	−0.8	−1.4	1.1	−0.1	−2.5	0.9	.
1975 IV Q	2.2	3.9	1.7	2.7	0.4	0.2	2.8	.
1976 IV Q	4.4	4.2	4.9	4.9	3.9	6.9	4.5	.
1977 IV Q	5.7	5.8	2.7	2.2	2.0	−0.8	3.0	.
1978 IV Q	5.8	5.3	3.5	4.7	2.0	5.6	3.6	0.3
1979 IV Q	1.4	5.3	4.2	3.1	1.1	5.8	2.9	3.8
1980 IV Q	−0.8	4.7	−0.3	−0.6	−2.6	0.6	0.6	2.9
1981 IV Q	2.0	2.7	0.6	1.8	−1.0	0.6	0.8	2.3
1982 IV Q	−1.7	3.7	−2.0	1.2	2.6	−2.4	−5.7	−2.5
1983 IV Q*	6.2	3.2†	3.2	.	.	−0.4†	6.6	.

*Preliminary
[1]From fourth quarter of the preceding year.   †To third quarter 1983.
.Not available.

Table 5. Real GNP (GDP)

The nominal gross national product (GNP) or gross domestic produt (GDP), the alternative measure preferred by France, Italy and the United Kingdom, measures the total *market* value of the output at prices that are current in the year being measured. Each component of output is then adjusted in order to answer the question: What would the market value of output be if each component is valued at price levels that prevailed in 1972, for example. Repeating this process, year by year, provides a series which measures the *real* rise in a country's GNP or GDP—a rise that eliminates the effects of inflation.

Table 6

Table 6
Annual Growth Rates of Employment, 1965-1983[1]
(Percent)

	U.S.	Japan	W. Germany	France	U.K.	Italy	Canada	Switzerland
1965 IV Q	3.0	1.0	1.2	-0.8	1.0	-3.9	6.8	-2.2
1966 IV Q	2.5	0.8	-2.9	0.3	0.4	0.9	3.5	-1.5
1967 IV Q	2.1	4.3	-5.8	-1.0	-2.6	1.1	-1.9	-1.3
1968 IV Q	1.7	4.0	4.0	-1.3	-0.3	3.5	1.1	-0.2
1969 IV Q	2.7	3.1	5.0	3.3	-0.4	2.2	1.8	0.2
1970 IV Q	0.1	3.8	2.1	0.7	-0.8	2.4	-3.6	-1.5
1971 IV Q	2.0	-0.9	-2.0	0.2	-2.0	0.1	0.7	-1.6
1972 IV Q	3.5	-1.7	-1.7	-0.2	2.0	-2.0	2.6	-2.9
1973 IV Q	3.9	0.9	0.7	1.1	1.7	3.2	5.9	0.2
1974 IV Q	0.4	-2.2	-4.7	0.5	0.4	1.4	-0.3	-1.4
1975 IV Q	-0.1	-4.8	-6.3	-2.9	-0.9	-0.2	-5.0	-12.3
1976 IV Q	3.6	-1.2	-0.2	0.1	1.8	-0.6	1.3	-3.0
1977 IV Q	4.5	-1.8	-1.1	-1.0	-2.0	-0.8	-1.1	0.4
1978 IV Q	4.0	-1.9	-0.5	-1.3	1.6	-0.7	2.9	-0.2
1979 IV Q	2.3	0.2	1.0	-1.5	0.5	2.1	2.0	0.2
1980 IV Q	-0.1	1.3	-0.4	-0.5	-3.8	-1.1	-2.4	1.9
1981 IV Q	0.6	1.0	-2.8	-2.8	-3.9	-1.3	-1.6	-0.3
1982 IV Q	-1.0	0.4	-4.0	-1.0	-2.2	-2.8	-12.2	-4.0
1983 IV Q*	3.5	0.4	-4.6†	2.6†	-0.7†	-2.0	.	-3.3†

*Preliminary
[1]From fourth quarter of the preceding year.   †To third quarter 1983.
.Not available.

Table 6. Employment

Data on the total number of persons employed in each country are not available on a uniform and timely basis; in some cases even annual data for this statistic are published only after long delays. The data shown in Table 6 refer to total employment only for the United States and the United Kingdom; the data for Canada, Japan and Switzerland refer to manufacturing employment; and those for France, West Germany, and Italy to industrial employment.

Table 7
Annual Growth Rates of Hourly Earnings, 1965-1983[1]
(Percent)

	U.S.	Japan	W. Germany	France	U.K.	Italy	Canada	Switzerland
1965 IV Q	3.8	8.4	6.5	5.7	7.1	.	7.5	5.0
1966 IV Q	3.6	12.7	6.3	6.0	5.2	.	4.7	5.7
1967 IV Q	5.3	13.5	4.0	6.0	5.4	.	8.9	5.4
1968 IV Q	5.0	16.5	5.5	16.5	7.3	.	8.2	4.1
1969 IV Q	6.3	17.6	10.0	8.2	5.9	.	7.5	3.9
1970 IV Q	6.0	21.2	15.4	10.8	12.6	.	7.0	8.3
1971 IV Q	7.0	13.6	7.8	11.5	11.0	.	9.8	8.9
1972 IV Q	6.6	18.5	8.5	11.5	16.8	.	7.5	8.5
1973 IV Q	6.2	28.2	10.3	15.6	12.2	.	9.7	9.1
1974 IV Q	10.5	30.2	12.3	20.5	22.1	.	16.5	10.3
1975 IV Q	8.4	9.3	7.7	15.9	29.6	.	13.0	6.0
1976 IV Q	7.8	10.2	5.6	14.1	12.3	.	13.5	1.2
1977 IV Q	8.1	7.0	7.2	12.1	4.0	.	10.2	2.1
1978 IV Q	8.3	4.6	4.8	13.4	25.1	.	6.9	3.7
1979 IV Q	8.5	5.7	4.4	13.1	14.4	.	9.4	2.6
1980 IV Q	11.3	8.0	7.0	15.2	13.8	.	11.2	6.3
1981 IV Q	8.3	5.1	5.1	14.8	8.8	.	12.4	5.9
1982 IV Q	7.1	5.4	4.0	12.5	6.0	.	9.5	6.3
1983 IV Q*	4.8	2.2†	2.9	12.4	5.3	.	.	.

*Preliminary
[1]From fourth quarter of the preceding year.   †To third quarter 1983.
.Not available.

Table 7. Hourly Earnings

For Canada, France, West Germany, Japan, the United Kingdom, and the United States: hourly earnings in manufacturing.

For Switzerland: hourly earnings in the entire economy.

Data for Italy are not available on a quarterly basis.

Table 8
Annual Growth Rates of Unit Labor Costs, 1965-1983[1]
(Percent)

	U.S.	Japan	W. Germany	France	U.K.	Italy	Canada	Switzerland
1965 IV Q	-1.5	6.3	4.1	2.8	5.1	.	2.3	.
1966 IV Q	3.0	-5.9	5.3	2.9	4.9	.	4.2	.
1967 IV Q	0.0	-2.1	-3.6	0.0	0.0	.	3.7	.
1968 IV Q	5.8	2.1	2.2	2.7	4.7	.	-0.6	.
1969 IV Q	4.1	0.0	6.8	2.7	6.7	.	4.2	.
1970 IV Q	3.9	12.5	10.7	5.1	7.7	.	5.2	.
1971 IV Q	-1.3	11.1	8.3	4.9	7.1	.	-2.3	.
1972 IV Q	1.3	1.7	4.3	7.0	5.0	.	4.2	.
1973 IV Q	5.1	8.2	10.0	8.7	7.9	25.0	5.9	.
1974 IV Q	14.5	40.9	11.0	24.0	27.9	20.7	17.2	18.6
1975 IV Q	4.2	10.8	1.4	9.7	21.8	24.5	11.6	14.5
1976 IV Q	4.0	-1.9	2.8	7.4	6.6	17.5	8.6	3.0
1977 IV Q	6.8	4.0	2.9	11.0	11.5	26.1	6.2	-0.3
1978 IV Q	5.5	-3.8	2.8	3.7	13.5	5.0	2.0	-0.1
1979 IV Q	8.6	-3.0	3.6	7.1	16.1	15.3	13.2	0.1
1980 IV Q	11.1	4.1	7.2	16.7	22.9	18.2	11.9	6.0
1981 IV Q	9.3	1.0	3.5	10.5	3.4	17.2	16.0	4.9
1982 IV Q	6.3	10.7	3.8	11.2	6.6	18.4	9.7	9.6
1983 IV Q*	2.0	0.0	0.0	.	2.5	15.6†	1.7	.

*Preliminary
[1]From fourth quarter of the preceding year.　　　†To third quarter 1983.
.Not available.

Table 8. Unit Labor Costs

The United States and the United Kingdom data refer to unit labor costs in manufacturing. For Canada, West Germany, and Japan, data refer to unit labor costs in the entire economy. Quarterly data are not available for earlier dates for Italy and Switzerland.

Table 9
Annual Growth Rates of The Monetary Base, 1965-1983[1]
(Percent)

	U.S.	Japan	W. Germany	France	U.K.	Italy	Canada	Switzerland
1965 IV Q	5.4	9.3	6.7	7.1	10.7	11.9	9.7	3.4
1966 IV Q	4.4	13.2	8.3	4.2	5.9	9.7	7.8	4.2
1967 IV Q	6.5	18.5	-5.0	7.5	4.7	12.3	5.8	6.9
1968 IV Q	7.0	18.9	9.3	7.2	3.9	8.0	8.2	15.7
1969 IV Q	4.0	19.6	3.1	-0.8	2.0	13.1	5.3	6.7
1970 IV Q	6.3	16.6	21.7	4.4	11.6	12.4	5.6	12.7
1971 IV Q	7.6	14.5	15.0	10.6	-5.1	17.0	15.2	18.5
1972 IV Q	8.0	29.0	26.4	31.6	21.2	10.0	15.6	7.9
1973 IV Q	7.8	34.3	7.4	7.5	31.5	21.4	16.1	3.8
1974 IV Q	8.8	16.1	-1.1	13.2	4.1	13.2	14.1	3.4
1975 IV Q	7.2	4.0	2.9	-21.7	11.4	44.3	15.5	2.3
1976 IV Q	7.7	8.6	10.2	7.4	20.1	21.0	9.3	7.7
1977 IV Q	8.5	8.4	7.9	8.8	5.2	17.4	12.2	3.6
1978 IV Q	9.3	14.9	13.1	12.3	10.0	25.7	11.8	17.4
1979 IV Q	8.2	7.5	5.2	6.6	9.8	15.0	8.6	-7.8
1980 IV Q	8.3	6.4	-3.7	15.4	-3.0	12.2	10.1	1.4
1981 IV Q	4.4	2.7	-1.6	4.3	3.9	13.5	2.3	-4.3
1982 IV Q	8.2	6.2	5.3	18.4	4.4	14.9	3.9	-13.5
1983 IV Q*	9.6	5.4	5.6	7.9+	7.9+	8.5+	1.4	24.2

*Preliminary
[1]From fourth quarter of the preceding year.

Table 9 and 10

The monetary base measures direct monetary liabilities of the government and the central bank of each country that is, the volume of currency issued *plus* central bank deposit liabilities to commercial banks (i.e., bank reserves).

The M-1 concept of money supply refers to currency and checkable deposits held by the public.

Table 10
Annual Growth Rates of Money (M1), 1965-1983[1]
(Percent)

	U.S.	Japan	W. Germany	France	U.K.	Italy	Canada	Switzerland
1965 IV Q	4.4	18.5	8.1	9.8	2.2	15.0	7.0	4.3
1966 IV Q	2.8	14.0	1.9	7.6	-0.1	14.8	8.0	2.8
1967 IV Q	6.4	14.1	7.1	4.5	8.6	13.2	8.7	8.1
1968 IV Q	7.3	14.2	7.4	8.1	5.6	13.6	5.9	11.6
1969 IV Q	3.9	21.8	8.1	1.1	0.2	15.9	3.7	12.0
1970 IV Q	4.9	15.9	6.5	4.9	8.8	25.4	4.3	-21.1
1971 IV Q	6.7	30.1	13.3	12.7	9.4	20.2	16.9	23.0
1972 IV Q	8.5	23.2	14.3	14.8	14.9	17.5	14.6	9.6
1973 IV Q	5.8	19.9	0.8	7.5	5.3	23.4	12.1	1.8
1974 IV Q	4.8	11.1	10.5	13.6	11.1	11.6	6.1	0.3
1975 IV Q	5.0	10.9	15.3	12.8	13.3	11.0	21.3	5.2
1976 IV Q	6.1	14.8	6.5	10.3	11.0	20.6	2.6	7.8
1977 IV Q	8.2	6.1	10.3	9.4	21.9	20.4	10.2	4.8
1978 IV Q	8.2	12.4	13.3	11.8	16.3	25.0	10.8	22.7
1979 IV Q	7.4	5.7	4.2	10.5	9.1	25.1	4.5	-2.6
1980 IV Q	7.2	-1.8	4.3	8.3	4.0	11.7	9.4	-4.6
1981 IV Q	5.1	9.2	-1.6	15.4	9.3	8.4	-3.1	-7.1
1982 IV Q	8.5	5.9	6.2	13.1	11.9	16.6	3.7	11.6
1983 IV Q*	10.0	0.1	9.2	6.9+	11.3	.	11.6	5.3+

*Preliminary
[1]From fourth quarter of the preceding year.   +To third quarter, 1983.
.Not available

Statistical Sources

The data in the Statistical Appendix are from the data-bank maintained by the Federal Reserve Bank of St. Louis and published by the bank in annual and quarterly issues entitled *International Economic Conditions* (Federal Reserve Bank of St. Louis, P.O. Box 442, St. Louis, Missouri, 63166).

Other major secondary sources of international data are:

(1) Organization for Economic Cooperation and Development (OECD). *Main Economic Indicators, 1960-1979.* Paris, OECD, 1970, and subsequent updates in OECD *Economic Outlook* (published semiannually).

(2) International Monetary Fund (IMF). *Monthly Statistics.*

(3) United States Department of Commerce *International Economic Indicators,* quarterly publication.

All three publications provide references to original data sources for each country.

About the Authors

Carl E. Beigie

Professor, University of Toronto and McGill University. In addition to his teaching, Mr. Beigie is a senior partner in St. Lawerence Economic Research Associates, Ltd. (Ottawa). He was the founding Executive Director of the C.D. Howe Institute and was its President from 1978 until 1982. He studied economics at Muskingum College in Ohio and the Massachusetts Institute of Technology. Mr. Beigie has worked at the Irving Trust Company in New York City; has held various industrial and governmental appointments; and has been an adviser to several non-profit organizations. A frequent lecturer and writer, he has focused most recently on inflation, Canadian-United States relations, and the role of government.

Alan P. Budd

Professor of Economics and Director, Centre for Economic Forecasting, London Business School. Alan Budd graduated in economics from the London School of Economics and studied for a Ph.D. at Cambridge University. He lectured on economics at Southampton University, and has been a visiting professor at Carnegie-Mellon University, Pittsburgh. He served in the U.K. Treasury from 1970 to 1974. He has been at the London Business School since 1974, and is the author of *The Politics of Economic Planning* and many articles on economic policy.

Michel Develle

Director, Economic and Financial Research and Chief Economist, Paribas, Paris. Michel Develle received his doctorate in economic sciences from the University of Aix-en-Provence, where he was assistant lecturer. He joined Paribas, France's leading merchant bank, in 1973 as chief economist and deputy director of economic and financial research, and became director in 1983. Dr. Develle is responsible for the bank's economic bulletin, *Conjoncture.* His articles have appeared in *Nouveau Journal, Revue Banque, Euromoney, Business Week,* and other publications.

Geoffrey Dicks

Senior Research Officer, Centre for Economic Forecasting, London Business School. Geoffrey Dicks graduated in Economics from Reading University (UK) and obtained his M.Sc. in economics and econometrics at Southampton University (UK). He joined the Centre for Economic Forecasting in 1976. Now Senior Research Officer, he is editor of *Economic Outlook* and *Exchange Rate Outlook*. His principal interest is in forecasting the world economy. To this end, he has developed a small monetary model *(European Economic Review,* 1983, vol. 21, pp. 261-285).

J. Paul Horne

First Vice President and International Economist, Smith Barney, Harris Upham & Co., Paris. A Yale University graduate, Mr. Horne worked in Rome as an economic-financial correspondent for *Newsweek* and *The Times* (London) for ten years. He subsequently worked in Rome and Brussels for the International Basic Economy Corporations, a Rockefeller financial services group. He joined Smith Barney, Harris Upham & Co. as that firm's international economist, based in Paris, in 1975. In addition to his analytical work, Mr. Horne writes on the European economies (particularly Italy) and on foreign exchange for financial publications, including the *Institutional Investor* and *Euromoney.*

Nobumitsu Kagami

Chief Economist and Adviser to the President, Nomura Investment Management Company, Ltd. Between 1981 and Spring, 1984, Mr. Kagami was Director, Jardine Fleming Investment Services. After graduating in economics from Hitotsubashi University in 1959, he joined the Tokyo office of Nomura Securities, Ltd. He earned the MBA degree from the Graduate School of Business, Stanford University, in 1963. Before going with Jardine Fleming in 1981, Mr. Kagami was with the Nomura Research Institute as Manager and Senior Economist in that organization's London office and, subsequently, Director and Senior Economist in London. Mr. Kagami writes extensively in both Japanese and English.

Nicolas Krul

General Manager, Gulf and Occidental Investment Company, S.A., Geneva. Nicolas Krul is a Ph.D. in international economics, and has advanced degrees in political science and law. He is a director of several multinational companies and an adviser to governments. Earlier, he was economic adviser to Lombard, Odier and Cy. and to the International Savings Banks Institute, and served in the Ministry of Foreign Affairs of the Netherlands. In addition to books on business-cycle policy, monetary policy, and financial structure, Dr. Krul is the author of numerous articles on money and finance.

Ezra Solomon

Dean Witter Professor of Finance, Graduate School of Business, Stanford University. Ezra Solomon graduated from the University of Rangoon in 1940 with a first-class degree in economics and served as an officer in the Burma Division of the British Royal Navy from 1942-1947. At the University of Chicago from 1948-1960, he received his Ph.D. from that school in 1950 and became professor of finance in 1956. He moved to Stanford University in 1961 as founding director of the International Center for the Advancement of Management Education, returning to full-time teaching and research in 1965 as Dean Witter Professor of Finance. In 1971-1973, Professor Solomon served as a member of the Council of Economic Advisers. He has written extensively, including twelve books.

Frank Wittendal

Senior Economist, The Conference Board. Dr. Wittendal received his Masters in econometrics from Paris-Pentheon University in 1969, and his doctorate in economics from Paris-Dauphine University in 1977. Before entering the private sector, he worked for the French Ministry (1966-1970). From 1970 to 1973, he was engaged in forecasting for banks and industrial companies. Frank Wittendal became chief economist of U.S.T.E.L., a steel manufacturers' association, in 1977. He has been with The Conference Board's Brussels offfice since 1980, and is responsible for the Board's *Economic Overview,* a medium-term forecast.